FROM SYNTAX TO TEXT

THE JANUS FACE OF FUNCTIONAL SENTENCE PERSPECTIVE

LIBUŠE **DUŠKOVÁ**

CHARLES UNIVERSITY IN PRAGUE
KAROLINUM PRESS, 2015

Reviewed by: Prof. PhDr. Jarmila Tárnyiková, CSc.
Prof. PhDr. Ludmila Urbanová, CSc.

CATALOGUING-IN-PUBLICATION – NATIONAL LIBRARY OF THE CZECH REPUBLIC

Dušková, Libuše
  From syntax to text : the Janus face of functional sentence perspective and intra- and interlingual study of English / Libuše Dušková. – First English edition. – Prague : Charles University in Prague, Karolinum Press, 2015
  ISBN 978-80-246-2879-0

811.111 * 811.162.3 * 81'367 * 81'37 * 81'42 * 81-115
English language
Czech language
syntax
functional sentence perspective
semantics
text linguistics
comparative linguistics
monographs

410 – Linguistics [11]

ISBN 978-80 246-2879-0
ISBN 978-80-246-2917-9 (pdf)

CONTENTS

PREFACE

This volume assembles my articles and treatises written since the turn of the century when my *Studies in the English Language* came out (1999). Two of the articles included among the chapters of the volume, "Syntactic forms of the presentation scale and their differentiation" (12), and "Textual links as indicators of different functional styles" (23), had in fact been written before 1999, but by the time they were issued the manuscript of the *Studies* had been submitted to the printers.

The twenty-four chapters making up the volume are divided into five parts that reveal the gradual progress from syntax to text. The evolvement of the subject matter reflects the two facets of functional sentence perspective: on the one hand syntactic structures as realization forms of the carriers of FSP functions and of communicative fields, and on the other the connection of FSP with the level of text, in particular the role of certain configurations of syntactic and FSP structures in the text build-up. That in the elaboration of the latter only a start has so far been made is evident from the unequal share of the two FSP facets in the content of the book: while the treatment of the relations between syntax and FSP accounts for a major section, viz. Parts I and II (*Syntactic Constancy* and *Syntax FSP Interface*), the studies devoted to the textual aspects, Part IV (*Syntax, FSP, Text*) and Part V (*Style*) take up much less space. Apparently, so does the modest extent of Part III (*FSP and Semantics*), to which only two chapters have been allocated owing to their primary semantic concern. In fact, this is not the only place where semantics is treated. Besides Part III, semantic aspects of FSP are taken into account if relevant to the treatment of other points of FSP dealt with elsewhere. Part V has been mediated through the textual level, to illustrate its differentiation into functional styles, even though an explicit link to FSP is here missing. Studies of the relations between syntax, FSP and style have already started and like the relations between syntax, FSP and text appear to offer further lines of FSP development.

As regards the relations between syntax and FSP, the idea of investigating interlingual syntactic constancy was instigated by the study "Basic distribution of communicative dynamism vs. nonlinear indication of functional sentence perspective," included in Part II (10). It examines in English the validity of the principle of end focus, whose operation with respect to the final sentence position coincides with the FSP concept of the basic distribution of communicative dynamism: the end of the sentence is in both approaches occupied by the informationally most important element, viz. the rheme in FSP terms. Since the principle of end focus is generally regarded as a universal principle of the organization of information structure, it can be expected to operate even in English in spite of its analytic character, and hence the primary grammatical function of English word order. Nevertheless, the two principles are often brought into conflict. Where this happens, another syntactic structure may come into play so that agreement between the two principles can be achieved. The study of the basic distribution of communicative dynamism vs. nonlinear indication of FSP has shown that in English the principle of end focus applies to a large extent even in the basic, non-transformed syntactic structures (in over 60% of all instances) and when the transformed structures (the passive, wh-clefts, existential construction and others) are added, this percentage considerably increases. A viable procedure for further investigation of this question that suggested itself was a comparison of English with Czech, an inflecting language whose word order is primarily governed by the FSP principle. The ensuing studies forming Part I were undertaken on the assumption that identical content can be interlingually presented in the same linear order, even though by different means: word order in Czech, against a different syntactic structure in English.

Accordingly, the aspects under study were the relations between syntactic function, FSP function and the linear arrangement of sentence elements. The choice of the material - samples of fiction in the original and their translations in the other language, was due to the fact that this is the only way to obtain rendition of identical content in two different languages. To mitigate the fallacies of translated texts, care was taken to include only instances in which all lexical items had counterparts in the other language, i.e. free translations have been excluded. Systemic relations between the two languages were primarily sought where the syntactic counterparts of original structures displayed distinct patterns recurrent in more than one source.

The main aim of all the studies of syntactic constancy was to ascertain the degree of syntactic divergence of different clause elements and the factors leading to the respective divergence. In the direction from Czech to English, one of these factors was assumed to be FSP. With a view to capturing all the factors that may be involved, the English-Czech direction was also included, mainly to test whether the divergence-conducive factors are the same in both directions or whether they differ and in which respects if they do. As shown in "Syntactic constancy of clause elements between English and Czech" (6), where the results of the studies of separate clause elements are summarized and compared, syntactic divergence in the Czech-English direction indeed involves FSP as a specific factor. The English sentence largely imitates the word order of the Czech sentence, which as a rule agrees with the basic distribution of communicative dynamism with the thematic element at the beginning and the rheme at the end. This was especially the case where the syntactic divergence involved the subject. In the case of postverbal clause elements, a major factor was found in different valency of the Czech verb and its English counterpart. In the English-Czech direction, with FSP playing no role, specific factors were found in the different status of the passive in the Czech verbal system and in the disposition of Czech to construe semantically adverbial elements in syntactically concordant realization forms, viz. as adverbials. It was partly the comparative and summarizing aspect of the study that led to its inclusion in the volume, albeit reiteration of the main findings of the separate studies could not be avoided. Another, more important reason was the fact that this is the only study in which the syntactic constancy of the object is treated. As shown by the Contents, a separate treatment of this clause element is lacking, because the research into syntactic constancy of the object has not been carried out by myself, but by a doctoral student of mine (cf. Valehrachová 2002, 2003).

The exclusion of the verb and the noun modifier from the summarizing comparative treatment was due not only to their later date, but more relevantly to their different nature. The verb has a specific status in both the sentence and the FSP structure. It is the only word class that in its finite form performs a single syntactic function, that of the predicate. The constitutive predicative function of the verb is reflected in its prototypical FPS function of transition. In both the sentence and FSP structure the verb forms a link, in the former between the subject and the rest of the sentence, in the latter between the other carriers of FSP functions. This largely dispossesses FSP of its capacity to act as a factor of syntactic divergence. On the other hand, specific syntactic aspects arose that had not been encountered in the treatment of other clause elements, such as drawing a line between convergent and divergent counterparts. As regards the noun modifier, it differs from all the other elements included in the study in being neither an immediate constituent of the sentence structure, nor of the clausal communicative field. It operates only within the structure of the noun phrase, whose syntactic and FSP functions are determined at the clausal level. The syntactic aspects of noun modification largely involved its realization forms, while divergent syntactic functions of the noun modifier at the clause level mostly represented concomitant shifts connected with syntactic divergence of the clause element in whose syntactic structure the modifier was included.

Even though the two variables under study in Part I have been the syntactic and FSP structure, the connection with the textual level, more exactly the hierarchically superordinate status of the textual level, emerged at such points as potential variation between the passive and active in the case of rhematic verb and context-dependent nominal elements. In English, the verb here appears in the medial position in both voices, the only effect of the voice alternation being an exchange in the positions of the two context-dependent participants in verbal action. Which of them is placed preverbally and which at the end depends on the position of the sentence in the text, viz. on what precedes and what follows.

Part II, *Syntax FSP Interface*, addresses diverse points of FSP including general ones, such as the hierarchical relationship between syntax and FSP, the question of potentiality, unavoidable in any treatment of FSP, and neutralization, a concept elaborated at the lower language levels but so far not with respect to the FSP structure.

Other points cover different realization forms of FSP structure and functions, word order both generally and in a specific case where the means of ordering elements in agreement with the basic distribution of communicative dynamism, offered by the language system, are confronted with their actual use in text. Inclusion in Part II of the study of the potential textual function of putative *should* (14) may appear, according to its title, inadvertent; however, the concern of the article is not the role of putative *should* in the text build-up, but its capacity to indicate context-dependence of the content of the clause within which it is contained.

The two articles in Part III, *FSP and Semantics*, deal with very different questions, the first (17) with the relationship between static and dynamic semantics, which has so far been elaborated only with respect to the presentation scale. Here the two semantics basically correspond. However, in the case of the quality scale the applicable dynamic semantic functions, specification and setting, cannot cover the variety of semantic roles of verbal complementation; the sentence semantics thus becomes obliterated. Here again a line of further research presents itself. The article on indefiniteness (18) is concerned with the interplay of semantics and FSP function of the indefinite article and other indefinite determiners and quantifiers. Although semantically disposed to operate in the rheme, indefinite determiners and quantifiers do not by themselves endow their head nouns with this FSP function. As in all other cases, the FSP function of nouns with indefinite determiners and quantifiers is determined by the interplay of all the FSP factors.

The studies included in Part IV, *Syntax, FSP, Text*, address two questions: theme development in terms of thematic progressions and the role of syntactic construction with a specific FSP structure in the text build-up. The last topic of this Part, "A textual view of noun modification" (22) draws attention to the capacity of alternative forms of noun modification to indicate the position of the modified noun phrase in the text: the more explicit form of postmodification at the first occurrence vs. the reduced modification structure in premodification as an indicator of context dependence.

In the final Part V, the leitmotif of all the studies collected in the volume, FSP, is not directly evident, since this part is concerned with style, as is indicated by the titles "Textual links as indicators of different functional styles" and "Noun modification in fiction and academic prose". In the latter, FSP is lacking even indirectly; the article has been included because of its subject matter, stylistic differentiation of academic prose and fiction, which links it with the other article "Textual links as indicators of different functional styles." Here, on the other hand, a direct link with FSP is present, even though not explicitly. The study of textual links basically elaborates the FSP factor of context dependence. All grammatical devices of textual cohesion here treated are anaphoric means referring to the left in the text, which presupposes a previous context.

Whether the content of the volume as outlined here will agree with the readers' interpretation of it is up to their judgment; the preface merely explains the author's starting point and conception of the shifts in the subject matter from syntax to text.

I would like to express my sincere thanks to both reviewers, Professors Jarmila Tárnyiková and Ludmila Urbanová, for their valuable comments, and to Lucie Gillová for meticulous assistance with the technical part of the book. I alone am responsible for the shortcomings of the book

I acknowledge with thanks the permission for reprints granted by the following publishers and representatives of the publishing institutions: Petr Valo, Karolinum, Charles University Press (*Prague Studies in English*, cf. 2, 7, 8, 18, 23; *Užívání a prožívání jazyka*, cf. 20); Karel Oliva, Institute of the Czech Language (*Linguistica Pragensia*, cf. 4, 5, 12, 14; *Slovo a slovesnost*, cf. 6, 17); John Benjamins, Ms. Patricia LePlae (*Language and Function*, cf. 1; *Travaux du Cercle Linguistique de Prague*, n. s. *Prague Linguistic Circle Papers* 3, cf. 10; *Travaux du Cercle Linguistique de Prague*, n. s. *Prague Linguistic Circle Papers* 4, cf. 11); V&R unipress GmbH, Ms. Marie-Carolin Vondracek (*The Prague School and Theories of Structure*, cf. 15); Jan Chovanec, Editor of *Theory and Practice in English Studies* and *Brno Studies in English*, Masaryk University in Brno (cf. 3, 9, 21, 24); Vice-Dean Vojtěch Kolman, Faculty of Arts, Charles University (*Shakespeare between the Middle Ages and Modernity. From Translator's Art to Academic Discourse*, cf. 19); Vice-Dean Marek Otisk, Faculty of Arts, Ostrava University (*New Chapters in Functional Syntax*, cf. 22); Vice-Dean Radka Závodská, Faculty of Education, The University of South Bohemia (*The Dynamics of the Language System, South-Bohemian Anglo-American Studies*, cf. 16); Vice-Dean Viera Žemberová, Faculty of Arts, Prešov University (*Proceedings of 6th Conference of British, American and Canadian Studies*, Prešov Part, cf. 13).

Prague, October 2014   *Libuše Dušková*

I. SYNTACTIC
CONSTANCY

1. CONSTANCY OF THE SYNTACTIC AND FSP FUNCTION OF THE SUBJECT

First published under the title "Constancy of syntactic function across languages" in Josef Hladký (ed.), *Language and Function. To the Memory of Jan Firbas. Studies in Functional and Structural Linguistics* 49, 2003, 127–145.

0. In this and the following chapters constancy of syntactic function is understood as identical syntactic rendition of a lexical item and its lexical equivalent in parallel texts taken from two (or more) different languages. Syntactic constancy conceived in this way is examined between English and Czech on the basis of original English texts and their Czech translations, and vice versa. Both instances of syntactic correspondence and instances of syntactic divergence are taken into account.

The following analysis is based on the assumption that syntactic structure is hierarchically subordinate to the information structure (functional sentence perspective, FSP henceforth); that is, given the universal validity of the principle of end focus, a translated text is assumed to present (or at least to show a tendency to present) the meaning content in the same perspective as the original, with changes in the syntactic structure, if need be, according to the respective grammatical rules. Accordingly, attention is focused on instances of syntactic divergence, which are examined with a view to ascertaining the underlying factors of the divergence.

The two languages on which this assumption is tested provide suitable ground insofar as the typological distinctions between English and Czech involve different hierarchies of the operating word order principles: owing to its analytic character, English employs word order primarily to indicate grammatical functions; on the other hand in inflectional Czech the grammatical principle plays a secondary role, syntactic relations being indicated by grammatical endings. Hence Czech word order is free to perform other functions among which indication of the FSP functions of the clause elements ranks highest. Considering these distinctions, similar linear arrangement of corresponding lexical items may be expected to involve differences in syntactic structure.

1. This chapter pursues some aspects of this assumption, taking as a starting point the findings of a diploma dissertation that investigated the constancy of the subject (Čermáková 1999). Commencing the investigation with the subject was motivated by the syntactic features of the subject in English, which in turn largely determine its role in FSP. Owing to the grammatical function of English word order, the English subject mostly occurs in initial position (78.5%, cf. Dušková 1975), which is as a rule the position of the theme. In Czech, on the other hand, the initial thematic position is often occupied by other clause elements, adverbials being nearly as frequent as the subject (29.3% and 33.5%, respectively, cf. Dušková 1975), while the subject fairly often assumes the function of the rheme, and stands at the end (22.4%, cf. Dušková 1986a; according to Uhlířová (1974), rhematic subjects account for one third of occurrences). The thematic nature of the English subject was first pointed out by Mathesius (1947a), whose ideas were further developed in later studies (Dušková 1975, 1986a). In Čermáková's (1999) treatise constancy of substantival and pronominal subjects is investigated in eight parallel texts, two English and two Czech contemporary novels, and their translations into the other language. Identical subjects (i.e. corresponding lexical items construed as the subject in both languages) were counted until the number of nonidentical counterparts of the subject in the other language reached the number 50. In this way the author obtained 100 instances of noncorrespondence in the English-Czech direction, and 100 instances of noncorrespondence in the Czech-English direction. In both directions, instances of correspondence overwhelmingly predominate: 2642 (96.15%) and 2378 (95.65%) as against 100 (3.85%) and 100 (4.35%), respectively (Čermáková 1999: 89, 96).

These results are directly comparable with the findings of another diploma dissertation based on the same methodology, investigating the constancy of the subject between English and German (Nekvapilová 1998). Allowing for language-specific features, German was assumed to behave in a similar way as Czech because it is also an inflecting language with a fairly free word order, at least as far as nominal and adverbial elements are concerned. In the German-English direction identical subjects accounted for 1994 (95.2%) instances, as against 100 (4.8%) instances of noncorrespondence, the respective figures for the English-German direction being 3086 (96.8%) and 100 (3.2%) (Nekvapilová 1998: 112, 119). A considerably lower degree of constancy between Czech subjects and their English counterparts was found by Klégr (1996: 92), viz. 446 (77.3%) instances of correspondence as compared with 131 (22.7%) instances of noncorrespondence. The difference is presumably due to the fact that Klégr's monograph, being concerned with the degree of interlingual constancy of the noun as a word class, covers only subjects realized by nouns, whereas the two diploma dissertations also include pronominal subjects.

In any case, the degree of interlingual constancy of syntactic function appears to be very high, and might thus seem to refute the initial assumption of the relation between syntactic and FSP structure. It should be noted, however, that despite typological distinctions, all three languages are members of the Indo-European family with a basically identical word class system and syntactic structure. Moreover, even the fixed grammatical structure of English (S—V—O, S—V—C$_s$, etc.) largely coincides with the principle of end focus. In Dušková (1999b) agreement between the grammatical word order principle and final placement of the focus in English was found in 62.2% of instances.

2. Turning attention to instances of noncorrespondence, let us first summarize the principal findings of Čermáková (1999).

2.1 The most frequent Czech counterpart of the English subject appeared to be direct object: 54 instances (absolute figures and percentages are the same). Next come integrated adverbials (16) and indirect object (13). All other clause elements have a frequency of occurrence below 10 (1 to 6) (Čermáková 1999: 91). Of these, the prepositional object (3 occurrences) should be included to complete the picture of the object complementation.[1]

The syntactic change of the English subject into the Czech object mostly involved a syntactic change in another clause element, and in 35 instances replacement of the English passive by the Czech active voice, cf.

(1) At dawn she was awakened by the sound of rain (BB, 56)
     Za svítání ji probudil déšť (BH, 62)
     [at dawn her$_{ACC}$ awakened rain$_{NOM}$]

Instances without a change in the voice mostly display, besides changes in non-verbal elements, replacement of the English *have* by a full lexical verb, or of *be* by *mít* 'have', cf. (2) and (3):

(2) she had toothache that morning (BB, 10)
     bolely ji to ráno zuby (BH, 13)
     [ached her that morning teeth]
(3) Her face was pale and long. (J, 27)
     Tvář měla bledou a podlouhlou. (S, 435)
     [face$_{ACC}$ she.had pale and long.]

Examples (4) and (5) illustrate the correspondence between the English subject and, respectively, an adverbial and the indirect object in Czech:

(4) her mouth opened to emit a sound (BB, 36)
     z pootevřených úst jí unikl zvuk (BH, 41)
     [from half-opened mouth her$_{DAT}$ escaped sound$_{NOM}$]
(5) Bernie hadn't after all owned the little house (J, 24)
     domek Berniemu vlastně nepatřil (S, 432)
     [little.house Bernie$_{DAT}$ after.all not.belonged]

---

1   The other Czech counterparts of the English subject with frequencies of occurrence below 10 were the verb (6 instances), no explicit syntactic counterpart (5), modifier (1), subject complement (1) and possessive determiner (1).

2.2 As regards the English counterparts of Czech subjects, the most frequent correspondence was again found between Czech subjects and direct objects in English (28 instances), largely with a concomitant change in another clause element, e.g.

(6) v každém muži je kus sobce (K, 23)
[in every man is piece egoist$_{GEN}$]
every man has a selfish streak in him (H, 14)

The next most frequent correspondence involves instances of Czech subjects without an explicit English counterpart (19 examples), cf. (7).

(7) že náš zpěv nikdo nezaslechne (K, 22)
[that our singing$_{ACC}$ nobody$_{NOM}$ will.not.hear]
our singing would go unheard (H, 13)

The correspondence ranking third on the frequency scale concerns Czech subjects reflected in possessive determiners in English (16 instances), cf. (8).

(8) v tom mám nejlepší postavu (K, 25)
[in it I.have best figure]
they show off my figure best (H, 15)

In 10 instances the Czech subject corresponds to a prepositional object, e.g.

(9) Ale jeho, bohužel, nepotkalo [štěstí] (F, 22)
[but him unfortunately it.not.met]
But he hadn't met with it [luck], alas (U, 20)

Indirect object as a counterpart of the Czech subject was found in three instances, cf. (10).

(10) měla jsem aspoň záminku mu zatelefonovat (K, 28)
[I.had at.least excuse him$_{DAT}$ phone]
it gave me an excuse to phone him (H, 18)

Of the other instances with frequencies of occurrence below ten,[2] the correspondence between the Czech subject and an adverbial in English needs to be mentioned insofar as the assumption of the superordinate role of the information structure applies to the correspondence between the English subject and a Czech adverbial, as in (4) (16 instances, see above), but not to the correspondence in the opposite direction. Of

---

2   The remaining correspondences with low frequencies of occurrence involved the subject in English counterparts of Czech subjectless sentences (9 occurrences), verb (4), and subject complement (2).

the nine attested instances, however, four represent passive counterparts of Czech active sentences whose subject appears as the *by*-agent in English, cf. (11).

(11) dveře mi otevřel předseda výboru (K, 40)
      [door$_{ACC}$ me$_{DAT}$ opened chairman$_{NOM}$ committee$_{GEN}$]
      I was let in by the chairman of the Party University Committee (H, 27)

In two of the other examples the adverbial construction of the Czech subject results from the introduction of a personal subject in English, which is lacking in the original. Cf. (12).

(12) Tudy vedla cestička vroubená ... (K, 33)
      [here led little.path flanked]
      I walked along the bank on a narrow path flanked by ... (H, 22)

Analyzing the factors motivating the attested syntactic changes, Čermáková points out the major role of functional sentence perspective, especially where the correspondence involves the subject in English vs. Czech direct object or adverbial. Generally, both English subject and Czech object or adverbial were contextually bound and represented the theme, whereas the postverbal elements in English (object or adverbial) represented the rheme and corresponded to the Czech verb or subject in final position (1999: 112). Among other distinct tendencies Čermáková points out the differences in the expression of the possessive relationship, and in verbal as against verbonominal expression of an action (1999: 112–113). Correspondences in the opposite direction moreover suggest the tendency of English to suppress the agent (1999: 114). The differences in the results between the English-Czech and the Czech-English approach are largely accounted for by the structural differences between the two languages (differences in the use of the passive, existential construction in English, subjectless sentences in Czech) (1999: 116). Of these findings, all of which call for further research, in what follows I shall attempt to expound the role of FSP from a different starting point, viz. the FSP function of the subject.

3. The concept of FSP adopted throughout is based on Jan Firbas's theory of functional sentence perspective, elaborated in a large number of studies, and synthetized in his *Functional Sentence Perspective in Written and Spoken Communication* (Firbas 1992). The FSP structure of the examples under consideration is determined on the basis of the interplay of the FSP factors, semantic, contextual, and linear modification (cf. Firbas 1992: 10–11, 115). Intonation, which constitutes an additional factor in the spoken language, plays a subsidiary role in written texts insofar as the position of the intonation centre (the nucleus) results from the interplay of the other three factors. For this reason, no capitals are used to indicate the nucleus bearer: the intonation centre is assumed to fall on whichever element is assigned the FSP function of rheme.

The starting point of the following discussion is the subject with the FSP function of rheme, treated with respect to: (a) its degree of interlingual constancy as compared with that of subjects examined only as syntactic functions; (b) the sentence position of rhematic subjects in the two languages and its effect on the syntactic and/or FSP structure in the other language; (c) the extent to which the syntactic changes contribute to the basic distribution of communicative dynamism (the order theme—transition—rheme, cf. Firbas 1992: 7–8, 10, 104–105, 118).

3.1 Given that rhematic subjects are more common in Czech than in English (the respective figures being 22.4% and 12.4%, cf. Dušková 1986a, Table 2), the degree of syntactic constancy among rhematic subjects may be supposed to be lower than among subjects counted without respect to their FSP role. To test this assumption, I collected 50 rhematic subjects from each original of Čermáková's sources and examined their syntactic counterparts in the other language.[3]

In both directions the percentage of constant subjects was considerably lower, and that of syntactically divergent subjects correspondingly higher, than in Čermáková's study: in the English-Czech direction constancy of the subject function was found in 78 instances (out of 100), in the opposite direction in 80 instances (out of 100). That is, nonidentical syntactic counterparts appeared in 22% of rhematic subjects in the English-Czech direction, and in 20% in the Czech-English direction.

Owing to being based on longer stretches of text (cf. note 3), Čermáková's list of examples contains a larger number of rhematic subjects. Her English source B provides 4 additional examples, while Source J is the only shorter text as compared with mine; the number of additional examples from her Czech sources amounts to 9. Accordingly, the following discussion of rhematic subjects with nonidentical syntactic counterparts takes into account 26 English and 29 Czech examples, of which 22 and 20, respectively, are identical in the two lists.

3.1.1 In the English-Czech direction, the relatively high degree of nonconstancy ascertained in 3.1 is surprising since Czech as a language with free word order, primarily governed by the principle of FSP, is able to place the rheme finally, whatever its syntactic function. That is, the syntactic structure of the original can be imitated, and the linear arrangement modified according to the FSP. Examining the 26 English examples (including Čermáková's additional 4) in this light, we find that 18 are accounted for by the existential construction. Here the problem of finding a Czech counterpart does not even involve a different linear arrangement since the notional subject in the existential construction occupies the postverbal position just as a rhematic subject does in Czech. The construction can be translated literally, as is often the case, cf.

---

3   The length of the texts used in my count, as compared with Čermáková's, proved to be somewhat shorter. In the case of the English originals 100 rhematic subjects were collected from 76 pages (BB, 33; J, 43), as against Čermáková's 93 pages needed for collecting 100 syntactically divergent subjects (BB, 52; J, 41), i.e. the difference was about 18%. However, it was largely due to one text (BB), the length of the other text being comparable in the two counts. As for the Czech originals, the difference was even greater, viz. 32%: 36 pages (F, 13; K, 23) as against Čermáková's 54 (F, 27; K, 27); again, largely on account of one text (F). Frequent use of final rhematic subjects appears to be a specific feature of Fuks's narrative style. As a result, the number of sentences needed for obtaining 100 rhematic subjects in English may be estimated at 2250 (Čermáková's figure 2742 minus 18%), the respective figure for Czech being 1680 sentences (Čermáková's figure 2478 minus 32%).

(13) There were lots of flowers. (BB, 21)
    Bylo tam plno kytek. (HB, 24)
    [was there lots flowers$_{GEN}$]

However, there is a tendency (also ascertained by Čermáková, see 2.) to use a transitive verb (often *mít* 'have') with rhematic object, which preserves the linear arrangement but changes the syntactic structure, cf. (14). Of the 18 examples with the existential construction the English rhematic subject corresponds to the object in Czech in 15 instances (83.3%).

(14) And there were other sources of income. (J, 22–23)
    A má ještě jiný zdroj příjmů. (S, 431)
    [and he.has still other source incomes$_{GEN}$]

The three existential constructions in which the subject has a counterpart other than the object are rare instances of correspondence between the English subject and the Czech subject complement or verb.

The remaining examples represent other forms of the presentation scale (cf. Firbas 1992: 66–69, 109–110, 134–140; Firbas 1966; and Chapter 12). In 5 instances the rhematic subject occupies initial position, its rhematic nature being indicated by the interplay of the other FSP factors, context independence and semantic structure, involving a verb of existence or appearance on the scene. As shown by (15), these factors here act counter to the linear arrangement. In Czech, examples like (15) can have parallel syntactic structure with the rhematic subject at the end.

(15) But now a heavy silence lay over it (J, 36)
    Ale v této chvíli byl ponořen do tíživého ticha (S, 442)
    [But in this moment was submerged in heavy silence]

The last three rhematic subjects appear in the structure Adv—V—S, which can in Czech be rendered literally including parallel word order, but the translator chose a transitive verb with an agentive subject, hence the English subject is again reflected in the final object.

3.1.2 On the other hand, as regards the 29 (20 + the additional 9 from Čermáková's list) syntactically divergent counterparts of Czech rhematic subjects, in agreement with the initial assumption the syntactic changes serve to preserve the linear arrangement of the original, i.e. final or late placement of the rhematic element. This is achieved by several means: a Czech intransitive verb followed by rhematic subject is replaced by a transitive verb followed by rhematic object (12 instances), as in (16); the rhematic subject appears as the *by-* or quasi-agent after a passive verb (4 instances), cf. (17); or the choice of a verb whose construction allows the Czech subject to be transposed into the object or another postverbal element in English (9 instances), cf. (18) and (19).

(16) proto, že z ní na mne čišel chlad (K, 33)
  [because from it on me blew cold$_{NOM}$]
  because it gave me the shivers (H, 22)
(17) a na dvou z nich seděli mužové se zakloněnými hlavami (K, 16)
  [and on two of them sat men with bent heads]
  Two of the chairs were occupied by men with heads bent back (H, 16)
(18) dr Proppera ranila mrtvice (F, 8)
  [dr Propper$_{ACC}$ struck stroke$_{NOM}$]
  Dr. Propper's had a stroke (U, 2)
(19) všechno zavinil můj neblahý sklon k hloupým žertům (K, 35)
  [all$_{ACC}$ caused my fatal penchant$_{NOM}$ to silly jokes]
  it all goes back to my fatal predilection for silly jokes (H, 22)

Final or late placement of the rhematic element resulting from a different syntactic structure is also found in the remaining pairs of examples, but again the particular correspondences are rare and produce no pattern (verb 1, C$_S$ 3 instances), cf. (20) and (21).

(20) kdy venku padal sníh. (F, 15)
  [when outside fell snow]
  when it was snowing outside. (U, 11)
(21) Za necelé dva měsíce měla být chanuka (F, 12)
  [in not-whole two months was.to be Hanukkah]
  In less than two months it would be Hanukkah (U, 8)

3.2 The second point to be considered is the sentence position of rhematic subjects with respect to its potential influence on the syntactic and/or FSP structure in the other language.

3.2.1 In my list of 100 English rhematic subjects (with syntactically both identical and divergent counterparts) the subject occurs in three positions: final (60 instances), medial (18), and initial (22). The final position is largely accounted for by the existential construction (45 instances), where either the subject is the last word, as in (25), or what follows constitutes postmodification, as in (13) and (14). The other 15 final subjects are found in the pattern Adv—V—S, cf. (22).

(22) behind the desk sat a man (J, 37)
  za ním seděl muž (S, 442)
  [behind it sat man]

The medial position of the subject is again accounted for by the existential construction in which the notional subject is followed by a scene-setting thematic adverbial (cf. Firbas's setting, 1992: 49–59, 61–62, 66–71), as in (23).

(23) There's a note on your desk. (J, 10)
    Na stole máte nějaký dopis. (S, 422)
    [on desk you.have some letter]

Initial rhematic subjects (including preverbal, preceded by a thematic adverbial) are found either in the presentation scale, as in (24) and (15), or with a focalizer, cf. (28).

(24) A memory came to her. (BB, 26)
    Přepadla ji vzpomínka. (BH, 30)
    [invaded her memory$_{NOM}$]

The additional 4 rhematic subjects from Čermáková's list occur in initial position (2 instances), medially (1) and at the end (1) as in (22).

The Czech counterparts of English rhematic subjects, whether construed as another syntactic element or as the subject, might be expected to occupy the final position. This applies to the nonidentical syntactic counterparts (26 instances, see 3.1.1), but of the remaining 74 instances, which display syntactic correspondence, 13 have the subject in initial or medial position, with the resulting loss of rhematic function. A half of these instances (7) are found in negative existential constructions, which may play a role, negation being semantically disposed to operate within the rheme. Yet the subject here is context independent, and with the verb of existence constitutes the presentation scale, which assigns it the role of rheme. Cf. (25).

(25) There weren't any mourners—no sons or anything. (BB, 8)
    Žádný truchlící pozůstalí se nevynořili—synové nebo podobně. (BH, 10)
    [No mourners not.emerged]

The Czech counterpart presents the subject as contextually bound, with the rheme constituted by the verb.

However, in two of these instances the subject does belong to the contextually bound part of the sentence, which is well worth noting, considering the fact that the existential construction is a special device for presenting a rhematic subject not only through its semantic structure, but also by the postverbal position of the subject. Cf. (26).

(26) There had been no other problem over the plaque (J, 9)
    Jiné problémy s firemním štítkem nenastaly (S, 421)
    [Other problems with plaque not.occurred]

Here the subject is contextually bound (the existence of problems with the plaque is mentioned in the preceding context, which is overtly reflected in the use of *other*), the only context independent element being negation (*no/nenastaly*).

Examples of the second group (5 instances) in which the Czech counterpart of the English rhematic subject does not stand in final position represent the specific English form of the presentation scale with the subject in initial position. Here its rhematic function is indicated by its context independence and the semantics of the verb (apperance/existence on the scene). These signals are easily missed by Czech speakers, who are used to looking for the rheme at the end, cf. (27).

(27) Distress at her own conciliatory nature rose in her throat (BB, 27)
Rozmrzelost nad vlastní pasivní povahou jí bobtnala v krku (BH,

In imitating the English word order the Czech sentence presents the final element as the rheme, whereas the rheme in the English sentence is constituted by the subject.

The last instance is a rhematic subject in initial position indicated by a focalizer, with parallel structure and word order in both languages, cf. (28).

(28) to which only she and he had a key (J, 14)
od níž jen oni dva měli klíče (S, 425)

Of special interest is one example of English subject in final position due to inversion, which is not rhematic despite its position and weightiness, these features being overruled by emphatic fronting of the subject complement. The Czech counterpart presents this element as the rheme in final position, cf. (29).

(29) Gone were the terracotta roofs of the farmhouses they had known, the stone sinks, the primitive wood-burning stoves. (BB, 17)
Terakotové střechy jejich bývalých venkovských domů, kamenné výlevky, primitivní plotny, kde se topilo dřevem, upadly v zapomnění. (BH, 19)

3.2.2 In my list of Czech rhematic subjects all subjects except one appear in final position. They are either the last word of the sentence, as in (18), or the words that follow invariably constitute postmodification of the subject, as in (17) and (19). The only exception displays the rhematic subject in initial position, but its rhematic nature is unequivocally indicated by contextual boundness of the verb and the focalizer that precedes it, cf. ex (30).

(30) tak mluvili i komunisté na svých vlastních schůzích, i Pavel tak mluvil (K, 25)
[even Pavel so talked]
even Communists went around talking like that at their meetings, and Pavel too (H, 15)

The 9 additional rhematic subjects from Čermáková's list are all found in the final position. Syntactic change as a means of achieving final or late placement of the English counterparts of Czech rhematic subjects accounts for 20 instances in my list of 100 rhematic subjects (cf. 3.1.2). Of the 80 examples whose English counterparts retain the subject function 56 (70%) have the subject in initial or preverbal position, cf. (31) and (32); 19 instances (23.75%) are rendered by the existential construction, cf. (33); and 5 instances (6.25%) display the pattern Adv—V—S, cf. (34).

(31) ale pak se stal zázrak (K, 22)
       [but then occurred miracle]
       but then a miracle occurred (H, 13)
(32) A tu ho náhle zachvátí jakási lítost (F, 8)
       [And now him suddenly seizes some pity$_{NOM}$]
       A wave of sudden pity came over him, (U, 3)
(33) bylo mnoho projevů a mnoho aplausů (K, 22)
       [was many speeches and many applauses]
       there were all kinds of speeches and applause (H, 12)
(34) nad vařičem visí kalendář (F, 13)
       [over burner hangs calendar]
       over the burner hung a calendar (U, 9)

Final or at least postverbal placement of the rhematic subject is thus found only in 30% of instances, the most frequent structure being constituted by rhematic subject in initial position, followed by a verb of existence or appearance on the scene, with the scene-setting thematic adverbial, if any, at the end (cf. Firbas 1966, 1992: 59-65). These findings suggest that in the case of rhematic subjects the principle of end focus is to a large extent overruled by the grammatical principle. Here the initial position of the rhematic element is counteracted by its context independence and the semantics of the verb.

However, since initial position is the regular position of thematic subjects (which are much more frequent, thematic subjects in English accounting for 85.8%, cf. Dušková 1986a, Table 2), we may inquire whether the change in the position (final in Czech vs. initial in English) may not result in a change of the FSP structure. This is the case in 8 instances, cf. (35), with 4 other unclear ones, cf. (36).

(35) tehdy panovala přísná morálka (K, 23)
       [then ruled strict morals]
       morals were pretty strict in those days (H, 14)

As against the presentation scale in Czech, which ascribes existence to *strict morals*, the English counterpart assigns the feature *strict* to the quality bearer *morals*: of these two elements only the former operates as the rheme, whereas the latter as the theme (cf. Firbas's quality scale, 1992: 66-69, 109-110).

There are some unclear instances, due to the uncertainty which sometimes arises where verbs implying existence or appearance on the scene may also be regarded as assigning some feature to the subject, and/or where it is not clear whether the subject is contextually bound or not, since the object it refers to is mentioned at some distance in the preceding context or is derivable from it, but in the particular sentence it also allows context-independent interpretation. Thus in (36) the Czech sentence resembles the presentation scale, while in the English counterpart the subject is ascribed a feature.

(36) Trhne rukou a začne mu tuhnout šíje. (F, 9)
     [he.jerks hand$_{INSTR}$ and begins him$_{DAT}$ stiffen neck]
     He snatched his hand back and his neck felt stiff. (U, 4)

Similarly in (37) the Czech sentence presents the subject as a phenomenon appearing on the scene (constituted by *his face and chest*), whereas in English the subject is conceived as contextually bound and the communication is perspectived to what is said about it. This is presumably due to the fact that the lampswitch is mentioned in the preceding context at a distance of ten lines.

(37) na jeho čelo a hruď dopadlo bledé světlo lampy (F, 7)
     [on his forehead and chest fell pale light lamp$_{GEN}$]
     the pale lamplight fell on his face and chest (U, 1)

Allowing for some degree of uncertainty in determining the FSP structure, a small number of instances appear to suggest that the initial position of the English subject, owing to its dual role in FSP, may be conducive to a divergent FSP structure in the other language.

3.3 To conclude the discussion of the FSP role of the subject with respect to syntactic change, consideration should also be given to thematic subjects. These have been obtained from Čermáková's (1999) list by determining their respective FSP roles.

3.3.1 In the English texts, thematic subjects account for 74 instances (cf. rhematic subjects in 3.1.1). All except 8 (i.e. 89.2%) appear in initial position, which testifies to the close connection between the English subject and the FSP role of theme. Six stand in preverbal position after an initial adverbial, also a component of the theme, as in (38). The two remaining instances display emphatic fronting of a rhematic adverbial, involving subject-verb inversion, cf. (39).

(38) The previous year his office had been plagued by an outbreak of obscene letters
     (J, 35)
     Vloni jeho kancelář zaplavila hotová průtrž obscénních dopisů (S, 441)
(39) at no time had Bernie been invited to ... (J, 39)
     a Bernieho nikdy nikdo nepožádal, aby ... (S, 444)

The Czech counterparts of the English thematic subjects occur in two positions, initial (29 instances), or they occupy the medial position after another thematic element or the verb (35). Where they follow the verb, which primarily functions as transition (cf. Firbas 1992: 70-73), the English word order is more consistent with the basic distribution of communicative dynamism than the Czech. In both these positions the Czech counterparts preserve the FSP role of theme, their syntactic function being mostly direct object (37 instances); the other syntactic functions involve adverbials (13 occurrences), O_i (12), O_{prep} (2), Verb (3), the genitive and possessive determiner (1 occurrence each), and 5 instances without an explicit counterpart. In 5 instances the Czech counterparts of English thematic subjects occur in the final position, with a change in FSP as a result. Compare (40), in which the English thematic subject appears in Czech as the rheme at the end.

(40) After all the lavatory was mended … (B, 54)
　　 Koneckonců opravil záchod … (BH, 59-60)
　　 [after all he.repaired lavatory]

Misinterpretation of the original FSP is also found within the rhematic section, as in ex (41), where the rheme is constituted by the final prepositional phrase, whereas in Czech by the counterpart of the direct object.

(41) [As tall as he] she fanned his face with her breath … (BB, 59)
　　 takže mu její dech vanul do tváře … (BH, 66-65)
　　 [so.that him$_{DAT}$ her breath blew into face]

In general, however, where the FSP structure of the Czech counterpart corresponds to that of the original, the two languages appear to display parallel linear arrangement to a remarkable extent. The only major difference, due to the grammatical function of word order in English, consists in the occurrence of thematic elements after the rheme.

3.3.2 Thematic subjects in Čermáková's Czech examples account for 61 instances, the remaining 10 sentences being constituted by subjectless verbal clauses (for rhematic subjects, see 3.1 and 3.1.1). In more than a half (35) the subject is expressed by the personal ending of the verb. Unlike English thematic subjects, Czech thematic subjects expressed by a pronoun or a noun occur in all positions in the sentence except at the end, the initial position being the most frequent (17 instances). The other positions are illustrated by (42), in which the subject follows an adverbial, and (43), where the subject is preceded by the verb and the object.

(42) … když se ve schránce něco bělá … (F, 7)
　　 [when in box something is.white]
　　 The minute I see something white in the letter box … (U, 1)
(43) … vadit jí to nebude … (K, 21)
　　 [matter her$_{DAT}$ it not.will]
　　 … she won't mind … (H, 11)

As regards the English counterparts, in 15 instances no explicit equivalent is found (cf. (43)). The most frequent syntactic counterparts are direct object, as in (44) (15 instances), and the possessive determiner, as in ex (8) (16 instances), other syntactic counterparts being found in Adv, O_{prep}, O_i, Vb and postmodification (with 5–1 occurrences).

(44) ... ale moje samota zůstává nedotčena. (K, 14)
    [but my solitude remains intact]
    ... but I keep my privacy intact. (H, 4)

Unless the FSP of the Czech sentence is misinterpreted (5 instances, cf. (45)), the English counterparts, whatever their syntactic function, retain the FSP role of theme.

(45) ... tam měl nejraději opice a slony ... (F, 9)
    [there he.liked best monkeys and elephants]
    ... the monkeys and the elephants were his favorites ... (U, 3)

Whereas in the Czech sentence the subject, indicated by the verbal ending, has the FSP role of theme, the rheme being constituted by the direct object, in the English counterpart it is reflected in the possessive determiner of the subject complement, which constitutes the rheme. Accordingly, the FSP structure is changed. However interesting these deviations may be in contrastive studies, they do not detract from the general finding that the FSP structure in the two languages even in the case of thematic subjects shows a high degree of correspondence.

3.4 The last point to be noted is the effect of syntactic change on the basic distribution of CD as against instances in which the syntactic structure of parallel sentences remains the same. Here a comparison is made only in the Czech-English direction, since Czech applies the principle of end focus as a matter of course. This has been demonstrated in the foregoing discussion by the almost exclusive final position of the rheme in the Czech examples.

Since the examples on which this study is based do not contain counterparts of thematic subjects without syntactic change, directly comparable instances are provided only by rhematic subjects.

In the list of Czech rhematic subjects with syntactically divergent counterparts in English (29 instances, cf. 3.1 and 3.1.2) the percentage of rhematic elements in the final position amounts to 86.2 (25 out of 29). In 4 instances the rheme is followed by a thematic adverbial or object, as in (20).

In the list of thematic subjects with syntactically divergent counterparts (see 3.3.2), including Czech subjectless sentences (i.e. 71 instances), and excluding 4 instances with a misinterpreted FSP (cf. (45)), which leaves a list of 67 sentences, basic distribution of communicative dynamism is found in 52 instances (77.6%). In 13 instances the rheme is followed by a thematic object or adverbial, as in (9) and (46).

(46) ... že při ofenzívách mají velké ztráty. (F, 35)
  [that during offensives they.have great losses]
  ... there were heavy losses during those big offensives. (U, 35)

The two remaining instances have the rheme at the beginning, one (a dependent exclamative clause) owing to emotive factors, the other representing an interesting case of initial rhematic subject in the presentation scale as a result of syntactic change, cf. (47).

(47) ... v šeru dálky zahlédne jakýsi povědomý dům. (F, 35)
  [in dark distance~GEN~ he.sees some familiar house]
  ... in the darkness ahead a familiar house stood out. (U, 35)

The lowest percentage of basic distribution of CD is found in the English counterparts of Czech rhematic subjects without syntactic change (cf. 3.2.2): here rhematic subjects in the final position account only for 22.5% (18 instances). In 56 instances (70%) they occupy the initial position, while postverbal placement of rhematic subjects followed by a thematic adverbial is found in 6 instances (7.5%). The prevalent structure displays the rhematic subject initially in the presentation scale, in which the order theme—transition—rheme is reversed. Accordingly, we find the highest percentage of basic distribution of CD among rhematic subjects with syntactic change, and the lowest percentage among rhematic subjects without syntactic change, whereas thematic subjects with syntactically divergent counterparts occupy an intermediate position.

4. In general, the initial assumption that the degree of interlingual constancy of the subject depends on its function in FSP has been confirmed by the findings of the present study in the Czech-English direction. Whether this relation between the syntactic and FSP structure also applies to other clause elements besides the subject remains to be investigated.

The final position of Czech rhematic subjects has proved to be a major factor conducive to syntactic change, whereas the initial position of English rhematic subjects, as shown by a few examples, may be a potential cause of misinterpreting the FSP structure. Syntactic change connected with the final position of Czech rhematic subjects moreover appears to contribute to the basic distribution of communicative dynamism in the English counterparts. This is due to the fact that without syntactic change final placement of a rhematic subject in English can be achieved only by the existential construction, which covers only some of the Czech rhematic subjects, and by the pattern Adv—V—S, deviant from the grammatical word order, and hence rare.

Syntactic change in the English-Czech direction appears to be due to other than FSP factors. Obviously, a language with free word order does not need syntactic change to achieve a different linear arrangement of sentence elements. Nevertheless, it is approximately as frequent as in the opposite direction. Here the factors involved partly consist in language specific modes of expression (predications with *mít* 'have' or other transitive verbs of a generally possessive or locative meaning as against predications with *be* in the other language), and partly in a different status of the Czech passive both in the verbal and the grammatical system, reflected in the uses of the passive in discourse.

Verification of the findings of the present study calls for larger corpora including counterparts of thematic subjects without syntactic change, and for a detailed examination of instances which lack the basic distribution of CD in spite of syntactic change.

SOURCES

[BB] Bainbridge, B. *The Bottle Factory Outing.* Glasgow: Collins, 1977.

[BH] Bainbridgeová, B. *Podnikový výlet v prodlouženém čase.* Translated by Hana Bělohradská. Prague: Odeon, 1981.

[J] James, P. D. *An Unsuitable Job for a Woman.* New York: Warner, 1972.

[S] Jamesová, P. D. *Povolání pro ženu nevhodné.* In 3× *Adam Dalgliesh.* Translated by Josef Schwarz. Prague: Odeon, 1986.

[F] Fuks, L. *Pan Theodor Mundstock.* Prague: Československý spisovatel, 1963.

[U] Fuks, L. *Mr. Theodor Mundstock.* Translated by Iris Urwin. New York: Ballantine, 1969.

[K] Kundera, M. *Žert.* Brno: Atlantis, 1991.

[H] Kundera, M. *The Joke.* Translated by Michael Henry Heim. Harmondsworth: Penguin Books, 1984.

2. SYNTACTIC CONSTANCY OF ADVERBIALS BETWEEN ENGLISH AND CZECH

First published in *Prague Studies in English* 23, *Acta Universitatis Carolinae, Philologica* 2, 2002 (issued in 2004), 111–126.

0. This chapter continues the study of interlingual constancy of clause elements.[1] The first clause element studied with a view to ascertaining its degree of interlingual constancy was the subject (cf. Chapter 1). Commencing the study with this clause element was motivated by notable differences between the two languages as regards its syntactic and FSP features. While the English subject, as a result of the grammatical function of word order, is largely confined to initial or preverbal position, and is hence prevalently thematic, the beginning of the sentence being the position of the theme, the Czech subject can occur at any place in the sentence according to its degree of communicative dynamism, not excepting the final position. Consequently, rhematic subjects are more frequent in Czech than in English (cf. Dušková 1986a). The initial study was thus prompted by the assumption that Czech rhematic subjects in final position might correspond to English final rhematic elements syntactically consistent with the postverbal position, viz. objects, adverbials or other complements of the verb, and this assumption was largely confirmed.

In the case of adverbials the situation is different. Being largely mobile also in English, they are disposed to occupy positions according to their degree of communicative dynamism in both languages. However, as regards English, this applies only to adverbials of certain semantic roles, while others, notably temporal and partly locative, tend to favour customary word order arrangements subsumable under grammatical ordering, which may deviate from the gradual increase in communicative dynamism. Moreover, linearity alone does not constitute the functional sentence perspective,

---

1 For interlingual constancy on the level of word classes, see Klégr (1996). One of the aspects dealt with in his monograph, which addresses the noun, concerns the non-correspondences between Czech nouns and their English equivalents in syntactic function, among them the syntactic correlates of the Czech adverbial (106–114).

but has to be considered in connection with the other FSP factors, semantic structure, contextual boundness (context dependence) and intonation (in speech).[2] All this suggests a different, more intricate pattern of correspondences and divergences involving additional factors and perhaps excluding some which play a role in the case of the subject.

1. This treatment is confined to adverbials realized by adverbs, noun phrases and prepositional phrases. Clausal and nonfinite verb forms of realization were excluded on the ground of presenting essentially different problems calling for separate treatment. The only exception was made in the case of the rare occurrence of these forms as translation counterparts of adverbials realized by adverbs, nouns or prepositional phrases in the original texts. Furthermore, the aim of the present study ruled out the inclusion of sentence modifiers as elements standing outside the syntactic relations established within the sentence. Accordingly, the adverbials under study comprise only elements integrated into the syntactic structure of the sentence (referred to as adjuncts and subjuncts in Quirk et al. 1985: 504–612; circumstance adverbials and adverbs modifying adjectives and other adverbs in Biber et al. 1999: 544–556; cf. also Huddleston and Pullum 2002, Chapter 8).

The procedure adopted was the same as in the study of the subject so that comparable results might be obtained. Eight parallel texts, two English and two Czech originals + their translations in the other language (see Sources) were excerpted for both corresponding and divergent adverbials until the number of divergent adverbials in each of the original texts reached fifty. The number of corresponding adverbials needed for the fifty divergent instances served as the measure of constancy. In this way a sample of 200 examples was obtained, 100 divergent instances in the English-Czech direction and 100 in the Czech-English.[3] With a view to the aim of the study, care was taken to base the data only on examples whose lexical elements had equivalent counterparts in the other language, i.e. instances of free translation were left out of account.

The counting of instances with adverbial function in both languages raised a number of questions whose solution had to be applied consistently in order to ensure identical treatment of analogous data. To begin with, only those adverbials were counted which had a counterpart in the other language, i.e. untranslated adverbials, as well as adverbials added in the translations were disregarded. Integrated adverbials included in the count comprised not only those functioning as clause elements but also those occurring within the structure of phrases as modifiers or intensifiers, e.g. *gratuitously spiteful*, *very odd*. Coordinated adverbials were counted as one instance, e.g. *with the permission and advice*. In general, the corresponding adverbials included in the count had the

---

2   For the FSP concepts, see Firbas (1992).

3   The data for the Czech-English part were collected in two seminar papers supervised by the present writer: Vladimíra Koubová, "Větněčlenská konstantnost příslovečného určení mezi češtinou a angličtinou" (Syntactic constancy of adverbials between English and Czech), Department of English and American Studies, Charles University, Prague 2002; Jana Komárková, "Constancy of Syntactic Function," Department of English and American Studies, Charles University, Prague 2000.

same semantic role, except a few instances, e.g. *She now asked a question.* (F, 52) *Jenom* ['only'] *se na něco zeptala* (Ž, 52). In the case of borderline instances between adverbials and other clause elements, notably objects and postmodification, the usual criteria were applied (the question test, passivization, word order rearrangement). Even so, some instances remained indeterminate. For the procedure adopted in the case of adverbs homonymous with particles constituting components of phrasal verbs, see 2.4.

A special problem was presented by clusters of adverbial expressions in regard to whether each adverbial should be counted separately or not. This was the case in sentences containing more than one temporal and/or locative expression, such as *It fell about her knees to the ground* (J, 29), counted as two adverbials (*about her knees* direction, *to the ground* ultimate location). On the other hand, the temporal expressions in instances like *It was beached as usual at the bottom of Tanner's Lane at five o'clock yesterday afternoon* (J, 32) were regarded as one adverbial since the time *when* is successively specified by all three components, in a way resembling restrictive modification.

The results of the count are presented in the Tables below.

Table 1: *English counterparts of Czech integrated adverbials*

	Kundera Žert (K1)		Kundera NLB (K2)		total	
	abs.	%	abs.	%	abs.	%
adverbials	579	92.1	1129	95.8	1708	93.95
non-adverbial counterparts	50	7.9	50	4.2	100	6.05
total	629	100.0	1179	100.0	1808	100.00

Table 2: *Czech counterparts of English integrated adverbials*

	Fowles (F)		P. D. James (J)		total	
	abs.	%	abs.	%	abs.	%
adverbials	644	92.8	754	93.8	1398	93.3
non-adverbial counterparts	50	7.2	50	6.2	100	6.7
total	694	100.0	804	100.0	1498	100.0

Three of the four samples show a comparable degree of adverbial constancy, two in the English-Czech direction (92.8 and 93.8) and one (K1) in the Czech-English direction (92.1). The higher adverbial constancy in sample K2 (95.8) is probably due to differences in the analytic procedures, texts Kl and K2 having been analysed by two different students (see Note 3). Significant differences in the author's language and/ or the translating procedure are not likely because the two texts were written by the same author and translated by the same translator.

As compared with the constancy of the subject, adverbial constancy appears to be lower: 93.95% in the Czech-English direction and 93.3% in the English-Czech direction, whereas the constancy of the subject was found to be 95.65% and 96.15%, respectively (cf. Chapter 1).[4] Although this difference plays a role with respect to the two clause elements in question, it appears insignificant in view of the typological distinctions between English and Czech, since both the constancy of the subject and that of the adverbial are found to be very high. This is to be attributed to the appurtenance of both languages to the Indo-European language family, which conduces to a basically identical word class system and syntactic structure.

2. The lower degree of adverbial constancy as compared with the subject appears to reject the assumption that the greater freedom in the placement of English adverbials may counteract syntactic divergence. However, an explanation will follow from the discussion of Tables 3 and 4, which list and classify the divergent counterparts.

When compared with analogous data obtained for the subject (presented in Chapter 1), Tables 3 and 4 suggest that the factors contributing to the lower syntactic constancy of the adverbial are to be sought in the representation of the premodifier in the Czech-English direction (Table 3) and in the group 'inclusion in the verb' in the English-Czech direction (Table 4). Whereas here these two categories rank high on the frequency scale (the premodifier as the second with 23% and inclusion in verbal meaning as the first with 29%), in the case of the subject these correspondences are lacking. More insight into the causes of the differences will be gained from a discussion of the particular divergent counterparts.

Table 3: Divergent syntactic counterparts of Czech integrated adverbials

	K1		K2		total	
	abs.	%	abs.	%	abs.	%
subject	6	12.0	12	24.0	18	18.0
object	25	50.0	19	38.0	44	44.0
premodifier	8	16.0	15	30.0	23	23.0
postmodifier	2	4.0	–	–	2	2.0
inclusion in the verb	3	6.0	2	4.0	5	5.0
verb	1	2.0	–	–	1	1.0
subject complement	4	8.0	1	2.0	5	5.0
other	1	2.0	1	2.0	2	2.0
total	50	100.0	50	100.0	100	100.0

4   Klégr's data for syntactic constancy between Czech adverbials and their English counterparts (1996, 107), which are based on realization forms containing a noun, show an even lower percentage, viz. 82.4.

Table 4: Divergent syntactic counterparts of English integrated adverbials

	Fowles		P.D. James		total	
	abs.	%	abs.	%	abs.	%
subject	8	16.0	18	36.0	26	26.0
object	11	22.0	9	18.0	20	20.0
premodifier	5	10.0	10	20.0	15	15.0
postmodifier	3	6.0	–	–	3	3.0
inclusion in the verb	18	36.0	11	22.0	29	29.0
verb	3	6.0	1	2.0	4	4.0
other	2	4.0	1	2.0	3	3.0
total	50	100.0	50	100.0	50	100.0

2.1 Starting with the most frequent divergent syntactic counterpart in the Czech-English direction, the object (44%), we largely find what appears to be a purely superficial change consisting in different verbal government, but in fact reflects the basically different character of the Czech and the English verb: whereas Czech has an intransitive verb followed by an adverbial, English displays a transitive verb with object complementation. The change is illustrated by example (1), other instances of this kind being *odejít z Prahy* [leave from Prague] > *leave Prague, odejít od někoho* [leave from somebody] > *leave somebody, vstoupila do mlhy* [she-entered into mist] > *she entered a mist, hladit (někoho) po hlavě* [stroke (somebody) on head] > *stroke (somebody's) head, nasednout do vlaku* [board into train] > *board the train, telefonovat do nemocnice* [telephone into hospital] > *ring up the hospital, být/potulovat se na ulici* [be/roam in street] > *roam the streets, chytit (někoho) za ruku* [seize (somebody) by hand] > *seize (somebody's) hand*, and the like.

(1) Stoupali jsme *po úzkém schodišti.* (K1, 14)
    [We-climbed on narrow staircase]
    We climbed *a narrow staircase.* (H1, 4)

As shown by the example, both the Czech adverbial and the English object occur in final position, with the FSP function of rheme. The syntactic divergence is not due to FSP, but neither does it have any effect on FSP, the two syntactic structures displaying analogous (basic) distribution of communicative dynamism with the theme at the beginning and the rheme at the end.

Among instances of this kind we also find word order arrangements, fairly common in English, with a thematic element following the rhematic object, due to the grammatical principle; here the FSP function of the last element is indicated by its anaphoric nature signalling context dependence. Compare the Czech and English word order in (2) and (3).

(2) A pak jsem se k němu *otočil zády.* (K1, 11)
 [And then $_{\text{auxiliary reflexive particle}}$ to him turned back$_{\text{INSTR}}$]
 ... *turning my back* on it. (H1, 2)
(3) Byla jsem u něho *celou hodinu.* (K1, 28)
 [I-was $_{\text{auxiliary}}$ with him whole hour]
 I *spent a full hour* with him. (H1, 18)

However, these instances do not affect the correspondence in FSP between the Czech adverbial and the English object: they merely demonstrate the primary function of the grammatical principle in English.

In the English-Czech direction the correspondence between adverbials and objects ranks third on the frequency scale (20%), i.e. it is by more than a half less frequent than in the opposite direction. The emerging patterns are less clearcut, some of the examples being individual solutions allowing no generalizations. The correspondence was also more difficult to determine since the borderline between objects and adverbials is sometimes indeterminate.

Two types of correspondence between English adverbials and Czech objects account for a half of the examples. The first again represents differences in verbal government, cf. (4):

(4) not a single servant had been *sent on his, or her* (...) *way.* (F, 52)
 ani jeden sluha nebo služka *nedostal nebo nedostala* (...) *výpověď.* (Ž, 51)
 [not-even one man-servant or maid-servant got ... notice]

The second type involves different expression of the possessive relationship: a prepositional phrase introduced by *with* in English against the Czech verb *mít* 'have' with object complementation, cf. (5).

(5) But now, *with luck,* it was promising to be quite an exciting holiday. (J, 18)
 když bude mít štěstí, zažije dovolenou pěkně vzrušující. (N, 221)
 [when he-will have luck ...]

The correspondences found in the remaining examples of this group derive from a more or less inexact lexical equivalent of the headword and occur only once or twice. Compare (6):

(6) along the half-mile that *runs round a gentle bay* to the Cobb proper. (F, 58)
 po stezce dlouhé asi půl míle, která *sleduje mělkou zátoku* až k Valu. (Ž, 57)
 [... which follows shallow bay as-far-as to Cobb]

As regards the functional sentence perspective, the divergent syntactic counterparts have the same FSP function as the adverbials in the original, but again the linear order may differ in the placement of another element (a thematic element at the end in English). Compare the analogous word order in the foregoing examples (4)–(6) with the order of elements in (7):

(7) Miss Sarah was *present at this conversation*. (F, 52)
   Slečna Sarah byla *té rozmluvě přítomna*. (Ž, 52)
   [Miss Sarah was that$_{DAT}$ conversation$_{DAT}$ present]

Evidently what has been said about the role of FSP in the case of the correspondence adverbial > object in the Czech-English direction applies here as well.

2.2 Counterparts of adverbials construed as premodifiers rank second in the Czech-English direction (23%, see Table 3) and fourth in the English-Czech direction (15%, see Table 4) on the frequency scale. The 5 instances of postmodification will also be considered to complete the picture. The correspondence between a Czech adverbial and an English premodifier predominantly displays the following pattern:

(8) a. A *mírně pootočila* křeslo. (K1, 17)
      [And gently she-turned chair]
      She gave the chair *a gentle turn*. (H1, 8)
   b. Pak jsme si *chvíli povídali*. (K1, 15)
      [Then $_{auxiliary\ reflexive\ particle}$ while$_{noun}$ we-chatted]
      Then we had *a short chat*. (H1, 5)
   c. *Pohlédl* na mne *dotčeně*. (K1, 13)
      [He-looked at me affrontedly]
      He gave me *an irritated look*. (H1, 3)

The Czech structure contains an adverbial modifying the verb, whereas the English construction is verbonominal: the verb is dissociated into the categorial and notional component, with the latter, an action noun, construed as the object. As a result, the modifier assumes the form and function consistent with a noun head. From the FSP point of view, the three examples listed under (8) are illustrative in showing the inflexibility of the English construction in comparison with the variability in Czech. Admittedly, even English can achieve parallel indication of the FSP structure by resorting to the verbal construction, but either the translator is not aware of the subtle distinctions signalled by the variations in the Czech word order, or the verbonominal construction is such an obvious counterpart as to be employed almost automatically.

All three examples listed under (8) display the usual Czech FSP structure with the rheme at the end. From the aspect of the order of the other elements, a perfectly fitting counterpart is provided in (8) b. In (8) a. the FSP of the English sentence differs from the Czech original: in the latter the rheme is the *chair*, in the former a *gentle turn*. In (8) c. a more common linear arrangement in Czech would be *Dotčeně na mne pohlédl*

[Affrontedly at me he-looked]. However, wherever the manner adjunct is placed, thanks to its almost general context-independence it is more dynamic than the verb (cf. Firbas 1992: 53), hence both Czech configurations basically display the same FSP structure, even though a manner adverbial in the final position is more dynamic than at the beginning. The FSP structure of the English verbonominal constructions is remarkably similar in that the lexical counterparts of the Czech verb and adverbial, the English object action noun and its adjectival modifier, occur at the end with the FSP function of rheme, within which the modifier is more dynamic than the head noun (see Firbas 1992: 84 for the FSP of the noun phrase). Nevertheless, the motivation of this syntactic divergence can be attributed to FSP only partly as the verbonominal construction primarily serves as a means of *aktionsart* (singling out one act of verbal action as against its unsegmented presentation by the verbal predication) and of facilitating modification and quantification where the verb does not lend itself to these processes easily.

Other examples of this correspondence obtained from the two sources, with different positions of the Czech adverbial, are *Hlasitě se rozesmála* [loudly ₑₑₓᵢ reflexive particle she-began-laugh] > *She burst into loud laughter*, *lekla se najednou* [she-scared $_{reflexive}$ $_{particle}$ suddenly] > *she had a sudden scare*, *odcházela často na záchod* [she-left often to toilet] > *she made frequent trips to the toilet*, *smály se úplně stejným smíchem*, [they-laughed $_{reflexive \; particle}$ completely same$_{INSTR}$ laugh$_{INSTR}$] > *they laughed the same laugh*, *některá udělala dřep špatně* [one did kneebend badly] > *one of us did a bad kneebend*, *několikrát telefonoval* [several-times he-called] > *he made several telephone calls* and the like.

In the English-Czech direction the correspondence between adverbials and premodifiers is less frequent (15%). It again displays one predominant distinct pattern due to a different headword. The correspondence is illustrated by (9).

(9) Maurice was always *very odd* and secretive, of course. (J, 30)
Maurice byl vždycky *velký podivín* a tajnůstkář. (N, 232)
[Maurice was always great eccentric$_{noun}$ and secretive$_{noun}$]

Unlike the original, in which the adverbial intensifies predicative adjectives, the translation employs copular predication with predicative nouns modified by an adjectival modifier, i.e. the lexical content of the subject complement is preserved, albeit in a different surface form.

English adverbials reflected in Czech adjectival premodifiers were found as components of different syntactic functions, cf. (10) and (11).

(10) The servants were permitted to hold evening prayers in the kitchen, under Mrs Fairley's eye and *briskly* wooden voice. (F, 54)
Služebnictvu se dovolovalo odbývat večerní modlitby v kuchyni za lhostejného dozoru paní Fairleyové a při zvuku jejího úsečného neohebného hlasu. (Ž, 53)
[... by sound {her brisk wooden voice}$_{GEN}$]

(11) But alas, what she had thus taught herself had been *very* largely vitiated by what
she had been taught. (F, 50)
Ale naneštěstí to, co se sama naučila bylo do *značné* míry pokaženo tím, co ji uči-
li. (Ž, 49)
[... was to large extent vitiated ...]

Other examples of this type are *we are very worried* > *mám velkou starost* [I-have great
worry], *the style is completely bogus* > *ten styl, to je vyslovený humbug* [that style, it is utter
humbug], *its highly fossiliferous nature* > *jeho mimořádná vhodnost k uchování otisků* [its
extraordinary suitability to preservation imprints$_{GEN}$] and others.

In all these instances the syntactic divergence involves only the internal structure
of a clause element, not a divergence in a clause element as such. As regards the FSP,
the FSP function of both the English and the Czech construction is subject to the FSP
function of the headword, within whose distributional subfield the component adver-
bial+adjective in English / adjective+noun in Czech displays parallel distribution of
communicative dynamism.

As regards adverbials reflected in postmodification (2 instances in the Czech-English direction and 3 in the opposite direction), the correspondence was difficult to
determine owing to the ambiguity of certain syntactic positions, in particular the position after the object, which may be occupied, besides postmodifying structures with
the object as head, by two separate clause elements, adverbial or object complement.
Here the boundary especially between adverbials and postmodification sometimes remains indeterminate as a result of their gradient nature. Cf. ex (12), which allows two
or more interpretations, largely depending on extralinguistic factors.

(12) she seemed to forget Mrs Poulteney's presence, as if she saw Christ *on the Cross
before her.* (F, 54)
... jako by viděla Krista před sebou na kříži. (Ž, 53)
[... as if she-saw Christ before her on cross]

The most likely interpretation of the first prepositional phrase is postmodification,
the unity of the concept being indicated by the capital C of the cross. However, from
the structural point of view adverbial interpretation is not ruled out. The second prepositional phrase may modify the cross or have the function of locative adverbial with
equal plausibility. Occasionally the problem is solved in the translation by a change in
the word order, as is the case here. The reordering of the two prepositional phrases is
partly justified by the thematic function of the PrepP *before her.* On the other hand,
adverbial interpretation of the first PrepP leaves room for doubt.

The 5 adverbials with postmodifiers as counterparts, included in the number of
divergent instances, are illustrated by (13) and (14).

(13) It was, in short, a *bargain struck between two obsessions*. (F, 59)
      Byla to zkrátka *dohoda mezi dvěma posedlostmi*. (Ž, 59)
      [Was it in-short bargain between two obssessions]

In the original the PrepP complements a verb, which is left out in the translation, hence the PrepP becomes directly dependent on the noun.
      Similarly in the opposite direction, cf. (14)

(14) Rozplakala jsem se štěstím. (K1, 24)
      [I-began-cry ~auxiliary reflexive particle~ joy~INSTR~]
      I cried tears *of joy*. (H1, 14)

2.3 The next correspondence according to the frequency of occurrence concerns adverbials rendered as subjects (18 Czech-English instances, and 26 English-Czech). In the former direction, this correspondence is the third most frequent, in the latter it ranks even higher as the second. In both directions a large majority of all instances displays a clearcut pattern illustrated by the examples listed under (15).

(15) a. *V těch pauzách* byla celá hrůza, která ... (K2, 70)
          [In those pauses was all horror which befell ...]
          Those pauses contained all the horror that ... (H2, 71)
      b. *Z hadic* tryskala rozprašovaná voda na trávník. (K2, 77)
          [From hosepipes jetted sprinkled water on lawn]
          The sprinklers were spouting jets of water over the lawn. (H2, 79)
      c. *Na dvou židlích* seděli mužové. (K1, 16)
          [On two chairs sat men]
          Two chairs were occupied by men. (H1, 6)

Here Czech thematic adverbials in initial position have English counterparts that preserve both the initial position and the thematic function, but diverge syntactically in being construed as subjects. Czech intransitive verbs are largely replaced by English transitive counterparts allowing the subject construction of the Czech adverbial. Example (15) c. illustrates this correspondence with a concomitant change in voice. In general, the syntactic divergence results in a sentence structure which also complies with the grammatical rules of English word order. Here the role of FSP as the motivating factor of the syntactic divergence is self-evident.
      As regards the Czech subject equivalents of English adverbials, again a distinctive pattern emerges, which is found in more than two-thirds of the examples. In all these instances the English adverbial, mostly a *by*-agent or quasi-agent, complements a passive verb, stands in postverbal position and constitutes the rheme or a component of the rheme. The structure is rendered by the active voice in Czech with the adverbial reflected in the subject, which preserves both the final position and the rhematic function. Compare the examples presented under (16).

(16) a. He found himself *greeted only by that lady.* (F, 43)
   Uvítala ho pouze tato *dáma.* (Ž, 41)
   [greeted him only this lady]
 b. the air was *torn by the scream of engines* (J, 10)
   vzduch *rozdrásalo ječení motorů* (N, 212)
   [air$_{ACC}$ tore scream$_{NOM}$ engines$_{GEN}$]
 c. the salt tang *borne* to him *on the wind* (J, 14)
   slaná příchuť vzduchu, *kterou* k němu *přinášel vítr,* (N, 217)
   [salt tang air$_{GEN}$ which$_{ACC}$ to him brought wind$_{NOM}$]

The remaining instances, illustrated by (17) a. and b., present the same pattern without a change in voice, i.e. a final or postverbal rhematic adverbial in English vs. an intransitive verb followed by rhematic subject at the end.

(17) a. Mrs Poulteney … realized Sarah's face *was streaming with tears.* (F, 54)
   Paní Poulteneyová … spatřila, že po Sařině obličeji *tečou proudem slzy.* (Ž, 53)
   [on Sarah's face streamed tears]
 b. Such an effect … *sprang from a profound difference* between the two women. (F, 54)
   Tento důsledek … *působil rozdíl* mezi oběma ženami. (Ž, 53)
   [This effect$_{ACC}$ caused difference$_{NOM}$ between both women]

There were two instances of thematic adverbials, one in final and the other in initial position, which were both reflected in initial thematic subjects in Czech, cf. (18) a. and b.

(18) a. There was nothing new to him *in this.* (J, 12)
   Ale *to* pro něj nebylo nic nového. (N, 214)
   [But this for him not-was nothing new]
 b. *Here* had been contrast indeed. (J, 21)
   Tohle byl věru pořádný kontrast. (N, 223)
   [This was indeed great contrast]

In the English-Czech direction the syntactic divergence cannot be ascribed to FSP. In all instances the preservation of the rhematic function of the adverbial, involving final position, can be achieved by imitating the syntactic structure of the English sentence. Where the FSP function of the English adverbial is thematic, again the syntactic function can be preserved, with one constraint on the position: the theme cannot stand at the end.[5] The largest group of examples, in which the syntactic divergence is accompanied by depassivization, is due to the nature of the Czech passive and its sta-

---

5   In sentences with objective word order in Mathesius' terms (Mathesius 1975: 83–84), i.e. unmarked sentences free of emotive or emphatic features.

tus in the Czech verbal system. Noting only features important from the contrastive point of view, the Czech participial passive is much rarer than the English passive, besides being marked as formal, while the reflexive passive as a rule does not allow the expression of the agent. Some of the other examples, as (17) a., show a difference in verbal government (here Czech does not allow the concomitant subject construction of the locative element). The changes in (18) a. and b. may be connected with the use of the verb *být* 'be'.

2.4 The last group of adverbials whose rendering in the other language is represented by a sufficient number of examples to display a distinctive pattern[6] comprises adverbials with no separate counterpart as a component of the sentence structure. The adverbials are expressed only within the morphosemantic structure of the verb into which they are incorporated. This correspondence, rare in the Czech-English direction (5 instances), ranks first (29 instances) from English to Czech (see Tables 3 and 4). As was mentioned in 2., inclusion of the English adverbial into the meaning of the Czech verb accounts for the lower degree of syntactic constancy of adverbials as compared with the subject. The notable difference between English and Czech in this respect is to be ascribed to the analytic vs. synthetic character of the two languages.

Identification of instances of this group involved drawing a line between phrasal verbs and free combinations of verb + adverb. In this procedure the usual tests were employed (semantic criteria and word order tests, cf. Quirk et al. 1985: 1152–55).

The 5 instances of this correspondence from Czech to English show that Czech occasionally displays analytic and English synthetic features, cf. (19).

(19) *Znovu se oženil.* (K1, 13)
  [Again ~reflexive particle~ he-married]
  He had *remarried*. (H1, 3)
(20) *Zvedl* jsem oči *vzhůru.* (K1, 16)
  [I-raised ~auxiliary~ eyes upwards]
  I *raised* my eyes. (H1, 7)

In (20) the upward direction is also expressed by the verb in Czech, which alone may serve as a counterpart of the English *raise*.

The 29 instances of this correspondence from English to Czech are illustrated by (21) a., b., c, d. Of these, types b. and c. were found to be the most frequent.

---

6 The only other sparsely recurrent correspondences were adverbial > subject complement in the Czech-English direction (5 instances), and adverbial > verb from English to Czech (4 instances, see Tables 3 and 4). The former correspondence appears to be due to the choice of a more idiomatic rendition, cf. *Začal se ke mě chovat jako kdysi dávno* (K1, 21) [he-began ~reflexive particle~ to me behave like once long-ago]—*He was his old self again* (H1, 11). An example of the latter is *Up this grassland [she might be seen walking], with frequent turns towards the sea* (F 58)— *Bývalo ji vidět, jak jde po travnatém svahu a často se otáčí směrem k moři* (Ž, 58) [it-was-usual her see as she-walks on grassy slope and often ~reflexive particle~ turns towards to sea].

(21) a. the dinghy ... *swung* slowly *round* (J, 10)
   loďka ... zvolna se *otáčela* (N, 212)
   [dinghy ... slowly $_{\text{reflexive particle}}$ turned]
 b. ... when his new book *comes out.* (J, 30)
   ... až *vyjde* jeho nová kniha. (N, 232)
   [... when out$_{\text{prefix}}$ goes his new book]
 c. Alice Kerrison ... *bounced down* from her seat (J, 19)
   Alice Kerrisonová ... *seskočila* z kozlíku (N, 221)
   [Alice Kerrisonová down$_{\text{prefix}}$ jumped from buggyseat]
 d. ... they *are always* difficult to find. (F, 44)
   ... *bývá* velmi obtížné je najít. (Ž, 42)
   [... it-usually-is very difficult them find]

Being incorporated in the verb, the adverbial also shares its FSP function. Thus in d. it is a constituent of the typical FSP function of the verb, the transition, while in a. *round*, the rheme proper of the English sentence, occurs as a component of the rheme proper constituted by the verb *se otáčela*.

2.5 In the observations on FSP as a factor involved in the different types of syntactic noncorrespondences discussed in 2.1–2.4, the particular syntactic divergence has been generally found to accord with the basic distribution of communicative dynamism (CD), i.e. the element affected by the divergence appeared in a position consistent with its degree of CD. This finding appears to confirm the assumption on which the study of interlingual syntactic constancy is based, viz. the subordinate status of syntactic structure with respect to the FSP (information) structure. Strictly speaking, what is involved in the syntactic divergences under discussion is not the FSP as such but the basic distribution of CD, i.e. the order theme—transition—rheme (or in the rheme-oriented terms the principle of end focus). However, for conveying the same FSP structure neither in the original nor in the translated text is the basic distribution of CD necessary. This applies primarily to English: here instances of thematic elements in final position were noted in (2) and (3) (cf. also (7), which shows this difference in linear arrangement in the opposite English-Czech direction). Another instance of deviation from the basic distribution of CD is illustrated by (22).

(22) Napravo od ní se svažoval k hladině břeh *zarostlý travou a plevelem.* (K1, 33)
   [On-right from it $_{\text{reflexive particle}}$ sloped to level (=of water) bank overgrown grass$_{\text{INSTR}}$ and weed$_{\text{INSTR}}$]
   To the right of the path *a mixture of grass and weeds* sloped down to the level of the water. (H1, 22)

Like (2) and (3), example (22) has a contextually bound thematic element at the end (cf. the medial position of this element in the Czech original), but unlike these examples, in which the rheme occurs in the final (postverbal) position, it has the rheme, realized by the subject, in preverbal position. As a result, the basic distribution of CD is reversed: rheme—transition—theme. Apart from the transition, constituted by the verb, the only element occurring in the position consistent with its degree of CD is the initial thematic adverbial, which connects the sentence with the preceding text. The configuration rheme—transition—theme constitutes one of the forms of the presentation scale (cf. Chapter 12 and Firbas 1992, 66–68). An instance of this form of the presentation scale was also found in the English original, cf. (23). Its Czech counterpart expectedly displays the basic distribution of CD (Th—Tr—Rh).

(23) and *dreadful heresies* drifted across the poor fellow's brain (F, 46)
a jeho mozek počaly pokoušet kacířské myšlenky (Ž, 44)
[and his brain$_{ACC}$ began tempt *heretic thoughts*$_{NOM}$]

Another instance of a different linear arrangement in the two languages is illustrated by (24). Here, however, the FSP appears to be changed. The sentence is given with its foregoing context (in square brackets) to show the interplay of all the factors determining the FSP functions in written language, context dependence, semantic structure and linearity.

(24) [Tomáš si tehdy neuvědomoval, že metafory jsou nebezpečná věc. S metaforami není radno si hrát.] Láska se může narodit *z jedné metafory*. (K2, 15)
[Love $_{reflexive particle}$ can be-born from one single metaphor.]
[Tomas did not realize at the time that metaphors are dangerous. Metaphors are not to be trifled with.] *A single metaphor* can give birth to love. (H2, 10)

As the context shows, *metaphor* is a context-dependent element, while *love*, even if occurring in the more distant context, is less recoverable and hence more dynamic. Nevertheless, the Czech sentence presents it in the theme, the rheme being constituted by the final adverbial consisting of a context-dependent noun and a new element, the rheme proper, in premodification. In the English translation, the FSP of the sentence consistent with unmarked intonation, i.e. with the nucleus (intonation centre) on the last element, presents *metaphor* as the theme and *love* as the rheme. Whether the translator misinterpreted the FSP of the Czech sentence or relied on contrastive stress on the subject for the interpretation, the result is infelicitous: in the former case there is a different focus, while the latter relies on immediate recoverability of *love* from the preceding context. As shown by the preceding context, however, *love* is not mentioned in the immediately preceding sentences.

However, these are rare exceptions. In general, what has been observed as the outcome of the syntactic divergence with respect to FSP is the achievement or preservation of the basic distribution of CD, which is significant mainly in the Czech-English direction. In Czech this is the primary word order principle in general. As far as English is concerned, syntactically divergent translation counterparts resulting in the basic distribution of CD testify to the universality of the principle of end focus and to the subordinate status of syntactic structure.

3. To conclude by summing up the principal findings of the foregoing discussion, the greater mobility of adverbials in English does not appear to dispose them to a higher degree of syntactic constancy as compared with syntactic constancy of the subject. The causes thereof are to be sought in the divergent syntactic counterparts specific to adverbials. In the Czech-English direction it is the noun modifier, predominantly the premodifier, in the opposite direction inclusion of the adverbial into the morphosemantic structure of the verb. These two types of correspondence account respectively, for 23% and 29% of all syntactically divergent instances. As counterparts of the subject, these correspondences have not been found.

As regards the role of FSP as a motivating factor of the syntactic divergence, three variables were considered: syntactic structure, FSP structure and linear arrangement.

Syntactic structure affected by FSP was found in the Czech-English direction in the case of Czech initial thematic adverbials reflected in English initial thematic subjects. Without the syntactic divergence the English sentence structure would deviate either from the grammatical word order or from the basic distribution of CD. As a result of the syntactic divergence it complies with both. In the case of the other syntactically divergent English counterparts of Czech adverbials, the syntactic divergence affects neither the FSP function of the respective element, nor its position, but largely preserves both. In the type of correspondence Czech adverbial > English object the divergence consists in different verb valency reflected in different verbal government. Similarly Czech adverbials corresponding to English premodifiers, mostly found in English verbonominal constructions, again display analogous FSP functions and linear arrangement.

In the English-Czech direction, syntactic divergence serving to achieve basic distribution of CD is not needed since FSP is the primary word order principle, and sentence elements can be linearly rearranged by mere movement. The ascertained correspondences between English adverbials and their Czech nonadverbial counterparts partly reflect systemic differences between the two languages, notably in the status and employment of the passive, partly derive from the synthetic character of Czech as opposed to the analytic character of English, as shown by incorporation of the meaning expressed by a separate English adverbial into the morphosemantic structure of a Czech verb. Moreover, they reveal minor tendencies favouring structures with nonadverbial components which call for further research.

SOURCES

[F]   Fowles, J. *The French Lieutenant's Woman.* London: Triad–Granada, 1983 (1st ed. 1969).
[Ž]   Fowles, J. *Francouzova milenka.* Translated by Hana Žantovská. Prague: Mladá fronta–Smena–Naše vojsko, 1976.
[J]   James, P. D. *Unnatural Causes.* London: Sphere Books, 1984 (1st ed. 1967).
[N]   Jamesová, P.D. *Z příčin nikoli přirozených.* Translated by J. Z. Novák. In *3x Adam Dalgliesh*, Prague: Odeon, 1986.
[K1] Kundera M. *Žert.* Brno: Atlantis, 1966.

[H1] Kundera, M. *The Joke.* Translated by Michael Henry Heim. New York: Harper and Row, 1984.
[K2] Kundera, M. *Nesnesitelná lehkost bytí.* Toronto: Sixty-Eight Publishers, 1985.
[H2] Kundera, M. *The Unbearable Lightness of Being.* Translated by Michael Henry Heim. London: Faber and Faber, 1999.

3. A SIDE VIEW OF SYNTACTIC CONSTANCY OF ADVERBIALS BETWEEN ENGLISH AND CZECH

First published in Jan Chovanec (ed.) *Theory and Practice in English Studies, Proceedings of the Seventh Conference of English, American and Canadian Studies*, Vol. 1, 19–34. Brno: Masaryk University, 2003. Reprinted without the introductory part.

0. This chapter follows up the findings of Chapter 2 with a view to verifying or modifying them by adopting a different approach. While in the latter, as in all other chapters concerned with syntactic constancy of clause elements in this volume, the investigation was based on instances of non-correspondence in the direction original – translation, here the direction of the divergence is reversed: adverbials in the Czech translations are examined with respect to the underlying elements in the English originals. This procedure suggested itself during the collection of the English-Czech material for Chapter 2, insofar as it displayed numerous instances of adverbials in the Czech translations that had non-adverbial counterparts in the English originals. To obtain comparable results, excerption and analysis of adverbials in the Czech translations were carried out in the same way as in the case of English adverbials – Czech translation counterparts.

1. To begin with, it was expected that the results would basically correspond to those obtained on the basis of English originals and Czech translations, presented in the previous chapter (cf. Table 4, p. 34). However, as follows from Table 1, this expectation proved to be unrealistic.

   1.1 The procedure from the Czech translation adverbials to the English non-adverbial counterparts yielded a substantially larger number of instances of non-correspondence.

Table 1 *Czech translation adverbials rendering English original non-adverbial elements*

Non-adverbial element in English texts J and F	Adverbial element in Czech translations			
	N	Ž	Total	
			abs.	%
premodifier	32	21	53	21.6
determiner	3	1	4	1.6
postmodifier	11	4	15	6.1
subject	18	11	29	12.0
object	15	20	35	14.2
subject complement	14	15	29	12.0
object complement	2	2	4	1.6
prefix/component of a compound	5	8	13	5.3
semantic feature of a verb or another word class	19 (+3)	15 (+6)	43	17.5
verb	5	6	11	4.5
cleft and pseudo-cleft sentence	1	5	6	2.4
disjunct clause	2	–	2	0.8
apposition	1	–	1	0.4
total abs.	131	114	245	–
%	53.5	46.5	100	100.0

Table 2 *English divergent counterparts of Czech adverbials*

English counterparts	Czech adverbials					
	K1		K2		total	
	abs.	%	abs.	%	abs.	%
subject	6	12.0	12	24.0	18	18.0
object	25	50.0	19	38.0	44	44.0
premodifier	8	16.0	15	30.0	23	23.0
postmodifier	2	4.0	–	–	2	2.0
inclusion in the verb	3	6.0	2	4.0	5	5.0
verb	1	2.0	–	–	1	1.0
subject complement	4	8.0	1	2.0	5	5.0
other	1	2.0	1	2.0	2	2.0
total	50	100.0	50	100.0	100	100.0

In comparison with Table 4 on p. 34 (non-adverbial English counterparts of Czech adverbials), reprinted here as Table 2 for convenience sake, instances of syntactic non-correspondence are more than twice as numerous (245 against 100). It may be argued that the source texts are different, viz. translated text vs. original text, and hence incomparable. However, one measure remains constant: the same two texts (J and F), which yielded each 50 instances of non-adverbial counterparts of adverbials in the translations, displayed, respectively, 131 and 114 such instances when the adverbials in the translations were considered with respect to whether or not they reflected non-adverbial elements in the originals. In the following discussion an explanation of this difference is sought, besides the differences between the quantitative data, in the differences between the registered types of non-correspondence.

1.2 As shown by Table 1, most of the types of syntactic non-correspondence are represented by more than ten occurrences. Starting with those that also appear in Table 2, we find among the best-represented the subject, object and premodifier. However, while in Table 2 the object is almost twice as frequent (44 occurrences) as the next element on the frequency scale, the premodifier (23 occurrences), here the representation of the object is not much higher than that of the subject and the subject complement (35, 29 and 29 occurrences, respectively). Moreover, in Table 2 the subject complement appears at the bottom end of the frequency scale, being represented only by five occurrences. Another quantitative difference between Tables 2 and 1 is found in the relative positions occupied by the two most frequent elements, the object and the premodifier, which are reversed, the premodifier being much more frequent than the object in Table 1.

1.2.1 Czech adverbial counterparts of objects in the English originals display two distinct patterns one of which is identical with that described in Chapter 2 (2.1), according to expectation. English transitive verbs with objects are reflected in Czech intransitive verbs modified by adverbials, as in (1).

(1) Alice Kerrison *drove the buggy* behind the fringe of trees (J, 19)
    Alice Kerrisonová *zajela s bryčkou* [the buggy] za hradbu stromů (N, 221)

This type accounts for about a half of the examples of this group. The other type, somewhat less frequent, also involves different government, in this case the government of transitive verbs. Compare (2).

(2) *seeing those around her* as fictional characters (F, 50)
    V osobách kolem sebe [In persons around her] spatřovala osoby z románů (Ž, 49)

This type is also found among the Czech object counterparts of English adverbials (listed in Table 2), but owing to the choice of lexical equivalents the examples are not so illustrative as in the data in Table 1. Example (3) is one of the more clear-cut ones.

(3) the situation of her cottage ... gave her every opportunity of keeping an eye *on things*. (J, 15)
místo, kde stojí její vilka, ... jí dává dokonalou příležitost mít pořád *všechno* [every-thing] na očích. (N, 218)

These two types account for a large majority of Czech adverbials rendering English non-adverbial elements. From the contrastive point of view, the former type is of more interest in that it shows the neutral nature of the English verb with respect to syntactic transitivity/intransitivity. Semantically intransitive verbs freely take objects which are semantically similar to adverbials. In inflectional Czech, on the other hand, the relationship between semantic and syntactic structure is much closer.

1.2.2 The correspondence between English modifiers and Czech adverbials, represented by 23 instances in Table 2, appears to be the most frequent type among the Czech adverbial counterparts of English non-adverbial elements (53 occurrences). The type described in Chapter 2 as the largely predominant one (cf. 2.2) is here represented by three examples only, cf. (4).

(4) for the first time since her arrival, she *gave the faintest smile* (F, 59)
poprvé od svého příchodu *se slabounce usmála* [fainly smiled] (Ž, 59)

The verbal meaning, which is decomposed into the categorial component (the verb) and the notional component (the object action noun) is expressed by a semantically corresponding verb in Czech, the English premodifier of the object action noun being concomitantly reflected in the adverbial modifier of the Czech verb.

Most instances of this group display a different pattern, illustrated by the examples listed under (5).

(5) a. at almost *the precise moment* (J, 11)
   přesně ve chvíli [precisely at moment] (N, 213)
   b. *the legal, certified* next of kin (J, 11)
   úředně potvrzená [legally certified] nejbližší příbuzná (N, 213)
   c. there was also a *daily* service—(F, 53)
   také se konala *denně* [daily$_{adverb}$] ranní pobožnost (Ž, 52)

In a. the modifier of the noun, reflected in the adverbial, is the only noun premodifier, in b. the first of two premodifiers, and in c. the difference is connected with the use of a full verb in Czech as the counterpart of *be* in English. Examples of this kind account for over a half of all instances of Czech adverbials reflecting English modifiers. Examples of the c. subtype show the more verbal character of Czech; the b. examples suggest a preference for subordination in multiple premodification at the cost of multiple coordination. Somewhat surprisingly, among English premodifiers reflecting Czech adverbials the c. subtype is marginal. For illustration, cf. (6).

(6) Když některá *udělala dřep špatně* [did kneebend badly] (K2, 22)
     If one of us *did a bad kneebend* (H2, 18)

Type b. also occurs among Czech premodifiers reflecting English adverbials (cf. Table 4 in Chapter 2), cf. (7).

(7) The servants were permitted to hold evening prayers in the kitchen, under Mrs
     Fairley's eye and *briskly wooden* voice. (F, 54)
     Služebnictvu se dovolovalo odbývat večerní modlitby v kuchyni za lhostejného
     dozoru paní Fairleyové a při zvuku jejího *úsečného neohebného* hlasu [brisk wooden
     voice]. (Ž, 53)

However, this is rare. Most instances are there connected with a difference in the word class of the headword, as in (8).

(8) they were *very* worried (J, 27)
     mají *velkou* [great (worry)] starost (N, 229)

In the type under discussion in this section, connection with a difference in the headword was observed in the small group illustrated by (4). A partly similar case is found where a premodified action noun in the English original is reflected in the corresponding verb + adverbial in the Czech translation, as in (9).

(9) without an accompanying lecture *on my inefficient housekeeping* (J, 22)
     aniž ji doprovodí kázáním, jak *neschopně hospodařím* [inefficiently] (N, 224)

In connection with English instances of premodification reflected in Czech adverbials mention should also be made of postmodification, which is marginal in Table 2, but represented by 15 examples in Table 1. Czech and English show a difference in this point in that a prepositional phrase following an object in English is often indeterminate between postmodification and adverbial function.[1] This is rare in Czech because an adverbial is as a rule indicated as such by its non-contiguous position. Compare (10).

(10) he likes to do *research for his books* in the Club Library (J, 228)
     pro své knihy [for his books] si rád dělá rešerše v klubové knihovně (N, 228)

1.2.3 Adverbials in the Czech translations reflecting the subject in the English originals are all found in the same pattern: the English subject stands in initial (or preverbal) position, is semantically equivalent to the Czech adverbial, and has the FSP function of the theme. Initial position and thematic function also characterize the Czech

---

1   Cf. the discussion of (12) in Chapter 2.

adverbials so that the original element and its translation counterpart differ only in the syntactic function. This is in agreement with what has been found in the Czech-English direction in Chapter 2. However, all examples discussed in this section represent the subtype with an active verb in both languages. Besides providing evidence in support of previous findings, they throw more light on the representation of semantic roles.

(11) *Cambridge* had not changed her. (J, 23)
   v Cambridgi [in Cambridge] se s ní neudála žádná změna. (N, 225)

Among instances of this group we even find the textbook example (12):

(12) *His bed* hadn't been slept in (J, 27)
   V jeho posteli [in his bed] nikdo nespal (N, 229)

The semantic role of most subjects/adverbials is locative, as in (11) and (12). Other semantic roles (means, reason, manner, time, and others, cf. (13) a. and b.) are represented by one or two instances.

(13) a. Once again *Sarah's simplicity* took all the wind from her swelling spite. (F, 59)
       Zase jednou jí Sarah *svou prostotou* [through her simplicity] vzala všechen vítr ze vzdutých plachet. (Ž, 58)
    b. and never once had *it* made him want to change his job (J, 25)
       ani jednou se mu *kvůli tomu* [because of it] nezachtělo změnit povolání (N, 227)

Examples of this kind show the perspicacy of Mathesius' observation, made many decades ago,[2] on the thematic character of the English subject (1947a: 278). In Czech, on the other hand, there is a closer relationship between syntactic function and semantic role. Semantic roles characteristic of adverbials do not as a rule appear in the subject construction.

1.2.4 The next clause element to be discussed on account of its frequency of occurrence is the subject complement (29 occurrences as in the case of the subject, see Table 1). In the Czech-English direction it ranks low on the frequency scale, being represented by five instances (see Table 3 in Chapter 2), which appear to be individual solutions allowing no generalizations.

On the other hand, the examples listed under subject complement in Table 1 clearly fall into two groups. In the first an English copula is reflected in a Czech full verb, with the concomitant correspondence subject complement : adverbial. The second group of examples demonstrates the different status of copulas in English and Czech: whereas English copulas constitute a fairly clearcut category, defined by both formal and

2   Mathesius (1947a) first appeared in *Časopis pro moderní filologii* 10, 244–48, in 1924.

semantic features, and represented by several subtypes, Czech copulas are virtually limited to *být* 'be' and *stát se* 'become', but even these lack clear structural character-istics. The two groups are illustrated, respectively, by (14) a. and b.

(14) a. How can you *be so sure?* (J, 28)
Jak to můžete *vědět tak jistě* [know so surely]? (N, 230)
b. Most of her listeners *looked stunned.* (J, 29)
Většina jejích posluchačů *vypadala udiveně* [wonderingly]. (N, 231)

Both the status of the copulas and examples of the a. type show the more verbal character of Czech, as compared with English.

1.2.5 Adverbials in the Czech translations as counterparts of verbs in the English originals account for 11 instances (see Table 1), as compared with one occurrence in Table 2. Leaving aside modal verbs reflected in Czech modal adverbials functioning as sentence modifiers, we find verbs modifying the main verbs, as in (15) a. and b., and verbs in adverbial clauses reflected in action nouns forming constituents of Czech adverbial prepositional phrases, as in (15) c.

(15) a. I *do* realize that. (J, 24)
To si *moc dobře* [very well] uvědomuju. (N, 226)
b. If her neighbours were so ill-advised as not *to keep her informed* (J, 15)
Když její sousedé jednají tak neuváženě, že ji *průběžně* [currently] *neinformují o* ... (N, 217)
c. *as he gazed* up at the lias strata (F, 47)
při pohledu [during look (at)] na vrstvy liasu (Ž, 46)

As shown by the c. example, it is sometimes Czech that displays nominal expres-sion as a counterpart of a finite clause in English, although the general tendency op-erates in the opposite direction (see Mathesius 1975: 146–52, Vachek 1961: 31–44 and Hladký 1961).

1.2.6 In the last two large groups of adverbials in the Czech translations which correspond to non-adverbial elements in the English originals a separate element un-derlying the Czech counterpart is missing. Here what appears as a Czech adverbial partly reflects a morpheme of a derived or a compound word, and partly corresponds to a semantic feature of a word, not expressed by a separate morpheme. The latter type is represented by considerably more examples (43 against 13, see Table 1, semantic fea-ture of a verb or of another word class, vs. prefix/component of a compound). In the Czech-English direction (Table 2) this type is listed under inclusion in the verb and ap-pears to be marginal (five occurrences). However, it is the most numerous group in the opposite direction: here inclusion of an English adverbial into the make-up of a Czech verb ranks highest (29 instances, cf. Chapter 2, Table 4 and 2.4). This is what might be expected, considering the analytical character of English and the synthetic character of Czech. The data in Table 1, however, modify previous findings.

Czech adverbials corresponding to prefixes or components of compounds in English are illustrated by (16) a. and b.

(16) a. but out of the *superimposed* strata of flint (F, 45)
　　　ale ve vrstvách křemene *ležících nad ním* [lying above it] (Ž, 43)
　　　a *fore-doomed* attempt (F, 47)
　　　předem odsouzený [beforehand doomed] pokus (Ž, 45)
　　b. framed by *shoulder-length* black hair (J, 23)
　　　orámovaný černými vlasy, *spadajícími až k ramenům* [falling as-far-as to shoulders] (N, 225)

Adverbials explicitly expressing a semantic feature of an English verb or of another word class occur in instances like (17).

(17) a. He *glimpsed* a dark head (J, 15)
　　　Letmo [fleetingly] *zahlédl* tmavou hlavu (N, 217)
　　　She may *be bringing* her niece. (J, 21)
　　　Celia *k nám* [to us] asi *veze* svou neteř. (N, 223–224)
　　b. There was also a *sleek* lawn (J, 16)
　　　Byl tam také *pečlivě* [carefully] *upravený* trávník (N, 218)
　　　the *mossy* banks of the little brook (F, 62)
　　　mechem porostlé [with-moss covered] břehy potůčku (Ž, 62)

Since this point is demonstrated in both translations, produced by different authors, it is presumably not a feature of the translator's technique, but reflects a more general aspect. Whether this is really the case remains to be investigated.

1.2.7 The only remaining point to be briefly commented upon is the cleft and pseudo-cleft sentence (6 occurrences, see Table 1). In the Czech-English direction, as a counterpart of a Czech adverbial, it occurred only once and was listed under the subject complement, cf. (18).

(18) Ne *z nenávisti* [from hatred] k nim. (K1, 26)
　　It wasn't hate that made me do what I did. (H1, 17)

The Czech counterparts of English cleft and pseudo-cleft sentences display the focalizer *právě* 'precisely', a device usually resorted to in Czech translations, cf. (19)

(19) a. *It was this place, … that* Charles had entered (F, 62)
　　　A právě v tato místa [And just in these places], … vstoupil Charles (Ž, 62)
　　b. *This latter reason was why* Ernestina had never met her at Marlborough House. (F, 56)
　　　Právě proto [Just therefore] se s ní Ernestina v Marlborough House nikdy nesetkala. (Ž, 56)

The use of a focalizer as a counterpart of the English construction, although Czech possesses a structural parallel, may be a reflex of acquired translating procedures, but even so it testifies to the basically synthetic nature of Czech.

1.3 As regards the FSP aspect, functional sentence perspective appears to play a role mainly in the Czech-English direction insofar as it fully displays the interaction of syntactic structure, FSP structure and word order, in dependence on the character of the language system (see Chapter 2, 2.3). Where the target language is Czech, as is the case in the opposite direction, the main point of interest is found in instances in which the word order in the English original differs from that in Czech. As far as Czech itself is concerned, word order is subordinate to the FSP structure while syntactic structure, being indicated by inflections, is largely free of word order constraints. The observations made in this section thus concern the differences in word order, or more exactly deviations from the basic distribution of communicative dynamism in English and their reflections in Czech. Some of these have been noted before, cf. (10), (11) and (15) a., in which a thematic element (*for his books, her, that*, respectively) occupies final or postverbal position, whereas in Czech it occurs early in the sentence. Other instances of a different linear ordering but similar FSP structure are illustrated by the examples listed under (20).

(20) a. A distant woodpecker drummed in the branches of some high tree (F, 62)
V dálce, v koruně některého z vysokých stromů, ťukal do větví datel (Ž, 62)
[In distance, in crown of-one of high trees, drummed into branches woodpecker]
a new species cannot enter the world (F, 47)
na světě se nemůže objevit nový druh (Ž, 45)
[in world reflexive particle cannot appear new species]
there was a charming domestic touch about the gay little equipage (J, 18)
Ta čilá, drobná ekvipáž působila líbezně domácky (N, 220)
[That sprightly, little equipage impressed charmingly domestically]
b. *Strange* as it may *seem* (F, 62)
Jakkoliv to *zní podivně* [However it sounds strangely] (Ž, 62)

The examples listed under a. have the same semantic structure in presenting a phenomenon on the scene, which, if context independent, functions as the rheme. In the existential construction, this is indicated not only by the semantic structure but also by the postverbal position of the notional subject. In the other two examples, the ordering of the sentence elements acts counter to the FSP structure, which, however, is clearly indicated by the semantic structure and context dependence and is reflected in the Czech word order. Similarly the b. example shows the dominance of the grammatical word order principle in English, which is again overruled by context, semantic structure, and in this case by syntactic structure as well, since the subject complement as a rule has the FSP function of rheme.

Instances of this kind form a small minority (some 16 per cent) in comparison with instances which have both a similar ordering of elements and a similar FSP structure in either language. This is shown by most of the adduced examples.

In a few instances a different or even similar ordering of elements displays a different FSP structure in the two languages, cf. (21).

(21) a. As if sensing the strong tug *of the on-shore current*, it began to move ... (J, 10)
Jako kdyby vycítila, že proud přílivu ji pevně *potáhne*, začala se pohybovat (N, 212)
[As-if she-felt that current of-tide her strongly will-tug, she-began reflexive particle move]

b. (a third party might well have wondered) what horror could be coming. (F, 60)
[Nezúčastněný divák by patrně nedýchal napětím], jaká hrůza tu vyjde najevo. (Ž, 60)
[what horror here will-come to-light]

In example a. the rheme proper is the final element in both English and Czech, but owing to divergent ordering, it is a different element. In b. the ordering is the same, but the semantic structure differs: while the English sentence presents horror as a phenomenon appearing on the scene, and hence has a rhematic subject, in the Czech sentence the rheme is the final adverbial complementing the verb. In general, however, these instances are very rare.

A final remark on FSP concerns English verbs one of whose semantic features is expressed by an added adverbial in Czech (see 1.2.6). The adverbial may be expected to share the FSP function of the verb, which means that where the verb is rhematic, the adverbial should function as the rheme proper. The latter case, illustrated by (22), is very rare. Normally, the verb has its characteristic FSP function of transition and the adverbial operates within it, as shown by (17) a.

(22) ... not through any desire on Sarah's part *to kill the subject*, but ... (F, 56)
... ne že by si byla přála *sprovodit* námět rozhovoru *ze světa*, ale ... (Ž, 56)

2. The findings of the present additional research, apart from providing more material confirming previous results, have brought out several points which appear worth further pursuit. The first point to note is the much lower constancy of adverbials than ascertained in the previous study.

Another point which appears in a different light is the tendency in Czech to verbal expression as against the tendency to nominal expression in English. Given that the tendencies hold in general, there also appear to be areas which show them to be reversed. Confirmation or refutation of this finding is a matter of further study.

The present treatment has also brought some findings about the subject complement, which has so far been noted only as a marginal counterpart of other syntactic elements. Since it is the next clause element to be treated in the study of interlingual syntactic constancy, the observations made here may be taken as a starting point.

As regards the basic assumption of the superordinate status of FSP structure with respect to syntactic structure, the findings obtained in the English-Czech direction are relevant in showing dissimilar word order arrangements resulting from the difference in the primary word order principle, in connection with semantic structure and similar/dissimilar syntactic structure. FSP is of course only one of the aspects that may play a role where different syntactic and similar FSP structures are observed. Other relevant factors of syntactic differences (verbal government, tendencies to verbal/nominal expression, analytic/synthetic language system) have been ascertained in almost all points under discussion.

SOURCES

Fowles, J. [F]. *The French Lieutenant's Woman*. London: Triad-Granada, 1983 (1st ed. 1969). 43-63.

Fowles, J. [Ž]. *Francouzova milenka*. Translated by Hana Žantovská. Prague: Mladá fronta-Smena-Naše vojsko, 1976, 41-63.

James, P. D. [J]. *Unnatural Causes*. London: Sphere Books, 1984 (1st ed. 1967), 9-30.

Jamesová, P. D. [N]. *Z příčin nikoli přirozených*. Translated by J. Z. Novák. In 3× *Adam Dalgliesh*, Prague: Odeon, 1986, 211-232.

Kundera M. [K1]. *Žert*. Brno: Atlantis, 1966, 11-33.

Kundera, M. [H1]. *The Joke*. Translated by Michael Henry Heim. New York: Harper and Row, 1984, 1-22.

Kundera, M. [K2]. *Nesnesitelná lehkost bytí*. Toronto: Sixty-Eight Publishers, 1985, 14-77.

Kundera, M. [H2]. *The Unbearable Lightness of Being*. Translated by Michael Henry Heim. London: Faber and Faber, 1999, 9-79.

4. SYNTACTIC CONSTANCY OF THE SUBJECT COMPLEMENT. PART 1: A COMPARISON BETWEEN CZECH AND ENGLISH

First published in *Linguistica Pragensia* 14/2, 2004, 57–71.

0. This chapter presents the results of an inquiry into syntactic constancy of the subject complement. It thus follows up the study of the clause elements treated in the preceding chapters, the subject (Chapter 1) and the adverbial (Chapters 2 and 3). The idea of investigating interlingual syntactic constancy is based on the assumption that syntactic structure is subordinate to the information structure (functional sentence perspective, cf. Firbas 1992; FSP henceforth) especially in respect of the general principle of end focus (Quirk et al. 1985: 1356–57) or end placement of the rheme.

In the previous studies this assumption has in general been confirmed. Apart from showing the extent to which FSP plays a role as a factor in syntactic divergence, depending on the clause element and the type of divergence involved, the studies also revealed other motivating factors of the divergence, some of them major ones and specific to a particular clause element. This had been expected, since FSP is regarded only as one of the potential motivating factors.

In the case of the subject complement two features, not encountered before, have to be taken into account. The FSP function of the subject complement, unlike the FSP functions of the clause elements treated so far, is almost exclusively rhematic (over 90%, see Uhlířová 1974). The other clause elements occur in both the theme and the rheme, the object and the adverbial with comparable representation, the subject favouring the function of the theme, but not to such a degree as the subject complement favours the rheme.

The other feature concerns the nature of the subject complement in Czech as compared with English. The syntactic delimitation of this clause element is inseparably connected with the class of copular verbs, which is much smaller in Czech insofar as it contains only two verbs, the counterparts of English *be* and *become*. The class of English copulas is larger (cf. Quirk et al. 1985: 1171–74), the criterion of a linking verb being the possibility of adjectival complementation (*she looks sad*) and a meaning reducible to *be* or *become* + some additional semantic feature (in the case of copulas other than *be* and *become: she looks sad* 'perceived through the sense of eyesight, she is sad'). Accordingly, an even more specific picture may be expected to emerge from an analysis of this clause element than has been obtained in the case of the clause elements treated previously.

1. The procedure adopted was the same as in the preceding studies so that comparable results might be obtained. Four parallel texts, two Czech originals + their translations into English (see Sources) were excerpted until the number of English divergent counterparts of the Czech subject complements in each sample reached fifty. At the same time the number of corresponding subject complements was noted. In this way a sample of 100 English divergent syntactic counterparts of Czech subject complements was obtained, the number of corresponding instances needed to obtain the fifty divergent ones in each sample serving as the measure of constancy. With a view to the aim of the study, care was taken to base the data only on examples whose lexical elements had equivalent counterparts in the other language, i.e. instances of free translation were left out of account.

2. In the classification of instances a problem arose how to treat translation counterparts in which a subject complement in the original appeared as a dependent component of a subject complement in the translation. This happened in the case of adjectival subject complements reflected in modifiers of subject complements realized by nouns. On purely formal grounds such instances qualify for inclusion among non-identical instances. From the semantic point of view, however, the classification is not so clear-cut.

    2.1 There were 28 instances of this kind, mostly found in the pattern Czech adjectival subject complement / English modifier of an added noun constituting the head of the subject complement (16 instances [57.1 %], 11 JI, 5 HA). In 3 instances the added head was constituted by the proform *one*, i.e. the semantic structure is identical with that of a subject complement realized by the adjective alone,[1] cf. (1).

(1) náš odjezd byl velmi kvapný (JI, 66)
    [our departure was very hurried][2]
    our departure had been a hurried one (C, 68)

    In 4 instances the head was realized by *thing* again in the function of a general substitute. To these may be added 1 example with *something* as the head and 1 with another categorial noun, *way*. Compare (2) a.,b.,c.

---

1   Cf. Mathesius' qualification by non-genuine classification, 1975: 114.
2   Square brackets in the examples are used for word-for-word translations.

(2) a. Věda je vznešená a krásná. (JI, 37)
    [Science is sublime and beautiful]
    Science ... was a sublime and beautiful thing (C, 39)
  b. bylo to hrozné (JI, 26)
    [was it terrible]
    It was something awful (C, 27)
  c. jsem na tom velmi špatně (HA, 87)
    [am on it very badly]
    I'm in a very bad way (S, 51)

In 5 cases the Czech noun is the anaphoric demonstrative *to* 'that' referring to the event/content qualified by the adjective constituting the subject complement. The English rendition is more explicit in that it names what is being referred to by the anaphoric pronominal subject. Cf. (3).

(3) Bylo to opravdu trochu drastické. (JI, 51)
    [Was that really somewhat drastic]
    It was indeed a drastic measure. (C, 53)

Similarly *pleasant* (*experience*), *foolish* (*suggestion*), *wisest* (*course*), *foolish* (*idea*). In 2 other examples of this kind the added noun refers to a personal subject: *nervous* (*wreck*), *worse* (*case*).

Instances in which a Czech adjectival subject complement appears as postmodification of an added head in English (7 altogether) are largely analogous: (*matter*) *of indifference*, (*state*) *of agitation*, (*way*) *of putting it*, (*kind*) *of release*, (*source*) *of amusement*, cf. (4).

(4) že jsem byl rozrušen (JI, 51)
    [that $_{\text{auxiliary}}$ I-was agitated]
    that I was in a state of agitation (C, 52)

Two instances deviate from this pattern in having the counterpart of a Czech quantifier or intensifier as the head: (*bit*) *of exaggeration*, (*height*) *of injustice*, cf. (5).

(5) že by bylo naprosto nespravedlivé, abych ... (JI, 48)
    [that it-would be grossly unjust]
    that it was the height of injustice that I should ... (C, 50)

The remaining instances display merger or splitting of the elements realizing the subject and the subject complement, as in (6) a. and b.

(6) a. že ... je loď malá (JI, 41)
    [that ... is boat small]
    it was a small boat (C, 42–43)

b. Kéž by to byla lichá obava (HA, 41)

[If-only$_{conditional\ particle}$ it was groundless fear]

let's hope out fears are groundless (S, 17)

The considerable frequency of occurrence of this pattern suggests a tendency of English to realize the subject complement by a noun phrase, albeit with an empty head, rather than by an adjective alone. However, this feature can be connected with the fact that predicative use of an adjective may be infelicitous with a particular subject.

2.2 If the instances discussed in 2.1 are included among identical counterparts, which appears plausible on semantic grounds, the percentages of identical and nonidentical English counterparts of Czech subject complements are as shown in Table 1.

Table 1

English counterparts	Czech subject complement					
	Jirotka (JI)		Havel (HA)		total	
	abs.	%	abs.	%	abs.	%
subject complement	212	80.9	232	82.3	444	81.6
divergent	50	19.1	50	17.7	100	18.4
total	262	100.0	282	100.0	544	100.0

If they are excluded from identical counterparts, the number of divergent instances rises to 67 (25.6%) in JI and 61 (21.6%) in HA, altogether by 5.2%, with a corresponding decrease in the number of identical instances, see Table 2.

As shown by the numbers of divergent instances in the two Tables, absolute figures comparable with those obtained for the other clause elements treated so far are presented in Table 1.

2.3 Proceeding to the unquestionably divergent syntactic counterparts of the Czech subject complement, we find the following distribution of syntactic functions (Table 3).

Table 3 shows the following representation of the divergent syntactic functions: inclusion of the subject complement in the verb (29%), followed by object and subject with comparable frequencies: 19% and 16%, respectively. Unlike these clause elements, which are well represented in both samples, the only remaining clause element with more than ten occurrences, the object complement (13%), occurs almost exclusively in one sample. Modifiers (of clause elements other than the subject complement) account together for 7%, the last clause element with a percentage above 5% being the adverbial (6%).

2.3.1 The best represented group, Czech copula + subject complement reflected in an English full lexical verb (29 instances) is mostly illustrated by the following examples.

Table 2

English counterparts	Czech subject complement					
	Jirotka (JI)		Havel (HA)		total	
	abs.	%	abs.	%	abs.	%
identical	195	74.4	221	78.4	416	76.5
nonidentical	67	25.6	61	21.6	128	23.5
total	262	100.0	282	100.0	544	100.0

Table 3

English divergent counterparts	Czech subject complement					
	Jirotka (JI)		Havel (HA)		total	
	abs.	%	abs.	%	abs.	%
Czech copula + Cs = English verb	11	22	18	36	29	29
object	10	20	9	18	19	19
modifier of object	3	6	1	2	4	4
subject	7	14	9	18	16	16
modifier of subject	2	4	1	2	3	3
object complement	12	24	1	2	13	13
adverbial	2	4	4	8	6	6
modal + verb	2	4	3	6	5	5
apposition	–	–	2	4	2	2
varia	1	2	2	4	3	3
total	50	100	50	100	100	100

(7) a. Jak spíš?—To je různé. (HA, 37)
   [How you-sleep?—That is different]
   How do you sleep?—It varies. (S, 15)
  b. Nebudu už jiný. (HA, 49)
   [I-will-not-be ever different]
   I won't change. (S, 24)
  c. Jsem rád, že jsme zajedno. (HA, 27)
   [Am glad that we-are of-one-mind]
   I'm glad we agree. (S, 7)

d. ... někomu, kdo toho není hoden (JI, 38)
   [... to-someone who of-it is-not worthy]
   ... upon anyone who didn't deserve them (C, 39)

As regards gradual increase of communicative dynamism, it remains preserved, the rheme retaining its final position in both languages. The syntactic divergence does not affect it, and cannot hence be regarded as a motivating factor.

From the contrastive point of view this group is of interest in another respect, viz. it contradicts the widely accepted view of the more nominal character of English as compared with the more verbal character of Czech.

In 5 instances of this group the divergence involved the use of an English modal verb reflecting the Czech copula + a modal adjective (*být schopen* 'be able', (*být*) *lze* 'be possible' / English *can*; *je nutno, třeba* 'be necessary' / English *have* or *need*, cf. (8).

(8) nebylo by ji nutno opatřovat záplatami (JI, 42)
   [it-would-not-be necessary it provide with-patches]
   it ... would not need to be patched up. (C, 44)

Here the modal component of the verb, whatever the means of expression, operates within the transition in both languages, i.e. both its FSP function and medial position remain preserved.

A point of FSP interest concerns 2 instances of this group in which the Czech subject complement is thematic (as was noted in 0., this FSP function of the subject complement is very rare). It appears in the initial position before the verb. Here the English verb reflecting the Czech copula + subject complement takes the passive form and the Czech postverbal subject is rendered as an adverbial *by*-agent, cf. (9).

(9) ale tím větší byla jeho radost ze získaných zkušeností (JI, 35)
   [but the greater was his pleasure from gained experience]
   However, this was outweighed by the pleasure of gaining experience. (C, 37)

This example is moreover of interest in that the divergence involves a linear arrangement of the corresponding lexical items which results in closer agreement with the basic distribution of communicative dynamism in English than in Czech (cf. the position of *tím větší* [the greater] in the original with that of *outweighed* in the translation). Rather exceptionally, the same linear arrangement in both languages can here be achieved by a more literal translation in English, the construction *the ... the* allowing subject-verb inversion, cf. *but the greater was his pleasure of gaining experience.*

2.3.2 The reflection of the Czech subject complement in the English object (19 instances) appears to result from a concomitant divergence in the valency of the verb, the English counterpart of the Czech copula appearing as a transitive verb, cf. the following examples.

(10) a. Tvrdí o něm, že je neobvykle nadaný. (JI, 33)
    [She claims of him that he-is unusually gifted]
    She claims that he has an unusual talent. (C, 34)

  b. Mnoho psů je zajícova smrt. (JI, 40)
    [Many dogs is hare's death]
    Many dogs mean the death of a hare. (C, 41)

  c. že mladá žena bude špatnou matkou (JI, 76)
    [that young woman will-be bad mother]
    that a young woman will make a bad mother (C, 77)

Most examples of this group have synonymous expression analogous to the Czech copular predication, cf. *have a talent / be gifted, make a good mother / be a good mother, mean the death of / be the death of.* In a few examples the lexical verb introduces an additional semantic feature, as in (11).

(11) a. dnešní mladé dámy jsou samý sport (JI, 76)
    [today's young ladies are all sport]
    young women nowadays only care about playing sport (C, 77)

  b. No tak to by byla delší debata (HA, 27)
    [Well so that would-be longer debate]
    Well, that would require some discussion. (S, 7)

Here FSP obviously does not play a role, but neither is it affected since both the Czech original and the English translation display the rheme at the end.

Where the Czech copula is reflected in a semantically full transitive verb, as in (11) a. and b., the type of the divergence again displays a tendency to more verbal expression, noted in 2.3.1.

2.3.3 The Czech subject complements reflected in the English subject (16 instances) mostly occur in two patterns: in the existential construction, or with an initial rhematic subject and a verb of appearance or existence on the scene (the specific English form of the presentation scale, cf. Firbas 1992: 135, 1966, and Chapter 12). Compare (12) and (13).

(12) a. je slyšet zvuk tekoucí vody. (HA, 75)
    [is to-hear sound of-running water]
    There is the sound of running water (S, 42)

  b. Je to nejkrásnější kousek světa, jaký jsem kdy viděl. (JI, 64)
    [Is it most-beautiful piece of-world which ever I-saw]
    ... there is no more beautiful place in the world (C, 66)

This pattern is represented by 8 examples, most of which, however, are recurrent instances of the type illustrated by (12) a. Here the Czech subject complement appears as the postverbal notional subject after existential *there*, which agrees with both the linear arrangement and the assignment of FSP functions in the original: the postverbal element is the rheme in either language.

The second pattern, represented by 2 instances, is also found in one example from the group Czech subject complement / English subject modifier, cf. (13) a. and b.

(13) a. bylo nesnesitelné dusno (JI, 65)
       [was unbearable closeness]
       an unbearable closeness set in (C, 66)
    b. Je to zlé (JI, 46)
       [Is it bad]
       A terrible thing has taken place (C, 48)

These examples show the primary grammatical principle of English word order to override the principle of end focus, which in other instances appears to be at least a contributing factor of the syntactic divergence. Here the syntactic divergence does not result in final placement of the rheme, but acts counter to the gradual increase in communicative dynamism.

Another instance in which the syntactic divergence does not conduce to final placement of the rheme is illustrated by (14).

(14) Ale je tomu právě naopak. (JI, 29)
      [But is to-it exactly opposite]
      But the very opposite is the case. (C, 30)

Here the rhematic function of the subject, rendering the Czech postverbal rhematic subject complement, is indicated not only by contextual boundness of the subject complement (*the case*), but also by the focalizer *very*, highlighting the subject.

In general, however, instances of this kind are rare. More frequently, the result of the syntactic divergence is a linear arrangement copying the original with the theme at the beginning and the rheme at the end.

In (15), illustrating a rare instance of a Czech thematic subject complement in the corresponding initial position, the Czech C_S and its English counterpart, the subject, agree in both initial position and thematic function.

(15) nejtrestuhodnější formou roztržitostí je, když se lidé zapomínají radovat ze života (JI, 43)
      [most-reprehensible form $_{instrumental}$ of-absentmindedness is when ... $_{subject\ clause}$]
      the most reprehensible form of absentmindedness comes about when people forget to enjoy life (C, 45)

A similar case was found in the group of Czech subject complements reflected in English subject modifiers, cf. (16).

(16) Hlavní bylo, že ji pozval. (JI, 55)
   [Main was that her he-invited]
   The main thing was that he had invited her. (C, 57)

Except for one instance, the remaining examples of English subject rendering a Czech subject complement contain a *wh*-word in the subject, which as a rule requires initial position, regardless of the FSP function.

The last example of this group deserves mention because it is the only one in which the syntactic divergence results in a different FSP structure, cf. (17).

(17) Zase bylo jednotvárné ticho. (JI, 65)
   [Again was uneventful silence]
   The uneventful silence returned (C, 67)

Although the overall perspective of the Czech and the English sentence is the same, the content being conveyed as given and presented as recurrent, the means employed differ. In Czech it is the initial adverbial *zase* 'again', in English the anaphoric definite article with the subject and the lexical meaning of the verb, which in fact reflects the Czech adverbial. However, within the two structures, the FSP functions are distributed in a different way, the Czech final C_S with the function of rheme corresponding to the initial thematic subject in English while the rheme is realized by the verb.

2.3.4 Of the 7 instances in which the Czech subject complement corresponds to an English premodifier (3 modifiers of the subject, 4 of the object, see Table 3), two have been mentioned in 2.3.3, cf. (13) b. and (16). Here the lexical content of the Czech subject complement is expressed by the modifier whose head is an added noun of a general meaning (as in the case of Czech subject complements corresponding to English modifiers of subject complement, cf. 2.1): *thing, something, matter, nature, fact, time*, as in (18).

(18) a. je nějaká špatná. (HA, 67)
      [she-is somehow~adjective~ bad]
      she's having a bad time (S, 36)
   b. Nejsou-li řeči doktora Vlacha zrovna osobní (JI, 27)
      [if-not-are speeches of doctor Vlach exactly personal]
      If Dr Witherspoon's speeches are not confined to personal matters (C, 28)

As can be seen, the rendition of the Czech C_S as the object modifier is connected with the use of a transitive verb in place of the Czech copula. The FSP is not affected, the Czech rhematic adjectival subject complement being reflected in the most dynamic component of the object noun phrase, the adjectival premodifier.[3] These examples show similar features as (11) a. and b., commented upon above.

---

3   For the FSP of the noun phrase, see Svoboda 1987.

2.3.5 Similarly in the case of the 6 adverbial counterparts of the Czech subject complement the divergence involves the use of a full verb in English, cf. (19).

(19) a. že co nevidět bude zase všechno v nejlepším pořádku (JI, 37)
[that very soon will-be again everything in best order]
that everything would very soon be working perfectly again (C, 38)
 b. jsem skutečně v krisi (HA, 51)
[am really in crisis]
I really am going through a crisis (S, 25)

As in most of the foregoing examples, FSP is here neither involved, nor affected. The type of divergence again testifies to the tendency of English to more verbal expression observed in 2.3.1, 2.3.2 and 2.3.4.

A counterpart of a structurally quite different kind appears in 2 instances in which the entire predicative part, the copula + C_S, is rendered by a sentence modifier (disjunct), the correspondence as such demonstrating the clausal scope of the English adverbial (specifically *je jasné, že* 'is clear that' / *obviously* in both cases), cf. (20).

(20) Je jasné, že nejsi nadčlověk. (HA, 43)
[Is clear that you-are-not superman]
Obviously you are not a superman. (S, 19)

2.3.6 Instances of subject complement reflected in the object complement (13 occurrences) are all except one drawn from one source (JI, see Table 3). This group displays a fairly straightforward picture due partly to the nature of the object complement itself, partly to the condensed structure of the English sentence, viz. nonfinite form of clausal propositions (cf. Mathesius 1975: 152–53, Vachek 1961: Ch. IV).

As regards the nature of the object complement, this clause element bears resemblance to the subject complement in that the relationship between the object and its complement is copular just as in the case of the subject and the subject complement. It is thus a copular relationship embedded in the sentence structure through its dependence on the superordinate verb.

The examples illustrate both the optional and the obligatory type. The optional type, replaceable by a finite clause in which the object complement appears as the subject complement, is illustrated by the superordinate verbs *find* (3 instances), *think* and *deem* (1 each), cf. (21) a., b., c.

(21) a. Myslím, že mu dokonce není vhod, že ... (JI, 38)
[I-think that to-him even not-is appropriate]
I believe he does not even find it appropriate that ... (C, 40)
 b. kdybyste si mysleli, že pohostinnost je cizí mé povaze (JI, 46)
[if to-yourselves you-thought that hospitality is foreign to-my nature]
if you were to think of hospitality as foreign to my nature (C, 50)

    c. Domnívala se prostě, že není nutno, aby sdělovala ... (JI, 48)
      [She-thought _{reflexive particle} simply that not-was necessary that she-divulged ...]
      she had not deemed it necessary to divulge ... (C, 50)

Examples (21) a. and b. explicitly demonstrate the condensed structure of the English sentence as is shown by the Czech original, where the English object complement construction appears in the form of finite clauses.

    After the verbs *make* (4 instances), *put* (2) and *get* (2), the construction is obligatory, cf. (22).

(22) a. že se můj výklad stal poněkud rozpačitým (JI, 31)
      [that _{reflexive particle} my explanation became somewhat diffident]
      that made my explanation somewhat diffident (C, 31)
    b. zdálo se, že je tím rozmrzelá (JI, 23)
      [it-seemed _{reflexive particle} that she-is through-it peevish]
      this seemed to have put her into a bad mood (C, 24)

This type again neither involves nor affects FSP, the factor in play being here found in the systemic difference between English and Czech sentence structure: non-finite vs. finite clauses, respectively.

2.3.7 The group listed in Table 3 as modal + verb includes verbs of sensory perception, *hear* and *see*. With respect to Czech, these verbs present a problem insofar as perception through the two senses (as well as perception through the other senses) is construed as a subjectless copular clause with the infinitive of the verb of perception constituting the subject complement. The structure as a whole implies a general human agent and the modal meaning of possibility.

    Hear has been mentioned in connection with the subject, see (12) a., where the English counterpart displays the existential construction, with the verb of perception reflected in the notional postverbal semantically cognate subject.

    A counterpart of another type is found in the correspondence discussed at this point: the modal meaning of possibility is expressed explicitly by the respective modal verb, and the Czech C_S corresponds to the lexical component of the verb phrase, cf. (23) a. and b.

(23) a. Saturnin se obrátil a snažil se mi něco říci, ale nebylo slyšet co. (JI, 73)
      [... tried _{reflexive particle} to-me something say but not-was to-hear what]
      Saturnin turned and tried to say something but no one could hear him (C, 75)
    b. Po celou následující scénu jsou oba vidět prosklenými dveřmi do kuchyně.
      HA, 73)
      [During whole subsequent scene are both to-see through-glass-panelled door to kitchen]
      During the rest of the scene both of them can be seen through the glass-panelled kitchen door. (S, 41)

As in the case of the object complement, it is again a structural difference between the two languages that the divergence is due to.

2.3.8 Czech subject complement reflected in apposition (2 instances) is illustrated by ex (24).

(24) Jste hnusní (HA, 53)
    [You-are abominable]
    You bastards (S, 26)

The three examples labelled as varia are individual instances outside the established groups.

3. The points emerging from the discussion of the divergent counterparts of the Czech subject complement largely confirm the findings of the previous studies in showing both the specificity of this clause element and the limits of FSP as a motivating factor of the divergence. They moreover somewhat modify the current view of the more verbal character of Czech as compared with the more nominal character of English insofar as the most frequent counterpart of the Czech subject complement, inclusion in a lexical verb, besides other, less represented types, suggests an opposite tendency, a tendency to more verbal expression. As regards the FSP function of the C_s, it was found to be overwhelmingly rhematic. Since this FSP function is connected with the final position in Czech and the grammatical position of all English postverbal complements, there is agreement in English between the grammatical principle and the principle of end focus, identical content being conveyed in the same linear arrangement in both languages.

Linearity has been found to come into conflict with the grammatical principle in English in the case of two instances of a Czech thematic, and hence initial, subject complement. Here in English the principle of end focus asserted itself against syntactic structure, the Czech initial thematic C_s being rendered as a subject in English which preserves both the initial position and the thematic function (cf. (15), (16)). The English translations under study thus do not display thematic subject complements.

A point which is found in both the Czech and the English texts under study concerns instances of subject complements operating within the transition. This was noted in the case of modal adjectives, rendered as modal verbs in English (cf. (8)). Here both the Czech subject complement and its English counterpart operate as modal exponents within the FSP function of transition (as transition proper, cf. Firbas 1992: 70–73). There being 5 instances of this kind, including the thematic C_s in (9) (2 instances), (15), and (16), the percentage of Czech rhematic subject complements amounts to 91%, which is in very good agreement with Uhlířová's finding (1974, over 90%).

As in the previous studies, even the present investigation has revealed instances, albeit rare, of syntactic divergence producing a linear order acting counter to the principle of end focus; the resulting structure displays a rhematic element (constituted by the subject) in the initial position (cf. (13) a., b.). More frequently, a thematic element is found after the rheme at the end (cf. (7) d.). Both these deviations from the basic distribution of communicative dynamism are due to the primary grammatical function of the English word order.

SOURCES

[HA] Havel, V. *Largo desolato. Largo desolato, Pokoušení, Asanace.* Prague: Artforum, 1990 (1st ed. 1985).
[S] Havel, V. *Largo Desolato.* Translated by Tom Stoppard. London: Faber and Faber, 1987.
[H] Jirotka, Z. *Saturnin.* Prague: Frant. Borový, 1943.
[C] Jirotka, Z. *Saturnin.* Translated by Mark Corner. Prague: Karolinum Press, 2003.

5. SYNTACTIC CONSTANCY OF THE SUBJECT COMPLEMENT. PART 2: A COMPARISON BETWEEN ENGLISH AND CZECH

First published in *Linguistica Pragensia* 15/1, 2005, 1–17.

0. This part deals with the constancy of the subject complement in the English-Czech direction. The treatment proceeds along the same lines as in Chapter 4, which approaches the point from the Czech side. That is, two English novels and their Czech translations (see Sources) were compared for syntactically divergent counterparts of the subject complement, which were excerpted until their number reached fifty in each translation. The measure of constancy was provided by the number of identical syntactic counterparts found in the same stretches of text as the two sets of fifty divergent instances.

1. As in Part 1, the first point to be considered concerns instances rendered in Czech by structures that as a whole perform the subject complement function, but whose internal arrangement differs, mostly in presenting the lexical counterpart of the English subject complement as a modifier of a head noun. In Part 1 these instances were included among identical counterparts on semantic grounds.

Obviously, in the present study the same solution had to be adopted, even though the point appears in a somewhat different light. The greatest difference is found in the respective frequency of occurrence: in the English-Czech direction these instances are almost five times less frequent than in the opposite direction (6 from English to Czech against 28 from Czech to English, cf. Tables 1 and 2 below, and in Chapter 4). The point is thus shown to play a minor role, insofar as the small number of examples provides no ground for either confirmation, or disproval of the tendency ascertained in the Czech-English direction.[1] Although in two English-Czech examples a general head

---

[1] The preference in English of what Mathesius (1975: 114) called qualification by non-genuine classification; it was on this ground that these instances were included among identical counterparts.

in the English subject complement is left out in Czech (cf. (1) a. and b.), in the other examples a head noun is added (cf. (2) a. and b.).

(1) a. She was *the first person* to see the bones ... (F, 44)
         Byla *první*, kdo spatřil kosti ... (Ž, 42)
         [She-was first who saw bones ...]
    b. For a moment the Cadaver Club was *a less agreeable place* (J, 26)
         Na chvíli se klub stal o něco *méně příjemným* (R, 34)
         [For while ~reflexive particle~ club became somewhat less agreeable]
(2) a. The ill was *familiar* (F, 43)
         Její nevolnost nebyla *nic mimořádného* (Ž, 41)
         [Her indisposition was-not nothing extraordinary]
    b. the fact that it was *Lyme Regis* had made his premarital obligations delightfully easy to support. (F, 43)
         právě *pobyt v Lyme Regis* činil z jeho předmanželské povinnosti věc přímo rozkošně snadnou. (Ž, 41)
         [precisely stay in Lyme Regis made from his premarital duty thing directly delightfully easy.]

However, examples (2) a. and b. are of a different kind: the added heads do not explicitly express a semantic feature already contained in the subject noun.

The type represented by the remaining two examples appears in Part 1 as well (see Chapter 4, (6) a. and b.). An adjective and a noun constituting the subject or C_S in one language are split between the two functions in the other language or vice versa, cf. (3):

(3) he supposed the *word* was *appropriate* enough (J, 23)
    předpokládal, že je to *vhodné slovo* (R, 30)
    [he-supposed that is it appropriate word]

2. Following the procedure in Chapter 4, Tables 1 and 2 below show the frequency of occurrence of syntactically identical and divergent counterparts of the English subject complement with the C_S modifiers included first among identical counterparts (Table 1) and then among divergent counterparts (Table 2).

Compared with the corresponding Tables in Part 1, these Tables display two noticeable points. The first concerns the fallacy of percentage comparisons without considering the respective absolute figures. In the Czech-English direction inclusion of subject complement modifiers among identical counterparts raised the number of identical counterparts, and hence the syntactic constancy by 5.2%, while from English to Czech this percentage amounts to 2.2, which obscures the actual difference in the representation of the pattern C_S>ModC$_S$ in the two directions, noted above, viz. 28 and 6, respectively.

Of more importance, however, is the other point emerging from a comparison of Tables 1 and 2 in the two parts, viz. the difference in the syntactic constancy of the sub-

Table 1

| Czech counterparts | English subject complement | | | | | |
| | Fowles (F) | | James (J) | | total | |
	abs.	%	abs.	%	abs.	%
subject complement	79	61.2	86	63.2	165	62.2
divergent	50	38.8	50	36.8	100	37.8
total	129	100.0	136	100.0	265	100.0

Table 2

| Czech counterparts | English subject complement | | | | | |
| | Fowles (F) | | James (J) | | total | |
	abs.	%	abs.	%	abs.	%
subject complement	76	58.9	83	61.1	159	60.0
divergent	53	41.1	53	38.9	106	40.0
total	129	100.0	136	100.0	265	100.0

ject complement between Czech and English on the one hand, and English and Czech on the other. In the case of the other clause elements investigated so far (subject: Cz>E 95.65%, E>Cz 96.15%, cf. Chapter 1; object: Cz>E 88.9%, E>Cz 85.7%, cf. Valehrachová 2003; and adverbial: Cz>E 93.95%, E>Cz 93.3%, cf. Chapter 2) the difference in the constancy of the respective clause element between the two directions was small (less than 3% in the case of object) or even negligible (less than 1% in the case of subject and adverbial). As regards the subject complement, the difference in syntactic constancy between the Czech-English and the English-Czech direction amounts to almost 20% (respectively, 81.6% and 62.2%). This involves another major difference, viz. while the syntactic constancy of C_S in the Czech-English direction, though ranking lowest of the four hitherto treated clause elements, does not appear to be separated from the nearest lowest element (the object) by a strikingly larger interval than the object from the adverbial (the latter by 5%, the former by 7.3%), the syntactic constancy of C_S from English to Czech displays a jump of 20%. The subject complement consequently appears to be the least constant syntactic element especially in the English-Czech direction.

3. An explanation will again be sought in the distribution of the divergent syntactic counterparts (see Table 3), and a qualitative analysis of each type of non-correspondence.

3.1 As shown in Table 3, the most frequent Czech divergent counterpart of the English subject complement is not a separate clause element, but the notional component of a verb whose inflectional suffixes (in some instances in conjunction with derivational prefixes) convey the categorial features expressed by the English copula. This type of non-correspondence also ranks highest in the opposite direction (cf. Table 3 in Part 1) with almost equal representation: 29 Cz>E instances against 33 E>Cz. While in the former direction this finding was surprising insofar as it showed English to favour verbal structure where Czech uses the verbonominal, from English to Czech this is what may be expected in consequence of the synthetic nature of Czech.

Instances of this group are illustrated by the following examples:

(4) a. he *had been in search* of information (J, 25)
      sháněl tady informace (R, 33)
      [he-sought here information]
   b. And who *is* actually *in charge* now? (J, 29)
      Kdo to tam vlastně teď *vede*? (R, 37)
      [Who it there actually now directs?]
   c. Linnaeus himself finally *went mad*. (F, 47)
      Linné se nakonec *zbláznil*. (Ž, 45)
      [Linné ~reflexive particle~ finally went-mad]

Table 3

Czech divergent counterparts	English subject complement					
	Fowles (F)		James (J)		total	
	abs.	%	abs.	%	abs.	%
English copula + C_S =Czech verb	12	24	21	42	33	33
adverbial	7	14	11	22	18	18
complement of *seem, look* = Czech adverbial	5	10	6	12	11	11
object	10	20	5	10	15	15
subject	11	22	5	10	16	16
modifier of subject	1	2	–	–	1	1
verb	1	2	2	4	3	3
object complement	2	4	–	–	2	2
apposition	1	2	–	–	1	1
total	50	100	50	100	100	100

3.1.1 A large majority of the examples contained the copula *be*, the resulting copula being represented by *get* (2 instances), *go* and *come* (1 instance each). It is noteworthy that in some cases, such as (4) c., English has no univerbal verb to express the concept. Other instances of this kind from this group are *be silent* 'mlčet', 'zmlknout' and *get used to* 'zvyknout si'. Here the English lexical system provides only analytical forms of expression. More frequently instances of copular predicates in the group under discussion are a matter of stylistic (or other) choice, cf. *be aware* (with 4 occurrences; the only other recurrent predicative adjective in this group was *dead*: 3 instances) / *realize*, *be enough* / *suffice*, *be convenient* / *suit*, *be amusing* / *amuse*, *be afraid* / *fear*, etc.

Gaps in the lexical system calling for an analytical form of expression can presumably be found even in Czech, even though for each example of this group in the Cz>E part there exists a univerbal synonymous verb. A noticeable point in connection with resulting copulas appeared in a few examples containing *be* in English, but a perfective verb in Czech, cf. (5).

(5) a. As soon as they *were* finally *alone* he said: (J, 28)
    Když konečně *osaměli*, řekl: (R, 36)
    [When finally they-became-alone, he-said]
  b. I thought he *was dead*. (J, 28)
    Já myslel, že už *zemřel*. (R, 36)
    [I thought that already he-died.]
  c. as she read the words she faltered and *was silent*. (F, 54)
    a když ta slova četla, zachvěl se jí hlas a **zmlkla**. (Ž, 53)
    [... faltered _{reflexive particle} to-her voice and she-became-silent]

While in (5) a. and b. *be* + adjective denotes a resultant state, a meaning which can be conveyed in addition to those of current state or quality (the Czech equivalent is thus derivable from the meaning of the construction alone), in (5) c. what is involved is change in a state, which is the semantic domain of the resulting copula. Here without the context of the sentence, the natural Czech equivalent would be imperfective *mlčela* 'was-silent'. The example is of interest in that it shows that even an inherently imperfective verb can be rendered perfective by context, cf. *I knew him* 'znal jsem ho' x *I knew him at once* 'Poznal jsem ho ihned'.

3.1.2 In both directions this group also included modal predicative adjectives: Cz>E 5 (*být schopen* 'be able', *lze* 'be possible' / *can*; *je nutno, třeba* 'is necessary / have or need*), E>Cz 1 (*be able* / *dovést* 'can'). The larger number of Cz>E examples is due to one source (JI 4, HA 1),[2] which may be a specific feature of the author's language. In any case, owing to the small number of examples these findings are inconclusive.

3.1.3 From the viewpoint of functional sentence perspective this type of syntactic non-correspondence does not appear to play a role in that neither the linear arrangement, nor the distribution of the FSP functions is affected. As noted in the Cz>E part, the subject complement overwhelmingly favours the FSP function of rheme (over 90%).

---

2   JI = Z. Jirotka, *Saturnin*; HA = V. Havel, *Largo desolato* (cf. sources in Part 1.).

This is the case of English subject complements in postverbal position, as shown by all adduced examples except (4) a. Here the only difference between English and Czech consists in the realization of temporal and/or modal exponents of the verb (TMEs), which operate as transition proper, and of the verb's notional component, which in the absence of complementing elements, if context independent, constitutes the rheme. In English the TMEs and the notional component of the predicate are decomposed into the copula and the C_s, while in Czech both are implemented by the verb alone, the former by the verb's inflections and the latter by its lexical component. Whatever the form of realization, in both languages the TMEs constitute the transition, and the notional element of the predicate (the lexical component of the verb / the C_s) implements the rheme.

Where the subject complement is expanded by further elements, as in (4) a., the rheme is constituted by the expanding element(s) while the English C_s / notional part of the verb in Czech implements the most dynamic component of the transition. In the case of a modal predicative adjective rendered by a modal verb in Czech (3.1.2), the modal element, whatever its form of realization operates within the transition proper. In both cases, if context independent, the transition is part of the non-theme (cf. Firbas 1992: 71–72).

In English the element following the subject complement may also be part of the theme. This is illustrated by (4) b., which contains a scene-setting thematic temporal adverbial at the end; compare its non-final position in the Czech translation. Temporal and locative adverbials acquire the FSP function of rheme only where they appear as specifications (cf. Firbas 1992: 49–53), which is reflected in their carrying the main stress. The preceding context of (4) b., however, indicates that *now* operates here as a scene-setting element (cf. Firbas's setting, *ibid.*).

3.2 The group of English subject complements rendered by Czech objects comprises 15 instances (see Table 3; in the opposite direction there were 19 instances of this type of divergence, see Table 3 in Part 1). As in the Cz>E direction, the divergence results from the use of a full verb in place of the copula, cf. (6).

(6) a. I realize how *busy* you *are* now. (J, 24)
     Dovedu si představit, co máš teď *práce*. (R, 32)
     [I-can to-myself imagine, how-much you-have now work]
  b. So I should not have *been too inclined to laugh* ... (F, 46)
     Takže bych sotva *měl chuť smát se* ... (Ž, 44)
     [So-that I-should hardly have inclination to-laugh _{reflexive particle}]

3.2.1 A recurrent verb was *mít* 'have' (5 instances, i.e. 33% of this group, cf. (6) a. and b.), which in general often alternates with existential or copular *být* 'be'. An instance of this kind occurred in the Cz>E direction (cf. (10) a. in Chapter 4: ... *že je neobvykle nadaný* [... that he-is unusually gifted], rendered as *that he has an unusual talent*. Here both languages allow alternative expression with the other verb, *have* and *be* respectively: ... *že má neobyčejný talent* [... that he-has unusual talent]; ... *that he is unusually gifted*. In the particular instances of the E>Cz group under discussion, however, copular expression was either altogether lacking (*be lucky* 'mít štěstí' [have luck] x *být šťastný* [be happy]), or blocked by stylistic and/or contextual factors (*be very busy* 'mít hodně práce' [have much work] (neutral) x 'být velmi zaměstnán' [be very busy] (formal; moreover, *zaměstnán* without an intensifier also means 'be employed as an employee').

3.2.2 Another recurrent type of the pattern English C_S > Czech object was found in the cleft sentence (3 inverted *wh*-clefts and 1 *it*-cleft). In the former the nominal relative clause constitutes the subject and contains the verb of the underlying proposition which is transitive; its right-hand participant is reflected in the C_S complementing the copula in the matrix clause. In Czech the proposition is construed as a single clause; hence the complement of the verb appears as object, cf. (7) a. The same pattern is found in the *it*-cleft: the verb appears in the subordinate clause, its complement constitutes the C_S in the copular matrix clause, and Czech displays a single-clause counterpart with the C_S construed as the object, cf. (7) b.

(7) a. He might perhaps have seen a very contemporary social symbolism ... ; but what he did see *was a kind of edificiality* of time. (F, 47)
   Snad by byl mohl spatřovat velmi současný sociální symbol ... On však *viděl jakousi velebnou budovu* času. (Ž, 46)
   [He however saw some majestic edifice of-time]
   b. It's *his ghost* that people claim to see, still scrubbing away at the stain. (J, 32)
   Prý tu lidé dodnes *vídají jeho ducha*, jak se snaží skvrnu odstranit. (R, 41)
   [it-is-said here people till-today often-see his ghost as ~reflexive particle~ he-tries stain to-remove]

Bi-clausal realization of one proposition[3] was moreover found in an instance which contained the verb in the matrix clause and its complement as C_S in a nominal relative clause which constituted the right-hand participant of the verb and syntactically operated as the object, cf. (8).

(8) Charles had already visited what *was* perhaps *the most famous shop* in the Lyme of those days (F, 44)
   Charles už také *navštívil* tehdy patrně *nejslavnější obchod* v Lyme (Ž, 42)
   [Charles already also visited then probably most-famous shop in Lyme]

As regards functional sentence perspective, apart from instances with bi-clausal realization of one proposition, the syntactic divergence has no effect. This is due to the FSP nature of the two verbal complements involved: both the subject complement and the object are postverbal elements which develop the semantic structure of the verb, and hence if context independent, inherently operate as the rheme (the rheme

---

3   For this point, see Daneš et al. (1987: 443, 536–537); Quirk et al. (1985: 1383–84).

proper if not complemented by further elements; part of the rheme where their semantic structure is further developed). The latter case is illustrated by (6) b., while in (6) a. the C_S / object operates as the rheme proper. Incidentally, this example illustrates the difference in the primary word order principle between English and Czech. In English the grammatical principle requires the entire *wh*-element constituting the rhematic C_S to be moved to initial position; hence the subordinate clause violates the principle of end focus, presenting the rheme at the beginning. In Czech the FSP word order principle overrides the grammatical to the extent that only the quantifier of the rhematic object (*co* 'what' = how much) is moved to the beginning, while the head noun (*práce* 'work'), the most dynamic element within the communicative subfield, retains the regular position of the focal element at the end.

In instances illustrated by (7) and (8) the situation is different. In English the bi-clausal realization of the propositional content produces two communicative subfields, which allows more explicit indication of the connection of the particular sentences with the preceding context. This is especially the case in the cleft sentences: in (7) *a kind of edificiality* is explicitly placed in contrast with the preceding part of the sentence *He might perhaps have seen a very temporary social symbolism* ... In Czech, although the object is also rhematic and appears at the end, the contrast is expressed only by the conjunction (*však* 'however'), which is present in English as well (*but*). Hence the connection with the context remains to be inferred.

Although structural counterparts of both *it*-clefts and *wh*-clefts exist in Czech, the English constructions are mostly rendered by single clauses, without clefting. In the renditions of *wh*-clefts the information structure is mostly indicated by word order alone. Even in speech the final rhematic element carries the nuclear tone without extra-strong stress. In one-clausal renditions of *it*-clefts the focus is prosodically highlighted (as in (7) b.) or reinforced by a focalizer (see (11) below). Among the identical counterparts drawn from my sources there was only one instance of an *it*-cleft with parallel structure in Czech, cf. (9).

(9) ... it was the Ca' Foscari which his architect had been instructed to build (J, 33)
Byl to Casa Foscari, podle něhož měl architekt vystavět dům (R, 42)
[was it Casa Foscari according-to which was architect to-build house]

3.3 English subject complements reflected in Czech adverbials (18 instances + 11 complements of *seem* and *look*, see Table 3) present a similar picture as the type of divergence described in 3.2 from both the syntactic and the FSP points of view.

3.3.1 In two-thirds of the examples the divergence is due to the rendition of the English copula by a full verb in Czech, as in (10).

(10) a. [Miss Sarah ...] had established that the girl *was* indeed not *well* (F, 53)
... zjistila, že děvče se skutečně *necítí dobře* (Ž, 52)
[... girl ~reflexive particle~ indeed not-feels well~[adverb]~]

b. ... a room which ... *was* surprisingly *restful.* (J, 28)
... po místnosti, která ... *působila* překvapivě *klidně* (R, 36)
[... which ... impressed surprisingly restfully]

3.3.2 There were four cleft sentences, all rendered by a single clause in Czech. It is presumably not accidental that one of the *it*-clefts in this type of divergence represents what has been called by Prince (1978) an informative-presupposition *it*-cleft. This type contains new information in the subordinate clause, even though presented as presupposed, and a highlighted element that would otherwise be thematic, mostly a thematic subject or a scene-setting adverbial, in the matrix clause (cf. Dušková 1993: 71–87, esp. 80–82). The sentence thus displays two information peaks (cf. divided focus in Quirk et al. 1985: 1384), a minor one in the matrix clause (the underlying thematic element highlighted by the construction) and the main focus on the new element in the subordinate clause, as in (11) a.

(11) a. it was in these more intimate ceremonies that Sarah's voice was heard at its best and most effective. (F, 54)
A právě při těchto důvěrnějších sezeních zněl Sářin hlas nejlépe a nejpůsobivěji. (Ž, 53)
[And precisely in these more-intimate sessions sounded Sara's voice best$_{adverb}$ and most-effectively]

b. It was not concern for his only daughter that made him send her to boarding-school, but obsession with his own ancestry. (F, 51)
Neposlal svou dceru do internátu z přílišné péče o ni, ale proto, že byl posedlý myšlenkou na vlastní předky. (Ž, 50)
[He-not-sent his daughter to boarding-school from excessive care for her, but therefore that he-was obsessed with-idea of own ancestors.]

The second *it*-cleft (11) b., illustrating the more common type with given information in the subordinate clause, explicitly states what the highlighted element in the matrix clause is contrasted with: the subject complement is a coordinated structure, with the second, discontinuous conjoint placed finally after the subordinate clause, so that the rheme proper is indicated not only by the syntactic structure, but also by sentence-final position. The *wh*-clefts focusing adverbials again represent the inverted type as those focusing objects (3.2.2). Note the use of a focalizer in the Czech counterpart of (12) b. (*právě* 'just') to give the rhematic part more prominence. In the Czech renditions of *wh*-clefts this is much rarer than in the counterparts of *it*-clefts.

(12) a. That's what he wanted to see me about. (J, 28)
Kvůli tomu si dal se mnou schůzku. (R, 37)
[Because-of it $_{reflexive particle}$ he-arranged with me meeting]

b. that's where it would all begin (J, 23)
začalo by to všechno právě tady (R, 31)
[began $_{conditional particle}$ it all just here]

It may be argued that where the focused element is an underlying adverbial, the matrix clause of the cleft sentence does not contain copular but lexical *be* ('happen'). If this view is accepted, *it*-clefts would display another anomaly in addition to that of eschewing assignment to any established type of complex sentence, viz. they would lack a constitutive feature of the syntactic and semantic structure of the matrix clause, which would then fail to contain a copular equative predication. It is on these grounds, the constitutive status of copular *be* in cleft constructions, that adverbials are here subsumed under subject complements.[4]

3.3.3 In two instances the English C_S realized by a modal adjective was reflected in a modal sentence modifier (epistemic disjunct) which replaced the entire copular clause, as in (13).

(13)   *it was possible* that the suicide story had also been embellished or untrue (J, 33)
     historka o sebevraždě byla *možná* přikrášlená nebo nepravdivá (R, 41)
     [story of suicide was maybe embellished or untrue].

3.3.4 The Czech counterparts of the verbs *seem* and *look* demonstrate the much narrower range of the category of copulas in Czech, there being only two copular verbs, *být* 'be' and *stát se* 'become'. The verb *zdát se* 'seem' in the sense 'appear' is intransitive, as shown by its capacity to be used without any right-hand complement. Hence its adjectival complement is syntactically classed as an adverbial. In the case of *vypadat* 'look' a complement expressed univerbally usually takes the form of an adverb, so that its status of a full verb is supported formally, cf. (14).

(14) a. it seems highly appropriate (F, 47)
       zdá se zcela pochopitelné (Ž, 45)
       [it-seems ~reflexive particle~ quite understandable]
    b. It should have looked incongruous (J, 33)
       Měl by vypadat nepatřičně (R, 42)
       [It-should ~conditional particle~ look incongruously]

As regards the FSP structure, the difference in the syntactic behaviour of the verb does not affect the rhematic function of the final element.

3.4 The 16 instances of the divergence English C_S > Czech subject (see Table 3; the same number of this non-correspondence was also found in the opposite direction, cf. Table 3 in Part 1) display two distinct patterns accounting together for three-quarters of all examples of this group.

3.4.1 In both subtypes the divergence involves, apart from the subject complement, also the subject in English. In the first subtype the English subject is reflected in a Czech adverbial. The linear arrangement in the original conforms to the basic distri-

---

4   In Quirk et al. (1985: 1174) *be* complemented by adverbials is regarded as a copula in general.

bution of communicative dynamism (CD), with the thematic subject at the beginning and the rhematic C_S at the end. In Czech the divergent syntactic counterparts retain the same sentence position as the clause elements in the original. Accordingly, specifically with respect to the basic distribution of CD, there is no change in the FSP structure. Compare (15).

(15) The room had obviously once been the kitchen (J, 27)
      V Koutku byla předtím očividně kuchyň (R, 34)
      [In Corner(room) was before obviously kitchen]

To these may be added two instances with a Czech rhematic subject rendering an English rhematic C_S, both in final position, without an adverbial element. In (16) the initial thematic subject is reflected in the pronominal dative; the other instance has an empty *it* in the subject with no counterpart in Czech.

(16) He was in no danger of ... (F, 48)
      Nehrozilo mu nebezpečí, že ... (Ž, 46)
      [Not-threatened him danger that]

It is to be noted that in this case English displays closer agreement with the basic distribution of CD than Czech, in which unstressed pronouns cannot occur initially.

Since the FSP structure again remains unchanged and the syntactic structure may be imitated, the actual Czech renditions are a matter of choice. It may thus be wondered why it was the divergent and not the parallel alternative that has been chosen. An explanation may be found in the tendency of Czech to construe elements with adverbial semantics as syntactic adverbials (cf. the locative meaning of the English subject in (15)).

In the other recurrent pattern of this group the subject and the C_S exchange their functions: the English initial thematic subject appears as initial thematic C_S in Czech, and the English final rhematic C_S is reflected in the Czech final rhematic subject, cf. (17).

(17) These last hundred years or more the commonest animal on its shores has been
      man—(F, 44)
      Za posledních sto let byl nejčastěji se vyskytujícím živočichem na tomto břehu
      člověk (Ž, 42)
      [In last hundred years was oftenest $_{reflexive\ particle}$ appearing animal$_{instr}$ on this shore
      man$_{nom}$]

In this type of divergence, the relations between the two languages are far from clear-cut. In (17) Czech displays a thematic C_S, which is in general rare; here it is presumably due to viewing the semantic structure of the sentence in a way that reverses the roles of quality bearer and quality. While in English the sentence structure assigns the former to the initial thematic subject, and the latter to the final rhematic C_S, in

Czech the role of quality, the intrinsic role of the subject complement, is ascribed to the initial element, as shown by its form in the instrumental case. The role of quality bearer is then assigned to the context independent final rhematic element which consequently appears as the subject.

Secondly, among the identical counterparts one English example displayed exactly the same structure as the Czech rendition of (17), cf. (18).

(18) but worst of all was the shrieking horror on the doomed creature's pallid face (F, 49)
Ale nejhorší ze všeho jsou k hrůznému výkřiku otevřená ústa v smrtelně bledém obličeji té ztracené duše (Ž, 48)
[But worst of all is to horrid shriek open mouth in deathly pale face of-that doomed soul]

This structure is deviant in two features: it is a deviation from grammatical word order (see Chapter 10), as well as from the usual rhematic function of the C_S; the latter feature being common to both English and Czech. These examples call for a more detailed study of the interaction between syntactic, semantic and FSP structure in both languages, taking into account instances of parallel syntactic and linear structure with the usual distribution of FSP functions, thematic subject and rhematic C_S.

3.4.2 The only other recurrent pattern in this type was again the *it*-cleft (2 instances), rendered by a single clause without a focalizer. The rhematic function of the subject is indicated by its final position, and its contrastive nature by stress, cf. (19).

(19) But it's Gerard who runs the firm. (J, 30)
Ale firmu vede Gerard. (R, 38)
[But firm$_{acc}$ runs Gerard$_{nom}$]

3.5 The remaining Czech divergent counterparts of English subject complements are represented by 1 to 3 occurrences: apposition and subject modifier (1 instance each, cf. (20) a. and b.), object complement (2 instances: (20) c.), and verb (3 instances: (20) d.).

(20) a. the one subject that cost her agonies to master was mathematics (F, 50)
Sarah prodělala muka při zvládání jednoho předmětu, a to matematiky. (Ž, 49)
[Sarah suffered agonies in mastering one subject, and that (=namely) mathematics]
b. this stone is not attractive (F, 44)
není na tom kameni nic přitažlivého (Ž, 41–42)
[not-is on that stone nothing attractive]
c. if mere morality had been her touchstone (F, 50)
kdyby považovala morálku za nejvyšší měřítko (Ž, 49)
[if she-regarded morality as highest yardstick]
d. Little seemed to have changed. (J, 25)

Téměř nic se tu nezměnilo. (R, 33)
[Almost nothing $_{\text{reflexive particle}}$ here changed]

As regards the divergence $C_S > C_O$, in contrast to the English-Czech direction, in which this pattern operated as a sentence condenser, here it results from the replacement of the copula by a full, complex transitive verb. The divergence English $C_S >$ Czech verb is in all three instances due to the omission of a counterpart of *seem*.

4. When compared with the picture presented by the opposite Cz>E direction, the foregoing discussion of Czech divergent counterparts of English subject complements yields similar, as well as different results. Starting with the latter, the problem of classifying English subject complements reflected in C_S modifiers as identical or divergent counterparts hardly arose, as there were only six instances of this kind. The tendency of English to use qualification by non-genuine classification rather than straightforward qualification could not be confirmed, there being only two instances of this kind.

The greatest, and presumably most important difference between the Czech-English and English-Czech directions appeared in the measure of constancy of this clause element. While in the latter the constancy, although the lowest of all clause elements investigated so far (81.6%) displayed a gradual decrease from the next element with lowest constancy (Czech counterparts of English objects 85.7%), in the English-Czech direction the decrease is very pronounced (62.2%). This high degree of syntactic non-constancy is largely due to three of the four divergent counterparts represented by more than ten occurrences: fusion of the copula and the subject complement in a lexical verb (the most frequent counterpart as in the opposite direction), adverbial, and object; together they account for 77% of all divergent instances. The divergence here results from the use of a full verb in place of the copula. The high percentage of this non-correspondence manifests unequivocally the more verbal character of Czech. Full verbs rendering copulas were registered as the most frequent type of divergence in the Czech-English direction as well, but the overall percentage of the same three divergence types (fusion of the copula and C_S in a lexical verb, object, adverbial) was lower: 54 (see Table 3 in Part 1). It is to be noted that in both languages the use of verbal or verbonominal form of expression is largely a matter of choice, and rarely a consequence of a systemic gap.

Other differences between the Czech>English and English>Czech direction are found in the diversity and relative frequency of the divergent counterparts. In the former direction, the divergent syntactic counterparts are more numerous, and of those that appear in both directions, the object complement shows a higher, and the adverbial a lower frequency of occurrence (see Table 3 in Part 1). On the other hand, apart from these two elements, the divergent counterparts ranking highest on the frequency scale, fusion of the copula and C_S in a lexical verb, object and subject, are identical in both directions.

A point specific to the English-Czech direction is the cleft-construction (both *it*-cleft and *wh*-cleft), found in ten instances. The fact that the construction did not occur among English counterparts of Czech subject complements is of course due to the nature of the subject complement: it can be focused neither by the *it*-cleft, nor by the *wh*-cleft. The underlying syntactic functions of the focused elements in the English-Czech part are the object, adverbial and subject. A Czech C_S rendered by an English C_S may here occur only where both languages display a 'focusing emphatic paraphrase',[5] and then it would be included among identical counterparts.

As regards the role of functional sentence perspective, in the case of counterparts constituted by postverbal elements the FSP appears as a concomitant feature of two syntactic structures, the original C_S and the divergent counterpart, which display the same FSP function and linear arrangement when content independent. Accordingly, the motivation of the syntactic divergence has to be sought elsewhere. Czech in general has no need to resort to syntactic divergence to achieve a different linear arrangement. The motivating factor here appears to be the more verbal character of Czech, one of the features of synthetic structure. The synthetic structure of Czech also asserts itself where English cleft constructions are rendered by one clause. In this case, however, there is a difference in the FSP. The decomposition of one propositional content into two clauses which constitute the cleft construction allows more explicit indication of the position of the sentence in the surrounding context, in particular the highlighting of a contrast. In the Czech rendition by one clause where no focalizer is present, this remains to be inferred from the context insofar as the rhematic element is indicated in the same way as non-contrasted rhemes (intonation playing a role primarily in speech).

In the case of the subject counterpart, the FSP is of particular interest owing to the different rules governing the behaviour of this clause element in English and Czech. A factor motivating the syntactic divergences from the English C_S appears to be the semantic structure or a different interpretation of the semantic structure. It may thus be concluded that syntactic divergences in the English-Czech direction are to be ascribed largely to two factors, the synthetic nature of Czech and the influence of semantic structure.

SOURCES

[F]   Fowles, J. *The French Lieutenant's Woman*. London: Triad–Granada, 1983 (1st ed. 1969).
[Ž]   Fowles, J. *Francouzova milenka*. Translated by Hana Žantovská. Prague: Mladá fronta–Smena–Naše vojsko, 1976.
[J]   James, P. D. *Original Sin*. London–Boston: Faber and Faber, 1995 (1st ed. 1994).
[R]   Jamesová, P. D. *Vraždy v nakladatelství*. Translated by Alena Rovenská. Prague: MOTTO, 1999.

5   The term used in Daneš et al. (1987: 537).

6. SYNTACTIC CONSTANCY OF CLAUSE ELEMENTS BETWEEN ENGLISH AND CZECH

First published in Czech under the title "Konstantnost syntaktické funkce mezi jazyky," *Slovo a slovesnost* 66/4, 2005, 243–260. Revised.

0. This chapter summarizes the results of the research into syntactic constancy of clause elements between English and Czech, presented separately in the preceding chapters. In addition to the elements treated therein, viz. the subject, adverbial, and subject complement, it also includes the object, with recourse to the studies by Valehrachová (2002, 2003). The four clause elements are compared with respect to the extent of their syntactic constancy and the factors motivating shared and specific types of syntactic divergence. Originally it had been intended to include other languages in addition to English and Czech; however, this project was realized only in the case of the subject, which was also compared with respect to its constancy between English and German (Nekvapilová 1998).

The aspects under study are the relations between syntactic function, FSP function and the linear arrangement of the elements of the sentence. The focus on this point stems from the specific situation in English, whose analytic character produces conditions for a potential conflict between the grammatical principle, which is its primary word order principle, and the universal principle of the organization of information structure, the principle of end focus. In terms of the theory of functional sentence perspective (Firbas 1992) the principle of end focus coincides with the basic distribution of communicative dynamism which arranges the elements of the sentence according to the gradual increase in communicative dynamism, with the least dynamic element at the beginning and the most dynamic element at the end. In English, despite its analytic character, the universal validity of the principle of end focus has been shown to apply to a large extent (cf. Chapter 10). Moreover, where the grammatical and the FSP principles operate counter to each other, final placement of the focal element can often be achieved by means of specific syntactic constructions (primarily with the help of the passive, see Mathesius 1975: 85, 101, 118–119; Dušková 1971). On the other hand, however, the final position often contains thematic elements (cf. Chapter 10; Firbas 1992: 42, 45, 49–50, 59–62; Sgall, Hajičová, Buráňová 1980: 121–127). Mathesius regarded these deviations, especially rhematic subjects in the initial position, as manifestation of a certain lack of susceptibility of English to the FSP principle. This view was rectified by Firbas (1966; 1992) by including among the FSP factors context in/dependence, semantic structure and in speech intonation.

As regards Czech, conditions giving rise to conflicts between grammatical and FSP structure generally do not arise since owing to its inflectional character the primary function of Czech word order is to indicate the FSP structure.

Consequently, given that the principle of end focus operates regardless of the grammatical system, identical content can interlingually be assumed to be presented in the same linear order, even though by means of differing syntactic structures. In other words, syntactic structure is assumed to be subordinate to FSP structure. This assumption has been investigated on the basis of translated texts, English originals and their Czech translations, and Czech originals and their English translations, largely drawn from fiction as the most plentiful source of research material for this aim.

Basing research on translated texts is not an ideal method insofar as there are usually more ways of translating and the translation counterpart may be influenced by the structure in the original. However, interlingual rendering of the same content cannot be obtained in any other way and anyhow, the method appears to be on the increase especially in connection with the growing number of aligned originals and their translations (cf. Johansson and Oksefjell 1998). As regards English and Czech, previous to studies of syntactic constancy the method was used by Klégr (1996) with respect to word-class constancy of the noun.

In the present research, excerpts include only instances which have non-clausal realisation forms and in which all lexical items have counterparts in the other language, i.e. free translations have been excluded. Instances making up the research material were examined especially in regard to translation equivalents displaying distinct patterns recurrent in more than one source. In such cases it can be supposed that the counterpart does not represent the translator's personal choice but reflects systemic relations between the two languages under study.

The interlingual constancy of the four clause elements, subject, adverbial, object, and subject complemet has been investigated by the same method: for each clause element, four samples were excerpted, two Czech and two English originals and their translations. Each clause element was examined on the basis of fifty divergent counterparts obtained from each sample, i.e. altogether on 100 examples in either language. The measure of constancy of each clause element was then determined on the basis of the number of syntactically concordant counterparts needed to obtain the 50 divergent ones.

The three aspects under study, syntactic function, FSP function and linear arrangement (sentence position of the clause elements) were found to display differences between English and Czech in the case of all clause elements under study, but to a differing degree. The differences in the behaviour of the particular clause elements were basically due to the character of the formal indicators signalling the respective syntactic function, which appeared to be a potential factor in the transfer of an FSP function from a clause element in the original to another clause element in the translation.

The English and the Czech subject differ in all three respects: in Czech the subject is signalled by morphological means, hence it is not restricted in regard to sentence position. The English subject is signalled by word order, hence its prevalent position is initial or preverbal. It appears in this position in almost 80% of all instances (78.5%, cf. Dušková 1975). In Czech, the initial position is often occupied by other clause elements, initial adverbials being nearly as frequent as the subject, 29.3% and 33.5%, respectively (Dušková 1975). The difference in the position of the subject entails differences in its FSP functions: Czech rhematic sujects (in the final position) are almost twice as frequent as rhematic subjects in English, respectively 22.4% and 12.4% (cf. Dušková 1986a). According to Uhlířová's study (1974) the percentage of Czech rhematic subjects is even higher: 33%. The thematic function of the English subject has already been pointed out by Mathesius (1947a) and subsequently confirmed by quantitative data: English thematic subjects are by almost 9% more frequent than Czech thematic subjects, 85.8% and 77.2%, respectively (Dušková 1986a).

In the case of the English object, the situation is similar in that its formal indicator is again the word order, viz. the postverbal position. Agreement or disagreement of this position with the object's FSP function depends on its relation to the context. Where the object is context-independent, hence rhematic, the grammatical position and the FSP function coincide. Where the object is context-dependent, hence thematic, the grammatical position and the FSP function fail to coincide. It is thus thematic objects and thematic adverbials in the postverbal position that represent the most frequent deviation from the basic distribution of communicative dynamism (cf. Chapter 10).

In contrast to subjects and objects, English adverbials are basically similar to Czech adverbials in all three respects. Their syntactic function is identifiable from their realization forms: adverbs or prepositional phrases. Like Czech adverbials, they are largely mobile and hence amenable to being placed according to their FSP function. There is merely one significant difference, as compared with Czech, viz. the disposition of English adverbials to be placed in compliance with their FSP function does not apply to all adverbial semantic roles: thematic temporal and locative adverbials are primarily placed at the end.

As regards the English subject complement, although lacking inflections and concord with the subject, its syntactic function is as a rule adequately indicated by the copular verb. Having almost exclusively rhematic function (over 90% according to Uhlířová 1974), its postverbal grammatical position and FSP function are basically in agreement. Accordingly, in the case of this clause element, the situation in English and Czech is in principle comparable.

1. From what has been said, the degree of syntactic constancy of the clause elements under discussion may be supposed to depend on the respective degree of interlingual differences. Quantitative data are presented in Tables 1 and 2.

Table 1: English syntactic counterparts of Czech S, Adv, O, C_S

Czech	same		different		total	
	abs.	%	abs.	%	abs.	%
subject	2378	95.65	100	4.35	2478	100
adverbial	1708	93.95	100	6.05	1808	100
object	801	88.90	100	11.10	901	100
subject complement (C_S)	444	81.60	100	18.40	544	100

Table 2: Czech syntactic counterparts of English S, Adv, O, C_S

English	same		different		total	
	abs.	%	abs.	%	abs.	%
subject	2642	96.15	100	3.85	2742	100
adverbial	1398	93.30	100	6.70	1498	100
object	599	85.70	100	14.30	699	100
subject complement (C_S)	165	62.20	100	37.80	265	100

According to the figures in Tables 1 and 2, however, the assumption of the relatedness between syntactic constancy of clause elements and the three aspects under study appears to be fallacious. Obviously, other factors come into play, which is what has been expected: the FSP function has been supposed to be only one of the factors inducing syntactic divergence.

Nevertheless, in the case of the subject, the most differing clause element as compared with Czech, its high degree of constancy led to an additional line of research in which the starting point was the subject's FSP function of rheme. Here the results showed a substantially lower degree of constancy, viz. in both directions about 80%: English > Czech 78%, Czech > English 80% (cf. Chapter 1). The other three clause elements were examined only with respect to the constancy of syntactic function.

The divergent syntactic counterparts of all clause elements under study are given in Tables 3 and 4. The subsequent discussion concentrates on their most frequent divergent counterparts with a view to determining the most important factors of the divergence.

1.1 In the case of the Czech subject, the most constant clause element (about 96% in both directions, cf. Tables 1 and 2), the most frequent divergent counterpart is the English object (Table 3, 45%), cf. (1); counterparts lacking an explicit equivalent (19%) , cf. (2), and possessive determiners (16%), cf. (3).

Table 3: English divergent syntactic counterparts of Czech S, Adv, O, C_s

English	Czech (abs. = %)			
	subject	adverbial	object	C_s
subject	9*	18	45	16
direct object	28	44	x	19
indirect object	3	–	5	–
prepositional O	10	–	x	–
prepositional object as second O	–	–	9	–
adverbial	9	x	11	6
verb	4	1	–	–
modal vb + verb	–	–	–	5
incorporation in verb	–	5	6	29
subject complement	2	5	14	x
object complement	–	–	–	13
noun premodifier	–	23	–	7
noun postmodifier	–	2	2	–
possessive determiner	16	–	8	–
apposition	–	–	–	2
no counterparts	19	–	–	–
varia	–	2	–	3
total	100	100	100	100

* subjects in English counterparts of Czech subjectless sentences

(1) a. V každém muži je kus sobce (K1C, 23)
     [In every man is piece of egoist]
     every man has a selfish streak in him (K1E, 14)
   b. proto, že z ní na mne čišel chlad (K1C, 33)
     [because from it on me blew cold]
     because it gave me the shivers (K1E, 22)
   c. dr. Proppera ranila mrtvice (FLC, 8)
     [Dr. Propper$_{acc}$ struck stroke$_{nom}$]
     Dr. Propper's had a stroke (FLE, 2)
(2) že náš zpěv nikdo nezaslechne (K1C, 22)
   [that our singing nobody will-not-hear]
   our singing would go unheard (K1E, 13)

(3) v tom mám nejlepší postavu (K1C, 25)
    [in that I-have best figure]
    they show off my figure best (K1E, 15)

Considering these three types of divergence from the viewpoint of the influence of FSP on syntactic structure, supportive evidence is found in the first. The linear arrangement of corresponding lexical items is similar, with the thematic element in the initial position and the rhematic at the end. Example (1) a. illustrates a notable feature of English, tolerance to thematic elements in the final position following the rheme (standing in the so-called post-IC [intonation centre] prosodic shade, cf. Firbas 1992: 160, 170–72, 192). This is a typical arrangement of the existential construction which primarily serves to place the rhematic element (the subject) after the verb, cf. (4):

(4) There is a note on your desk. (J2E, 10)

Example (2) also demonstrates the influence of the rhematic function of the final element on the syntactic divergence: the use of a copular verb complemented by an adjective derived from the past participle of the counterpart of the Czech verb whose negative polarity is conveyed by the negative prefix of the participle, serves to place the rheme, constituted by the finite verb form in Czech and the negated past participle in English, at the end. If the structure of the Czech sentence were imitated, the rhematic verb would precede the thematic object: *that nobody would hear our singing.*

Instances with a possessive counterpart of the Czech subject like (3) call for further study. In this case the syntactic divergence does not lead to final placement of an identical element, cf. *postavu* [figure] in Czech and *best* in English. However, since in a modified noun phrase with a context-independent modifier it is the modifier that carries a higher degree of CD (cf. Svoboda 1968), the FSP structure of both wordings is the same, with a difference in the composition of the rhematic section: one clause element in Czech (modified object within whose FSP subfield the rheme is the modifier) against two elements in English, object + adverbial of manner, which in effect follows the gradual increase in CD more closely than the Czech original in having the rheme proper at the end.

The Czech divergent counterparts of the English subject (Table 4) present even more distinctive patterns. In Czech, however, they cannot be attributed to the principle of end focus since final position of rhematic elements can be regularly achieved by mere changes in word order.

The divergence English subject > Czech object is represented nearly twice as much as in the Czech-English samples, viz. by 54 instances as compared with 28 in the opposite direction. The other two divergent Czech counterparts with frequencies of occurrence higher than 10% are the adverbial and indirect object (16 and 13 instances, respectively, see Table 4).

Table 4: Czech divergent counterparts of English S, Adv, O, Cs

Czech	English (abs. = %)			
	subject	adverbial	object	Cs
subject	x	26	22	16
direct object	54	20	x	15
indirect object	13	–	–	–
prepositional object	3	–	–	–
adverbial	16	x	42	18
verb	6	4	–	3
complement of *seem* and *look*	–	–	–	11
incorporation in verb	–	29	30	33
subject complement	1	–	3	x
object complement	–	–	–	2
noun premodifier	–	15	–	1
noun postmodifier	–	3	2	–
no counterparts	5	–	–	–
apposition	–	–	–	1
varia	2	3	1	–
total	100	100	100	100

It is hardly accidental that the correspondence between English subjects and Czech objects mostly involves a change in the voice of the verb (35 instances out of 54), as in (5).

(5) At dawn she was awakened by the sound of rain (BE, 56)
   Za svítání ji probudil déšť (BC, 62)
   [At down her awakened rain]

Instances without the change of voice mostly display a different verb. In (6) the English verbo-nominal construction *have + ache* is rendered by a full verb *bolet* and in (7) Czech *mít* corresponds to *be* in English.

(6) she had toothache that morning (BE, 10)
   bolely ji to ráno zuby (BC, 13)
   [hurt her that morning teeth]

(7) Her face was pale and long. (J2E, 27)
   Tvář měla bledou a podlouhlou. (J2C, 435)
   [face she-had pale and long]

These divergences reflect systemic difference between the two languages, in the case of the passive a different status of the passive voice in the Czech verbal system, instances without the change of voice reflecting the more verbal character of Czech. The correspondence between Czech *mít* [have] + object and English *be* + C_s is fairly common and calls for further study.

The adverbial and indirect object as counterparts of the Czech subject are illustrated by (8) and (9).

(8) her mouth opened to emit a sound (BE, 36)
   z pootevřených úst jí unikl zvuk (BC, 41)
   [from half-opened mouth her$_{dat}$ escaped sound]
(9) Bernie hadn't after all owned the house. (J2E, 24)
   domek Berniemu vlastně nepatřil (J2C, 432)
   [cottage to-Bernie$_{dat}$] actually not-belonged

Example (9) reflects differences in verbal government: English *own sth.*—Czech *patřit* + dative. Example (8) illustrates a deeper difference between English and Czech: due to the inflectional character of Czech, clause elements largely display correspondence between their syntactic functions and semantic roles. The initial thematic element in (8) denotes the place from where the sound issues, hence it is construed as an adverbial, whereas in English the thematic function of an element tends to induce subject construction. Consequently, the semantic roles of the English subject also include typical semantic roles of adverbials whose Czech counterparts often disallow subject construction, cf. (10).

(10) The roof of the tunnel was seeping water.
   Stropem tunelu prosakovala voda.
   [Through-roof of-tunnel seeped water]

1.2 The third column in Tables 3 and 4 gives divergent counterparts of the adverbial, which appeared to be the second most constant clause element (Tables 1 and 2, between 93–94%).

In the Czech-English direction the three most frequent English counterparts of the adverbial are the object (44%), premodifier (23%) a subject (18%). The most frequent counterpart, the object, reflects differences in verbal government. Czech intransitive verbs with adverbial modification appear in English as transitive verbs with objects. Here a major factor of syntactic divergence is to be sought in the neutral character of the English verb, noted already by Mathesius (1975: 76–77). In this case the neutral character of the English verb involves transitivity / intransitivity, cf. the transitive use of *climb* in (11), besides intransitive uses such as *the road climbed steeply*, which is rarely found in Czech, where the change from transitivity to intransitivity and vice versa largely involves a different form of the verb or even a different verb. This feature of the English verb is ultimately to be ascribed to the analytic character of English.

(11) Stoupali jsme po úzkém schodišti. (K1C, 14)
    [We-climbed up narrow staircase]
    We climbed a narrow staircase. (K1E, 4)

The frequent correspondence Czech adverbial > English premodifier (23%, see Table 3) is a concomitant feature of the word-class divergence, and hence also of the syntactic function of the head word, cf. (12).

(12) a. Pak jsme si chvíli povídali. (K1C, 15)
        [Then we $_{auxiliary\ reflexive\ particle}$ while$_{noun}$ chatted]
        Then we had a short chat. (K1E, 5)
    b. A mírně pootočila křeslo. (K1C, 17)
        [And gently she-turned chair]
        She gave the chair a gentle turn. (K1E, 8)
    c. Pohlédl na mne dotčeně. (K1C, 13)
        [He-looked at me irritably]
        He gave me an irritated look. (K1E, 3)

This divergence arises from a deeper difference between Czech and English, noted by Mathesius (1975: 43, 105) and other Czech authors (cf. Dušková 2012), viz. the more nominal nature of English as compared with the more verbal character of Czech. In Czech the adverbial modifies the verb, while in English the verbal action is dissociated into the categorial and notional component. The action is expressed by an action noun, construed as the object, with the Czech adverbial modifier reflected in the adjectival modifier of the object noun. From the FSP viewpoint (12) a., b., c. illustrate invariable structure regardless of the Czech original. While the Czech original in (12) c. displays a word-order alteration with effect on the FSP structure, the English counterpart preserves the same structure, although the same distribution of communicative dynamism could be achieved by the corresponding verbal structure, cf. *He looked at me testily / irritably*. Examples (12) a. and b. display the same FSP structure in both languages, in (12) b. with closer adherence to the basic distribution of communicative dynamism in English than in Czech insofar as the placement of the context-independent modifier *gentle* is more consistent with its degree of communicative dynamism than the initial position of *mírně* [gently] in Czech. However, the compliance of the English construction with the FSP structure is a by-product of the primary function of the construction, viz. singling out one act of verbal action, i.e. it serves as an aspectual device. Moreover, it is also effective in making quantification and modification easier.

The last type of syntactic divergence of the Czech adverbial with a frequency of occurrence over 10, English subject (18%, see Table 3) also displays a distinctive pattern, cf. the examples listed under (13).

(13) a. V těch pauzách byla celá hrůza, která ... (K2C, 70)
     [In those pauses was all horror that ...]
     Those pauses contained all the horror that ... (K2E, 71)
   b. Na dvou židlích seděli mužové ... (K1C, 16)
     [On two chairs sat men ...]
     Two chairs were occupied by men ... (K1E, 6)

Unlike the two preceding types, this pattern clearly shows that the English divergent syntactic structure is due to the FSP factor. The initial position in the Czech sentences is occupied by a thematic adverbial reflected in the English initial thematic subject. This divergence makes it possible to construe the rheme in the postverbal, here final position (respectively, as object and adverbial/*by*-agent).

In the opposite direction (Table 4), the Czech divergent counterparts of English adverbials with the highest number of occurences (29) illustrate a hitherto unrevealed factor: the adverbial has no separate counterpart, but is incorporated in the morphemic-semantic structure of the verb.

(14) a. the dinghy swung slowly round (J4E, 10)
     loďka se zvolna otáčela (J4C, 212)
     [dinghy ${}_{\text{reflexive particle}}$ slowly turned-round]
   b. they are always difficult to find (FJE, 44)
     bývá velmi obtížné je najít FJC, 42)
     [it-usually-is very difficult them find]

Most instances of this group represent the type illustrated by (14) a. This divergence is due to the synthetic nature of inflectional Czech, in contrast to analytic English. In the opposite direction this type is marginal (5 occurrences, see Table 3, and (15)).

(15) Znovu se oženil. (K1C, 13)
    [Again ${}_{\text{reflexive particle}}$ he-married.]
    He had remarried. (K1E, 3)

The divergent counterpart ranking next in the frequency of occurrence is the subject (26 instances, see Table 4). The most recurrent correspondence here involves an English rhematic *by*-agent in a passive clause and a Czech rhematic subject, both placed finally, cf. (16) a. The correspondence illustrated by (16) b. is less frequent.

(16) a. The air was torn by the scream of engines (J4E, 10)
     vzduch rozdrásalo ječení motorů (J4C, 212)
     [Air${}_{\text{acc}}$ tore scream${}_{\text{nom}}$ of-engines]

b. Sarah's face was streaming with tears (FJE, 54)
po Sařině obličeji tečou slzy (FJC, 53)
[down Sarah's face run tears]

The divergence involving the change of voice results from the status of the passive in the Czech verbal system. Type (16) (b) achieves the same linear arrangement of identical semantic elements by the use of a verb facilitating adverbial construction of the initial element and subject construction of the final element.

The third most frequent divergent counterpart of an English adverbial is the object (20 occurrences, see Table 4). In spite of being relatively well represented, this type presents individual solutions of different instances, rather than distinctive patterns.

(17) not a single servant has been sent on his or her way (FJE, 52)
ani jeden sluha nebo služka nedostal nebo nedostala výpověď (FJC, 51)
[not one servant or maid did-not-get$_{masculine}$ or did-not-get$_{feminine}$ notice]

The last divergent counterpart of an English adverbial with a frequency of occurrence over 10 is the Czech premodifier (15 instances, see Table 4). This divergence largely displays the same pattern based on the divergence of the head element: English adjectives modified or intensified by an adverbial are reflected as Czech nouns modified by adjectives, with concomitant changes in syntactic functions. Compare (18).

(18) Maurice was always very odd and secretive   (J4E, 30)
Maurice byl vždycky velký podivín a tajnůstkář (J4C, 23)
[Maurice was always great eccentric$_{noun}$ and secretive-man]

This type of divergence has also been registered in the opposite direction from Czech to English, cf. (12), where it appears to manifest the more nominal character of English as compared with Czech. Here, however, the divergence merely represents a stylistic choice between a more formal and neutral expression. The literal translation "byl vždycky velmi podivínský a tajnůstkářský", though possible, contains the formal intensifier *velmi*, which moreover calls for the use of the stylistically higher form *vždy* instead of *vždycky*.

1.3 The fourth column in Tables 3 and 4 gives the divergent counterparts of the object. In the direction from Czech to English the three most frequent counterparts are the subject (45 instances), subject complement (14 instances) and the adverbial (11 instances). As shown by these data, a large majority of all instances is accounted for by the rendition of the Czech subject by the object in English. The correspondence illustrated in (19) and (20) has already been noted in the case of the divergent counterparts of the Czech subject, cf. (1) a. and b., which moreover illustrate a concomitant syntactic divergence in the other nominal or adverbial element in the sentence.

(19) Můj prvotní úlek vystřídal vztek (VC, 10)

[My initial fright$_{acc}$ substituted outrage$_{nom}$]
My initial fright gave way to outrage (VE, 8)
(20) celou místnost rozdělovala dlouhá knihovna (VC, 28)
[entire room$_{acc}$ divided long bookcase$_{nom}$]
the entire room was divided in two by a long bookcase (VE, 28)

What was said about (1) a. and b. also applies here: the Czech initial thematic element, here the object, is reflected in the English initial thematic subject and the Czech final rhematic subject in an English postverbal rhematic element. The factor motivating this divergence is obviously the principle of end focus, which assigns the thematic element to the initial and the rhematic element to the final sentence position.

The reflection of the Czech object in the English subject complement, illustrated by (21) again involves a concomitant replacement of the Czech *have* by *be* in English, as has been noted before in (7):

(21) Měl jen euforickou náladu (SC, 153)
[he-had only euphoric mood]
he's just been in a euphoric mood (SE, 48)

The adverbial counterparts of the Czech object are illustrated by (22).

(22) Jiřík si trochu posmrkal sako. (VC, 25)
[Jirik to-himself a little mucus-soiled jacket]
Jirik managed to sneeze some mucus on to his jacket. (VE, 24)

As both the object and the adverbial occupy the postverbal position, the order of the semantic elements remains the same, and so does the rheme, the only change consisting in the syntactic divergence. This is due to a lack of an exact English counterpart of the Czech verb, whose meaning is hence expressed periphrastically.

In the opposite direction (Table 4) English objects are most frequently reflected as Czech adverbials (42 instances), followed by incorporation in the semantic structure (which may be indicated by the morphemic structure) of the verb (30 instances) and the subject (22 instances). The correspondence between an English object and a Czech adverbial is illustrated by (23).

(23) [she] left the dance floor (J3E, 3)
odešla z parketu (J3C, 7)
[she-went-off from dance-floor]

This divergence is a mirror image of a pattern noted among the divergent counterparts of the adverbial in the opposite direction, viz. from Czech to English, cf. (11). Notably, even the quantitative data are similar: Czech adverbial > English object 44%, English object > Czech adverbial 42%. As noted above, a major factor of syntactic divergence is here found in different verbal government. An English transitive verb with an object is reflected in a Czech intransitive verb and an adverbial. This difference is due to the neutral character of the English verb with respect to transitivity / intransitivity, cf. *she left—she left the floor,* as against two different verbs in Czech *odešla z parketu x opustila parket.* Ultimately this feature of the English verb stems from the analytic character of the English grammatical system.

The correspondence type ranking second in the frequency of occurrence is the incorporation of an English object in the semantic structure of the Czech verb (30 instances), cf. (24).

(24) They've had a row (J3E, 5)
    Hádaly se (J3C, 10)
    [They-quarrelled]

This type of correspondence has been noted in the opposite direction in the case of incorporation of English adverbials in the Czech verb, cf. (14). This divergence is again due to the analytic nature of English, verbal meaning being often dissociated into the categorial (verbal) and notional (nominal) component. In the direction from Czech to English it is rare (6 instances, see Table 3, and (25)).

(25) Pokrčil jsem omluvně rameny (VC, 26)
    [I-shrugged apologetically with-shoulders]
    I shrugged apologetically (VE, 26)

It is to be noted that the analytic form of expression is here more accommodating with respect to the basic distribution of communicative dynamism than the synthetic verbal expression.

The third of the most frequent syntactically divergent counterparts of the English object, the Czech subject (22%, see Table 4), largely occurs in the pattern illustrated by (26).

(26) The guest list had chiefly comprised their most prestigious writers (J3E, 14)
    Na seznamu hostů byli především nejvýznačnější spisovatelé (J3C, 19)
    [On list of-guests were chiefly most-prestigious writers]

This type has been noted in the case of the adverbial in the Czech-English direction, cf. (13). However, the motivation of the divergence in the Czech-English and English-Czech direction differs, cf. (13) and (26). While in the former direction the divergence clearly shows the operation of the FSP factor, here the divergence results from the choice of the verb. The English sentence has the basic distribution of communicative dynamism with the thematic subject at the beginning and rhematic object at the end. Although the same syntactic structure (and basic distribution of CD) can be imitated with the use a verb like *obsahovat* 'contain', the translator here resorted to the frequent pattern *být* 'be' and the concomitant changes in syntactic functions of the elements involved. Similarly in most of the examples of this group, the divergence is due to the choice of the verb. All except four have a final rhematic object in English reflected as a final rhematic subject in Czech. On the other hand, English thematic objects, appearing in their regular postverbal position, are reflected in Czech thematic subjects placed within the initial thematic section, cf. (27).

(27) The Commissioner wouldn't like it (J3E, 13)
     že by se to panu komisaři nezamlouvalo (J3C, 18)
     [that~conjunction~ ~conditional~ ~particle~ ~reflexive~ ~particle~ it to-Mister Commissioner not-appealed]

From what has been said the correspondence between English objects and Czech subjects appears to involve additional, largely specific factors. In the English-Czech direction it reflects distinctions in the valency structure of the English and the Czech verb and the analytic tendencies of English. In the Czech English direction the operation of the FSP factor again comes to the fore, the English subject as the counterpart of the Czech object preserving both the latter's FSP function and position, which corresponds to the respective degree of CD.

1.4 The last of the syntactic elements here discussed, the subject complement, is the least constant of all: 81.6% in the Czech-English direction and 62.2% from English to Czech. As shown by the percentages, it also differs from all the other elements by displaying a substantially different degree of constancy in each direction. While in the case of the other clause elements the difference in constancy between the two directions was small (less than 3% in the case of the object: Czech > English 88.9%, English > Czech 85.7%) or negligible (less than 1% in the case of the subject: Czech > English 95.65%, English > Czech 96.15%; similarly the adverbial Czech > English 93.95%, English > Czech 93.3 %), here the difference amounts to nearly 20%, cf. Czech > English 81.6%, English > Czech 62.2%. This involves another difference: while in the Czech-English direction the syntactic constancy of the treated clause elements decreases gradually without conspicuous jumps, in the opposite direction the two least constant clause elements, the subject complement and the object, are separated by a gap large enough to contain an intermediate element between them. The causes giving rise to this novel feature are indicated by the distribution of the divergent syntactic counterparts of the subject complement in Tables 3 and 4.

Returning in this connection to the assumption of a relationship between the formal, syntactic and FSP characteristics of the clause elements on the one hand and their degree of syntactic constancy on the other, it needs to be recalled that the subject complement has been described as being essentially comparable in the two language. The similarity was primarily found in the FSP function of the C_s, insofar as its function is rarely other than rhematic. However, there is a considerable difference between English and Czech in the conception of the copula. In contrast to the two Czech copulas *být* 'be' and *stát se* 'become', the class of English copulas is considerably larger (cf. Quirk et al. 1985: 1171–74). The criterion of a copular verb is the adjectival form of the complement (*she looks sad*) together with the meaning paraphrasable by *be* or *become* + another semantic feature: 'perceived by sight she is sad'. These instances obviously appeared only in the English-Czech direction and are noted as a special group within the correspondence English C_S > Czech adverbial, see Table 4.

Another specific problem in the case of the subject complement was the classification of its counterparts into identical and different where the counterpart constituted a component of the subject-complement structure as a modifier of a different head. Such instances are frequent in the Czech-English direction (28 occurrences) and from the formal point of view should be classed as different. However, most instances represent structures illustrated by (28): the Czech predicative adjective is reflected in the modification of an added head realized either by an anaphoric pronoun coreferential with the subject or a categorial pronoun or noun.

(28) a. náš odjezd byl velmi kvapný (JIC, 66)
    [our departure was very hurried]
    our departure had been a hurried one (JIE, 68)
  b. Věda je vznešená a krásná. (JIC, 37)
    [science is sublime and beautiful]
    Science … was a sublime and beautiful thing (JIE, 39)
  c. bylo to hrozné (JIC, 26)
    [was it awful]
    It was something awful (JIE, 27)
  d. jsem na tom velmi špatně (HAC, 87)
    [am on it very badly]
    I'm in a very bad way (HAE, 51)

This type of qualification, illustrated by *Mrs. Smith was a clever woman*, is described by Mathesius (1975: 114) as qualification by non-genuine classification and characterized as more idiomatic than qualification by an adjective alone. The relatively high representation of this structure, attested in both sources, supports his view. A contributive, if not the primary, factor is moreover found in restrictions on the predicative use of many adjectives, whether semantic (as in *most visitors are occasional ones*) and/ or formal, cf. here in (28) a. Since in the registered instances the added head of the C_S hardly ever introduces an additional semantic feature into the semantic structure of the sentence, these instances were classed as identical counterparts. In the opposite direction this type is rare (6 diverse instances).

As shown in Table 3, the most frequent counterparts of the Czech subject complement are found in the incorporationof the Czech C_S into the semantic structure of the English verb (29%), object (19%) and subject (16%). The only other divergent counterpart with more than 10 occurrences, object complement (13%), is drawn almost exclusively from one source (JIC).

Incorporation into the semantic structure of the verb (29%) is illustrated by the following examples.

(29) a. Jak spíš?—To je různé. (HAC, 37)
        [That is different.]
        How do you sleep?—It varies. (HAE, 15)
    b. Nebudu už jiný. (HAC, 49)
        [I-won't-be already different]
        I won't change. (HAE, 24)
    c. Jsem rád, že jsme zajedno. (HAC, 27)
        [... that we-are at-one]
        I'm glad we agree. (HAE, 7)
    d. ... někomu, kdo toho není hoden (JIC, 38)
        [... someone who of-it is-not worthy]
        ... upon anyone who didn't deserve them (JIE, 39)

As regards the FSP structure, this type of divergence does not basically affect it: the Czech rhematic subject complement is reflected in the English final rhematic verb, the only difference consisting in the dissociation of the two FSP functions, transition and rheme, into the copula and C_S in Czech, whereas in English both FSP functions are carried by the final verb. FSP as a motivating factor of this divergence type was detected only in two rare instances containing a thematic C_S in the initial position. By means of the passive with an expressed *by*-agent, the English counterpart achieves final placement of the element corresponding to the Czech final rhematic subject, cf. (30).

(30) ale tím větší byla jeho radost ze získaných zkušeností (JIC, 35)
    However, this was outweighed by the pleasure of gaining experience. (JIE, 37)

This divergence type is of interest from the contrastive point of view insofar as nominal forms of expression are in general characteristic of English rather than of Czech. Here, on the contrary, it is Czech that appears to be more nominal than English. It is to be noted, however, that not all English instances of this kind have an equally acceptable alternative form copula + adjective, mostly for lack of a suitable adjective.

The second most frequent divergent counterpart of the Czech subject complement, the object (19 instances) is a concomitant feature of the use of a transitive verb, albeit mostly a light one, viz. a verb like *have, be, make*:

(31) a. Tvrdí o něm, že je neobvykle nadaný. (JIC, 33)
        [... that he-is unusually gifted]
        She claims that he has an unusual talent. (JIE, 34)
    b. že mladá žena bude špatnou matkou (JI, 76)
        [that young woman will-be bad mother]
        that a young woman will make a bad mother (JIE, 77)

Most instances of this kind have a synonymous alternative form of expression corresponding to the Czech copular predication, cf. *have a talent / be gifted, make a good mother* / *be a good mother*; they are thus to be ascribed to the translator's choice. Where English has a lexical verb, as in (32), it again displays a more verbal form of expression than Czech.

(32) No tak to by byla delší debata (HAC, 27)
    [Well so that would-be longer debate]
    Well, that would require some discussion. (HAE, 7)

As shown by the adduced examples, here the syntactic divergence has no impact on the FSP structure, the rheme remaining at the end in both languages.

The next divergent counterpart, the correspondence Czech C_S > English subject (16 instances) was found in two structures: in the existential construction, cf. (33) (8 instances), and with a verb of appearance or existence on the scene and a rhematic subject in the initial position, cf. (34) (2 instances, to which can be added one example reflecting the Czech C_S as a modifier of the English C_S, cf. (34) b.

(33) a. je slyšet zvuk tekoucí vody (HAC, 75)
    [is to-hear sound of-running water]
    There is the sound of running water (HAE, 42)
  b. Je to nejkrásnější kousek světa, jaký jsem kdy viděl. (JIC, 64)
    [Is it most-beautiful piece of-world which I-have ever seen]
    ... there is no more beautiful place in the world (JIE, 66)
(34) a. bylo nesnesitelné dusno (JIC, 65)
    [was unbearably oppressive]
    an unbearable closeness set in (JIE, 66)
  b. Je to zlé (JIC, 46)
    [Is it bad]
    A terrible thing has taken place (JIE, 48)

These instances, though innumerous, deserve mention on the ground of demonstrating the primacy of the grammatical word order principle in English, which here overrides the principle of end focus. While the FSP structure of the Czech and the English sentence remains the same, the two versions differ in respect of the distribution of communicative dynamism: the Czech sentence displays a gradual increase in CD with the rheme at the end, viz. the basic distribution, whereas in English the linear arrangement is reversed, the rheme coming first. Among the syntactically divergent counterparts this is rare because instances involving divergence in pre- and postverbal elements are precisely those that patently show the operation of the FSP principle, cf. (1), (13), (19) (20), (30).

In the case of the correspondence Czech C_S > English subject, the role of the FSP factor is obvious in 2 instances containing a thematic subject complement in the preverbal position, cf. (35) a. and b.

(35) a. nejtrestuhodnější formou roztržitosti je, když se lidé zapomínají radovat ze
       života (JIC, 43)
       [most-reprehensible form$_{INSTR}$ of-absentmindedness is when people ...]
       the most reprehensible form of absentmindedness comes about when people
       forget to enjoy life (JIE, 45)
    b. Hlavní bylo, že ji pozval. (JIC, 55)
       [Main was that her he-invited]
       The main thing was that he had invited her. (JIE, 57)

In all instances of syntactic divergence discussed so far, whatever factor may have
been at the root of it, the original and its counterpart in the other language displayed
the same FSP structure. The only instance where the divergence results in a different
FSP is (36):

(36) Zase bylo jednotvárné ticho. (JIC, 65)
     [Again was uneventful silence]
     The uneventful silence returned. (JIE, 67)

Both versions describe the same recurrent event, but their rhemes differ. While in
Czech it is the subject complement (*ticho*) in a subjectless sentence, in English it is the
verb (*return*).
   The last divergent counterpart of the Czech subject complement, the English object
complement (C_O, 13 instances), displays in all instances a close relationship between
the C_S and the C_O, underlying the different realization forms of complex transitive
complementation, cf. (37).

(37) a. Myslím, že mu dokonce není vhod, že... (JIC, 38)
       [I-think that to-him even not-is convenient that ...]
       I believe he does not even find it appropriate that ... (JIE, 40)
    b. Domnívala se prostě, že není nutno, aby sdělovala... (JIC, 48)
       [She-supposed $_{reflexive particle}$ simply that is-not necessary that she-divulged ...]
       she had not deemed it necessary to divulge... (J1E, 50)
    c. že se můj výklad stal poněkud rozpačitým (JIC, 31)
       [that $_{reflexive particle}$ my explanation became somewhat diffident]
       that made my explanation somewhat diffident (JIE, 31)

The last column in Table 4 gives the divergent counterparts of the English subject
complement in Czech. As in the opposite direction, the counterpart that ranks highest
in the frequency of occurrence is incorporation of the English C_S into the Czech verb
(33 instances), cf. (38).

(38) a. he had been in search of information (J1E, 25)
       sháněl tady informace (J1C, 33)
       [he-gathered here information]

    b. And who is actually in charge now? (J1E, 29)
       Kdo to tam vlastně teď vede? (J1C, 37)
       [Who it there actually now runs]
    c. Linnaeus himself finally went mad. (FJE, 47)
       Linné se nakonec zbláznil. (FJC, 45)
       [Linné $_{\text{reflexive particle}}$ finally became-mad]

As shown by (38) c., English sometimes lacks a univerbal expression of a verbal meaning. Other registered instances of this kind are, e.g., *be silent / mlčet, zmlknout, get used to / zvyknout si*. Here the English stock of words supplies only analytic forms of expression. However, there are also instances of choice between a copular predication and a synonymous verb, cf. *be aware / realize, be enough / suffice, be convenient / suit, be amusing / amuse, be afraid / fear*, etc. As for free variation of the two alternatives in identical contexts, it is presumably rare, actual choices in particular contexts largely involving diverse syntactic, semantic and other factors, not to mention the translator's preferences and idiolect.

The next three most frequent Czech counterparts of the English subject complement, the object, the adverbial and the subject, have comparable frequencies of occurrence, viz. 15, 18 and 16 instances, respectively (see Table 4). In the case of the object, as in the opposite direction, this divergence results from the rendition of the English copula by a transitive verb in Czech.

(39) a. I realize how busy you are now. (J1E, 24)
      Dovedu si představit, co máš teď práce. (J1C, 32)
      [I-can to-myself imagine what-a-lot you-have now of-work]
    b. So I should not have been too inclined to laugh … (FJE, 46)
      Takže bych sotva měl chuť smát se … (FJC, 44)
      [So-that I-would hardly have desire to-laugh $_{\text{reflexive particle}}$]

There were 5 occurrences of the verb *mít* 'have' as a counterpart of existential or copular *be*, which has also been noted in the opposite direction, cf. (31) a. As shown by this example, both languages here have a choice, cf. *mít talent / být nadaný—to have an unusual talent / be unusually gifted*, but more frequently one of the forms of expression is lacking, e.g. *be lucky / have luck—mít štěstí x být šťastný* 'be happy'.

Another recurrent instance was the Czech object as a counterpart of the English C_s in the cleft and pseudo-cleft sentence (4 occurrences):

(40) a. He might perhaps have seen a very contemporary social symbolism … ; but
      what he did see was a kind of edificiality of time. (FJE, 47)
      Snad by byl mohl spatřovat velmi současný sociální symbol … On však viděl
      jakousi velebnou budovu času. (FJC, 46)
      [He however saw some majestic edifice of-time]
    b. It's his ghost that people claim to see, still scrubbing away at the stain. (J1E, 32)

Prý tu lidé dodnes vídají jeho ducha, jak se snaží skvrnu odstranit. (J1C, 41)
[allegedly here people until-today often-see his ghost as it tries stain to-remove]

As regards adverbial counterparts of the English subject complement (18 instances) they also include the translation equivalents of the complements of *seem* and *look* (11 instances, see Table 4). This type of divergence is similar to the reflection of the English C_S in the Czech object, most instances here displaying adverbial modification as a concomitant feature of the replacement of a copula by a full verb, cf. (41).

(41) ... a room which ... was surprisingly restful (J1E, 28)
... po místnosti, která ... působila překvapivě klidně (J1C, 36)
[about room which impressed surprisingly restfully]

This counterpart of the English C_S was again found in the Czech translation equivalents of the English cleft sentence.

(42) it was in these more intimate ceremonies that Sarah's voice was heard at its best and most effective. (FJE, 54)
A právě při těchto důvěrnějších sezeních zněl Sařin hlas nejlépe a nejpůsobivěji. (FJC, 53)
[And just at these more-intimate ceremonies sounded Sarah's voice best and most-effectively].

An adverbial corresponding to the complement of the copula *look* is illustrated in (43):

(43) It should have looked incongruous (J1E, 33)
Měl by vypadat nepatřičně (J1C, 42)
[It-should look incongruously]

The last divergent counterpart of the English C_S with a frequency of occurrence over 10 is the Czech subject, with the same representation as in the opposite direction (16 instances, see Tables 3 and 4). The collected instances can be grouped into two patterns both of which show a divergence in the rendition of the English subject in addition to the correspondence English C_S > Czech subject. The first pattern contains the English subject construed as a Czech adverbial. The linear arrangement in the original preserves the basic distribution of communicative dynamism with the theme at the beginning and the rheme at the end. The Czech divergent counterparts retain the same linear arrangement so that both versions display not only the same FSP structure but also the same linear arrangement, cf. (44).

(44) The room had obviously once been the kitchen (J1E, 27)
V Koutku byla předtím očividně kuchyň (J1C, 34)

As the English syntactic structure displays the basic distribution of CD and can be readily imitated in Czech, a reason for the divergence can hardly be sought among syntactic or FSP factors. As has already been noted (cf. (8)), divergence of this kind appears to be due to the disposition of Czech to construe elements with adverbial semantics in syntactically corresponding realization forms, viz. as adverbials.

In the second pattern, the two divergent elements exchange their syntactic functions, the English initial subject being reflected in the initial Czech C_S, and the English rhematic C_S in the final position as the final rhematic subject in Czech, cf. (45).

(45) These last hundred years or more the commonest animal on its shores has been man (FJE, 44)

Za posledních sto let byl nejčastěji se vyskytujícím živočichem na tomto břehu člověk (FJC, 42)

[During last hundred years was oftenest occurring animal$_{instr}$ on this coast man$_{nom}$]

In the case of this divergence the relations between English and Czech call for further research including not only counterparts displaying syntactic divergence as (45), but also rare instances (represented by 1 occurrence in the research material of this study) displaying identical syntactic structure, illustrated by (46):

(46) but worst of all was the shrieking horror on the doomed creature's pallid face (FJE, 49)

Ale nejhorší ze všeho jsou k hrůznému výkřiku otevřená ústa v smrtelně bledém obličeji té ztracené duše (FJC, 48)

[but worst of all is for horrible shriek open mouth in deadly pale face of-that lost soul]

The initial position of the subject complement in English is made possible by the formal distinctiveness of the superlative *worst*, which is thus identified as an adjective and as such cannot implement the subject. If this position were occupied by a noun, it would be interpreted as the subject. Example (46) represents an exceptional instance of a specific English form capable of indicating the same syntactic function, viz. the subject complement, as the Czech instrumental case.

It remains to consider what are the causes of the high degree of divergence of the subject complement in the English-Czech direction (62.2%). They can be found in three of the four most frequent divergent counterparts: incorporation of the C_S in the semantic structure of the verb, adverbial and object, which together account for 77% of all the divergent counterparts. All three are connected with the use of a full lexical verb in place of an English copula, their high total percentage evidently attesting to the more verbal character of Czech. Even though the use of full lexical verbs in place of copulas has also been noted in the English-Czech direction, the overall percentage of the same three types of divergence (incorporation in the verb, object, adverbial) was considerably lower: 54%. Notably, in a number of instances both languages have a choice between verbal and verbonominal expression, instances of lexical gaps—at least in the material under study—being rarer.

2. In general, the factors involved in syntactic divergence largely appear to be specific for each direction. The only factor that has been found to play a role in both directions is different verbal government. Although this feature is primarily a matter of the surface structure, it reflects intrinsic differences in the semantic structure of the verb that ultimately result from the different character of the English and the Czech grammatical systems.

A specific factor of syntactic divergence in the Czech-English direction was found to be functional sentence perspective. The study has shown that the English sentence largely imitates the word order of the Czech sentence, which as a rule agrees with the basic distribution of communicative dynamism with the thematic element at the beginning and the rheme at the end. The operation of this factor has been attested especially where the syntactic divergence involves the subject ((1), (13), (19), (20), (30), (35)). It is to be noted, however, that although syntactic divergence largely leads to a linear arrangement in accordance with the basic distribution of CD, this is not invariably the case, as shown by (34) a., (34) b., which have the rheme at the beginning.

Where the syntactic divergence involves postverbal clause elements, viz. one postverbal element is reflected in another postverbal element, functional sentence perspective plays no role. A third specific factor in the Czech-English direction has appeared in the manifestation of the nominal tendencies of English, cf. (12).

In the English-Czech direction, the FSP factor plays no role. As regards manifestations of the synthetic/analytic nature of the two languages, Czech appears to be more synthetic, cf. (14), but not exclusively so, English often displaying synthetic forms as well, cf. (29). In the case of Czech, specific factors have been found in the different status of the passive in the Czech verbal system, reflected in its textual uses ((5), (16) a.), and in the disposition of Czech to construe semantically adverbial elements in concordant syntactic realization forms, viz. as adverbials (cf. initial locative or temporal adverbials corresponding to English subjects in (8), (13), (26), (44)).

The last point concerns the high degree of constancy of the subject. The cause is presumably to be sought in its being the first participant in verbal action, which appears to be closely connected with this syntactic function. Hence conditions for its syntactic divergence as a rule arise only in the presence of other participants in, and/or circumstants of, verbal action. Even under these conditions syntactic divergence of the subject primarily occurs where the linear arrangement deviates from the basic distribution of communicative dynamism, which, though not uncommon in English, does not invalidate in it the principle of end focus as the universal principle of the organization of information structure.

SOURCES

BE   Bainbridge, B. *The Bottle Factory Outing.* Glasgow: Collins, 1977.

BC   Bainbridgeová, B. *Podnikový výlet v prodlouženém čase.* Translated by Hana Bělehradská. Prague: Odeon, 1981.

FLC   Fuks, L. *Pan Theodor Mundstock.* Prague: Československý spisovatel, 1963.

FLE   Fuks, L. *Mr. Theodor Mundstock.* Translated by Iris Urwinová. New York: Ballantine, 1969.

FJE   Fowles, J. *The French Lieutenant's Woman.* Granada: Triad, 1983 (1st ed. 1969).

FJC   Fowles, J. *Francouzova milenka.* Translated by Hana Žantovská. Prague: Mladá fronta, 1976.

HAC Havel, V. *Largo desolato.* In: V. Havel, *Largo desolato. Pokoušení. Asanace.* Prague: Art- forum, 1990 (1st ed. 1985).

HAE Havel, V. *Largo desolato.* Translated by Tom Stoppard. London–Boston: Faber and Faber, 1987.

J1E   James, P. D. *Original Sin.* London: Faber and Faber, 1994.

J1C   Jamesová, P. D. *Vraždy v nakladatelství.* Translated by Alena Rovenská. Prague: Nakladatelství MOTTO, 1999.

J2E   James, P. D. *An Unsuitable Job for a Woman.* New York: Warner, 1972.

J2C   Jamesová, P. D. *Povolání pro ženu nevhodné.* In: *3× Adam Dalgliesh.* Translated by Josef Schwarz. Prague: Odeon, 1986.

J3E   James, P. D. *Devices and Desires.* London: Faber and Faber, 1989.

J3C   Jamesová, P. D. *Plány a touhy.* Translated by Luba and Rudolf Pellarovi. Prague: Odeon, 1993.

J4E   James, P. D. *Unnatural Causes.* London: Sphere Books, 1984.

J4C   Jamesová, P. D. *Z příčin nikoliv přirozených.* Translated by J. Z. Novák. Prague: Odeon, 1986.

JIC   Jirotka, Z. *Saturnin.* Prague: František Borový, 1943.

JIE   Jirotka, Z. *Saturnin.* Translated by Mark Corner. Prague: Karolinum Press, 2003.

K1C   Kundera, M. *Žert.* Brno: Atlantis, 1966.

K1E   Kundera, M. *The Joke.* Translated by Michael Henry Heim. New York: Harper and Row, 1984.

K2C   Kundera, M. *Nesnesitelná lehkost bytí.* Toronto: Sixty-Eight Publishers, 1985.

K2E   Kundera, M. *The Unbearable Lightness of Being.* Translated by Michael Henry Heim. London: Faber and Faber, 1999.

SC   Stýblová, V. *Mne soudila noc. Skalpel, prosím.* Prague: Československý spisovatel, 1990.

SE   Stýblová, V. *Scalpel, Please.* Translated by John Newton. Prague: Orbis Press Agency, 1985.

VC   Viewegh, M. *Výchova dívek v Čechách.* Prague: Český spisovatel, 1994.

VE   Viewegh, M. *Bringing Up Girls in Bohemia.* Translated by A. G. Brain. London: Readers International, 1997.

7. SYNTACTIC CONSTANCY OF THE VERB BETWEEN ENGLISH AND CZECH

First published in *Prague Studies in English 24, Acta Universitatis Carolinae, Philologica 2*, 2005 (issued 2006), 19–44.

0. In this chapter the term verb is used to denote its syntactic function, i.e. not as a word class term but as a term designating the clause-constitutive element. Specifically, it refers to verb phrases containing a finite verb, whether alone or in a compound form which incorporates, in addition to the finite verb, one or more non-finite forms. The verb thus defined (this limitation being necessary with regard to the syntactic functions of non-finite verb forms) differs from the nominal and adverbial clause elements in two respects: first in its relationship to its regular realization form, the finite verb form, which has only this one function. Secondly, it differs in its predicative force: in regular sentences it is the element that constitutes the predicative act. The first of these features is reflected in the FSP function of the verb, the second in the major types of its syntactically divergent counterparts.

Within the framework of the study of syntactic constancy of clause elements as displayed by English and Czech parallel texts (cf. the preceding chapters and Valehrachová 2003) the verb occupies a special position even from the viewpoint of its role in FSP, which again differs from the nominal and adverbial elements. While both these elements constitute the two principal poles of the FSP structure, the theme or the rheme[1] in dependence on the context and semantic structure, the verb intrinsically operates as transition, a link between the thematic and the rhematic section, its only other FSP function being rarely the rheme.[2] The only other clause element which also basically performs one FSP function, the subject complement, aligns itself,

---

1   In certain semantic roles and as sentence modifiers, i.e. where they are semantically affinitive with the modal or temporal exponents of the verb, adverbials also occur as transition-proper oriented elements (cf. Firbas 1992: 77–79).

2   According to Uhlířová (1974: 210) the verb performs the FSP function of transition in over 90% of its occurrences.

through its nominal nature, with the other nominal elements. In contrast to the verb its greatly predominant FSP function is the rheme (over 90%), and only marginally the theme (cf. Chapter 4 and 5, and Uhlířová 1974). Even more marginal is the subject complement in the FSP function of transition, which is restricted to verbonominal predicates whose notional component complementing a copula is a modal adjective. The FSP function of transition thus appears to be specific to the verb.[3]

1. The following treatment is based on parallel texts drawn from English and Czech fiction and the respective translations into the other language (see Sources).

1.1 Examples in the English-Czech direction were collected in the same way as in the preceding chapters. Syntactically divergent counterparts of English finite verbs, were excepted until their number reached fifty, the measure of constancy being provided by the number of corresponding counterparts within the same length of the text.

The Czech-English part relies on the findings of a diploma dissertation (Strnadová 1998), see Section 2.

1.2 The classification of excerpts into syntactically corresponding and divergent counterparts produced a gradient rather than a clear-cut division. At one end there are instances classifiable as fully corresponding, at the other the counterparts of finite verbs which display a different syntactic function, with several types of shifts in between. Instances classified as fully corresponding comprise pairs of English and Czech finite verbs that deviate in none of the verbal categories (tense, mood, voice) and represent interlingual synonyms. The latter criterion applies to all counterparts included in the study. Finite verbs differing only in their formal make-up, such as phrasal and prepositional verbs, were included among the fully corresponding counterparts (e.g. *set out / vyjít, put away / odkládat, take for / považovat za, account for / vysvětlit* and the like). Similarly differences between the analytic vs. inflectional morphological devices were disregarded (compound perfect and progressive forms, as well as other compound forms vs. Czech inflectional).

1.3 Comparison of the two texts has shown that the number of finite verb forms in the original and translation considerably differs. Instances without a counterpart have been noted, but not included, the analysis being based only on finite verb forms which had corresponding finite-verb counterparts and syntactically divergent counterparts.

1.3.1 In the Czech translation the added finite verbs outnumber the English instances without a Czech counterpart more than three times: 86 and 27, respectively. Compared with the total number of finite verbs with counterparts (1272), the Czech translation appears to contain 4.6% (59) additional instances.

---

3   This applies to the clause level. According to Svoboda (1989: 85–87), the FSP function of transition also appears in the communicative subfield of the noun phrase and other subfields.

The prevalence of added finite verbs over their omission is presumably due to a general feature of translated texts, viz. their greater explicitness, cf.

(1) Only one art has ever caught such scenes—*that of the Renaissance.* (F, 63)
Atmosféru podobné scény dovedlo postihnout umění jediného období. *Byla to renesance.* (Ž, 63) [It was Renaissance].

However, it may also reflect the more verbal nature of Czech, entailing a less condensed structure. Among the 86 added finite verbs, there were several recurrent types the most frequent of which (11 instances) reflected an English noun phrase or a prepositional phrase with an action noun or another deverbal noun, as in (2):

(2) normally she would have guessed *his tease at once*[4] (F, 75)
jindy by ihned poznala, že ji škádlí [that her he-teases] (Ž, 75)

Two other recurrent counterparts reflect English apposition (see (1) above) and non-clausal modification of nouns (6 and 8 instances, respectively), cf. (3).

(3) Mary spoke in a dialect *notorious* for its contempt of pronouns and suffixes. (F, 70)
Mary mluvila nářečím, *které proslulo* [which became-known] naprostým pohrdáním ke gramatickým osobám a zájmenům. (Ž, 70)

As regards the less represented types, of contrastive interest are clausal counterparts of verbless sentences and non-clausal disjuncts.[5]

(4) A thousand apologies. (F, 65)
Prosím tisíckrát za prominutí. [I beg thousand-times for pardon.] (Ž, 65)
(5) that she could therefore, *just conceivably,* be ignorant of ... (F, 83)
A že proto *není vyloučeno,* že neměla tušení ... (Ž, 83)
[And that therefore is-not excluded that she-not-had knowledge]

Most of these types of non-correspondence also occurred among the divergent syntactic counterparts, cf. 1.7.

As regards recurrent instances of English finite verbs without a Czech finite-verb counterpart, they mostly involve omission of a clause containing *be*, and some coordinate structures of verbs rendered only by one of the conjoints, cf. (6) and (7).

(6) Sam did most of the talking, *though it was mainly* to the scrubbed deal of the long table. (F, 94)

---

4   In the examples, capitalization and punctuation follow the original, i.e. where an example starts with a lower case letter and/or a full stop is lacking, the example is an extract from a longer sentence.
5   The term disjunct is used according to Quirk et al. (1985: 612 ff.).

většinou mluvil Sam, *i když zdánlivě* do vydrhnuté desky dlouhého stolu. (Ž, 94)
[even though apparently to scrubbed deal of-long table]
(7) as he *had sweated and stumbled* his way along the shore. (F, 71)
když *klopýtal* [he-stumbled] podél pobřeží. (Ž, 71)

1.3.2 Another source of additional finite verbs in Czech was found in English non-finite constructions reflected in Czech finite clauses. Here again the more verbal and less condensed nature of Czech has come to the fore. There were altogether 151 instances of this kind.

1.3.2.1 Most finite counterparts of English nonfinite verb forms reflected English infinitive constructions (72 instances). The Czech finite verbs largely occurred in clauses which retained the syntactic function of the infinitive: object, adverbial of purpose, adverbial of result, subject. Compare a. and b. in (8), (9), (10) and (11), respectively.

(8) a. I wish *to be told* at once. (F, 71)
     b. přeji si, *abyste mi to* ihned řekla, [that to-me it you-said] (Ž, 71)
(9) a. Charles set out *to catch her up* (F, 77)
     b. Charles spěchal, *aby ji dostihl* [so-that her he-caught] (Ž, 78)
(10) a. she now decided that she disliked Charles sufficiently *to be rude to him.* (F, 93)
     b. rozhodla se, že Charles je jí natolik nesympatický, *aby k němu mohla být hrubá.*
         [so-that to him she-could be rude] (Ž, 93)
(11) a. it is a pleasure *to see you.* (F, 91)
     b. jak mě těší, že vás vidím, [how me it-pleases that you I-see] (Ž, 91)

However, this correspondence in syntactic function often gives way to coordinate clauses, as in (12):

(12) she rose at once *to leave the room.* (F, 90)
     Sarah se okamžitě zvedla *a chtěla odejít z pokoje.* [and wanted leave from room]
     (Ž, 90)

Coordination is the regular equivalent of the infinitive with temporal function (called "non-genuine purpose" in Czech grammar), cf. (13).

(13) She turned, *to see him hatless, smiling;* (F, 78)
     Otočila se a *viděla ho tu stát usměvavého s kloboukem v ruce.* (Ž, 78)
     [and saw him here stand smiling with hat in hand]

1.3.2.2 The gerund was rendered by a finite clause in 29 instances.

(14) instead *of continuing* on her way (F, 78)
     místo *aby pokračovala* v cestě [instead that she-continued] (Ž, 78)
(15) Still *without looking at him,* she inclined her head (F, 78)

Pořád ještě na něho nepohlédla, sklopila hlavu [Still yet at him she-not-looked] (Ž, 78)

1.3.2.3 The participle (*ing*-participle: 33 instances including two perfect forms) is of particular interest insofar as it also occurs in the English-Czech direction as a frequent divergent counterpart of an English finite verb (16 instances). However, this mirror image is only partial: of the 33 *ing*-participles only seven have the postmodifying function, as in (16):

(16) a. he saw *a man hoying a herd of cows* (F, 76)
         spatřil *muže, který vyháněl* [who hoyed] stádo krav (Ž, 76)
     b. the ordeal *facing* travellers (F, 89)
         obřad, *jaký čekal* cestovatele [such-as awaited] travellers (Ž, 89)

Most *ing*-participles rendered by finite clauses in Czech (26, i.e. 78.8%) functioned as adverbials or object complements, cf. (17) and (18).

(17) Sarah scrambled to her feet, *gathering her coat about her* (F, 65)
     Sarah prudce vstala, *zapnula si plášť* a [she buttoned to-herself coat and] (Ž, 65)
(18) She saw Charles *standing alone* (F, 73)
     Všimla si, že Charles *stojí sám* [that Charles stands alone] (Ž, 73)

In the case of the past participle the postmodifying function prevails (11 instances out of the total of 17, i.e. 64.7%), but again, the mirror image is only partial: against four English finite verb forms rendered by Czech adjectives derived from past participles (see 1.7.1, (53) b.), there are 11 English past participles reflected in Czech finite verb forms, as in (19).

(19) no wife *thrown at Charles's head* would ever touch his heart. (F, 73)
     žádná žena, *jež bude Charlesovi vnucována* [who will-be on-Charles forced], se nikdy nedotkne jeho srdce. (Ž, 73)

Example (20) illustrates rendition by a finite clause of a past participle functioning as object complement.

(20) why she should not *wish it known* (F, 79)
     proč si nepřála, *aby se vědělo* [that it-was-known] (Ž, 79)

As stated above, none of these additional finite verb forms found in the Czech translation have been included in the count.

1.4 Proceeding to the intermediate groups between fully corresponding and divergent counterparts, the first point to be noted is shifts in the verbal categories. Since these shifts do not affect the syntactic function of the verb as such, instances of this kind qualify as corresponding counterparts, albeit deviant in one (exceptionally more) categorial features. Shifts in categorial features have been extended to include shifts in polarity.

1.4.1 Shifts of this type most frequently concerned the category of voice. This is not accidental, since while shifts in the rendition of the other verbal categories largely lack systemic grounds, in the case of the passive the shift reflects the different status of this category in the Czech verbal system (cf. Dušková 1999: Part 1, Chapter 7). Rendition of numerous English passives by the Czech active is thus only to be expected: out of the 74 finite passives in the original 57 (77%) had active counterparts, cf. (21) a. and b.

(21) a. The door *was opened* by Mary; (F, 79)
    Dveře *otevřela* Mary, [door$_{acc}$ opened Mary$_{nom}$] (Ž, 79)
  b. *I was reminded* of some of the maritime sceneries (F, 79)
    Připomnělo mi to [it to-me reminded] některá přímořská místa (Ž, 80)

Among the passive counterparts of the English passives, all of which evidently qualify as fully corresponding, it is the compound form, a structural parallel of the English passive, cf. (22) a., that prevailed over the reflexive form, cf. (22) b. (12 and 5 instances, respectively, i.e. 70%). This may raise the question to what extent a translated text is influenced by the original.

(22) a. The visitors *were ushered in.* (F, 90)
    Návštěvníci *byli uvedeni.* (Ž, 90)
  b. that *was generally supposed* (F, 58)
    jak *se všeobecně předpokládalo* [as $_{reflexive\ particle}$ generally it-supposed] (Ž, 59)

1.4.2 Shifts in mood (cf. (23)) and temporal reference (cf. (24)) were found to be far less frequent (9 and 8 instances, respectively).

(23) To the ignorant *it may seem* that (F, 58)
    Nezasvěceným lidem *by se mohlo zdát*, že [it-might seem] (Ž, 58)
(24) Mrs Poulteney thought she *had been* the subject of a sarcasm (F, 83)
    paní Poulteneyová zatrnula, že *je* [is] obětí sarkasmu (Ž, 84)

In some of these instances the shift did not materially affect the meaning, cf. the shift in mood (indicative vs. imperative) in (25), and in tense in (26):

(25) you *will* kindly *remember* (F, 71)
    Napříště si laskavě *pamatujte* [remember] (Ž, 71)
(26) *Is something wrong, Mrs Poulteney?* (F, 82)
    Stalo se [happened] něco, paní Poulteneyová? (Ž, 82)

1.4.3 Shifts in polarity, illustrated by (27), were also infrequent (7 instances):

(27) Yet there *had remained* locally a feeling that (F, 80)
  Přesto však v městečku *nikdy nezanikl* pocit, že (Ž, 81)
  [In-spite-of-that however in village never not-expired feeling that]

1.4.4 A somewhat different type of shift was found in phasal and modal modification, i.e. in predicates containing a phasal or modal verb as the finite component and the main verb in non-finite form.

As regards phasal modification (13 instances), the shifts concerned the inceptive (initial) and durative (continuative) phases (7 and 4, respectively), the remaining 2 instances being accounted for by shifts in iterativeness. In 8 instances phasal modification was added, in 5 it was omitted. All phasal meanings were more frequently expressed correspondingly in both languages, and included among the fully correponding instances, cf. (28) a., b. and c.

(28) a. Ernestina *began to cry* again; (F, 75)
      Ernestina se zase *rozplakala*; [roz- prefix denoting initial phase] (Ž, 75)
  b. it *remains to be explained* (F, 80)
      zbývá vysvětlit [it-remains to-explain] (Ž, 80)
  c. she *would throw herself* into his arms (F, 89)
      vrhala [iterative, cf. semelfactive *vrhla*] *se* mu do náručí (Ž, 89)

The following examples illustrate counterparts with phasal shifts:

(29) a. It [her mouth] *fell* open. (F, 60)
      Zůstala dokořán otevřená [It-remained widely open] (Ž, 60)
  b. Mrs Poulteney *began to change* her tack. (F, 83)
      Paní Poulteneyová *změnila* [changed] taktiku. (Ž, 83)
  c. He accordingly *described* everything that had happened to him; (F, 79)
      A tak *začal popisovat* [began describe] všechno, co se mu přihodilo. (Ž, 79)

Shifts in modal modification were more numerous (56 instances), but even more numerous were instances of full correspondence (61+6 where the modal verb is reflected in a modal adverbial), as in (30) a.–c.

(30) a. I *cannot possess* this for ever (F, 63)
      Nemohu to *mít* navždy (Ž, 63)
  b. It was very clear that any moment Mrs Poulteney *might go off* (F, 81)
      Bylo nad slunce jasnější, že paní Poulteneyová *může* každým okamžikem *vybuchnout* (Ž, 85)
  c. She *must have heard* the sound of his boots (F, 77–78)
      Určitě slyšela [certainly she-heard] klapot jeho okovaných bot (Ž, 78)

The shifts in modal modification were of three kinds: most frequently the modal component was omitted (22 instances), cf. (31), less frequently (15 instances) a modal verb was added, as in (33), and in 19 instances there was a change in the modal meaning, cf. (35) a. and b.

(31) not what you *may think* of as a family Bible (F, 81)
      ne to, co si pod tím pojmem *představujete* [you-imagine] (Ž, 82)

Omission of *can* is regular in the case of verbs of perception and where it expresses ability reflected in a perfectivizing prefix in Czech, cf. (32) a. and b.

(32) a. a man with a broken leg *could* shout all week and *not be heard* (F, 62)
        člověk se zlomenou nohou by mohl křičet celý týden a *nikdo by ho neuslyšel* [nobody would him not-hear] (Ž, 62)
     b. Yes, he was welcome to as much milk as he *could drink*. (F, 76)
        Ano, může mít tolik mléka, kolik *vypije* [drinks up] (Ž, 76)

An added modal is illustrated by the following example.

(33) But what *is* the sin in walking on Ware Commons? (F, 82)
     Ale proč by *měl být* [should be] hřích chodit na Wareskou občinu? (Ž, 82)

In some cases the added modal, together with the particular lexical verb, captured the meaning of the verb in the original, cf. (34):

(34) when she *was spared* the tracts (F, 57-58)
     když *nemusela roznášet* [she-did-not-have-to distribute] traktáty (Ž, 57)

Changes in modal meaning involved different kinds of modality:

(35) a. We *must* never fear what is our duty. (F, 60)
        Nikdy se *nemáme* [we-not-should] bát svých povinností. (Ž, 60)
     b. he would not tolerate it in the girl he *was to* marry (F, 94)
        Nebude nic takového trpět u děvčete, které si *chce* [wants] vzít. (Ž, 94)

Examples (32) and (34) demonstrate the fluent borderline between fully and partially corresponding counterparts.

There were two examples of emphatic *do* without an explicit reflex, which were added to shifts in modality:

(36) But they *do think* that. (F, 58)
     Ale oni si to *myslí* [think]. (Ž, 58)

1.4.5 In a small number of instances (6) the shift concerned catenative verb phrases one component of which (attitudinal or notionally modal) appeared in a non-verbal form in Czech, as in (37) a. and b.

(37) a. I *prefer to walk* alone. (F, 78)
    Chodím raději sama. [I-walk more-gladly alone] (Ž, 78)
 b. Mrs Tranter *chanced to pass* through the hall (F, 79)
    paní Tranterová šla náhodou kolem [passed by-chance] (Ž, 79)

1.4.6 The last group of shifts includes instances which still qualify in respect of the correspondence English finite verb > Czech finite verb, but the interlingual synonymy is on the level of the whole sentence, rather than on the level of the verb alone, as a consequence of shifts in the assignment of syntactic functions and/or semantic roles. Two subgroups may be distinguished here, one preserving a verbal predicate in both languages, the other involving an additional shift between verbal and verbo-nominal predication.

1.4.6.1 The first subgroup is represented by 23 instances out of which two distinct patterns emerge: (a) possessive predicate in one language vs. existential sentence in the other (6 instances, i.e. nearly 25% of this group):

(38) a. *She had* infinitely the most life and infinitely the least selfishness; (F, 68)
    Bylo v ní [was in her] daleko nejvíc života a daleko nejméně sobectví. (Ž, 68)
 b. *There had been* Charles's daffodils and jonquills (F, 67)
    Měla [she-had] sice Charlesovy žluté a bílé narcisy (Ž, 67)

The two constructions are often interchangeable within one language, cf. *She had Charles's daffodils*, where the actual choice is presumably due to the semantic difference. In other instances the sentence structure may favour only one: in (38) a. *in her* in the existential construction would have to be placed either after a weighty coordinated subject or, if placed according to its degree of communicative dynamism, it would violate the grammatical word order principle. In Czech the choice appears to be even more restricted (cf. Chapter 9, 1.3).

(b) The second subgroup involves instances of shifts between object and subject. The most frequent pattern presented an English object rendered as the subject in Czech, both elements operating as rhemes, with the subject invariably in final position; the position of the English object was most frequently postverbal but penultimate before a thematic element. Compare (39) a. and b.

(39) a. It [= Lovers' Lane] drew *courting couples* every summer. (F, 81)
    Každé léto se sem táhly *milenecké párky*. (Ž, 81)
    [Every summer ~reflexive particle~ here gathered courting couples]
 b. I brought up *Ronsard's name* just now; (F, 68)

Před nedávnem tu padlo *Ronsardovo iméno*: (Ž, 68)
[Before not-long here appeared Ronsard's name]

1.4.6.2 The second subgroup involves an additional shift between verbal and verbo-nominal predicates. It might be added to the last group, treated in 1.5, but owing to displaying other syntactic shifts it has been included as a subtype in 1.4.6.

This subgroup is represented by 43 instances, most of which (27) display the same type of syntactic divergence, consisting in an object or adverbial counterpart of an English subject complement as a concomitant feature of a full verb in place of the copula. In some instances, additional syntactico-semantic shifts appeared, connected mainly with the choice of the subject.

(40) a. Ware Commons *was public property*. (F, 80)
Wareská občina *patří všem*. (Ž, 81)
[Wares Commons belongs to-all]
b. *It's no matter*, sir. (F, 78)
Nic se nestalo [nothing not-happened], pane. (Ž, 78)

Significantly, all instances but one displayed the verbo-nominal predicate in English whereas only one English verbal predicate appeared as a copula + subject complement in Czech, cf. (41):

(41) Some said that after midnight *more reeling than dancing took place*; (F, 81)
Někteří tvrdili, že po půlnoci *je to spíše potácení než tanec*. (Ž, 81)
[after midnight is it rather reeling than dancing]

It is to be noted that the Czech construction conduces to final position of the rheme, which in English occurs before the verb.

Mít 'have' as a counterpart of *be* or *být* 'be' against *have* (*be/být* as a copula or lexical verb other than existential) again occurred in several instances (6), cf. (42) a. and b.

(42) a. It *was on the tip of his tongue* (F, 80)
Měl to zrovna na jazyku [he-had it just on tongue] (Ž, 80)
b. Its cream and butter *had a local reputation*; (F, 76)
Zdejší smetana a máslo *byly pověstné v celém okolí*; [were renowned in whole area] (Ž, 76)

1.5 Unlike the shifts discussed in 1.4, which displayed more (in 1.4.1–1.4.4) or less (1.4.5, 1.4.6) correspondence between finite predicates, examples of this group involve addition or deletion of a clause element, and may hence be classed in different ways. The shift concerns the correspondence between verbal and verbo-nominal predicates, the clause element verb being reflected in a copula + subject complement and vice versa. This shift was found in both directions. Apart from copular predications (1.5.1, (43); 1.5.2 (a)) it appeared functionally and semantically justifiable to include in this group all instances where the verb has a decomposed make-up consisting of a semantically weakened or indeterminate verb and a nominal component which shapes the meaning of the whole construction (1.5.1, (44) a., b.; 1.5.2 (b)–(e)).

1.5.1 The shift between an English verb and a Czech copula + subject complement was found in 6 instances, cf. (43).

(43) he *did not know* this. (F, 63)
    nebyl si toho *vědom,* [not-was aware] (Ž, 63)
(44) a. Certainly I *intended* at this stage ... to tell all (F, 85)
    Zajisté jsem *měl v úmyslu* [I-had in intention] na tomto místě ... vypovědět všechno (Ž, 85)
   b. the first disagreement that *had* ever *darkened* their love (F, 95)
    první neshoda, která *vrhla stín* [threw shadow] na jejich lásku (Ž, 95)

1.5.2 Czech univerbal expression of English verbo-nominal predication altogether accounts for 68.76% of this shift, the number of Czech verbal counterparts being 55 (as compared with 26 English verbal predicates rendered by the Czech verbonominal). This quantitative difference again testifies to the more verbal character of Czech (cf. Chapters 4 and 5).

English verbonominal constructions with Czech verbal counterparts were of several types.

(a) The most frequent type is constituted by a copula + subject complement (21 instances, i.e. 38.2% of all registered English verbo-nominal constructions), cf. (45).

(45) she knew he *was attractive* to women. (F, 67)
    Věděla, že *přitahuje* [attracts] ženy. (Ž, 67)

Besides *be*, the most frequent copula in this group (16 instances, i.e. 76.2%), there were 4 occurrences of *become; fall* (open), *make* (sure), *grow* (like) were each represented by one occurrence.

(46) a. Sarah went less often to the woods than she *had become accustomed to* (F, 87)
    Sarah chodila do lesa méně často, než *si* předtím *navykla* [to-herself she-accustomed] (Ž, 87)
   b. Her coat *had fallen open* (F, 64)
    Kabát *se jí rozevřel* [coat ~reflexive particle~ to-her opened] (Ž, 64)

(b) The second type displays transitive copulas in the pattern V—O$_d$ (12 instances, i.e. 21.8% of the registered verbo-nominal constructions). The verbs found in this constructions were *make* (*advances, a nod, a response, a pretence, inquiries;* 5 instances), *give* (*a wink, a smile*; 2 occurrences), *have* (*the desire, revenge, fear*; 3 instances), with *bear* (*resemblance*) and *do* (*the talking*) represented once.

(47) a. she ... *made an infinitesimal nod;* (F, 91)
     nepatrně pokývla [infinitesimally she-nodded] (Ž, 91)
   b. For the first time since her arrival she *gave the faintest smile.* (F, 59)
     poprvé od svého příchodu se *slabounce usmála*, [faintly she-smiled] (Ž, 59)
   c. Charles resolved that he *would have his revenge* on Mrs Poulteney (F, 94)
     Charles se rozhodl, že *se pomstí* [he-will-revenge himself] paní Poulteneyové (Ž, 93–94)
   d. Sam ... *had borne very little resemblance* to the mournful and indignant young man who (F, 70)
     Sam ... *se velmi málo podobal* [very little resembled] tomu nasupenému rozhořčenému mladíkovi, který (Ž, 70)

(c) The next type differs from (b) in one of two features: a semantically weak or indeterminate verb is complemented by a non-action noun, or an action noun complements a full verb (*set foot/eyes, one's heart on* x *pick exits, come to one's senses*) (13 instances, 23.6%).

(48) a. the gentleman *had set his heart* on having an arboretum in the Undercliff. (F, 80)
     šlechtic *si umínil* [resolved], že na Spodním útesu zřídí jakousi botanickou zahradu vzácných stromů. (Ž, 80)
   b. He *came to his senses* of what was proper. (F, 65)
     Uvědomil si [he-realized], co se sluší a patří. (Ž, 66)

(d) The ditransitive type $V—O_i—O_d$ is represented by 4 examples (7.3%), all containing the verb *give*.

(49) He *gave his wife a stern look.* (F, 77)
   Přísně se podíval na ženu.[6] [Sternly he-looked at wife] (Ž, 77)

(e) the last type displays the pattern $V—O—C_o$ (5 instances, 9.1% of the verbo-nominal constructions):

(50) Mrs Poulteney, *whom* the thought of young happiness always *made petulant* (F, 90)

---

6   For the FSP aspect of this point, see also Chapter 2., 2.2 and Dušková 2012. In (49) the Czech equivalent deviates from the FSP structure of the original. Both the subject and the indirect object are context-dependent, hence the rheme is constituted by the verb + the manner adjunct. However, the Czech counterpart presents the thematic object as the rheme. If the sentence were construed verbally in English, the rhematic section, the verb + the manner adjunct, would be dissected by the thematic object. The English verbo-nominal construction here serves to achieve the basic distribution of communicative dynamism.

paní Poulteneyová, *kterou* pomyšlení na mladé štěstí vždycky *podráždilo* [whom ... annoyed] (Ž, 90)

Considering these shifts from the viewpoint of the options offered by the target language, structural parallels may be found in all types, albeit not in particular instances, but verbal expression largely prevails in Czech (68.76% of these shifts, see above). The only exception is found in 1.5.2 type (c), where the number of examples rendered univerbally in Czech (13) is outnumbered by English verbs which have two-component Czech counterparts (20 instances, cf. 1.5.1 (44) a., b.).

The type most amenable to variant expression appears to be copula + subject complement, cf. *be attractive – přitahovat* (cf. *to attract*), *být přitažlivý*; *be jealous*[7] *– žárlit, být žárlivý*; *be aware – vědět* (cf. *to know*), *být si vědom*, etc.

The use of a verbo-nominal construction instead of verbal expression may be due to the interplay of the syntactic-semantic features of a given sentence, as shown by the following example. In (51) it is presumably the need to express the intensifier (*very* > *velmi*) that determines the choice.

(51) Ernestina *had been very silent* on the walk downhill to Broad Street. (F, 95)
      Ernestina *byla* při chůzi z kopce dolů do Broad Street *velice mlčenlivá*. (Ž, 95)

In type (b), illustrated by the examples listed under (47), the option largely depends on the verb: while the counterparts of *make* and *have* + action noun sometimes offer a choice (*make an offer – nabídnout, učinit nabídku*, but *make a nod* – only *přikývnout, make a pretence* – only *předstírat; have no fears – neobávat se, nemít obavy*, but *have one's revenge* – only *pomstít se*), *bear* and monotransitive *give* are less amenable to alternative expression, cf. *bear resemblance – podobat se, give a wink – mrknout, give a smile – usmát se*. On the other hand type (d), represented by ditransitive *give*, displays, apart from verbal rendition, several instances of verbo-nominal construction. Compare (49) with the following examples:

(52) a. Mrs Poulteney *gave her a look of indignation*. (F, 82)
         Paní Poulteneyová *na ni vrhla pohoršený pohled*. [at her threw indignant look] (Ž, 82)
      b. Ernestina *gave Charles a sharp, reproachful glance*; (F, 93)
         Ernestina *vrhla na Charlese přísný, vyčítavý pohled*. [threw at Charles stern, reproachful glance] (Ž, 93)
      c. He *threw an angry look at the bearded dairyman* (F, 77)
         Vrhl hněvivý pohled na vousatého sedláka [he-threw angry look at bearded farmer] (Ž, 77)

---

7   For systemic gaps in this type, see Chapter 5, 3.1.1.

It is to be noted that here the usual verbal counterpart would not display the FSP structure as distinctly as the verbo-nominal form which is decomposed into the categorial (transitional) and notional (rhematic) component. If the verb alone is used, both the categorial and the notional component are expressed in one form which hence realizes two FSP functions (see Firbas, 1961). While the Czech counterparts of (52) a. and b. faithfully follow the FSP structure of the original, in (52) c. the translation again deviates from the FSP structure of the original, *the bearded dairyman* being context-dependent, and accordingly thematic (cf. Note 6).

Type (c) mostly comprises idiomatic constructions in English which seldom have a parallel Czech counterpart, cf. *have one's eye on sb./sth.*, *set one's heart on sth.*, but *set eyes on sth.* – *spatřit, spočinout na něčem zrakem, set foot in a place* – *vkročit, vkročit nohou*. Here especially the verbo-nominal variant is shown to be more formal or literary, which is a fairly general feature of this type of constructions in Czech.

In type (e), prevalently realized by *make* in the complex transitive construction, Czech may resort to a causative verb, as in *make sb. petulant* (in (50), cf. *to pomyšlení způsobilo, že byla podrážděná* [the thought caused that she was petulant]), but hardly in instances like *make sth. clear*, and the like.

As has been noted in 1.5, from the purely syntactic point of view shifts between verbal and verbo-nominal predicates involve a divergence consisting in the addition or deletion of a clause element, but from the semantic and functional point of view verbal and verbo-nominal predicates may be regarded as equivalent. This is especially shown by systemic gaps such *be jealous, be silent*, where verbal expression is lacking. Assignment of this group to corresponding or non-corresponding counterparts respectively enhances or lowers the interlingual syntactic constancy of the verb by 5.1%, see Table 1.

Table 1: Czech counterparts of English finite verbs

fully corresponding		1222	77.6%
	voice	57	3.6%
	mood	9	0.6%
	tense	8	0.5%
	polarity	7	0.4%
with shifts in	phasal modification	13	0.8%
	modal modification	56	3.6%
	catenative verb phrases	6	0.4%
	syntactic structure	66	4.2%
with shifts between verbal and verbo-nominal predicates		81	5.1%
divergent		50	3.2%
total		1575	100.0%

1.6 Table 1 shows the total number of English finite verbs and their Czech counterparts found within the stretch of text that supplied 50 syntactically divergent counterparts.

In addition to the fully corresponding counterparts, most of the groups involving shifts qualify to be regarded as corresponding rather than divergent counterparts, specifically the groups involving shifts in the verbal categories, polarity, phasal and modal modification and catenative verb phrases, which together account for 8.8%.

With this correction, syntactic constancy of the verb would appear to be 86.4%. Moreover, the discussion in 1.4.6 has shown that even the type displaying correspondence between English and Czech finite verbs whose interlingual synonymy involves the sentence level may justifiably be classed with the corresponding rather than the divergent counterparts. Syntactic constancy then rises to 91.6%. If even the most problematic group of shifts between verbal and verbo-nominal predicates is included, syntactic constancy of the verb, viz 96.7%, appears to be higher than that of the subject, which has so far ranked as the most constant clause element: 96.15% (see Chapters 1 and 3).

1.7 Table 2 presents the syntactic functions of the 50 divergent couterparts of the English verb, obtained from the analysed texts.

Table 2: Czech divergent counterparts of the English verb

modifier		18	36%
	premodifier	1	
	postmodifier	17	
adverbial		17	34%
adverbial reflecting a cleft sentence		10	20%
subject		2	4%
object		1	2%
varia		2	4%
total		50	100%

1.7.1 The most frequent syntactically divergent counterpart of the English finite verb is the noun modifier (18 occurrences). Except one example, all instances of English finite verbs as noun modifiers are found in postmodification which is further expanded. The realization form of the modifier is prevalently the present participle (12 instances, see (53) a.), the past participle accounting for four instances. The only instance of premodification displays an adjective derived from the latter form, see (53) b.

(53) a. the one remaining track *that traverses* it is often impassable. (F, 62)
     jediná cesta *procházející* [traversing] těmito místy je často neschůdná. (Ž, 62)

b. Part of her hair *has become loose* and half-covered her cheek. (F, 65)
   Pramen rozpuštěných vlasů [strand of loosened hair] jí pokrýval část obliče-
   je. (Ž, 65)

In (54) the postmodifier is expressed by an agent noun derived from the present participle in the genitive case, the remaining instance displaying an adjective.

(54) which [= a ledge] hid her from the view of any but one *who came* ... to the very
   edge. (F, 64)
   jejíž výběžek ji chránil *před očima každého příchozího* [from the eyes of-every ar-
   riving-one] vyjma toho, kdo ... postoupil až úplně na okraj. (Ž, 64)

This group of counterparts is characterized by one common feature, viz. the finite
verb reflected in the modifier occurs in a subordinate clause that as a whole performs
the postmodifying function. It is thus only on the level of this clause that the counterparts display a divergence. On the level of the head noun, which is a constituent of
the superordinate clause, the difference consists only in the form of realization (finite vs. non-finite or non-verbal form).

Since non-finite realization forms of syntactic functions serve to condense sentence structure, the Czech counterparts here display a features which is usually pointed out as characteristic of English. As was shown in 1.3.2, this is indeed the case. It is
to be noted, however, that English participles rendered by Czech finite clauses within
the same stretch of text (33 instances of the *ing*-participle and 17 occurrences of the
past participle, see 1.3.2.3) considerably outnumber English finite clauses rendered by
Czech participles (16 instances). The discussion in 1.3.2.3 moreover shows that English
participles rendered by Czech finite clauses also occur in other than the modifying
function, notably the adverbial (23 instances). Here the structural parallel (*přechod-
ník* 'transgressive') has largely disappeared from Modern Czech in favour of finite
realization.

In two instances the choice of participial postmodification is presumably due to the
fact that otherwise there would be two or three relative clauses in close proximity. Since
Modern Czech has virtually one relative for the subject function (*který* 'who/which'),
cumulation of relative clauses may be felt undesirable for stylistic reasons.

(55) She had ... physical charms to match ... *corn-coloured hair* and delectably wide
   grey-blue eyes, eyes *that invited* male provocation (F, 68)
   Bylo v ní ... mnoho fyzického půvabu ... *vlasy, které připomínaly barvou zralé zrno*
   [hair which resembled by-colour ripe corn], a široké, šedě modré oči, *vyzývající*
   [inviting] mužské dvoření (Ž, 68)

1.7.2 The second well represented divergent counterpart is the adverbial. In Table 2
it is presented in two separate groups, as adverbials and explicit counterparts of the
cleft sentence.

The counterparts of the first group of adverbials (17 instances) display two distinct patterns.

(a) The English finite verb is reflected in a temporal adjunct (as defined by Quirk et al. 1985: 504–505) (6 instances), cf. (56).

(56) the little scene that took place with a pleasing regularity *when they got back to Aunt Tranter's house.* (F, 89)
    malý výstup, který se odehrával s příjemnou pravidelností *po návratu* [after return] do domu tety Tranterové. (Ž, 89)

The temporal adjunct is realized by a prepositional phrase containing an action noun derived from, or semantically affinitive with the finite verb of the corresponding English clause. As in the case of the modifier, the syntactic divergence is found on the level of the subordinate temporal clause, since in the structure of the superordinate clause both the prepositional phrase and the subordinate clause operate in the same syntactic function, as a temporal adjunct. Accordingly, the divergent feature is again only the realization form. This type of non-correspondence appears to be specific to the verb and is due to its predicative nature.

(b) The second pattern reflects finite verbs occurring in comment clauses with the function of attitudinal disjuncts (4 instances). Both the comment clause and the adverbial operate as a sentence modifier, the syntactic divergence being restricted to the level of the comment clause alone.

(57) a. But it was not, *I am afraid*, the face for 1867. (F, 69)
        Bohužel [unfortunately] to však nebyl obličej pro rok 1867. (Ž, 69)
    b. So also, *Charles was not pleased to note*, did Ernestina. (F, 91)
        A také Ernestina si *k Charlesově malé radosti* [to Charles's small pleasure] počínala stejně. (Ž, 91)

This pattern reflects the differences in the status of comment clauses and disjuncts in general between English and Czech.

(c) Another type of interlingual relations based on systemic differences between the two languages was observed in the rendition of the verbal proform *do* by the sentential adverb *ano* 'yes' (2 instances), cf. (58).

(58) Travelling no longer attracted him; but women *did*, (F, 74)
    Cestování už ho nelákalo, ale ženy *ano* [yes] (Ž, 74)

Of the remaining instances one displays a correspondence which may be classed with type (b), cf. (59).

(59) *It so happened* that the avalanche ... was appointed to take place at Marlborough House (F, 89)

Zvláštní náhodou [by-strange chance] čekala Charlese ... lavina právě v Marlborough House. (Ž, 89)

Here the structure of the sentence with the main clause which modifies the content of the subordinate clause like a content disjunct, cf. *accidentally*, represents the underlying form out of which comment clauses have developed.

Two instances display syntactic divergence even on the level of the higher clause; however, they seem to be individual solutions chosen by the translator rather than patterns reflecting systemic relations.

(60) *There were times*, if cook had a day off, when Mrs Tranter sat and ate with Mary alone in the downstairs kitchen. (F, 69)
   Občas [occasionally] když kuchařka měla volný den, jedla paní Tranterová s Mary sama dole v kuchyni. (Ž, 69)

Here the temporal content of the main clause appears as a subordinate element, a temporal adjunct, in the clause which has subordinate status in the original, but has been raised to the status of the main clause in the translation.

Similarly one of the two instances completing this group is an ad hoc solution while the last is a case of recategorization and subsequent lexicalization in Czech:

(61) one day it was discovered ... that a gang of gipsies had been living there ... *for nobody knew how many months*. (F, 80)
   jednoho dnes se přišlo na to, že se tu ... zdržovala *bůhvíkolik* [god-knows-how-many] měsíců ... banda cikánů. (Ž, 81)

1.7.3 The last type of divergent counterparts represented by recurrent examples (10 instances) was found in explicit devices reflecting the focusing function of the cleft sentence (8 *it*-clefts and 2 *wh*-clefts). It is discussed as a separate type, rather than having been included among the other adverbial counterparts, on the ground of its homogeneous nature: all counterparts of the *it*-clefts are focusing adjuncts and the counterparts of the *wh*-clefts reflect the meaning of *be* + the following *wh*-word. Functionally the English and the Czech devices are equivalent; syntactically they display a major divergence which provides another reason for treating them as a separate group. The divergence involves a reversal of the relation of subordination: the focusing adjunct reflects the copular verb in the main clause of the cleft sentence, but in the resulting sentence which replaces the bi-clausal construction of one propositional content, the constitutive feature of the cleft sentence, it appears as a subordinate element.

The most frequent counterpart of an English *it*-cleft contains the focalizer *právě* 'just', 'precisely' (4 instances).

(62) *It was Mrs Tranter who* made me aware of my error. (F, 78)
   Právě paní Tranterová [precisely Mrs Tranter] mě upozornila na můj omyl. (Ž, 78)

The *wh*-clefts contained in the excerpted text also illustrate a well-established counterpart, cf. (63).

(63) *This is why* we cannot plan. (F, 86)
     Proto [therefore] nemůžeme plánovat. (Ž, 86)

Besides *právě*, illustrated in (62), the counterparts of *it*-clefts included *teprve* 'only' rendering *it was not unti l... that* (attested once), which even more than *právě* appears to be generally used to render this construction.

(64) *It was not until towards the end of the visit* that Charles began to realize (F, 91)
     Teprve ke konci návštěvy [only towards end of-visit] svitlo Charlesovi, že (Ž, 92)

In the remaining instances the devices chosen as focalizers are contextual, ad hoc choices: *tedy* 'thus', 'then' and *v jádru* 'in core'.

(65) If I have pretended until now to know my characters' minds and innermost
     thoughts, *it is because* I am writing ... in a convention universally accepted at the
     time of my story. (F, 85)
     Jestliže jsem dosud předstíral, že vím, co se děje v mysli mých osob, v jejich nej-
     skrytějších myšlenkách, *tedy* [then] proto, že píši ... v mezích konvence běžně
     uznávané za časů, kdy se můj příběh odehrává. (Ž, 85)

In this elliptical *it*-cleft (*it is because I am writing in a convention universally ac-cepted ... that I have pretended ...*) *tedy* functions as an emphasizer. Similarly the expression *v jádru* 'in core' in the following example:

(66) but *it was* really *Charles's heart of which* she was jealous. (F, 68)
     ale *v jádru* žárlila spíše *na Charlesovo srdce*. (Ž, 68)
     [but in core she-was-jealous rather of Charles's heart]

Here it may be argued that *v jádru* renders *really*, but then *spíše* [= rather] remains to be accounted for.

This brief account of explicit Czech reflexes of the cleft sentence needs to be comple-mented by noting instances which lack an explicit counterpart of the focusing function of the main clause of the *it*-cleft. Within the excerpted text, there were 8 such instances.

(67) It was to banish such gloomy forebodings ... that Ernestina fetched her diary (F, 71)
     Aby zahnala teskné předtuchy ... přinesla si Ernestina deník (Ž, 71)
     [so-that she-banished gloomy forebodings ... brought to-herself Ernestina diary]

In a few *it*-clefts, the focusing function is expressed twice in that they also con-tain an adverbial focalizer. On the other hand the Czech counterpart expresses the fo-cusing function only once through the equivalent of the adverbial focalizer.

(68) *it was only then that he realized* whom he had intruded upon. (F, 65)
  teprve v té chvíli si uvědomil [only in that moment he-realized], na koho to vlastně
  narazil. (Ž, 65)

These three types account for 90% of all the divergent counterparts.

1.7.4 The remaining instances are represented by one or two examples, and accordingly do not lend themseslves to generalizations.

In two instances the divergent counterpart is the subject:

(69) a. *She was not standing at her window* as part of her mysterious vigil for Satan's
  sails; (F, 84)
  Její hlídka u okna neměla nic společného s mystickým čekáním na Satanovy
  plachty; (Ž, 84)
  [her vigil at window not-had nothing in-common with mystic waiting for Satan]
  b. *what has changed is that* we are no longer the gods of the Victorian image
  (F, 86)
  hlavní změna je v tom, že [main change is in that, that] už nejsme bohové k viktoriánskému obrazu (Ž, 86)

The b. example is a noninverted *wh*-cleft, but without an explicit counterpart in Czech of its focusing function. Since it displays the syntactic divergence discussed at this point, it has not been included among instances like (67). The example is moreover of interest for illustrating a frequent textual function of *wh*-clefts, viz. to express a contrast with the preceding context.[8] This is reflected in the adjective *hlavní* 'main' added to the nominalized subject, cf. the preceding context: *The novelist is still a god, since he creates … ; what has changed is that we are no longer the gods of … (F, 86).*

In one instance the English verb is reflected in a Czech object:

(70) I have decided to leave England. For the rest of my life *I shall travel.* (F, 75)
  Rozhodl jsem se odjet z Anglie a *věnovat zbytek života cestování.* (Ž, 75)
  [I-decided leave from England and devote rest of-life to-travelling]

Example (71) illustrates a regular equivalent which preserves both the optative function and the stylistic (formal and archaic) characteristic: the Czech optative particle *kéž* rendering the verb of the main clause *would.*

(71) *Would* that it did not (F, 60)
  Kéž by se netýkalo (Ž, 60)
  [optative particle it-would-not-concern]

---

8   For this point, see also Chapter 5, 3.2.2.

The last divergent example is an ad hoc counterpart (*it seemed* rendered as *jakoby* 'as if', (F/Ž 78)).

1.8 Attempting to summarize the results of the foregoing discussion, what appears to have been clearly shown is the unique nature of the verb, specifically its clause-constitutive function. Most of the divergent counterparts represent reduction of clauses, cf. participial modification vs. adjectival relative clause, nominalization of adverbial clauses, and reflexes of English finite verbs in the subject and object. In all these types the verbal element remains preserved either in the respective non-finite form or an affinitive action noun in the respective noun phrase or prepositional phrase. The syntactic divergence is largely found only on the level of the subordinate clauses; on the level of the superordinate clause both the finite subordinate clause and its restructured counterpart display the same syntactic function. A similar picture emerges where an English finite verb occurs in a comment clause, rendered as a sentence adverbial (disjunct) in Czech.

A second distinct relationship emerging from the divergent counterparts displays differences between the two languages in focusing devices, which confirm earlier findings (cf. Chapter 5).

2. The Czech-English part draws on the data obtained from a diploma dissertation (Strnadová 1998) dealing with constancy of the verb as a word class. Although the treatise pursues a different aim, and adopts a different approach following the methodology of *The Noun in Translation* (Klégr 1996), in consequence of the close relationship between the finite verb and its syntactic function it largely covers the same ground as the preceding part.

The study is based on three Czech novels and their English translations (see Sources) which provided 828 finite verbs. Elimination of finite verbs that lacked an equivalent (31 instances) and finite verbs whose finite counterparts displayed too complicated equivalence relations (34 instances, cf. Strnadová 1998: 16–17) reduced the original number by 65 instances, i.e. to 763. These Czech finite verbs were found to have finite counterparts in 90.1% (687 instances), the remaining 76 Czech finite verbs being accounted for by 65 (8.5%) non-finite verb forms and 11 (1.4%) non-verbal forms. Syntactic constancy of the finite verb was accordingly attested in 90.1%, the non-finite and non-verbal counterparts displaying syntactic functions other than that performed by the finite verb (see Tables 4 and 5).

2.1 The group of instances classed as fully corresponding in the English-Czech direction is here represented by the basic group denoted as simple predicates (=verb phrases constituted by lexical verbs); copulas, modal and phasal verbs are treated as separate groups termed complex predicates. In the English-Czech part modal and phasal predicates that preserved these components were included among the fully corresponding counterparts. Nevertheless, a comparable group of fully corresponding English counterparts of Czech finite verbs can be arrived at by adding to the group of simple predicates copular, modal and phasal predicates with the same structure in English. This is made possible on the basis of detailed treatment of each of these groups in which the divergent instances are specified and discussed. According to Table 3.1.4 in Strnadová (1998: 19) from the total of finite predicates (687 instances, 100%) 53 (7%) display some kind of deviation in the verb phrase: 18 simple predicates, 8 copular, and 27 modal (there is no deviation in the rendition of phasal predicates), see Table 3.

Table 3: English counterparts of Czech finite verbs

Czech finite verbs	English counterparts		
	same	different	total
simple predicates (lexical verbs)	503	18	521
copular predicates	93	8	101
modal predicates	34	27	61
phasal predicates	4	0	4
total	634	53	687

Although there are differences in the conception of modal verbs in the two approaches, the figure 634 is essentially comparable with the group of fully corresponding counterparts of English finite verbs: 1222 (77.6%), see Table 1 in 1.6. Within the total of 763 Czech finite verbs including syntactically divergent counterparts (65 non-finite and 11 non-verbal forms, according to Table 3.1.2 in Strnadová 1998: 17), the group without divergent copular and modal predicates accounts for 81.1%. Syntactic constancy of Czech finite verbs with respect to their English counterparts thus appears to be higher by 3.5% than in the English-Czech direction. However, compare the commentary on Table 1 in 1.6, where predicates with shifts between verbal categories are considered with respect to their potential for being included among corresponding counterparts.

2.2 As regards the divergent counterparts in each of the groups listed in Table 3, they more or less mirror the shifts treated in 1.5 and 1.4.4.

Czech finite lexical verbs were found to have 18 divergent counterparts, of which 15 correspond to copular predications (Table 3.2.1 in Strnadová 1998: 23). As compared with the total of comparable counterparts obtained from Table 3 (634 instances), these copular counterparts represent 2.3% (the percentage of 15 from 634+15). In the opposite direction this percentage is more than four times smaller: 6 Czech copular predicates reflecting English finite verbs (see 1.5.1) as compared with 1222 structurally parallel counterparts, i.e. 0.5%.

The 15 copular counterparts of Czech finite lexical verbs include four which display the same type of shift as was noted in 1.4.6, (38) b., (42) a., viz. predicates with *mít* 'have' reflected in predicates with *be*, as in (72).

(72) *měla* vzteklou tvář [she-had livid face] (KM, 134)
    her face *was* livid (H, 125)

Two instances are of interest from the FSP point of view: the copular predication here conduces to preserving the same linear order of the nominal elements as in the original. As a result, both the Czech sentence and its English counterpart display the basic distribution of communicative dynamism.

(73) a. jehož korbu *tvořila* poloviční popelnice (KI, 11)
  [whose body$_{acc}$ formed half dustbin$_{nom}$]
  a hand cart whose body *was* half a dustbin (O, 5)
  b. Z prostředního patra ... *vznikl* soud (L, 227)
  [from middle floor ... arose courtroom]
  The middle floor ... *was* now a courtroom (W, 93)

In the group of copular predicates (101 instances) there are altogether 8 divergent counterparts, all but one of which are reflected in a finite lexical verb, cf. (74).

(74) čím *budeš* k lidem *důvěřivější* (L, 231)
  [what$_{instr}$ you-will-be to people more-trusting]
  the more you *trust* people (W, 98)

As compared with the 21 instances of English copular predications rendered uni-verbally by a lexical verb in Czech (cf. 1.5.2 (a)), this type of shift appears to be much less frequent from Czech to English, which supports the generally held view of Czech as the more verbal of the two languages.

2.3 The divergences in modal predicates (27 out of 61, see Table 3), which appear to be very frequent, in fact reflect a different conception of the modal verbs in English and Czech: in the latter, the class of the modals is conceived more broadly. As a result, entirely parallel structures are regarded differently, e.g. verbs like *přát si* 'wish', *chtít* 'want', *mínit* 'mean' are classed as modal in Czech but as lexical in English. In a few other instances similar shifts were noted as in 1.4.4 (omission or addition of a modal component), cf. (75) (and the comment on (34) in Part 1).

(75) *musil za trest* ... očišťovat městské ulice (KI, 12)
  [he-had for punishment to-clean city streets]
  He *was* ... *sentenced* to clean the streets (O, 5)

2.4 As regards the verbal categories discussed in 1.4.1–1.4.3, voice, mood and polarity, they are mentioned in connection with the specification of the code system, but not included among the points under detailed discussion.

2.5 For the present purpose the most relevant part of the study is the treatment of the non-finite and non-verbal counterparts (the quantitative data are presented in Table 3.1.2, Strnadová 1998: 17).

The figure 687 (90.1%) includes not only the simple predicates, but also the complex groups, i.e. copular, modal and phasal. Consequently, it is comparable with the percentage 96.7 in 1.6, in which the predicates involving shifts between verbal and ver-bo-nominal structure are included in the syntactically corresponding counterparts. Without this group, the percentage of syntactic constancy from English to Czech is 91.6 (see the commentary on Table 1 in 1.6). This figure is then comparable with the total of Czech finite verb forms 687 from which copular counterparts of simple predicates (15) and univerbal lexical counterparts of copular predicate (7), see below, have been subtracted, i.e. 665. This lowers the percentage of syntactically corresponding counterparts in the Czech-English direction to 87.1, i.e. by 3%.

Table 4: English counterparts of Czech finite verbs

finite verb forms	687	90.1%
non-finite verb forms	65	8.5%
non-verbal forms	11	1.4%
total	763	100.0%

Table 5: English divergent syntactic counterparts of Czech finite verbs

		total	%
adverbial	13 gerunds 11 *ing*-participles 3 infinitives 1 noun	28	36.9
noun modifier	10 *ing*-participles 4 *ed*-participles 1 infinitive 2 nouns 3 preposition *with* 1 preposition *like* 1 derivational morpheme -*like*	22	28.9
object	12 infinitives (complements of verbs) 3 infinitives (complements of adjectives) 3 gerunds 1 noun	19	25.0
object complement	3 *ing*-participles	3	3.9
subject	3 infinitives	3	3.9
subject complement	1 infinitive	1	1.4
total		76	100.0

2.6 Table 5 is based on Supplement 1 of the Czech-English study (3.2.3), in which all non-finite counterparts of Czech finite verbs are listed. The non-verbal counterparts are exhaustively treated by Strnadová in 3.2.4 (1998: 48–50). The examples are first classified according to the realization form: non-finite (infinitive, gerund, *ing*-participle, *ed*-participle) and non-verbal (noun, preposition, derivational morpheme), and then according to syntactic function. To be comparable with Table 2 in 1.6, Table 5 is arranged according to the syntactic function within which the different realization forms are listed.

At first sight, Table 5 differs from Table 2 in two major respects. The first concerns the degree of syntactic constancy, which appears to be considerably lower than in the English-Czech direction. The English divergent forms, though obtained from a smaller material (763 against 1575 instances) substantially outnumber the Czech divergent counterparts (76 against 50), thus displaying a higher density as a concomitant feature.

This difference is closely connected with the second major point of non-correspondence, viz. the forms of realization of the syntactically divergent counterparts. Of those listed in Table 5 only the participles and the noun (mostly in prepositional phrases) are also found from English to Czech (see 1.7.1 and 1.7.2). The third major realization form is here the adverb (1.7.3), which is not attested in the Czech-English direction. The Czech-English direction largely displays divergent counterparts constituted by specific realization forms, viz. infinitives, gerunds, prepositions (except for the preposition *with*/Czech *s*, see the comment on (77) d.) and a bound morpheme. Of the last two realization forms only the preposition *with* appears to be based on systemic relations.

Table 5 also shows that the two most significant factors conducing to the higher degree of syntactic non-constancy of Czech finite verbs in English are the infinitive and the gerund, i.e. the non-finite forms whose syntactic behaviour parallels that of the noun.

In general the non-finite verb forms as counterparts of Czech finite verbs play a specific and decisive role in this direction insofar as the English-Czech approach entirely excludes them: the starting point being the syntactic function of the finite verb, the non-finite forms are a priori ruled out by their syntactic functions which assign them to syntactic nouns, adjectives and adverbs.

The different syntactic functions of the Czech divergent counterparts are illustrated by the following examples.

Adverbial: a. gerund, b. *ing*-participle, c. infinitive, d. noun.

(76) a. *aniž* to pokladní *věděla* (L, 230)
   [without$_{conjunction}$ it cashier knew]
   without her *knowing* about it (W, 97)
   b. *Sedl jsem si na lavici ... a držel jsem* [and clutched] koženou taštičku (KI, 7)
   I sat down on a seat ... *clutching* a small leather bag (O, 1)
   c. *Abych dokázal* [in-order-that I-showed] dobrou vůli, chopil jsem se největší lopaty. (KI, 11)
   To show my good will I took the biggest shovel. (O, 5)
   d. To všechno byly dostatečné důvody, *že se mu říkalo Voltaire*. (KM, 132)
   [that all were sufficient reasons that he-was-called Voltaire]
   – reason enough *for his nickname*. (H, 123)

Noun modifier: a. *ing*-participle, b. *ed*-participle, c. preposition *like*, d. preposition *with*, e. derivational morpheme *-like*.

(77) a. z mraků, *které visí* [which hang] nad městem (L, 231)
from the clouds *hanging* over the city (W, 97)
b. výbuchů žárlivosti, *za nimiž následoval* [after which followed] ostych (L, 233)
explosions of jealousy *followed by* shyness (W, 99)
c. zvenčí našité *kapsy připomínaly neforemná pouzdra na pistole* [sewn-on pockets resembled shapeless holders for pistols] (KI, 7)
sewn-on *pockets* rather *like misshapen pistol holders* (O, 1)
d. Toho, *co má* [that has] tak velký zuby? (L, 232)
The one *with* the big teeth? (W, 98)
e. co na pokladní *připomínalo zvíře* (L, 228)
[what in cashier resembled animal]
it was the only *animal-like* thing about her (W, 96)

The correspondences illustrated by (77) a. and b. were also found in the English-Czech part, but with lower frequency (see 1.7.1). A special recurrent realization form is here illustrated by (77) d., which demonstrates two different forms of expressing the possessive relationship: the verb *mít* 'have' and the preposition *with*. This type is also found in Czech, cf. *dívka s dlouhými vlasy* 'the girl with long hair'; in (77) d. *mít* is presumably preferred in Czech to avoid two instrumental forms with the Common Czech ending *-ama*.

Object: a. infinitive as verb complement, b. infinitive as adjectival complement, c. gerund, d. noun.

(78) a. dožadovali se, *abych vysvětlil* [they-asked that I-explained] (KI, 8)
they asked me *to explain* (O, 2)
b. jak ráda to pro tebe *udělám* [how gladly it for you I-will-do] (L, 227)
how *glad* I am *to be able to do* this for you (W, 95)
c. vyhnout se ... *aby ho znechutila* [that him she-repelled] ... informacemi (KM, 129)
to avoid *repelling him* ... with the ... directions (H, 120)
d. naslouchal jsem ... *jak oheň vítězně hučí* [how fire victoriously roars] (KI, 12)
I'd ... listen ... *to the victorious roar of the fire* (O, 6)

Type (d) realized by a prepositional phrase with an action noun was also noted in Part I, cf. 1.7.2.

Object complement: *ing*-participle

(79) Student *cítil, jak mu hoří tváře* [how to-him burn cheeks] (KM, 134)
The student *felt his cheeks burning* (H, 124)

Subject: infinitive

(80) představení, na které se dostaly [for which could-be-obtained] jen málokdy vstu-
penky těsně před zahájením (L, 228)
when *it was impossible to get* the tickets just before the film began (W, 95)

This example also illustrates the shift between a prepositional phrase with an action noun (*před zahájením* [before beginning]) and a finite clause (*before the film began*)
as in (78) d., but here in the Czech-English direction (cf. 1.7.2).
Subject complement: infinitive

(81) nezbývá, než *aby si paní Kristýna vymyslela* [that Madame Kristýna thought-up]
záminku (KM, 130)
the only possibility was *for Kristyna to think up* an excuse (H, 120)

Similar features between Tables 2 and 5 are found in the relative frequency of occurrence of the different syntactic functions: in both Tables the two syntactic functions ranking highest are the adverbial and the noun-modifier. In the case of the latter,
this appears to be largely due to the close relationship between participial postmodification and postmodifying finite clauses, which is found in both languages. The third
most frequent counterpart of English finite verb forms, an explicit adverbial device
conveying the focusing function of a cleft sentence, is specific to this direction. On the
other hand the relatively high frequency of occurrence of the object function from
Czech to English is to be ascribed to the infinitive and the gerund as the realization
forms.

3. The conclusions which can be drawn from the foregoing discussion point to the specific status of the verb in both the sentence structure and the FSP structure. As regards
its syntactic constancy, the finite verb involves problems connected with drawing a
line between corresponding and non-corresponding counterparts, not encountered in
the case of other clause elements (except in a much lesser degree, yet significantly, in
the case of the subject complement, cf. Chapter 4). In particular, a modal or phasal component in a verb phrase does not affect the syntactic function of the verb as a whole,
but if left out or added in the counterparts, it detracts from full correspondence. An
even more involved problem is presented by shifts between verbal and verbo-nominal
predicates which are functionally and semantically equivalent but involve addition or
omission of a clause element, the subject complement.

Another specific feature of the verb is the coincidence of the finite verb form and
the syntactic function of predicate. In the English-Czech direction this relationship
excludes inclusion of non-finite verb forms, which in the opposite direction play a
major role as the realization forms of divergent syntactic functions. In consequence,
the syntactic constancy of the finite verb is higher from English to Czech than in the
Czech-English direction.

Divergent counterparts of the finite verb moreover largely display yet another specific feature consisting in syntactic correspondence on a higher sentence level. This is found especially where the difference between the verb and its divergent counterpart involves a condensation process whereby a finite subordinate clause is reduced to a non-finite or non-verbal structure. Non-correspondence of this kind is often found where the finite verb appears in a subordinate postmodifying clause reflected in participial postmodification. Similarly finite verbs in subordinate adverbial clauses reflected in prepositional phrases containing an action noun represent syntactic divergence only on the level of the subordinate clause, the prepositional phrase being an instance of nominalization. These patterns, apart from some others, were found in both directions, but in Czech the reduced structures appear to be less frequent, which testifies to its more verbal character.

The role of functional sentence perspective as a factor conducive to syntactic divergence, which has proved to be significant in the case of the nominal elements and adverbials, appears to be marginal in syntactic divergence of the finite verb. In the material under study it was noted in a few instances where a different predicate structure served to preserve the basic distribution of communicative dynamism in copying the word order of the Czech sentence. This finding only confirmed the initial assumption based on the specific role of the verb in the syntactic and the FSP structure. On both these levels the verb forms a constitutive link between the left-hand and right-hand sentence components, which largely determines its FSP function of transition.

SOURCES

[F]   Fowles, J. *The French Lieutenant's Woman.* London: Triad–Granada, 1983 (1st ed. 1969).
[Ž]   Fowles, J. *Francouzova milenka.* Translated by Hana Žantovská. Prague: Mladá fronta–Smena–Naše vojsko, 1976.
[KM] Kundera, M. *Kniha smíchu a zapomnění.* Toronto: Sixty-Eight Publishers, 1981.
[H]   Kundera, M. *The Book of Laughter and Forgetting.* Translated by Michael Henry Heim. New York: Penguin Books, 1981.
[KI]   Klíma, I. *Láska a smetí.* Prague: Československý spisovatel, 1990.
[O]   Klíma, I. *Love and Garbage.* Translated by Ewald Osers. London: Penguin Books, 1991.
[L]   Lustig, A. *Neslušné sny.* Prague: Hynek, 1995.
[W]   Lustig, A. *Indecent Dreams.* Translated by Paul Wilson. Evanston: Northwestern University Press, 1990.

8. NOUN MODIFICATION IN ENGLISH AND CZECH: A CONTRASTIVE VIEW

First published in *Prague Studies in English 25, Acta Universitatis Carolinae, Philologica 1*, 2008 (issued 2010), 117–140.

0. A modified noun is here understood as a noun phrase operating in any of its syntactic functions which contains a pre- and/or a postposed modifier (modifiers), i.e. a head noun and a modifier dependent on it. Structures of this kind are studied on the material of parallel texts (a Czech novel and its printed English translation) with a view to ascertaining in which respects English and Czech correspond and in which they differ. From this viewpoint this chapter contributes to the enquiries into syntactic constancy presented in the preceding chapters. However, owing to the nature of the subject matter, the underlying hypothesis necessarily differs. The studies of syntactic constancy carried out so far have been concerned with clause elements, which have not only a function in the syntactic structure of the sentence, but also a function in its information structure, the functional sentence perspective, clause elements being carriers of FSP functions. A major point aimed at in the treatment of clause elements has been to find out to what extent the FSP function of a clause element contributes to its syntactic divergence. In the case of noun modification the situation is different in that the FSP function on sentence level is performed by the head noun, with the modifying element(s) operating only in the FSP subfield of the noun phrase. In other words, the FSP subfield of the noun phrase is not an immediate constituent of the FSP structure of the sentence and does not determine the FSP function of the head noun. In the hierarchically superordinate communicative field of the sentence the FSP function of the modified NP, in any of its syntactic functions, depends on sentence position, semantic structure of the sentence, context dependence and intonation in spoken language. On this level the modification of the NP may play some role through its semantic structure and context dependence or independence, but ultimately the FSP function of the modified NP as a whole is the result of the interplay of the factors operating on the higher sentence level. Accordingly, although the FSP aspect is duly taken into account, it is not supposed to be one of the major factors of syntactic divergence. These are primarily sought in the typological distinctions between the two languages under study.

As regards the syntactic aspect of noun modifiers, a point to be noted is the difference between the British and the Czech approach. While the former treats them as an exclusive feature of the noun phrase (cf. Quirk et al. 1985: Chapter 17), the status of clause element being assigned to subject, verb, object, subject and object complement, and adverbial (*ibid.* pp. 49–50), in Czech grammar the noun modifier is included among the other clause elements (cf. Daneš et al. 1987, *Mluvnice češtiny*, Atribut (noun modifier) in Section C, Větné členy (clause elements), 41–160). As the subject under study is the modifying component of the noun phrase, this theoretical distinction on the sentence level plays no role.

1. The typological distinctions between Czech and English are reflected in the subject matter itself, the structure of the English and the Czech noun phrase. While the former contains two obligatory elements, a determiner and a head noun, the latter is constituted by the noun alone, insofar as Czech lacks the category of determiners, above all an article system. Even this distinction has no effect on contrastive treatment of the modifying element and may be left out of account. The only exception is made in the case of the determinative function of the English possessive genitive in order to distinguish it from its modifying function.

The following analysis concentrates on the proportion and types of identical and non-identical instances of noun modification, with the aim of establishing the factors of divergence.

1.1 The largest group of examples (220 instances) displays correspondence not only in the syntactic function but also in the form of realization, cf. Table 1. Within the total number of the analysed noun phrases this group accounts for 70.3%, cf. Table 4.

1.1.1 Expectedly, in both English and Czech, modification is mostly expressed by adjectives (104 instances, cf. Table 1). Owing to the typological differences between the two languages instances of adjectival modification regarded as formally identical correspond only on the level of word classes, i.e. in both languages the modified NP contains an adjective and a noun. Correspondence in gender, number and case distinctions is ruled out by the non-existence of these categories in the English adjective, the lack of number distinctions moreover excluding agreement in number with respect to the head noun. Thus defined, correspondence in adjectival modification is illustrated by the following examples:

(1) v *poloprázdné* kavárně / in a *half-empty* café, *krásný* den / a *lovely* day, *bílé* vrány / *white* crows, *osamělí* jezdci / *lonely* riders, *tělesné* proporce / *bodily* proportions etc.

Correspondence was also found in multiple adjectival modification, cf. (2):

(2) v *malém, tichém* bytě / in a *small, peaceful* flat, *svobodný a poměrně mladý* člověk / a *single and relatively young* chap, *příjemné a uklidňující* šero / a *pleasant and reassuring* twilight, *klidný a střízlivý* život / a *quiet and sober* existence, etc.

An interesting example of correspondence in multiple adjectival modification is shown in (3), where the correspondence extends to the placement of the coordinated adjectives in pre- and postposition:

(3) *hezký, světlovlasý* člověk, *poctivý, spolehlivý* a velmi *chytrý* / a *handsome fair-haired* fellow, *honest, reliable* and very *intelligent*.

This example explicitly illustrates the communicative subfield of the noun phrase, which was first described by Svoboda (1968)[1] as having a thematic head noun irrespective of its context dependence or independence and a rhematic modifier if context independent. The rhematic function of the modifier is due to its semantics which is as a rule more informative than that of the head noun. This conception is in accordance with the largely accepted transformational relation between an adjectival modifier and the predicative function of the adjective in the underlying clause where if context independent, the adjective is invariably rhematic. Example (3) demonstrates not only the rhematic function of the modifying constituent, but also the gradual increase in communicative dynamism (information load) of the successive adjectival components, which is evident in the linear arrangement including the postposition of the last three adjectives, even though this is also motivated stylistically; five preposed adjectives would appear too weighty. With respect to the head noun, however, the example is less typical in that the context dependence of the head noun derives from the semantic structure of the clause in which the noun phrase occurs: *Byl to hezký, světlovlasý člověk, poctivý, spolehlivý a velmi chytrý.* / *He was a handsome fair-haired fellow, honest, reliable and very intelligent.* The features 'human' and 'adult' being derivable from the subject, the head noun is semantically redundant and can be left out without affecting the semantic structure. For that matter, the use of the head noun may have been motivated by the multiplicity of the adjectival string.

A modified NP whose communicative subfield has a semantically relevant, context independent thematic head noun and a rhematic context independent modifier is illustrated by (4). This example also demonstrates the subordinate role of the NP's FSP structure in the hierarchical superordinate communicative field of the sentence where the NP as a whole, in the syntactic function of subject complement, constitutes the rheme:

(4) Venku je *krásný den.*
    It is a *lovely day* outside

---

1   In a later study Svoboda (1987) adopted a different solution based on a parallel between the FSP function of the verb in a clause and that of the head noun in a complex noun phrase. In accordance with Firbas (1992: 84, 95) I subscribe to Svoboda's original proposal.

The importance of semantics and context independence for the rhematic function of the modifier within the FSP of the noun phrase stands out when considered in connection with the other FSP factors, intonation and linearity. Both these factors here operate counter to the other two. As regards the prosodic factor, not only the adjective, but also the noun carries the word stress, which contradicts the usual placement of the intonation centre on the rheme. As for linearity, both English and Czech belong to the adjective—noun type. In English this order is largely obligatory for lack of inflections, cf. *he was a handsome fellow* vs. **he was a fellow handsome*, whereas in inflectional Czech anteposition is optional,[2] cf. *byl to hezký člověk / byl to člověk hezký*. In Czech the basic position of the adjective before the noun runs counter to the primary principle of Czech word order, the functional sentence perspective. Nevertheless it is the unmarked, usual order, whereas postposition of an adjective in the noun phrase is a marked order emphasizing the importance of the attributed quality (cf. Daneš et al. 1987: 161–162).

The marked character of a postposed adjective in Czech is reflected in its comparatively rare occurrence. Among the 104 adjectival noun modifiers in the Czech source text only nine instances, including (3), occurred in postposition. One of these was a technical term (*daň důchodová* 'tax return'), where the postposition is the usual order. The English counterparts of the remaining instances are of special contrastive interest in that four of them display some kind of compensation. Compare the examples listed under (5):

(5) a. Začal jsem být považován za *člověka šíleně odvážného* [man recklessly daring]
I had begun to acquire stature as *a person of reckless daring*.

b. V dešti se ještě nikdo neutopil a na *věci nepříjemné* člověk zapomíná [things unpleasant one forgets].
No one is drowned by rain and one is apt to forget *the unpleasant things that have happened*.

c. Strastiplná cesta sněhovou vánicí zdá se vám z <u>*časového odstupu*</u> dobrodružstvím docela zajímavým [some time later adventure quite interesting]
A miserable journey through a snowstorm seems to have been *an interesting adventure when recalled <u>some time later</u>*.

d. ... kdy budu nucen řešit *situaci naprosto nevídanou, senzační a obyčejně velmi málo příjemnou* [situation entirely unexpected, sensational and usually very little pleasant].
... when I will be forced to deal with *a wholly unexpected situation*
Something unbelievable could happen any hour of the day, and despite its sensational character, the event would in all likelihood afford me very little pleasure.

2 Grammatical anteposition applies only to adjectives lacking inflectional endings.

Of these solutions a fairly clear instance of the options offered by the respective language systems is (5) a., where postposition of the modifier in English is achieved by a realization form available for this position (a postposed adjective in Czech → prepositional phrase in English). This type of compensation was found in two cases (for the other instance, see (12) a. i.). A modified version of another systemic realization form occurring in postposition, a relative clause (cf. a possible form *a person who is recklessly daring*) is presented in (5) b. The adjective here remains in its grammatical position before the noun and a relative clause is added. The semantics of the added clause does not expand on the content being expressed, but merely presents the occurrence of the unpleasant things as a separate proposition. However, by making the modification structure weightier the relative clause increases the importance of the modification, and thus achieves a similar effect as the postposition of the adjective in Czech.

Example (5) c. partly employs the same device, viz. postposition of a subordinate clause, which in this case conveys the meaning of the temporal adverbial that in Czech stands before the final rheme. This position is in full agreement with its role in the semantic structure of the sentence since the change of a negative quality into a positive one is due to a lapse of time. At the same time it reflects the thematic function of the adverbial, temporal elements usually constituting the temporal scene of the event; they are thus part of the thematic section. In English the temporal element is expanded into a clause and placed finally. Owing to the role of the adverbial in the semantic structure of the sentence, this does not essentially affect its thematic function. As a result, the rheme proper—the opposite quality—presented in the penultimate position before a thematic element, is brought into relief and thus intensified.

Example (5) d. illustrates elaboration of the content, decomposing each qualification into a separate clause, and hence calls for comment on the textual level.

In three examples the English adjectives occur in the regular anteposition without any compensating devices, the emphasizing function indicated by the postposition of the adjective in Czech thus lacking a reflection, cf. (6).

(6) Opustil místo po výstupu *téměř absurdním* [after scene almost absurd]
     He'd abandoned the position after *an almost absurd* scene.

1.1.2 The form ranking second in the frequency of occurrence after adjectival modification is the postposed Czech genitive case rendered by the *of*-phrase in English (42 instances, cf. Table 1). This structure is regarded as an identical form of realization partly on account of the postposition, which is obligatory in both languages, but more importantly because of the functional equivalence. Where the preposition in the genitival *of*-phrase expresses only relational meaning, the phrase as a whole represents an analytic form of the primary function of the inflectional genitive. The English possessive case, though inflectional in form, appears to be a divergent, rather than a corresponding equivalent of the Czech genitive insofar as it mostly functions as a Czech possessive adjective (cf. Vachek 1955).

The correspondence Czech genitive → English *of*-phrase is illustrated by the following examples:

(7) neobvyklá dávka *bláznovství* / an unusual degree *of lunacy*, místo *sluhy* /the position *of manservant*, vážnější čtenáři *novin* / the more serious-minded readers *of the newspaper*, místo činu / the scene *of the crime*, proudy *deště* / streams *of rain*, etc.

As regards the other prepositional phrases, correspondence was more frequently found even in the use of the same preposition (*s/with* 5 instances, *bez/without*, *proti/against*, *v/in* (2 instances), *z/from*, *mezi/between* (altogether 11 instances), see (8) a. Correspondence on the level of the word class appeared in the case of the prepositions *o* 'about', which had three different English counterparts *concerning, of, about*; *na* 'on' → *at, of*; and *pro* 'for' → *of* (altogether 6 instances), see (8) b. Although the number of examples is small, leaving aside instances of different government, the instances of correspondence and non-correspondence between the particular prepositions show that prepositions with more specific meanings are more likely to occur as their dictionary equivalents than prepositions with a more general meaning.

(8) a. Příhoda *s lupičem* / An incident *with a burglar*, člověk *bez fantazie* / a person *without imagination*, filipika *proti něčemu* / a diatribe *against something*, obrazy *v širokých starodávných rámech* / pictures *in broad and ancient frames*, vysvědčení *z posledního místa* / a report *from his last place*, debata *mezi Saturninem a naším dodavatelem paliva* / an argument *between Saturnin and our fuel supplier*.
   b. ustálené mínění <u>*o*</u> *debatách* / a definite opinion <u>*concerning*</u> *debates*, při pohledu <u>*na*</u> *ty koblihy* / at the sight <u>*of*</u> *the doughnuts*, smysl <u>*pro*</u> *komiku* / sense <u>*of*</u> *the comic*.

1.1.3 Other identical realization forms registered in the source texts were relative clauses (28 occurrences), participles (past and *-ing* participles 13 and 7 instances, respectively) and nominal *that*-clauses (9 instances), cf. examples (9) a., b., c.:

(9) a. krátké období svého života, *které jsem nedávno prožil*
      The short period of my life *which I have recently lived through*
      za podmínek, *které jsem mohl přijmout*
      under conditions *which I felt able to accept*
   b. i. policie, *povolaná* telefonicky
         the police, *summoned* by telephone
         křik *poplašených* vran / the cries of *frightened* crows
         s černými vlasy *rozdělenými* pěšinkou / with black hair *parted* in the middle
      ii. duše se mu naplní *skličujícími* představami
         his soul filled with *depressing* thoughts
         vzrušující příhoda / *exciting* incident
   c. Později jsem dospěl k *přesvědčení, že se tím prostě baví.*
      Later I arrived at *the conviction that he simply enjoyed it.*

Correspondence in these realization forms is found only on the categorial level. English relative clauses have a more varied repertory of realization forms than is the case in Czech, notably different relatives for animate and inanimate antecedents, the zero relative in syntactic functions other than the subject and discontinuity between a preposition and the relative, to mention only the major differences. For the present discussion these differences are largely irrelevant since they affect neither the syntactic aspect, nor the syntax—FSP interface. What calls for mention is the position of the postmodifying relative clause with respect to its head noun. The source texts provided two instances of discontinuous postmodification in the English counterparts of Czech relative clauses placed in their regular position after the head noun, cf. (10) a. and b.

(10) a. Jisto je, že by se v Čechách našlo _velmi málo mladých mužů, kteří by měli svého sluhu_, ...
   Certainly no one can deny the fact that _not many young men_ can be found in Bohemia _who have their own gentleman's gentleman._
   b. Po jakýchsi zmatených formalitách došlo _k souboji, ve kterém byl lupič zraněn._
   After somewhat confusing opening formalities _the duel_ commenced, _during which the burglar was wounded._

Here, as in other instances of this kind,[3] the English discontinuous construction represents one of the ways of reconciling the conflict between the grammatical word order principle and the principle of FSP (the principle of end focus). In both sentences the subject is rhematic, which—if the principle of end focus or the basic distribution of communicative dynamism is to be complied with—should be placed at the end. The rhematic function of the subject results from the semantic structure of the sentence and the subject's context independence. Both sentences are presentation sentences in which the subject is a phenomenon first appearing on the scene, while the verbs perform the presentation function. However, the primary grammatical function of English word order assigns to the subject the preverbal position. The solution of the conflict is found in the weightiness of the subject which allows dissociation of the head noun and the postmodification in such a way that the head noun (with premodiers) takes the regular preverbal position and the postmodifying relative clause is postponed after the verb, thus achieving end position. The relative clauses in the two examples illustrate another point relevant to the FSP subfield of the noun phrases. The fact that postmodifiers occur after the head noun does not necessarily mean that they constitute the NP's focal component. As noted above, the modifier is more informative than the head only if it is context independent. In (10) a. the content of the relative clause is given, the only new element in the subject head noun being the quantifier. Nevertheless, the clause is still a component of the rheme and as such is

---

3   For a discussion of discontinuous constructions, see Dušková 1995.

duly placed after the thematic locative adverbial. The relative clause in (10) b. conveys new content, and hence constitutes the rheme proper on the level of both the noun phrase and the sentence. Besides the FSP aspect, a contributing factor is here the weightiness of the subject.

Czech in contrast shows the solution offered by an inflecting language. Since its word order is as a rule not constrained by grammatical factors, the syntactic functions of clause elements being indicated by inflectional endings and grammatical agreement, it is primarily determined by the FSP structure. Accordingly the subject is placed as a whole at the end of the superordinate clause and no discontinuity arises.

Table 1: Noun modification

Identical instances in Czech and in English			
Adjective		104	47.3%
Prepositional phrase		59	26.8%
Czech genitive → English *of*-phrase	42		
Other identical prepositions	11		
Other non-identical prepositions	6		
Relative clause		28	12.7%
-ed participle		13	5.9%
-ing participle		7	3.2%
Nominal *that*-clause		9	4.1%
Total		220	100.0%

1.2 The next group of examples retains the syntactic function of noun modifier but displays a different form of realization (62 instances, 19.8% of the total, cf. Table 4).

1.2.1 Czech adjectival modifiers were reflected in non-correspondent realization forms in 31 instances (cf. Table 2). Among these the most numerous group was represented by the type Czech adjective → English converted noun (12 instances, excluding lexicalized formations such as *coffee-house, houseboat, snowstorm*). Here the only indicator of the syntactic dependence and modifier function of the English noun is the position before another noun, i.e. word order, cf. (11).

(11) za *nedělního*$_{adjective}$ dopoledne—on a *Sunday* morning, *sloní*$_{adjective}$ kly—*elephant* tusks, blízko řetězového$_{adjective}$ mostu—near to a *suspension* bridge.

Other types of non-correspondence in the case of Czech attributive adjectives were Czech adjective → English *of*-phrase (9 instances), *-ing* and *-ed* participles (respectively, 4 and 2 instances), and generic possessive case (4 instances), cf. (12) a., b., c. and d.

(12) a. i.　pohled *naprosto nechápavý* [look utterly obtuse]—a look *of utter incom-*
　　　　　prehension
　　　ii.　pověst *výjimečného muže* [reputation of exceptional man]—reputation as a
　　　　　man of exceptional character,
　　　　　delší [rather-long] *řeč*—*a speech of some length;*
　　　iii.　ostatní *mozkové*~adjective~ *závity*—the other *parts of our brains.*
　　b.　nebýt této *rušivé*~adjective~ příhody—despite this one *disturbing* event
　　c.　fasádami, *plnými*~adjective~ štukatérské práce—facades *filled* with ornamental
　　　　stucco
　　d.　[měl] placatou *námořnickou*~adjective~ čepici—[wearing] a flat *sailor's* cap

As regards the type Czech adjective → English *of*-phrase, most of the Czech examples have the regular order adjective—noun, while only a few display postposition, cf. (5) a., b., c. and (12) a. i. In these instances the English prepositional phrase
may be regarded as a compensational device. All other Czech examples in this group
have the adjective before the noun. As explained in 1.1.1, this position does not prevent the adjective, if context independent, from functioning as the rheme within
the communicative subfield of the noun phrase in which it operates as the modifier. Compare the preposed adjective in Czech with the English postposed prepositional phrase in (12) a. ii., where the linear arrangement of the English counterpart is
more consistent with the increasing degree of communicative dynamism than in
the Czech original. An opposite case is presented by (12) a. iii., in which the adjective is context dependent, cf. the context of the sentence *He explained that we have
all hitched up* <u>our brains</u> *to the service of narrow, specialised occupations and that we try
with all our strength to let* <u>the other parts of our brains</u> *atrophy.* It is hence less dynamic
than the head noun irrespective of pre- or postposition. In the other examples of this
group the preposed adjectives, rendered as prepositional phrases, are context independent and thus more informative than the head nouns, again irrespective of their
position.

　　Participial counterparts of Czech adjectives demonstrate the affinity between
these two categories with a fluent boundary between them, the adjectival status of
many participles being often fully lexicalized.

　　Example (12) d. Czech adjective → English generic possessive case clearly illustrates the adjectival character of the latter, demonstrated by the presence of another
modifier before it, cf. *a* <u>flat</u> *sailor's cap,* where *flat* does not modify *sailor* but *cap,* viz.
'a flat cap, such as are worn by sailors'. This excludes the determiner function of the
possessive case, insofar as the regular position of the determiner in a noun phrase
is before the modifier. However, the univocal structure of this example is due to its
lexical realization. Where the meaning of the modifying adjective is compatible with
both nouns, the structure is inherently ambiguous, cf. *an old man's cap* = 'the cap of
an old man', with the possessive case operating as determiner or 'an old cap such as
are worn by men', as in (12) d.

1.2.2 Other non-correspondent realization forms of Czech and English modifiers were found in the case of Czech prepositional phrases, genitives, relative clauses, nominal content clauses and past participles (cf. Table 2).

In the case of Czech prepositional phrases and genitives (7 instances each), the only recurrent non-correspondent English counterpart was a converted noun (4 instances in both groups).

(13) a. v tom *výstřižku z novin*/in this *newspaper* cutting,
 přiznání k dani/*tax* return
 b. *chytání pstruhů*/*trout* fishing, [o hlavy pokojných] *návštěvníků kavárny*
 /[around the heads of peaceful] *café guests*

The other English counterparts in these two groups occurred only once, e.g. an English relative clause and a prepositional phrase rendering Czech genitives are illustrated in (14) a., and b.; an English participle rendering a Czech prepositional phrase in (15). For the other types, see Table 2.

(14) a. *číslo* asi dva roky *starých novin*/*a newspaper which* must have been about two years old
 b. *boj dvou* nestejně vyzbrojených soupeřů/*a duel between two* unequally armed combatants
(15) *číslo* ... *starých novin s článkem* [with article] o .../a newspaper ... *containing an article* about ...

Some recurrent types of non-correspondence were also found in the case of other Czech modification structures: English past participles in the case of Czech relative clauses (4 instances), see (16) a.; gerundial and infinitive constructions rendering Czech nominal content clauses (3 and 2 instances, respectively), cf. (16) b.; *-ing* participles as counterparts of Czech past participles (3 tokens, 2 types), cf. (16) c.

(16) a. *přirovnání* a *podobenství, kterými* [by which] doktor Vlach *proplétá* [interweaves] své temperamentní řeči
 parables and comparisons *interwoven* into Doctor Witherspoon's intemperate speeches
 b. i. *vzpomínka na to, že jsem udělal* [recollection of that (= to) that (= že) I did] něco tak neobvyklého
 the mere recollection of having done something so strange
 ii. *že* má jakousi chorobnou *touhu, aby se stal* [need that he become] sluhou nějakého dobrodruha džentlmena
 he had a kind of pathological *need to become* the servant of some gentleman adventurer
 c. i. uhnul *roztočené* [swung] kouli/to dodge the *swinging* ball
 ii. velmi *zmatené* [confused] teorie/a very *confusing* theory

In the case of participles the English realization forms present the head noun as the agent, while Czech presents it as the patient.

Table 2: Noun modification

Different forms of realization			
Czech		English	
Adjective	31 (50.0%)	converted noun	12 (38.7%)
		of-phrase	9 (29.0%)
		ing-participle	4 (12.9%)
		-ed participle	2 (6.5%)
		generic 's genitive	4 (12.9%)
		total	31 (100.0%)
Prepositional phrase	7 (11.3%)	converted noun	4 (57.1%)
		ing-participle	1 (14.3%)
		-ed participle	1 (14.3%)
		other forms	1 (14.3%)
		total	7 (100.0%)
Genitive	7 (11.3%)	converted noun	4 (57.1%)
		prepositional phrase	1 (14.3%)
		relative clause	1 (14.3%)
		other forms	1 (14.3%)
		total	7 (100.0%)
Relative clause	7 (11.3%)	-ed participle	4 (57.1%)
		prepositional phrase	2 (28.6%)
		other forms	1 (14.3%)
		total	7 (100.0%)
Nominal clause	5 (8.05%)	gerund	3 (60.0%)
		infinitive	2 (40.0%)
		total	5 (100.0%)
Past participle	5 (8.05%)	-ing participle	3 (60.0%)
		adjective	1 (20.0%)
		other forms	1 (20.0%)
		total	5 (100.0%)
Total	62 (100.00%)		

All types of non-correspondent realization forms are summarized in Table 2.

The unspecified forms of realization, viz. other forms, include diverse counterparts that occurred only once and appear to represent the translator's ad hoc solution of a particular case, e.g. when *(cválají)* <u>rozblácenými</u> [muddy] *cestami* is rendered by *(gallop) along paths* <u>caked with mud,</u> where the meaning of the modifier is decomposed into a verbal and a nominal component, with the verb introducing an additional semantic feature and the noun expressing the core of the meaning. In other instances a non-recurrent rendition may indicate a systemic tendency, e.g. when a complex sentence with three subordinate clauses is split into two sentences, in the second of which a relative clause (recorded under another form) appears as the main clause at the beginning. However, since in the case of noun modifiers this was a unique instance, the point was not further pursued.

The representation of the different types of non-correspondent realization forms shows two notable points. The most frequent non-corresponding counterpart of all Czech non-clausal realization forms (adjective, prepositional phrase and genitive) is the converted noun (altogether 20 instances out of the total of 45, i.e. 44.4%, with all the other divergent realization forms in these three groups ranking considerably lower). The second point concerns the recurrent non-corresponding counterparts of modifying finite clauses: 75% of Czech relative and nominal clauses are here rendered by gerunds, infinitives and participles.

The first feature is to be assigned to the analytic character of English, the second to the tendency to condense sentence structure, making use of a full-fledged system of non-finite verb forms.

2. The third group of examples differs not only in the form of realization, but also in the syntactic function. Czech noun modifiers are reflected in other syntactic elements in English. These can be divided into two subgroups according to whether the divergence is found in the same clause element that contains the respective noun modifier in the Czech text, or whether the divergence involves another clause element (cf. Table 3).

2.1 The subgroup where the divergence occurs in the same clause elements displays several types.

2.1.1 First there are instances showing a reversal of the syntactic relations where the Czech modifier appears as the head of the noun phrase and the Czech head noun takes the place of the subordinate element (modifier), cf.

(17) a. *pokus loupeže* [attempt of-burglary] → *an attempted burglary*
     b. *štukatérská práce* [stucco work] → *ornamental stucco*

The Czech noun modifier replaces the entire noun phrase in *za člověka velmi výstředního* [as man very excentric] → *as a notable excentric.*

In this type the nouns reflecting the Czech adjectives mostly express quantity or quality partition (cf. Quirk et al. 1985: 249), as in (18).

(18) a. _některé_ [some] _cenné zlatnické starožitnosti_ → _a number_ of valuable old antiques
   b. _různé_ [various] _kožešiny_ → _an assortment_ of animal skins[4]
   c. (že má) _jakousi_ [some] _chorobnou touhu_ → (that he had) _a kind_ of pathological need

Although these nouns look like the head of a noun phrase, they can be regarded as multi-word wholes functioning as determiners in the case of the quantitative expressions and as adjectives where they denote a partitive quality. This view is supported by the frequent plural agreement in the case of (18) a., cf. _a number of valuable antiques were stolen_, and alternative constructions in the case of (18) c., cf. _this kind of people, people of this kind, these kind of people._ Example (19) is in fact another instance of this kind, with ellipsis of the qualified noun, cf. _this category of people, people of this category._

(19) _lidi tohoto druhu_ [people of this kind] → _this category_

2.1.2 Another subtype of the first group was found in noun phrases with two premodifying adjectives the first of which appears as an adverbial modifier of the second, cf. (20). Example (20) c. illustrates the reflection of a noun modifier in an adverbial as a separate clause element.

(20) a. Po _jakýchsi_ [some] _zmatených_ formalitách → After _somewhat_ confusing opening formalities
   b. _takový_ [such] _menší_ byt → a _fairly_ modest flat
   c. do _jisté_ míry → _partly_

Coordinated vs. subordinated construction was also noted in two instances of noun phrases with complex modification structures, cf. (21) a. and b.

(21) a. na tom názorném _příkladu s kavárnou, člověkem a mísou koblih_ něco je
   [in that graphic example with café, man and plate of-doughnuts]
   In his graphic _tale of a fellow in a café with a plate of doughnuts_
   b. jako _tyč a kouli_ na řetěze [pole and ball on chain]
   a _pole_ with a ball and chain

2.1.3 To complete the picture of this subgroup mention should be made of an isolated instance of the non-correspondence Czech noun modifier → English preposition (_po celý zápas_ [during whole fight] _throughout the battle_) and a recurrent instance of a purely theoretical distinction, viz. the difference in the noun phrase structure consisting in the absence of the category of determiners in Czech. This difference

---

4   The type _animal skin_ is discussed in section 3.1

sometimes gives rise to the rendition of Czech modifiers by English determiners, which was found in the case of the English 's genitive in the function of determiner, as in (22).

(22) teorie *doktora Vlacha* [theory of Dr. Witherspoon_modifier] → *Dr. Witherspoon's* theory
ve vile *profesora Ludy* [in villa of Professor Luda_modifier] → at *Professor Luda's* villa

This also applies to instances where the Czech modifer is a preposed possessive adjective, as in (23).

(23) *Saturninovo* [adjective derived from *Saturnin*] počínání → *Saturnin's* behaviour

This type was altogether represented by six instances.

2.2 Syntactic divergence of the Czech noun modifier involving another clause element was found in the following cases (cf. Table 3).

2.2.1 In five instances the Czech noun modifier appeared as the object, cf. (24).

(24) a. paní Suchánková měla <u>uplakané</u> oči [Mrs. Sweeting had red-from-tears eyes]
Mrs. Sweeting had <u>*tears*</u> in her eyes.
   b. ... která prý se ... baví představou, <u>*co by se dělo*</u>, kdyby ...
[who allegedly enjoy thought what would happen]
... enjoys *reflecting on <u>what it would be like</u>*
   c. každý rozumný tvor musí být jat údivem, <u>*že se takoví lidé mohou vyskytovati*</u> i mimo ústavy [astonishment that such people can be]
any reasonable person would be *astonished <u>to see people of this sort anywhere</u>* outside an institution
   d. *Radu*, že jsem se mohl ... <u>*postavit mimo skluzavku*</u> mohl by mi dát jen člověk, jenž neví ... [Advice that I could stand beyond icepatch]
Only a person with no knowledge ... would *say <u>that I could have left the ice patch</u>*
   e. a zdálo se mi o tom, že slyším pláč <u>milenky</u> [that I-hear crying of-mistress]
and *dreamt of <u>a mistress</u>* crying

In (24) a. English has no exact equivalent of the adjective *uplakaný*, derived from the verb *plakat* 'to weep', with the meaning 'showing signs of having wept'. The nearest English equivalent would be *Mrs. Sweeting's eyes were red from weeping*. The divergence is thus due to the way in which the meaning of the Czech adjective is transposed into English. Here the FSP structure does not change since the adjective is context independent in Czech and hence more dynamic than the head noun *oči* 'eyes'. The end position of the latter in the English version does not affect its thematic function which primarily results from its partial context dependence (it is derivable from the subject, viz. eyes are a person's inalienable possession).

The second example of the rendition of a Czech noun modifier by an object in English is a concomitant feature of a different head, viz. a gerund which is complemented by an object, whereas the Czech head, a noun, takes a modifier. Examples (24) c. and d. are instances of verbo-nominal predication in Czech *být jat údivem* 'to be taken by astonishment' = *to be astonished*, *dát radu* 'to give advice' = *to advise*, where the noun takes a modifier whereas the verbal expression in English calls for object complementation.

In (24) e. the divergence is due to the use of a different verb in whose complementation the components of the Czech noun phrase are decomposed into two clause elements, the object which reflects the Czech modifier, and the object complement, representing the original head noun. In this case the FSP structure of the two versions differs in that the rheme in the Czech construction is the postmodifier whereas in the English construction it is the object complement, i.e. the less dynamic element in Czech.

2.2.2 In three instances the Czech noun modifier was reflected in an adverbial, cf. (25):

(25) a. Saturnin *hledal inzerátem v novinách* místo sluhy [looked-for by-advertisement in newspapers position of-servant]
Saturnin *advertised in the newspapers* for the position of manservant

b. střídal *místa sluhů* [he-changed position of-manservant]
he moved *position as a manservant*

c. svou *překvapenou zaměstnavatelku* hodil ... do nádrže vodotrysku [he-threw surprised employer into ... fountain]
taking his employer by surprise threw her into a fountain.

In all examples the divergence is due to the semantic structure of the verb which opens syntactic positions for different clause elements. In (23) a. the Czech verb phrase *hledat inzerátem* 'look for by means of an advertisement' is rendered univerbally in English, viz. 'to advertise'; hence the Czech noun component of the phrase is incorporated in the English verb and its modifier appears as an adverbial in English. Similarly in (23) b. the different syntactic functions are due to the difference in the meanings of the verb: *change, transpose* vs. *move*. In (23) c. the divergence results from the expansion of the Czech premodifying participle into a participial clause.

2.2.3 Two other examples may be grouped together on the basis of the verb *be*, which is in both followed by a divergent counterpart of the Czech noun modifier, the subject complement in (26) a. and the past participle of the passive verb in (26) b.

(26) a. Měl vůbec *humor nepřijatelného druhu* [He-had really humour of-unacceptable kind]
His *sense of humour* was really *beyond the pale*.

b. že jsou to *pocity zděděné po předcích* [that are it sentiments inherited from ancestors]
that such *sentiments are inherited* from our ancestors

In these two examples the FSP structure again partly differs. In (25) a. the Czech object which constitutes the rheme includes the noun *humour*, which appears as the modifier of the subject in English, the subject as a whole constituting the theme. In other words, a complex rhematic element is decomposed into its less dynamic component, which owing to its syntactic function and the concomitant position becomes the theme. This singles out the rheme-proper part of the rhematic section, the postmodifier, as the only component of the rheme, with the result of a different distribution of the degrees of communicative dynamism. Similar decomposition of the Czech rhematic section with the same effect on the FSP structure is found in the English version of (26) b., although the syntactic structure is different: auxiliary + past participle constituting the passive vs. copula + subject complement. The reason for grouping the two examples together is their FSP aspect.

2.2.4 The remaining examples of divergent syntactic counterparts of the Czech noun modifier occurred only once: object complement, cf. (27) a., apposition, cf. (27) b., and two counterparts included in "other" in Table 3: the head noun of an adverbial prepositional phrase, cf. (27) c., and the subject, cf. (27) d.

(27) a. mluvil něco o tom, že mám *chatrné* zdraví [that I-have frail health]
      he said something about my *health* being *frail*
  b. Ovzduší těchto *domů s fasádami*, plnými štukatérské práce
      [atmosphere of-these houses with facades full of-stucco work]
      The atmosphere of these *houses – facades* filled with ornamental stucco
  c. v *první* chvíli [in first moment]
      at first
  d. *Teorie* doktora Vlacha [theory of Doctor Witherspoon]
      Doctor Witherspoon offers a theory.

In (27) a. the syntactic divergence results in a different linear arrangement but does not affect the FSP structure since the premodifier in the Czech construction is context independent and hence more dynamic than the head noun. Example (27) b. differs only in the type of modification, apposition being syntactically independent, its qualifying role and FSP function remaining the same. The divergence in (27) c. is a phraseological matter.

Example (27) d. is a sentence from the title of a chapter summarizing its contents, the next sentences being structured in the same way in both languages (*Přijal jsem sluhu / I engage a servant, Příhoda s lupičem / An incident with a burglar* etc.). The primary factor affecting the wording is here the textual aspect, which is presumably what motivates the divergence. However, the FSP structure in the two renditions of the content is different. Since both comply with the principle of end focus, their rhemes differ: *doktora Vlacha* in Czech vs. *theory* in English.

Table 3: Noun modification

Divergent syntactic counterparts of Czech noun modifiers			
Divergence in the same clause element	17	Czech noun modifier → another clause element	14
Reversal of syntactic relations	6	Object	5
Subordination vs. coordination	2	Adverbial	3
Possessive determiner	6	be + adjective/past participle	2
Preposition	1	Object complement	1
Adverbial	1	Apposition	1
Other	1	Other	2
Total	31		

Table 4: Noun modification

Distribution of noun modifiers with identical and non-identical forms and functions		
Identical function and form	220	70.3%
Divergent form	62	19.8%
Divergent function	31	9.9%
Total	313	100.0%

3. Considering the small, statistically insignificant number of syntactically divergent English counterparts of Czech noun modifiers, an additional source of examples was sought in the opposite direction, viz. in syntactically divergent Czech counterparts of English noun modifiers. Here a different picture emerges.

3.1 In general, the English text contains more noun modifiers than the Czech source text. This is partly due to instances where a modifier is added while Czech has none, as in (28).

(28) Nikomu se při tom *nic* nestalo [To-nobody then nothing happened]
     Nothing untoward took place

Other instances of this kind were, e.g., *vysvědčení z posledního místa* [report from last place]—*a report from his last place of employment*, *tento druh lidí* [this kind of people]—*this second group of people, temperament - good temperament, sprcha neobvyklých událostí* [shower of unusual events]—*a passing shower of unusual events, vzpomínka* [recollection] *na to, že jsem udělal - a mere recollection of having done, předmětem vyšetřování* [subject of investigation]—*the subject of further investigation, po jakýchsi zmatených formalitách* [after some confusing formalities]—*after somewhat confusing <u>opening</u> formalities, do vily historika a sběratele profesory Ludy* [of historian and collector Professor Luda]—*into the villa of professor Luda, historian and collector <u>of fine objects</u>*. There were about twenty instances of this kind, all serving to express the meaning of the original more explicitly, which appears to be a general feature of translated texts. Sometimes, an entire noun phrase containing a modifier was added, as in the last example.

Another source of modifiers without explicit Czech counterparts was provided by instances in which the meaning of a Czech de-adjectival noun is decomposed into the respective adjective and a general noun that in fact serves as the substantival suffix in Czech. Compare *dynamika* [dynamics] → *dynamic passions*, *výstřednosti* [excentricities] → *peculiar ways*, *ztřeštěnost* [hare-brainedness] → *hare-brained schemes*. Still other instances were multi-word denominations, such as *big game = šelma*, *animal skin = kožešina*, *roof beams = krov*, *props manager = rekvizitář*, lexicalized to a different degree, cf. *punch-line = pointa*. All these instances testify to the analytic character of English. They are regarded as multi-word denominations and are not included in the count.

An FSP point worth mentioning in this connection is the English equivalent of Czech *klouzačka = patch of ice*, whose form demonstrates the context independence of the modifier by postposition when it occurs for the first time, while at a second occurrence (distanced by two sentences) the context dependent modifier moves to the anteposition, viz. *ice patch*, cf. *I was like someone who ... steps onto a patch of ice ... Only a person with no knowledge of what it is ... would say that I could have left the ice patch at any moment ...*

The opposite case was rare, e.g. *údolní přehrada* [valley dam] → *dam*, *visuté lešení* [suspended scaffolding] → *scaffolding*, *tržná rána na hlavě* [ripped wound on head] → *head injury*, *ostře nabitým revolverem* [with-live-shell loaded revolver] → *with a loaded revolver*.

3.2 Even without the instances noted in 3.1. the number of Czech syntactically divergent counterparts of English noun modifiers was nearly twice as large, viz. 31 divergent counterparts in the Czech → English direction (cf. Table 3) vs. 52 in the English → Czech direction (cf. Table 5). Subtracting the six occurrences of English determinative *'s* genitives as counterparts of Czech modifiers, which had no effect on the structure of the respective noun phrases, Czech divergent counterparts outnumber the English more than twice. Moreover, the larger number of divergent counterparts provides ground for the emergence of patterns characterizing the different divergent types.

3.2.1 A large group of English noun modifiers correspond to adverbials in Czech (18 instances, 34.6% of all divergent counterparts, see Table 5).

A Czech adverbial recurrently appears as a concomitant feature of a verbal predicate where English has a verbo-nominal structure in which the English noun modifier modifies the head noun of different clause elements according to the type of the verb, cf.

(29) a. you will *subject* the doughnuts *to a dull and thoughtless* gaze
        budete se na ty koblihy *dívat tupě a bezmyšlenkovitě*
        [you will at doughnouts gaze dully and thoughtlessly]
   b. I *am* in *full* agreement
        úplně souhlasím [fully I-agree]
   c. she *showed* quite a *maternal* concern for my welfare
        starala se o mne docela *mateřsky* [she-looked after me quite maternally]
   d. *to engage in a desperate* battle—*zápasit zoufale* [struggle desperately]

A verbal noun + modifier vs. a Czech verb + adverbial also occur in (30).

(30) because *a search of the whole boat* failed to disclose his whereabouts
        Protože jsem ho marně *na celé lodi* hledal [because in vain on whole boat I-looked-
        for him]

Another recurrent pattern of English modifiers reflected in Czech adverbials was
found in manner adjuncts expressed by a prepositional phrase with a noun denoting
the semantic role and the modifier as the qualifying component:

(31) a. I hardly behaved *in a very dignified* manner.
        nechoval jsem se nijak zvlášť *důstojně* [I-not-behaved in-no-way especially
        dignifiedly]
   b. he did so [= he expressed himself] *in a derogatory* manner
        vyjadřoval se ... *velmi hanlivě* [he-expressed himself very derogatorily]

Decomposition of the meaning into a noun and a modifier was also found with
nouns denoting other categorial meanings, cf.

(32) a. with *a paean of praise* velmi *pochvalně*
        [very laudatorily] (intensifying near-synonym)
   b. In *a* fit *of rage v zuřivosti* [in rage] (partitive)
   c. Then he collected together various hunting trophies for the flat, such as buf-
        falo horns, ... and *similar* objects.
        Potom mi nanosil do bytu různé lovecké trofeje, jako buvolí rohy, ... a *po-
        dobně.* [similarly] (general category of things)

In several instances the modifier corresponding to an adverbial in Czech expressed
intensifying or limiting meaning, as in (12) a. i. and (33).

(33) a. you never had the *slightest* intention of discussing
        o čem jste *vůbec* neměli v úmyslu hovořit [about which at all you had-not in in-
        tention to-talk]
   b. This is the *only* way I can explain
        Jen tak si mohu vysvětlit [only so I-can explain]

   c. In the _very_ first week
      hned v prvním týdnu [immediately in first week]
   d. to the service of _narrow_, specialised occupations
      do služeb _úzce specializovaných_ povolání [to service of narrowly specialised occupations]

The remaining instances were ad hoc solutions of particular structures.

3.2.2 An almost equal number of English noun modifiers appear as objects in Czech (17 occurrences, 32.7% of all syntactically divergent counterparts, see Table 5). Several patterns can again be distinguished in which the same factors as in the previous case play a role.

English noun modifiers of deverbal nouns in verbo-nominal predicates appear as adverbials in Czech verbal predicates, cf. (34).

(34) a. I would like to _make the observation that my own experience_ ...
     Chci podotknout, že mé zkušenosti ... [I want to-observe that ...]
   b. I will not _give the name of the lady_ concerned
     Nebudu _jmenovat dámu_, o kterou šlo ... [I will-not name lady who was concerned]
   c. in the course of _his conversations with Mrs. Sweeting_
     když o mně _mluvil s paní Suchánkovou_
     [when about me he-talked with Mrs. Sweeting]

Other instances of deverbal nouns + modifiers in English vs. Czech objects are illustrated in (35).

(35) a. that he was _the recipient of a systematic and by no means superficial education_.
     že se mu _dostalo hlubokého a systematického vzdělání_
     [that (= že) was-given to-him of-profound and systematic education]
   b. No man can abide _doubts about his Courage_
     Žádný muž nesnese, _aby bylo pochybováno o jeho statečnosti_
     [No man not-abides that was doubted about his courage]

Both Czech sentences in (35) are subjectless, the object in (35) a. being in the genitive case, in (35) b. in the prepositional locative.

In most other examples of the correspondence English noun modifier → Czech object the respective noun phrases contained nouns that had no explicit counterparts in Czech. The semantics of the nouns were partly the same as in the case of adverbials, cf. (36).

(36) a. in which he elaborated upon _the notion that a duel between two combatants ... was hardly cricket_
     ve které se snažil _vyložit lupiči_, že _boj dvou ... soupeřů není fair_.

[in which he-tried to-explain to-burglar that duel of two ... combatants is-not fair]

b. I have pondered in vain *the reasons <u>why Saturnin does this</u>*
Marně jsem *přemýšlel, <u>proč to Saturnin dělá</u>*
[In vain I-pondered why it Saturnin does]

c. Of course I haven't the faintest *idea <u>what spiritual maturity has in common with doughnuts</u>*
Já si ovšem *nedovedu představit, <u>co má společného s duševní vyspělostí představa koblih</u>*
[I to-me of-course cannot imagine what has in-common with spiritual maturity idea of doughnuts]

d. *His sense <u>of humour</u>* was really almost beyond the pale.
Měl vůbec <u>*humor*</u> nepřijatelného druhu
[He-had humour of-unacceptable kind].

In other instances the noun makes the meaning more explicit or conveys information implicit in the Czech text but entirely lacking in the case of a non-Czech reader.

(37) a. The tune on a musical grandfather clock *marked <u>the passing of time</u>* during my quiet evenings
Sloupkové hodiny s hracím strojkem *odměřovaly* čas [measured time] za klidných večerů

b. I used to ... read *the romantic novels <u>of Václav Beneš Třebízský</u>*.
a četl jsem <u>*Václava Beneše Třebízského*</u> [and I-read Václav Beneš Třebízský].

3.2.3 The third Czech most frequent divergent counterpart of an English noun modifier was the subject complement (9 instances, 17.3%, cf. Table 5). This correspondence displayed two patterns. In the first the modifier was a component of a subject complement that contained a noun without a counterpart in Czech. Most nouns in this case denoted general categories, conveying little additional meaning, cf.

(38) a. It was an <u>*unpleasant*</u> experience
bylo to <u>*nepříjemné*</u> [it was unpleasant]

b. that it would not be a <u>*good*</u> idea
že by nebylo <u>*dobré*</u> [that it would-not-be good]

c. It was a <u>*foolish*</u> thing to do
Bylo to sice <u>*nesmyslné*</u> [it was it-is-true foolish]

As in the case of the object, there were also instances where the head noun expresses the meaning more specifically, cf. (39).

(39) it even seems ... too like a *character <u>in a novel</u>*
Zdá se to dokonce ... příliš <u>*románové*</u> [it seems even ... too novel-like]

The other recurrent pattern was a complex subject complement with a relative clause whose antecedent was a general noun denoting the semantic role of the respective adverbial in Czech, cf. (40)

(40) a. he claimed that ... it was *a place where* he felt everything collapsing
       Říkal ... že *tam* na něho všechno padá
       [he-said that there on him everything falls]
   b. *Such is the manner in which* he runs away from every serious discussion.
      On vám[5] od každé vážnější debaty *takhle* uteče.
      [He to-you from every more-serious debate so runs-away]
   c. This is *the* only *way* I can explain the fact that ...
      Jen *tak* si mohu vysvětlit to, že ...
      [Only so to-me I-can explain that ...]

Two points are to be noted in these examples. The decomposition of the superordinate communicative field into two subfields, that of the superordinate copular clause and the subfield of the relative clause, alters the FSP structure when compared with the corresponding Czech clauses. These have only one clausal communicative field, while the English construction produces two rhemes, one in each clause. In the superordinate clause the rheme is the subject complement whose least dynamic element is the head noun and the rheme proper is contained in the relative clause. In the communicative subfield of the relative clause the rheme is in the postverbal part, viz. the final word in a., the complex object noun phrase including the modifying nominal clause (which again has its own communicative subfield) governed by *explain* in c., and the verb in b., the final element in b. being partly context dependent. In the case of (40) c. the use of the construction may be motivated by the focalizer *jen = only* highlighting the initial manner adjunct, which thus carries a secondary focus whose reflection can be seen in the rhematic function of the English counterpart. The other point concerns the linear arrangement. As shown by the literal translations (especially of (40) a.), corresponding placement of the English adverbial acts counter to the rules of English word order. Hence the decomposition of the adverbial into two parts achieves a linear arrangement that places the adverbial in the initial part of the superordinate communicative field of the whole sentence, consistent with its thematic function in Czech. In this respect these constructions resemble reversed *wh*-clefts which can be regarded as systemic counterparts of Czech sentences with initial thematic scene-setting adverbials, cf. *Tady se to stalo* [here it happened] = *this is where* [= *the place where*] *it happened*.

3.2.4 The remaining divergent counterparts of English noun modifiers were the verb, the subject (three occurrences each), a main clause and apposition, which both occurred once.

---

5   This form is a dativus incommodi, a type of free dative which denotes a participant unfavourably affected by verbal action. In some cases it has an English counterpart in the prepositional phrase with *on*, cf. *she walked out on him*.

In the case of the verb all three occurrences displayed the same pattern:

(41) a. I find *many things to wonder at*
musím *se divit* mnoha věcem [I-must wonder-at many things]
b. I had *nothing to complain about*
Na nic jsem si *nemohl stěžovat* [about nothing I-could-not-complain]
c. I had *nothing to complain about* in my new abode
nemohl jsem si *na nové obydlí* stěžovat [I-could-not-complain about new abode]

The common feature of these constructions is to be sought in the modal component of the Czech verb and the implicit modal meaning of the English postmodifying infinitive. However, the FSP structure in (41) a. differs in the rheme, which is the object in Czech, but the entire object noun phrase in English, with the context independent, and hence more dynamic, element at the end.

The subject as a counterpart of an English noun modifier occurred in the following instances:

(42) a. he is well aware of *my success in satisfactorily completing* ...
ví, že *se mi povedlo správně vyplnit* ...
[he-knows that to-me succeeded correctly to-complete ...]
b. The unexpected speeches of Dr. Witherspoon will sometimes *be responsible for the existence of a chapter* treating of criminality at the beginning and criminality at the end, while ...
Neočekávané proslovy doktora Vlacha někdy *způsobí*, že *kapitola*, začínající pojednáním o kriminalistice, *skončí* pojednáním o kriminalistice, ačkoliv ...
[Unexpected speeches of Dr. Witherspoon sometimes cause that chapter beginning with treatment about criminality ends with ...]
c. On dark autumn nights, when ... a whirlwind tears the leaves off the trees, and the *shrieks of a howling gale* encircle the towers of old castles ...
Za tmavých podzimních nocí, kdy ... studený vichr rve listí ze stromů, *meluzína skučí* kolem věží starých hradů [when ... gale howls around towers of-old castles]

As shown by the literal translations, only (42) a. can be classed with instances that reflect any systemic features. English again contains an action noun where Czech has a verb, cf. *success* vs. *povést se = succeed*, with the concomitant feature, viz. noun modifier in English vs. subject in Czech, the subject function being due to the syntactic construction of the verb's participants.

Examples (42) b. and c. display alterations of sentence structure, which would require many more examples if recurrent differences in coordination and subordination in construing mutiple sentences are to be ascertained.

Example (43) illustrates a relative clause where Czech has a main clause. This is also (and presumably more often) found in the opposite direction, cf. 1.2.2.

(43) I was once woken up during the night by a man in an official cap *who explained to me* ...

Tak jsem byl například jednou probuzen mužem v úřední čepici *a bylo mi vysvětleno* ... [and it-was to-me explained]

The last example, relative clause in English (discontinous like (10) a. and b.) vs. apposition in Czech, is similar in that English displays subordination where Czech has coordination.

(44) that *a third category of people* existed, *the members of which* are as rare as white crows.

že se vyskytuje ještě *třetí druh lidí, takové jakési bílé vrány*

[that is-found still third kind of-people, such white crows].

The divergent syntactic functions are summarized in Table 5.

Table 5: Noun modification

Divergent syntactic counterparts of English noun modifiers		
Adverbial	18	34.6 %
Object	17	32.7 %
Subject complement	9	17.3 %
Verb	3	5.8 %
Subject	3	5.8 %
Main clause	1	1.9 %
Apposition	1	1.9 %
Total	52	100.0 %

4. In conclusion the findings obtained from the foregoing discussion appear to present the following picture. The initial assumptions concerning both the syntactic and the FSP aspects of the noun modifier have been largely confirmed. The data for the Czech → English direction show that Czech and English noun modifiers are basically similar. The syntactic function is preserved in 90% of all instances and a high degree of agreement was also found in the form of realization (70%). This is due to the membership of both languages in the same language family. The results obtained in the English → Czech direction need to be verified by examining an original English text and its Czech translation.

As regards the FSP aspect, again the two languages behave in a very similar way. This follows from the primary ordering of the prototypical word class whereby the noun modifier is realized, viz. the order adjective—noun, which applies to both languages. The adjectival form of realization was found in nearly a half of all identical instances, with all the other realization forms ranking much lower. The second factor acting in the direction of similarity is the FSP structure of the noun phrase, where linearity plays a very minor role. A context independent modifier is more dynamic than the head noun irrespective of its position and of the context dependence or independence of the head noun. Since the contextual factor is a general one, the same conditions again apply to both languages. As a communicative subfield on the phrase level the FSP of the noun phrase does not play an essential role on the clause level. Here the FSP function of the modified noun phrase is determined by the FSP structure of the higher level of the clause. A point of contrastive interest emerges from the rare instances of reversal of the basic order adjective—noun in Czech, some of which have English counterparts displaying some kind of compensation. This shows that even an analytic language has means to achieve this order.

The differences between Czech and English noun modifiers appear to be primarily due to the typological distinctions between the two languages. Both in the case of the different realization forms and in the case of divergence in syntactic function the operative factors were found in the analytic and nominal character of English. The most frequent different realization form of all Czech non-clausal noun modifiers was a converted noun—a formally indeterminate word class acquiring its syntactic function from its position. Another manifestation of the analytic character of English appeared in frequent instances of decomposition of a Czech de-adjectival noun into two components, an adjective expressing the meaning and a general noun performing the same function as the derivational suffix in Czech. Here English is shown to have a limited degree of derivational capacity. As regards evidence of the nominal character of English, more than two-thirds of all Czech noun modifiers realized by finite clauses were reflected in non-finite forms (infinitives, participles and gerunds). This testifies not only to the nominal character of English, but also to the tendency towards condensed sentence structure. Both the analytic and the nominal feature of English manifest themselves even more clearly in the syntactically divergent Czech counterparts of English noun modifiers. The higher number of divergent counterparts in the English → Czech direction appears to be mainly due to the use of modification structures with general nouns as heads where the heads have no explicit counterparts in Czech. The second main factor of the divergences was found in the different form of predication, viz. verbo-nominal in English vs. verbal in Czech, with the concomitant feature modification vs. complementation. As for the FSP aspect, its role as a factor causing divergence in form or function was marginal and of contrastive interest only in special cases.

SOURCES

Jirotka, Z. *Saturnin*. Prague: Fr. Borový, 1943, pp. 7–9.
Jirotka, Z. *Saturnin*. Translated by Mark Corner. Prague: Karolinum Press, 2003, pp. 7–20.

II. SYNTAX
FSP INTERFACE

9. FROM THE HERITAGE OF VILÉM MATHESIUS AND JAN FIRBAS: SYNTAX IN THE SERVICE OF FSP

First published in Jan Chovanec (ed.), *Theory and Practice in English Studies, Proceedings from the Eighth Conference of English, American and Canadian Studies*, Vol. 3, 7–23, Brno: Masaryk University, 2005.

0. As the title of this chapter indicates, the following reflections have been initiated by two Czech scholars, Vilém Mathesius and Jan Firbas. However, to do the aspect of FSP full justice, the name of another Czech scholar should have been included in the title, viz. the name of Josef Vachek. The reason why he does not appear alongside the other two is that FSP was not the primary concern of his work. On the other hand, the reason why he cannot in the present context remain unnoticed is that but for him, Jan Firbas might never have taken up FSP as the leitmotif of his linguistic pursuits. Jan Firbas was of course familiar with and inspired by the works of Vilém Mathesius from his previous studies, but it was Josef Vachek who suggested FSP as a promising line of research, and this suggestion became seminal for further development of the FSP theory.

The subtitle "syntax in the service of FSP" implies the hierarchy of the two levels, which is not meant to purport that serving FSP is the only concern of syntax. In fact only a small number of syntactic constructions have been noted and/or partly treated as specific FSP devices. Apart from those discussed in what follows (the passive, the cleft sentence and the existential construction), attention has been paid to pseu-do-clefts, fronting (of both thematic and rhematic elements, also sometimes referred to, respectively, as topicalization and focus movement), left dislocation, raising, emphatic and end-focus motivated word order configurations, alternative constructions of the verb's actants, and some minor types (Grzegorek 1984; Sgall et al. 1980: 4.25).

However, more detailed treatment of the FSP aspects of most of these points is lacking. The reason for choosing the passive, the cleft sentence and the existential construction is obviously due to the initiators of this treatment: all three points have been addressed, to a greater or lesser extent, by both Vilém Mathesius and Jan Firbas, and moreover, they have received a good deal of attention in further research. Consequently, an outline of a fairly complex picture can now be presented.

1. Of the three constructions, Czech writers have been most concerned with the passive.

1.1 In Mathesius' work (Mathesius 1915, 1947a, 1975) it was a recurrent point, approached from different aspects. Mathesius' consistently functional conception of language even led him to disregard form to the extent of classing some active forms as special types of the passive: apart from formally passive forms (such as *The play is performed by our best actors, I have been told that ..., He will be well taken care of*) he regarded as passive, constructions like *to be subject to, to be the subject of,* further what he called adverbial predications, e.g. *the ship is under construction,* and possessive predications, e.g. *he had his reward at once.* The last type was of particular interest to him where it involved an indirectly affected subject: *persons who had relatives going out, I had one Colossus bulging over my shoulders* (1975: 108–114). Some of these constructions are also mentioned in connection with FSP as means facilitating movement in the position of sentence elements. However, the type of the passive which appears to be a word order device par excellence is the passive with an expressed *by*-agent, illustrated by (1).

(1) The play is performed by our best actors.

In his account of English word order Mathesius (1975: 157) states, "In English ... the grammatical principle asserts itself especially with regard to the expression of the relation between the subject and the finite verb. The usual word order of the English sentence, viz. subject—finite verb—object cannot be changed at will. Hence in such a case the grammatical word order fails to comply with the principle of functional sentence perspective ... English resolves this conflict by resorting to the passive *At home I am helped by Father / Zu Hause hilft mir der Vater.*" This sentence is part of an often quoted passage which appears in Mathesius' account of the function of the subject in English (1975: 101–103).

(2) Jan velmi dobře prospíval. Ve škole horlivě naslouchal každému slovu svých učitelů a *doma mu pomáhal otec* [at-home him helped father], kdykoliv mu byla nějaká úloha příliš těžká. Práce všeho druhu se mu velice dařila a říkalo se o něm, že pracuje stejně přirozeně, jako dýchá.

John prospered very well. At school he eagerly listened to every word of his teachers. *At home he was helped by his father* whenever he found his task too difficult. He was successful in any kind of work. He was said to be working as naturally as he was breathing.

As the passage demonstrates, Mathesius was primarily concerned with the thematic function of the English subject, which he also demonstrated in other types of the passive, and in the constructions of verbs of perception.

1.2 Firbas's contribution to the insights into the functions of the passive (1966, 1992: Chapters 4 and 7) was initiated by Mathesius' views, which Firbas on the whole endorsed, except for one point: the insusceptibility of ModE to the requirements of FSP. Mathesius had come to this view on the basis of the occurrence in many English sentences of non-thematic subjects, of which he was well aware despite the strong tendency of ModE to express the theme of the sentence by means of the grammatical subject. It was precisely this point, the non-thematic subjects, which led Firbas to perceive another function of the passive, a function hitherto entirely unnoticed. In contrast to Mathesius, who regarded word order as the only means of FSP, Firbas demonstrated the operation of two other factors in written language, context and semantic structure. Non-thematic subjects are indicated by context independence and semantic structure expressing existence or appearance on the scene. The latter feature is basically due to the semantics of the verb conceived on a fairly general level. This is well known, but what needs to be noted in the present connection is the conception of the semantic aspect from the level of general sentence semantics, which allows disregard of the grammatical form, and even of the basic lexical meaning. Only in this way could the following passives be included among the different surface realizations of what Firbas later called the presentation scale:

(3) a. Sometimes a terrible cry was to be heard (when the doctor was pulling out the teeth of some little boy).
   b. New Zealand apples were being sold, or rice-brooms from Australia were exhibited or a billiard-table manufactured in the Bermudas. (Firbas 1966)
   c. Quite a number of houses have been built in our town.
   d. Powerful machines have been constructed.
   e. An uncanny impression is thereby created.
   f. A new method has been developed.
   g. Ingenious new schemes have been devised in various institutes.
   h. Monuments will be erected in the centre of the city. ... (Firbas 1992: 62)

These sentences can also be perspectived in a different way, but where the adverbial (if there is any) serves as a setting and the subject as the phenomenon to be presented, the meaning conveyed by the verbal forms is fully compatible with appearance / existence on the scene.

Firbas concludes that these observations do not disprove the well-known fact that in a majority of cases the passive participates in perspectiving the sentence away from the subject.

1.3 Significantly, the different functions of the passive demonstrated on the one hand by Mathesius, and on the other hand by Jan Firbas, are closely connected with the respective types of the passive: whereas Mathesius described the most frequent

FSP structure of passives with an expressed *by*-agent, i.e. a transitive verbal structure with two participants that exchange their positions, Firbas was concerned with agentless passives, i.e. transitive verbal structures whose first participant is deleted owing to its general nature or irrelevance in the particular context.

1.3.1 According to statistical data English passives with an expressed *by*-agent account for some 10 per cent (10.53 per cent) of passive forms (63 out of 598 instances of passive forms from a total of 5 000 finite verb forms, cf. Dušková 1971). In addition to the 63 instances of passives with a *by*-agent, there were 21 passives with a quasi -agent, construed with a preposition other than *by*, and 15 janus-agents. Nearly all of these examples testify to Mathesius' interpretation of the interaction of FSP and English grammatical word order, i.e. the subject is thematic and the *by*-agent rhematic, as in:

(4) Such situations are characterized by varying degrees of bilingualism.

Nevertheless, in a small number of passives (less than 10, some 12 per cent) the construction displays a thematic *by*-agent and a rhematic subject, which in the active would exchange their positions; their linear order would then be consistent with their degree of communicative dynamism (CD), i.e. in accordance with the basic distribution of CD.

(5) a. In the six years 1956–61, a total of 81,079 applications for disablement benefit were made by coal miners.
   b. In the six years 1956–61, there was a total of 81,079 applications for disablement benefit made by coal miners.

The *by*-agent of this sentence is context dependent (coal miners are what is spoken about in the preceding sentences), and there is no contrast with workers from other fields. Note that the verb in the passive is one of those displayed by Firbas's examples. The only context independent element in the sentence is the quantifier in the subject, which is what makes it rhematic, since miners' applying for disablement benefits has also been mentioned. The reason why the passive and not the active is used is presumably textual: since the rhematic subject is the only element that contains new information, it is expedient to introduce it as early as possible; all that follows merely repeats what is being discussed. The FSP structure of (5) a. would be indicated more distinctly by the corresponding existential extension of the sentence, adduced in (5) b.

1.3.2 Textual factors typically assert themselves where both participants of a transitive verb are context dependent, and the rheme is constituted by the verb, as in the following examples:

(6) a. The sight of this harmless vanity depressed him. (James OS, 342)
   a.' He was depressed by the sight of this harmless vanity.
   b. Her initial testiness had surprised him. (James OS, 350)
   b.' He was surprised by her initial testiness.

The change in the voice hardly affects the FSP structure, the context dependence of both noun phrases being clearly indicated by anaphoric devices and by the non-contrastive character of the context. The passive forms of the sentences are slightly more consistent with the basic distribution of CD in that the preverbal noun phrase is the theme proper and the postverbal element is the diatheme, while in the active the diatheme precedes the theme proper. But this is often the case in English, especially in sentences with initial adverbials followed by pronominal subjects. In these examples the choice of voice appears to be due to textual aspects which clearly manifest themselves in the following example, showing the hierarchically superordinate status of the text build-up with respect to the FSP structure within a sentence:

(7) a. ["Are you all right, Blackie? I mean, do you want someone to go home with you?"] The thought appalled Blackie. (James OS, 195)
  b. Blackie was appalled by the thought.

The subject resumes the most activated element from the immediately preceding context (*do you want someone to go home with you*), whereas the object refers to an element further to the left (more distant) in the text. Both noun phrases are context dependent, and have the same form of realization: there is no modification, and both are definite. Their respective positions appear to be due to the position of the sentence in the text: they present a mirror image of the order in which their antecedents occur in the preceding textual string.

In examples like the following a motivating factor is presumably to be sought in the more frequent use of the passive, due to the attitudinal meaning of the particular verbs: they form statal passives, whose past participles tend to recategorize as adjectives.

(8) a. She was delighted at the news.
  b. I am so terribly upset by all this.

1.3.3 Returning to (5), which illustrates the configuration of a rhematic subject with a thematic *by*-agent, i.e. a presentation scale implemented by a passive with an expressed *by*-agent, it appears to be rare. Thematic *by*-agents themselves, though essentially less frequent than rhematic *by*-agents, more often occur with thematic subjects where the rheme is constituted by some other clause element. Examples (8) a. and b. demonstrate rhematic verbs. The following examples illustrate rhematic adverbials other than *by*-agents.

(9) a. The problem was extensively debated in 'naturalistic' ... terms by the Greek philosophers, and was of considerable importance in the development of traditional linguistic theory. It has been discussed at various times by philosophers since then, notably in the eighteenth century. (Lyons, 6)
  b. ... Philosophers have discussed it at various times since then, notably in the eighteenth century.

c. ... Philosophers have since (then) discussed it at various times, notably in the eighteenth century.

d. ... Since then philosophers have discussed it at various times, notably in the eighteenth century.

In (9) a. the first sentence contains the prototypical passive with a thematic subject and a rhematic *by*-agent. In the second sentence the only new element is the temporal specification whose rhematic function is reinforced by the focusing subjunct *notably* in the further specification. The active counterpart would be more consistent with the basic distribution of CD, cf. the active alternatives (9) b., c. and d., but interferes with the presentation of the content as a thematic progression with constant theme, reflected in the maintenance of the same subject through several successive sentences. This tendency of English has also been pointed out by Mathesius in connection with (2) (cf. also 1947a). The next example displays a similar structure:

(10) The thesis of linguistic egalitarianism is now less widely accepted by linguists than it was a generation ago. (Lyons, 7)

The passage discusses the attitudes of linguists to egalitarianism, the new element being the specification of degree: *less widely*. Of particular interest is the following example which contains a *by*-phrase in initial position:

(11) By the productivity of human language is meant its unboundedness, or, to use a looser but suggestive term, its 'open-endedness' ... (Lyons, 14)

The sentence deviates from grammatical word order in displaying subject—verb inversion after an initial adverbial. The deviation is clearly motivated by the principle of basic distribution of CD: the initial *by*-phrase is thematic, and the final position displays the rheme, realized by the subject. However, the verb can hardly be interpreted as presentative: the conveyed meaning indicates equative relationship between the two noun phrases. Obviously, the *by*-phrase does not represent a *by*-agent but an adjunct of means modifying an agentless passive whose agent is implied by the preceding paragraph:

(12) By duality of structure linguists refer to the fact that ... (Lyons, 4)

1.3.4 Firbas's presentation scale involving a passive verb is mainly found in passive sentences without an expressed agent, containing verba efficiendi. The prototypical verb is illustrated in (13) a. and b. Apart from these, presentation sentences also display other verbs, cf. (13) c. and d.

(13) a. One more specific point should be made in this context. (Lyons, 2)

b. Two general points may be made about recent developments in this area. (Lyons, 11)

    c. Near one of the posts, a hammer and a few nails had been left behind.
       (Adams, 18.)
    d. At the moment of his departure, a telegram was handed to him.

The relative frequency of occurrence of the different types of the passive can be illustrated by a brief quantitative probe into the uses of the passive in Lyons's Introduction to *New Horizons in Linguistics* 2. The first 16 pages display 108 passive clauses, the majority of which represent agentless passives: 86 (80 per cent), the remaining 22 (20 per cent) being agentive. The percentage of agentive passives is here higher as compared with the data of a more extensive study (Dušková 1971), but owing to the much smaller size of the Lyons sample this may not be conclusive. Among the non-agentive passives there are two instances of the presentation scale (see (13) a. and b. above; note that both contain the verb *make*). Sentences with agentive passives (22) include no instance of a presentation scale, but there are 2 instances (10 per cent) of agentive passives with a thematic *by*-agent, cf. (9) a. and (10).

These and the previously adduced results show that what Mathesius pointed out was the prototypical type of a passive with an expressed *by*-agent, while Firbas demonstrated the surface nature of the syntactic form by applying the same methodological apparatus to passive sentences as in the case of the active. Application of this approach has provided further evidence to show that the passive is not an automatic device for placing the rheme at the end, but a structure subject to the operation of the same interplay of FSP factors as sentences in the active. Any element of a passive sentence may constitute the rheme—the subject, the verb, an adverbial, not only *by*-agents, but also other semantic roles, just as any element may be thematized by the context. As regards the basic distribution of CD, passive sentences display similar deviations as active ones, thematic elements in final position being fairly frequent in both, cf. (14).

(14) This was accepted between them. (Adams, 18)

However, against this background the two types of patterning revealed by Mathesius and Firbas are clearly discernible.

A new finding of further research is the operation of textual factors which may override linear ordering determined by the FSP structure alone.

1.3.5 The last point to be mentioned in this section is the passive of ditransitive verbs (cf. Brůhová 2015). Here the subject appears to be prevalently implemented by the thematic element, whichever object in the active it may be. Compare the following examples:

(15) a. there is no reason why these assumptions and expectations should not be given full theoretical recognition from the outset. (Lyons, 2)

b. All these men had applied for compensation, but it had been granted to only two.[1]

In the small sample the distribution of direct and indirect object as the subject of the passive does not greatly differ, a moderate predominance being shown by direct object: 56.76 per cent against 43.23 per cent accounted for by indirect object. Brůhová's (2015) results based on a much larger sample show an opposite tendency, viz. a slight preponderance of the indirect object as the subject of the passive. Moreover, there appear to be major differences in the frequency of occurrence of the two passives in the case of different verbs.

It may be concluded that the FSP function of the passive, primarily found in the type with an expressed *by*-agent and in the passive of ditransitive verbs, appears to be a major function, but should be seen against the background of a variety of other uses. Passive sentences are found to be subject to the operation of the same FSP factors as active sentences without a focusing device. In other words syntactic form, though serving as an FSP device, overrides neither context dependence, nor semantic structure, but is subordinate to both.

2. The second construction to be discussed, the cleft sentence, figures prominently in the work of Firbas, while Mathesius gave it only a brief mention in connection with strengthening and emphasis (1975: 165).[2]

2.1 Mathesius describes the cleft sentence as a specific English device expressing emphasis by means of a whole clause after the fashion of the French construction, cf. (16).

(16) a. It is not conscience that makes me do so.
    b. It was he who advised the King not to do so. (Mathesius 1975: 165)

Firbas was concerned with the cleft sentence from the FSP point of view, expounded in his article 'It was yesterday that ...' (Firbas 1967). The full form of the sentence is adduced in (17):

(17) It was yesterday that George flew to Prague.

He first considers the question of the rheme, and assigns it to *yesterday* as the most natural interpretation. The *It-is ... that*-construction singles out *yesterday* for particular attention, throwing it into relief. At the same time he points out the conspicuous deviation from the basic distribution of CD: the rheme is found in the first part of the sentence. Assigning the other FSP functions to the remaining elements of the sentence, Firbas shows that the transition, the copula *be*, mediates between the subject

---

1   For this example and a more detailed discussion of the passive, see Dušková (1971).
2   In this volume the cleft sentence is treated from the textual viewpoint in Chapters 11 and 21; this aspect is further developed in Dušková (2015); for the syntactic and FSP aspects, see also Dušková (1993).

it (the theme proper) + *that George flew to Prague* (the rest of theme) on the one hand, and *yesterday* (the rheme) on the other. The subordinate clause constitutes a communicative subfield of its own, in which respect it differs from the underlying non-cleft sentence where the rheme is signalled—in this case—by extra-strong stress: *George flew to Prague YESTERDAY*. In the article this point is not specifically mentioned, but it was made explicit in a discussion.

As for the syntactic aspect, Firbas considers it from the viewpoint of potential ambiguity of the subordinate clause with a relative clause, illustrated by (18):

(18) a. It is the country that suits my wife best. (Firbas 1967)
    b. She likes to spend her holidays in Italy. It (viz. Italy) is the country that she likes best.

The disambiguating factor is found in the FSP function of the subordinate clause: in the cleft sentence it is thematic—compare the question *What is it that suits her best?* Here *country* is put in contrast with town life. On the other hand, the relative clause carries new information, and constitutes the rheme in that it specifies the particular country with respect to other countries. This is reflected in the prosodic structure: in the cleft sentence the intonation centre (the nucleus) is on *country*, whereas if the subordinate clause is relative, the intonation centre is on *best*.

Just as Mathesius revealed the prototypical case of the passive that serves as a syntactic device of FSP, Firbas identified, and insightfully interpreted the prototypical use of the cleft sentence: a structure involving one rhematic element, contained in the main clause and constituted by the subject complement in an identifying copular predication, and a presupposed, given subordinate clause, forming one FSP unit with the subject of the main clause, the initial *it*.

As regards the distinction between the subordinate clause in the cleft sentence and a relative clause, apart from the FSP aspect demonstrated by Firbas there is a difference in the function of the initial *it*. In the cleft sentence it is a syntactic component of the cleft construction anticipating the subordinate clause; in other words, the initial *it* and the subordinate clause constitute one syntactic unit. Actually in one approach (Carlson 1983: 230) the subordinate clause is regarded as an obligatorily extraposed relative clause whose head is the subject of the main clause *it*. On the other hand if the subordinate clause has relative function, its antecedent is the element that precedes it. The initial *it* in the main clause is referential, either anaphoric, pointing back in the text to what precedes, or exophoric, identifying an object in the situation of utterance. Hence it can be replaced by its antecedent or an explicit denomination of the object/notion being referred to. Compare (18) b.

Further distinctions between the subordinate clause in the cleft sentence and the relative clause are found in their constructional properties (cf. Quirk et al. 1985: 1386–87; Huddleston and Pullum 2002: 1034–1035, 1046, 1055–1057, 1414–1420).

2.2 As regards textual studies of the cleft sentence, it has been shown that contrary to the general view which associates the focused element with new information, there are two major types of *it*-clefts, one containing new information in the main clause and the other in the subordinate clause (Prince 1978; Dvořáková 1988). If the main clause contains new information and the subordinate clause is context dependent, the degree of communicative dynamism in the main clause greatly exceeds that of the subordinate clause. This is the type described by Firbas, which is regarded as the prototypical use of the cleft sentence. According to statistical data, this type somewhat predominates over the type with given information in the main clause and new information in the subordinate clause (55 per cent and 45 per cent, respectively, cf. Dvořáková 1988, and Note 15 in Dušková 1993). Prince (1978) characterized these two types of *it*-clefts as stressed-focus *it*-clefts in which the subordinate clause conveys given information, and hence is weakly stressed; and informative-presupposition *it*-clefts which have a normally stressed subordinate clause and a short main clause focusing an anaphoric element (cf. discourse-old and discourse-new presupposition in Huddleston and Pullum 2002: 1424). The information in the subordinate clause, though new, is presented as presupposed. The concept of presupposition thus appears to be distinct from that of familiar information (Huddleston and Pullum 2002: 1424).

Inquiries into the syntactic function of the focused element in the underlying non-cleft sentence suggest that *it*-clefts are used to give prominence to what would in the non-cleft sentence stand at the beginning and be mostly thematic, whether context-dependent or not. The most frequently focused element is the subject, which in English favours the FSP function of theme. This is due to its being largely bound to the initial or preverbal part of the sentence, i.e. to the position of the theme. The second most frequently focused element is the adverbial. Firbas's example illustrates an adverbial operating as a specification; there are also *it*-clefts displaying a focused scene-setting, i. e. thematic adverbial, which would stand at the beginning in the non-cleft form, cf.

(19) a. [The servants were permitted to hold evening prayer in the kitchen ... Upstairs, Mrs Poulteney had to be read to alone;] it was in these more intimate ceremonies that Sarah's voice was heard at its best and most effective. (Fowles, 54)
   b. in these more intimate ceremonies Sarah's voice was heard at its best and most effective
   A právě při těchto důvěrnějších sezeních zněl Sařin hlas nejlépe a nejpůsobivěji. (Žantovská, 53)
   [And precisely in these more-intimate sessions sounded Sara's voice best_adverb and most-effectively]

In the cleft form the sentence acquires two information peaks, a minor one in the first part after the copula, and the main focus at the end of the subordinate clause. This structure explicitly indicates the relation to the preceding context, in resuming the element that further develops the paragraph theme. At the same time the presentation of the new information contained in the subordinate clause achieves a climax.

Apart from these two major uses (the type with discourse-old and the type with discourse-new presupposition), there are minor types illustrated by (20) a. and b. Example (20) a. illustrates proverbial clefts (cf. Huddleston and Pullum 2002: 1417); (20) b. and c. illustrate stylistic clichés (cf. Quirk et al. 10985:1384)

(20) a. It is a long lane that has no turning.
    a.' A lane that has no turning is a long one.
    b. It was a very troubled wife that greeted Henry on his return that night.
    b.' The wife that greeted Henry on his return that night was a very troubled wife.
    c. It was late last night that a group of terrorists attacked an army post.
    c.' Late last night a group of terrorists attacked an army post.

Examples (20) a. and b. lack one of the defining features of the cleft construction: they do not represent the equative, identifying type of copular predication but ascribe a quality to the subject, cf. (20) a.' and b.' Example (20) c. presents the event as given and the time of the event as the most important item, whereas the opposite applies, cf. (20) c.'

Yet another use of the *it*-cleft is found in sentences with multiple postverbal adverbials, as in the following example:

(21) a. It was not by chance that Mrs S. arrived in town so early that morning.
    b. Mrs S. did not arrive in town so early that morning by chance.
    c. That morning Mrs S did not arrive in town so early by chance.

Here the use of the *it*-cleft relieves the cumulation of adverbials in the postverbal section -there would be four in the non-cleft form—and at the same time gives additional prominence to what would be the rheme proper even in the underlying form. The only other option is to place the temporal setting at the beginning, but then it would acquire a higher degree of CD within the thematic section, uncalled for from the textual point of view.

2.3 The last two points are the counterparts of the cleft sentence in Czech, and the distinction between the cleft sentence and the passive.

2.3.1 The first point is presented in the light of syntactically divergent Czech equivalents of the English subject complement. In Chapter 5, 3.3.2 a recurrent Czech counterpart of the English cleft construction was found in non-cleft, one-clause sentences. This interlingual relation appears to be fairly general despite the fact that a structural counterpart of *it*-clefts (*vytýkací důrazový opis* [the emphatic focusing periphrastic construction], Daneš et al. 1987: 537) does exist in Czech. The prevalence of one-clause counterparts is hardly surprising, considering that Czech is a synthetic language, whereas English is analytic. Compare (19) a. and the following examples.

(22) a. It's his ghost that people claim to see, still scrubbing away at the stain. (James
    OS, 32)

> Prý tu lidé dodnes vídají jeho ducha, jak se snaží skvrnu odstranit. (Rovenská, 41)
> [it-is-said here people till-today often-see his ghost as _reflexive particle_ he-tries stain to-remove]

   b. It was not concern for his only daughter that made him send her to boarding-school, but obsession with his own ancestry. (Fowles, 51)

> Neposlal svou dceru do internátu z přílišné péče o ni, ale proto, že byl posedlý myšlenkou na vlastní předky. (Žantovská, 50)
> [He-not-sent his daughter to boarding-school from excessive care for her, but therefore that he-was obsessed with-idea of own ancestors]

   c. But it's Gerard who runs the firm. (James OS, 30)

> Ale firmu vede Gerard. (Rovenská, 38)
> [But firm$_{acc}$ runs Gerard$_{nom}$]

These instances reveal a difference not only in the FSP, but also in the explicitness of indicating the textual relations, as has already been noted in connection with (19) a. In English the bi-clausal realization of the propositional content produces two communicative subfields which allow more explicit indication of the connection with the preceding context, especially the signalling of a contrast. In the Czech rendition by a single clause, where no focalizer is present, this remains to be inferred from the context alone since the rhematic element is indicated in the same way as a non-contrastive rheme (intonation playing a role primarily in speech). In the case of informative presupposition it-clefts, the contrastive function also involves an underlying thematic element, highlighted by the construction. In the material of this chapter the information structure is mostly indicated by word order alone, and less frequently with the support of a focalizer (as in (19) a.). There was only one instance of an it-cleft with parallel structure in Czech, cf. (23).

(23) a. … it was the Ca' Foscari which his architect had been instructed to build. (James OS, 33)

   b. byl to Casa Foscari, podle něhož měl architekt vystavět dům. (Rovenská, 42)

> [was it Casa Foscari according-to which was architect to-build house]

2.3.2 The last point concerns the potential overlap between a passive with an expressed by-agent and a corresponding it-cleft.

(24) a. The book was written by X. Y.

   b. It was X.Y. who wrote the book.

The two constructions differ in the presupposed part: in the case of the passive it may involve more or fewer elements, whereas in the case of the it-cleft the presupposed part generally involves all elements except one. In the passive, the only presupposed element may be the subject, as in answer to the question

(25) What do you know / What can you say about *The Castle of Otranto?*
    a. *The Castle of Otranto* / It was written by Horace Walpole.
    b. *It was Horace Walpole who wrote *the Castle of Otranto*.

In FSP terms, the only context dependent element is the subject, whereas the entire predicate is context independent. The cleft sentence is here a textual misfit.

A different FSP structure appears when the two constructions are used as answers to the question

(26) Who wrote *The Castle of Otranto?*
    a. *The Castle of Otranto* was written by Horace Walpole.
    b. It was written by Horace Walpole.
    c. Horace Walpole.
    d. It was Horace Walpole (elliptical cleft: who wrote it)

Since here the only context independent element is the author, the question arises whether this is not an instance of overlap between the cleft sentence and the passive, cf. (26) d. However, in the passive there is no suggestion of a contrastive context. The question presupposes the existence of a writer, and the answer specifies the individual within the respective class.

On the other hand, the cleft sentence presupposes a contrast not between the class of authors and a singled-out writer, but one between two singled-out writers:

(27) Who wrote *The Castle of Otranto?* — (*The Castle of Otranto* was written by) Mrs Radcliffe.
    a. I'm afraid you're mistaken: It was Horace Walpole who wrote *The Castle of Otranto.*
    b. No, *The Castle of Otranto* was written by Horace WALPOLE.

The passive is conceivable here if contrastively stressed, cf. (27) b.

3. The last point to be briefly discussed is the existential construction.

3.1 Mathesius describes it as "another device [besides the passive] that helps to reconcile the conflicting requirements of functional sentence perspective and the English grammaticized word order" (1975: 119). He points out that here both the subject and the predicate, construed as postmodification, frequently express something new.

(28) a. There is a strong wind blowing outdoors.
    b. There was no possibility of escape. (Mathesius 1975: 119)

3.2 Firbas mentions existential *there* in connection with the immediately relevant situational context (1992: 24), described in terms of non-linguistic referents. Existential *there* is classed together with such notions as speaker/writer, listener/reader, people in general, nature in general, i.e. *I, you, one, it*, which can be introduced into discourse directly, without an antecedent. "With due alterations, the same applies to the pronoun, or rather proadverb, *there* of the existential construction. Though semantically very weak, it is not totally stripped of all meaning. As an integral part of the existential construction, it acts as an indicator of the scene expressed by a genuine adverbial of place.

(29) There were books on the table / There were books there."

The existential construction is noted at a further point, more relevant to the present discussion, in the Chapter "The semantic factor," subsection "The context-independent subject" (1992: 59). "In the absence of any of the successful competitors so far discussed [=object, subject complement, object complement, and adverbial] the verb shows a strong tendency to recede into the background and to be exceeded in CD in the presence of a context independent subject."

(30) a. A boy came into the room.
    b. There was a boy in the room.
    c. In the centre of the room ... stood ... old Jolyon himself.
    d. A very sweet look had come into the old lady's face.
    e. There was little sentimentality about the Forsytes. (Firbas 1992: 59)

"In each sentence, the notional component of the finite verb expresses appearance or existence on the scene. ... The subject is context-independent and conveys the information towards which the communication is perspectived. (In the case of the *there*-clause, this applies to its 'notional' subject). ... The adverbial elements serve as settings. ... under the circumstances the subject carries the highest degree of CD irrespective of sentence position ... " (*ibid.*) The existential construction is here presented as one of the forms of the presentation scale. As shown in Chapter 12, this realization form of the presentation scale is not only the most frequent, but also the only neutral form in the sense of being unmarked with respect to deviation from both the grammatical word order and the basic distribution of communicative dynamism.

3.3 Treatments of the existential construction in the literature are mostly concerned with other aspects than the role played by existential *there* in FSP, specifically with the relations between existential and non-existential sentences:

(31) a. A friend of yours is at the door.
    b. There is a friend of yours at the door.
(32) a. No one was waiting.
    b. There was no one waiting

Furthermore, attention is paid to semantic aspects, including the relations between locative, possessive and existential sentences, and to the type of definiteness conveyed by the notional subject (Breivik 1983; Huddleston and Pullum 2002: 1390–1401; Quirk et al. 1985: 1402–1414; Grzegorek 1984: 29–30, 76–84). Rather as an exception, the FSP aspect is also taken into consideration by Grzegorek (1984: 78), who discerns two FSP structures in locative-existential sentences according to whether the locative element belongs to the focus or is context dependent. However, the only observation made in this respect concerns the difference between the two types in intonation: where the locative element belongs to the focus, it carries a secondary intonation centre; if context dependent, the sentence stress is on the notional subject alone.

(33) a. There's a strange looking WOMAN in the HOUSE,
    b. There's a strange looking WOMAN in the house,
    b.' In the house, there's a strange looking WOMAN. (Grzegorek 1984, 78)

Only the type with a context dependent adverbial allows the adverbial to be placed initially ([33] b.'). It is this type that appears to be the major one (cf. Dušková 1977). Evidently, Jan Firbas again described the prototypical case. The low degree of CD of such adverbials is occasionally reflected in a deviant word order configuration, displaying the adverbial element before the notional subject. Such word order arrangement is clearly motivated by the respective degrees of CD that the sentence elements carry. They are then found in positions consistent with the basic distribution of CD. Compare:

(34) a. There was about the place that dead silence indicative of an untenanted house.
    b. There were in his in-tray no fewer than thirty unpaid bills. (Huddleston and Pullum 2002: 1392)
    c. There was in the vicinity a helpful doctor. (Quirk et al. 1985: 1404)
    d. Despite all the intellectual activity of the time, there was in print no guide to the tongue, no linguistic vade-mecum, no single book that Shakespeare or Marlowe or Nashe, … or any of their other learned contemporaries could consult. (Winchester, 71)

This position of a scene-setting adverbial is the least frequent one. Though mostly thematic, locative and temporal adverbials in existential constructions are commonly found at the end, cf. the following examples. The final position of thematic elements is here nothing exceptional, thematic elements in final and postverbal position being fairly frequent in English in general.

(35) a. There was nothing alarming there. (Adams, 15)
    b. Of course there were real mad dogs in those days. (Raverat, 51)
    c. here is note on your desk. (James UJ, 10)

Initial adverbials are less common than final, but more common than medial. Compare (36).

(36) Here there was a delay. (Adams, 19)

The relatively rare placement of a context dependent adverbial in the initial position is doubtless connected with the fact that any initial clause element other than the subject is more or less marked: it is more prominent than in its regular position, hence this position involves some motivation. In the case of initial adverbials a concomitant factor is frequently found in their connective function. It is to be noted that the position which is most consistent with the gradual increase in CD, illustrated by the examples listed under (34), is the least frequent, whereas the most deviant position in this respect ((35) a., b., c.) is to be regarded as the most regular. This clearly manifests the primary principle of English word order, grammatical function. In this case it asserts itself in the customary order of the clause elements.

While the sentence position of scene-setting adverbials does not affect their thematic function (just as the sentence position does not affect the rhematic function of context independent subjects construed with verbs of existence or appearance), there are also instances where the position of an adverbial in the existential construction is decisive for its FSP function. This is manifestly connected with the semantics of the adverbial which disposes it to operate as a specification. Compare (37).

(37) a. Everywhere there were clusters of dry droppings. (Adams, 15)
    b. There were clusters of dry droppings everywhere.

If placed finally, the adverbial acquires the function of a specification and constitutes the rheme proper, cf. (37) b.

The importance of the semantics of the adverbial is shown by the following example which contains a final adverbial whose rhematic function is reinforced by a focalizer:

(38) At this height there was no risk of prying eyes even from the top desks of buses. (James OS, 340)

Without the focalizer, in written language the FSP function of the final adverbial would be ambiguous. In speech, the ambiguity would be resolved by intonation.

Example (37) b. in itself does not disprove the defining features of the notional subject in the existential construction, viz. its context independence, and hence its rhematic function. In fact the most dynamic element is frequently not the subject itself, but its postmodification. Characteristically, notional subjects in existential constructions are expanded; there is then an extensive rhematic part, introduced by the head of the subject construction, as in (34) a. and d., (35) a., and (39).

(39) But there was a second bout of worship to be got through. (Fowles, 54)

However, modification does not constitute a separate FSP unit but operates within the FSP function of its head. As regards existential constructions with final rhematic adverbials, their FSP structure is similar to that of existential sentences with final postmodification of the notional subject as long as the notional subject is context independent. The only difference concerns the composition of the rhematic part which includes two FSP units instead of one, as in (37) b.

However, a question arises how to regard the FSP structure of existential constructions whose notional subject is context dependent; in particular whether the communication is perspectived away from the subject, as in (40) b. in contrast to (40) a.

(40) a. A girl entered the room.
     b. The girl entered the room. (Firbas 1966)

This question presents itself in both the bare existential and the existential locative sentences. Confining ourselves to the latter case, let us consider (41).

(41) a. There is a restaurant on the top floor.
     b. On the top floor there is a restaurant.
     c. nejhořejším poschodí je restaurace.
         [On top floor is restaurant]

According to the context, the notional subject can be introduced into discourse for the first time, e.g. when describing the building and the services offered on the top floor. Only in this case can the adverbial be placed initially (cf. (41) b.). In Czech, this is reflected in word order, cf. (41) c.

However, in answer to the question *Is there a restaurant in the building?*, which asks about the existence of an object in a particular place, the object is introduced in the question, and can thus be regarded as context dependent.

(42) Is there a restaurant in the building?
     There is a restaurant on the top floor.
     Restaurace je v nejhořejším poschodí.
     [Restaurant is on top floor]

The answer responds to two points: it asserts the existence of the object and specifies its location. In respect of asserting the existence the Czech equivalent is defective because it answers only the part about the location and might also be used in answer to *On which floor is the restaurant*: the existence of the restaurant in the Czech answer is presupposed, and hence presented as given. The Czech sentence is locative, not existential-locative.

The existential construction in answer to the question in (42) may be replaced by a non-existential form, cf. (43).

(43) Is there a restaurant in the building?
    a. There is a restaurant on the top floor.
    b. A restaurant is on the top floor

In the literature, the pair of sentences illustrated by this example is mostly discussed from the viewpoint of semantic and/or pragmatic constraints which may rule out the non-existential form (Grzegorek 1984: 79–80; Huddleston and Pullum 2002: 1396–1397). The semantic restrictions mainly concern abstract entities, as in (44).

(44) a. There's plenty of room on the top shelf.
    b. *Plenty of room is on the top shelf. (Huddleston and Pullum 2002: 1397)

However, even physical entities may block the non-existential use, cf. (46).

(45) a. There is one performance at noon.
    b. One performance is at noon. (*ibid.*)
(46) a. There is a fireworks display tonight.
    b. *A fireworks display is tonight. (*ibid.*)

As pointed out by Huddleston and Pullum (2002: 1397), the acceptability of the non-existential form requires connection to prior discourse. In terms of FSP, the subject must be context dependent. Accordingly, ex. (45) b. represents an instance illustrated by ex. (43), whereas (46) b. is a case of (41). What is pragmatically determined is the likelihood of a previous, connection-establishing context. Ex. (46) b. is unacceptable because it does not contain any indication of being connected to prior discourse.

From what has been said it follows that existential and non-existential forms are not synonymous: the former asserts the existence of an object in a location, whereas the latter asserts the location of an object which has some relationship to previous discourse. The FSP of the non-existential form is straightforward: the subject is thematic and the final adverbial is the rheme. All the three factors operating in written language act here in the same direction: semantic structure (viz. a quality scale, or rather a combined scale with telescoped phenomenon and quality-bearer function, cf. Firbas 1992: 66–67), context dependence and linearity.

In the case of the existential sentence the situation is more involved inasmuch as the semantic structure still implements the presentation scale, but previous mention of the phenomenon whose existence is being established flouts the requirement of context independence. The contextual factor being as a rule hierarchically superordinate, the question arises whether the existential construction is an exception or is subject to the customary interplay of the two factors. Explicitly, is the notional subject a component of the rheme or is it thematic? If the latter, the sentence must be interpreted as a quality scale, i.e. not as presenting a phenomenon, but as assigning a feature to it, in this case localization at a particular place. However, this interpretation is flouted by the semantic structure. On the other hand if the sentence is a presentation scale, the notional subject must be a component of the rheme. An argument in favour of this interpretation may be found in discerning a feature in which the referents of *restaurant* in the question and the answer differ. In other words the objects denominated by the subject noun phrase in the question and in the answer are not identical: in the question, *restaurant* is used in the categorial sense, the indefinite article being non-specific. There is no existential presupposition: there may be no restaurant in the place. On the other hand, the indefinite article in the answer is specific, in referring to a particular, though unspecified object.

This is demonstrated if the answer responds to each of the points of the inquiry separately (note that we cannot ask about existence and location at the same time: *Where is there a restaurant in the building?*):

(47) Is there a restaurant in the building?
    a. Yes, there is a restaurant in the building. It is on the top floor.
    b. Yes, there is one. It is on the top floor.
    c. Yes, there is. (It is) on the top floor.
    d. Yes, on the top floor.

In the last form the stages indicated in a., b., c. are ellipted but unequivocally implied. An argument in favour of context dependence as hierarchically superordinate to syntactic and semantic structure can be adduced from Firbas's conception of the presentation scale, including realization forms implemented by the passive. However, the problem can hardly be resolved without taking into account bare existentials, which were not included for lack of data. At this point, the question of the FSP structure of the case illustrated by (42) can only be answered tentatively to the effect that the rheme includes, apart from the adverbial specification, the polarity of the verb asserting the existence of the object, as shown by (47). As for the notional subject, the elliptical, as well as the pronominal form indicate thematic function.

4. What has been added to the findings of Mathesius and Firbas is far from exhaustive and calls for further study. All three points promise further findings from taking into account textual aspects; in the case of the passive with an expressed *by*-agent a line of further study that presents itself is the potential overlap with the *it*-cleft; the FSP structure of the existential construction, including both existential-locative and bare existential sentences, may be insightfully illuminated by a contrastive approach, with respect to the reflection of context dependence in the free Czech word order. The contrastive approach promises worthwhile findings in general, especially when based on parallel texts. However, the point which I have attempted to make in this chapter is that without the early insights of the two scholars whose work has inspired the foregoing reflections we might still be puzzling over some of the essential points whose nature they had revealed.

SOURCES

Adams, R. *Watership Down.* Harmondsworth: Penguin Books, 1974.

Fowles, J. *The French Lieutenant's Woman.* London: Triad–Granada, 1983 (1st ed. 1969).

James, P. D. *Original Sin* (OS). London: Faber and Faber, 1994.

James, P. D. *An Unsuitable Job for a Woman* (UJ). New York: Warner, 1972.

Lyons, J., R. Coates, M. D., and G. Gazdar (eds) *New Horizons in Linguistics* 2. Harmondsworth: Penguin Books, 1987.

Raverat, G. *Period Piece.* London: Faber and Faber, 1952.

Winchester, S. *The Surgeon of Crowthorne.* London: Penguin Books, 1999.

10. BASIC DISTRIBUTION OF COMMUNICATIVE DYNAMISM VS. NONLINEAR INDICATION OF FUNCTIONAL SENTENCE PERSPECTIVE

First published in E. Hajičová, T. Hoskovec, O. Leška, P. Sgall, and Z. Skoumalová (eds), *Travaux du Cercle Linguistic de Prague* n. s. *Prague Linguistic Circle Papers*, Vol. 3, Amsterdam: John Benjamins Publishing Company, 1999, 249–261.

0. This chapter is concerned with the interaction of two word order principles, the grammatical and functional sentence perspective (FSP). The respective hierarchic status of the two word order principles was first examined by Mathesius (1929, 1975: 153–160), who by comparing English and Czech revealed an essential difference in that English word order primarily serves to indicate grammatical relationships, whereas Czech word order is primarily governed by FSP. By functional sentence perspective is meant the distribution of information, or degrees of communicative dynamism (CD), over the elements of a sentence. Here a general principle is found in a gradual increase in CD, culminating in end focus (Quirk et al. 1985: 1356–57). Where the sentence structure is consistent with this gradual increase in CD, i.e. where the least dynamic element, the theme, occurs initially, and the most dynamic element, the rheme, or focus, is found at the end, with transitional elements coming in between, we speak of basic distribution of communicative dynamism (Firbas 1992: 10).

1. The following discussion concentrates on different types of interaction between grammatical word order and the principle of FSP as they appear in English. Attention is paid to the following types:

First, instances displaying both grammatical word order and basic distribution of CD.

Secondly, instances with deviations from grammatical word order traceable to the principle of FSP, i.e. word order arrangements in which the grammatical word order principle is overriden by the principle of end focus.

Thirdly, deviations from the basic distribution of CD due to the grammatical principle; here indication of FSP is to be sought in non-linear devices.

Finally, instances with basic distribution of CD achieved by means of special syntactic constructions. These constructions are considered with respect to whether they are complementary or interchangeable, and, in the latter case, with respect to which factors influence the choice.

These points were investigated in three samples of contemporary fiction (see Sources), each providing 500 clauses taken from continuous text, i.e. a total of 1 500 clauses. To obtain a textually homogeneous sort, attention was paid only to the authors' monologues, whereas direct speech was left out. The exclusion of direct speech was moreover motivated by the fact that spoken language involves intonation as one of the means indicating FSP. In written language, on the other hand, intonation largely operates as a concomitant feature of an FSP structure indicated by other means. Accordingly, FSP was determined on the basis of syntactico-semantic structure, contextual boundness and linear arrangement (Firbas 1992; Sgall, Hajičová and Panevová 1986).

An FSP analysis was carried out on the level of clauses, mostly finite, but nonfinite and verbless clauses were also included, provided they contained complementation or modification. The selection of communicative fields constituted by clauses appears to be justified by the fact that it is in clauses that different word order arrangements are primarily revealed. For this reason the higher communicative fields of complex sentences, as well as the communicative subfields of phrases (cf. Svoboda 1987) were left aside.

1.1 The first point involves clauses displaying both grammatical word order and basic distribution of CD. By grammatical word order are meant not only word order arrangements in which position is the primary indicator of syntactic function, but also arrangements which are customary: S—V—O—Adv(s), S—V—Cs—Adv(s), S—V—O—Co—Adv(s),[1] etc.

A problem was presented by adverbials insofar as their position in a sentence is relatively free, and subject to their degree of CD. Yet even adverbials tend to occur in certain positions, and this tendency may act counter to their degree of CD. These instances are treated in section 3 as deviations from the principle of FSP, due to the operation of the grammatical word order principle; this principle here represents the more customary, albeit not obligatory, order. Where adverbials occur in positions consistent with their degree of CD, they are included, together with examples without adverbials, under the respective type. This notably applies to initial adverbials (120 instances, i.e. 8 % of the total) and adverbials in mid-position.

Basic distribution of CD is conceived rather broadly in that all clauses with the thematic elements in the initial part and with the rhematic elements at the end are regarded as instances of this arrangement. Whether or not the intermediate ele-

---

[1] C_S = subject complement (complementation of a copula); C_O = object complement (second complement of a transitive verb in copular relation to the object).

ments are strictly ordered according to their degree of CD or whether in the thematic section the diatheme precedes the theme proper is considered of minor importance.[2]

Bearing these limitations in mind, the first group may be characterized as follows. Clauses displaying both grammatical word order and basic distribution of CD accounted for 62.2 % of all instances (933 out of the total of 1 500 clauses). Grammatical word order, as well as basic distribution of CD, was found not only in clauses with the subject in initial position, as in (1), but also in clauses with initial object or another postverbal element, appearing in this position as a result of relativization, cf. (2). Example (3) illustrates basic distribution of CD in a clause with an initial thematic adverbial (diatheme).

(1) He was a nice funny little man. (Raverat, 121)
(2) (Benger's food,) which we called 'Uncle Richard's porridge' (Raverat, 124)[3]
(3) In this respect they are much the same as primitive people. (Adams, 28)

The relatively high percentage of clauses displaying correspondence between grammatical word order and basic distribution of CD without the use of special re-ordering devices is presumably due to the fact that most instances of this group have a simple sentence structure with only one postverbal element: S—V—Cs (1) and (3), S—V—O (4) and S—V—Adv (5).

(4) they breathed the cool air which gave the illusion of country freshness (James, 340)
(5) The gate led into the lane. (Adams, 15)

Where more than one element occurred in postverbal position, the last represents a further specification, i.e. the rheme proper cf. (6) and (7).

(6) (a smartness) which carefully combined professional competence with sexual allure (James, 349)
(7) the two rabbits went up to the board at a hopping run (Adams, 19)

1.2 Proceeding to the second group, constituted by deviations from grammatical word order traceable to the operation of FSP, we find altogether 47 instances (3.2 % of the total). These may be classified into three distinct subtypes.

---

2   For the concepts of theme proper and diatheme, see Firbas (1992: 79–81) and Svoboda (1981).
3   Where the preceding or following context is needed, it is added in brackets. All examples preserve the punctuation as found in the source, i.e. in the case of excerpts of clauses (components of sentences) they have no final punctuation mark and the first word is not capitalized.

1.2.1 Reversal of the customary order of postverbal elements, viz a prepositional object, object complement or an adverbial before direct object, or an adverbial before the subject complement, cf. (8) to (10).

(8) while the mourners pressed on him the traditional cooked ham and rich fruit cake
     (James, 343)
(9) anyone seeing this … has seen at work the Angel (which drove the first Crusade
     into Antioch) (Adams, 28–29)
(10) Mrs Pitt-Cowley looked for a moment slightly embarrassed (James, 357)

This subtype of deviant word order was the most frequent (30 instances out of 47, i.e. 63.8 %, and 2.1 % of the total).

1.2.2 Another subtype of deviant word order was found in clauses with an initial adverbial, inverted word order and final subject, cf. (11) and (12).

(11) Behind the ornaments were two coloured photographs. (James, 341)

There were altogether 12 instances of this word order arrangement, i.e. 0.8 % of the total.

1.2.3 A third subtype was constituted by instances of a fronted direct or prepositional object (5 instances, i.e. 0.3 %), cf. (12) and (13).

(12) One of these, Buckhorn, Hazel knew well. (Adams, 30)
(13) But of one thing I am certain. (Raverat, 122)

In all three subtypes the deviation is due to the principle of FSP. The final element is invariably the rheme proper. The elements preceding the rheme in (8)–(10) carry a lower degree of CD because of contextual boundness, as in (8), or owing to the semantic factor, as in (10). Apart from the operation of the principle of end focus, a contributing factor is found in the principle of end weight, as in (8) and (9).[4]

Example (11) illustrates the presentation scale (Firbas 1992: 66–69) with a contextually bound, scene-setting initial adverbial, a verb of existence on the scene, and a phenomenon being introduced on the scene, constructed as the subject in final, rhematic position.

As regards fronting, all instances are in accordance with "the function of so arranging clause order that end-focus falls on the most important part of the message as well as providing direct linkage with what has preceded." (Quirk et al. 1985: 1377)

It should be noted that in none of the subtypes of deviant word order does the particular word order arrangement interfere with the grammatical function of the elements involved. In subtype 1.2.1 the syntactic function of the transposed elements is

---

4   For the principle of end weight, see Quirk et al. (1985: 1361–62).

indicated by their forms (prepositional object, adverbial.) Subtype 1.2.2 involves an intransitive verb with only one participant, the subject, and in subtype 1.2.3 the subject is indicated by its position with respect to the verb, the syntactic function of the initial element being again signalled by its form, as in (13), and/or the valency of the verb.

The FSP structure of examples of this group suggests that the deviations are entirely due to the principle of FSP since what is achieved by each subtype of deviation is the basic distribution of CD. English here appears to display signs of free word order.

1.3 Examples of the third group, deviations from basic distribution of CD due to the operation of the grammatical principle, account for 13.8 % (207 out of the total). They again fall into three distinct subtypes.

1.3.1 First, there are clauses with a thematic object, placed in its regular postverbal position. Whether or not the object is followed by a more dynamic element, it is invariably less dynamic than the verb, and hence in the interpretative (Firbas 1992: 12), or deep, word order its position is within the thematic section. This subtype is represented by most instances of this group: 136, i.e. 65.7 % (9 % of the total). The thematic function of the object is invariably due to contextual boundness, mostly reflected in the object's pronominal form, cf. (14) and (15).

(14) The sight of this harmless vanity depressed him. (James, 342)
(15) he talked to me (as if I were quite grown up) (Raverat, 121)

Contextual boundness of thematic objects realized by nouns was indicated by anaphoric devices. Cf. (16).

(16) Surely few people could pray that prayer with any sincerity. (James, 343)

Where contextual boundness failed to be signalled by overt devices the thematic function of the object resulted from its having been mentioned in the immediately relevant preceding context, as in (17).[5]

(17) (Aunt Etty wrote to Charles ... asking him to look in the Down family Bible ...) He was not able to find the Bible at once. (Raverat, 124)

1.3.2 The next subtype comprises instances with a thematic postverbal adverbial (43, i.e. 21.7 % of this group and 2.9 % of the total). Where the thematic function of the adverbial is due to contextual boundness, this subtype is similar to 1.3.1. Cf. (18).

(18) a great deal of illness was left undiagnosed in those days (Raverat, 122)

---

5   For the concept of immediately relevant context, see Firbas (1992: 23–25).

Unlike subtype 1.3.2 there are also instances like (19) where the postverbal adverbial is not contextually bound, but whose thematic function is due to semantic structure; the adverbial operates as a setting, not as a further specification (cf. Firbas 1992: 49–59).

(19) only just to be allowed to draw a little picture sometimes (Raverat, 129)

1.3.3 The last subtype of deviation from basic distribution of CD includes instances with rhematic subject in initial position (Firbas 1966). This is one of the possible realizations of the presentation scale, in which FSP is primarily indicated by semantic structure; contextual boundness or non-boundness of a scene-setting adverbial, where present, does not play a role. This subtype is represented by 28 instances, i.e. 13.5 % of this group and 1.9 % of the total.

(20) Hundreds of letters of Grandmamma's exist, and hundreds of Aunt Etty's (Raverat, 121)
(21) and a tiny, frail figure, in a red dressing-gown and a white shawl, appeared at the end of my bed (Raverat, 133)
(22) a kind of telepathic feeling has to flow through them (Adams, 28)
(23) Roosting birds rustled overhead (Adams, 34)
(24) here and there a dead twig fell (Adams, 34)

All instances contain a context-independent subject, and a verb of appearance or existence on the scene (or a verb implying this meaning), which is less dynamic than the context-independent subject. Example (20) illustrates a presentation scale without a scene-setting adverbial, in (21) and (22) the scene-setting adverbial is contextually bound, whereas in (23) and (24) it is not, its thematic function being due to the semantic factor. Whether the thematic adverbial occurs in initial position, as in (24), or finally, as in (21), (22) and (23), its FSP function remains the same. On the whole, final placement of a scene-setting adverbial appears to be the more common (10 as against 3 instances). In this case there is a complete reversal of the basic distribution of CD, viz R—Tr—T. The deviation is thus the most pronounced. On the other hand where the scene-setting adverbial is placed initially, at least the placement of the theme is in agreement with the basic distribution (T—R—Tr).

2. The last group of examples includes clauses with special devices serving to change the order of elements in the underlying, simpler structure. Among these devices, the passive ranks the highest (127 instances, i.e. 8.5 % of the total). All the other devices had much lower frequencies of occurrence: existential construction 39 (2.6 %), extraposition 15 (1.0 %), cleft sentence 13 (0.9 %), tough movement and right dislocation 2 (0.1 %) and 1 (0.06 %), respectively. Also included were clauses with subjects of a semantically adverbial nature since these elements can also be constructed as adverbials, which usually involves a different sentence position (9 instances, i.e. 0.6 %).

2.1 As shown in Chapter 9, the passive is a major device serving to achieve final placement of the rheme and preverbal placement of the theme. In all but three instances the subject, i.e. the object of the corresponding active clause, is thematic, and it is by means of the passive that the preverbal position of this element is achieved. Where the agent is expressed (in the form of *by*-agent or quasi-agent in postverbal position: 50 instances, i.e. 39 % of the passive clauses), it is invariably rhematic, cf. (25).

(25) But her interest was never tinged by self-pity. (Raverat, 123)

In agentless clauses with the verb as the final element, the rheme is constituted by the verb, as in (26).

(26) A little way in front of them, the ground had been freshly disturbed. (Adams, 18)

Deviations from grammatical word order in passive clauses (three instances of thematic adverbials in postverbal position, as in (27)) do not interfere with the function of the passive on the FSP level insofar as the passive involves only the participants in verbal action.

(27) this was accepted between them (Adams, 18)

Of more importance in considering the function of the passive in the FSP structure is the occurrence of the three rhematic subjects, cf. (28)–(30).

(28) Near one of the posts, a hammer and a few nails had been left behind. (Adams, 18)
(29) If the truth must be told (still now, in my dreams at night, I am generally a young man). (Raverat, 129)
(30) But some attempt, even if misguided, had been made to make the room inviting. (James, 344)

Here the use of the passive results in a deviation from the basic distribution of CD, whereas the corresponding active is in agreement with it. All three examples contain a context-independent subject which would stand in postverbal position in the active. All are instances of the presentation scale with a passive verb (cf. Chapter 9). Example (30) moreover illustrates discontinuous infinitival postmodification by means of which the most dynamic component of the thematic subject, the postmodifier, achieves final placement (cf. Dušková 1995). An explanation of these counter-examples of the function of the passive in FSP may be sought in the primary function of the passive, viz. the suppression of the agent.

2.2 The existential construction is one of the realizations of the presentation scale (cf. Chapter 9) in which existential *there* in the subject position serves to achieve postverbal placement of the notional, rhematic subject. In this respect, it contributes to the basic distribution of CD. Where the clause also contains an adverbial, its function in the presentation scale is to set the scene, i.e. it is thematic. Nevertheless, scene-setting adverbials are mostly found in final position (16 final as against 9 initial adverbials). With one exception, where the final adverbial is given prominence by means of a focalizer, all final adverbials are thematic. Hence the existential construction here deviates from the basic distribution of CD in having the diatheme after the rheme, cf. (31). Where the scene-setting adverbial occurs initially, as in (32), the clause displays basic distribution of CD. Example (33) shows that where the final adverbial belongs to the rheme, it has to be reinforced by a focalizer.

(31) there is some strain of the Woodhouses of Hartfield in us (Raverat, 122)
(32) everywhere there were clusters of dry droppings (Adams, 15)
(33) At this height there was no risk of prying eyes even from the top desks of buses (James, 340)

2.3 Of the remaining devices, which have all too low frequencies of occurrence to allow generalizations, mention should be made of the subject construction of an adverbial element because it may provide an alternative for the expression of the presentation scale (see section 4). It is characterized by basic distribution of CD in having the theme at the beginning and the rheme at the end, cf. (34) and (35).

(34) A few seconds brought him to the oak (Adams, 35)
(35) (the roll-top desk) which held her portable typewriter (James, 341)

Owing to its adverbial semantics the element constituting the subject can also be constructed as an adverbial:

(34)'In a few seconds he came to the oak.
(35)'in which she kept her portable typewriter

3. Apart from the groups discussed so far, there was a small number of instances (2.2 %) whose FSP structure did not lend itself to unambiguous interpretation. The difficulty in assigning an FSP function to a clause element was mostly due to an uncertainty about the degree of contextual boundness. Thus in (36) the rheme proper is probably the object since it contrasts with *her house and husband* in the preceding context, but climax on the final prepositional phrase is also conceivable (in dependence on whether or not *manage* implies success).

(36) (she had nothing on which to spend her ... energy except the management of her house and husband;) and she could have ruled a kingdom with success. (Raverat, 123)

Examples of this kind were left out of account. So were four other constructions on account of involving special problems of different kinds: clauses with transitive phrasal verbs (29 instances; 1.9 %) and with ditransitive verbs (21 instances; 1.4 %) since they allow variable position of object / particle and indirect object / direct object, respectively; clauses containing lexical focalizers (14 instances; 0.9 %); and clauses with ellipted predication or predicate (10 instances; 0.7 %).

4. The last point to be discussed is the mutual relationship between the different types of word order arrangements and reordering devices.

Most of the subtypes treated in sections 1–3 appear to be complementary rather than interchangeable.

Subtype 1.2.1 (reversal of the customary order of postverbal elements) has an alternative only where the final element has no postmodification. In (8) and (10) the reversed postverbal elements can be reordered in accordance with the grammatical principle without a change in FSP:

(8)′ while the mourners pressed the traditional cooked ham and rich fruit cake on him
(10)′Mrs Pitt-Cowley looked slightly embarrassed for a moment

Example (9), however, offers no such alternative.

Subtype 1.2.2 (initial adverbial—verb—subject) alternates with the existential *there* construction. Another alternative may occasionally be found in subtype 2.3. As shown by (37), these variants may be used as a stylistic device.

(37) In the top drawer of the desk there was a file labelled investments ... In another file was a copy of her will ... Another file contained papers relating to her divorce fifteen years earlier. (James, 347)

Replacement by subtype 1.3.3 (rhematic subject—verb of appearance or existence on the scene—scene-setting adverbial) is ruled out in the case of *be* insofar as the presentation structure changes into locative, cf. (11) and (11′).

(11)′ Two coloured photographs were behind the ornaments.

Subtype 1.2.3 (fronting) theoretically suggests the passive as an alternative. However, where passivization is possible, as in (12), it results in a different FSP structure. While a fronted object acquires a certain degree of prominence (its FSP function being that of the diatheme, i.e. the most dynamic element within the thematic section), the subject of the passive is usually the theme proper (the least dynamic element of the thematic section). Other constraints arise from the necessity to express the agent.

As regards subtype 1.3.1 (thematic objects), again the passive suggests itself as an alternative, and indeed, passivization is often possible, as in (14) and (16):

(14)' He was depressed by the sight of this harmless vanity.
(16)' Surely that prayer could be prayed by few people with any sincerity.

However, where the subject of the passive is a personal pronoun, as is often the case, passivization is unlikely since personal pronouns rarely transform into *by*-agents, and omission of the agent is usually ruled out for semantic reasons. Moreover, the passive again displays a somewhat different FSP structure, which may be a textual misfit (in (14)' the connective function of the subject is lost in the passive).

Type 1.3.2 (thematic postverbal adverbials) coincides with type 1.2.1 where the reversal of the customary order of postverbal elements involves an adverbial. The relative frequencies of occurrence of the two subtypes indicate a preponderance of the grammatical word order (43 instances as against 30, the latter including not only adverbials but also prepositional objects and object complements).

Subtype 1.3.3 (the presentation scale) where it includes a locative adverbial may alternate with subtype 1.2.2 (adverbial—verb—subject), e.g. (21) is conceivable in the form of (21)'.

(21)' At the end of my bed appeared a tiny, frail figure in a red dressing-gown with a white shawl.

As shown by (37), different forms of the presentation scale (cf. Chapter 12) are found to co-occur for stylistic variation. Of the other types under discussion, alternative forms were found in some instances of the passive.

5. The points emerging from the foregoing discussion may be summed up as follows.

In most instances the interaction of the two major word order principles, the grammatical and FSP, appears to be cooperative, i.e. grammatical word order is in agreement with basic distribution of CD.

Where the two principles act counter to each other, English on the one hand resorts to special devices whereby the conflict is resolved (as in the case of the passive, 9%), or more or less resolved (in the existential construction, 2.6%). On the other hand, in about 17% of all instances the conflict between the two word order principles remains unresolved. While deviations from the basic distribution of CD account for 13.8%, deviations from grammatical word order represent only 3.2%. The preponderance of deviations from basic distribution of CD shows the importance of non-linear means for indicating the FSP structure.

The different types and devices that have been discussed largely show a complementary distribution. Where alternative structures are available, they appear to serve as a stylistic device for varying the expression of the same semantic content.

SOURCES

Adams, R. *Watership Down.* Harmondsworth: Penguin Books, 1974.
James, P. D. *Original Sin*. London: Faber and Faber, 1994.
Raverat, G. *Period Piece.* London: Faber and Faber, 1952.

11. SYNONYMY VS. DIFFERENTIATION OF VARIANT SYNTACTIC REALIZATIONS OF FSP FUNCTIONS

First published in Hajičová, E., P. Sgall, J. Hana, and T. Hoskovec (eds), *Travaux du Cercle Linguistic de Prague* n. s. *Prague Linguistic Circle Papers*, Vol. 4, Amsterdam: John Benjamins Publishing Company, 2002, 251–261.

0. This chapter deals with the second participant in verbal action as it appears on the syntactic level and the level of functional sentence perspective (FSP).[1] The interaction between the two levels will be considered where the second participant in verbal action has the FSP function of theme.[2] This involves contextual boundness[3] of the second participant insofar as context-independent second participants are as a rule rhematic.[4] The constructions under consideration include the passive, in which a thematic second participant appears as the subject, active clauses with the second participant as thematic object occupying the regular postverbal position, and active clauses with the second participant constructed as fronted object. Fronted objects moreover raise the question of their relation to the passive, and the cleft sentence in which the second participant appearing as thematic object in the underlying non-cleft form is focused.

The aim of this chapter is to find out to what extent these structures are interchangeable, and if differentiated, to ascertain the features to which the differentiation is due.

---

1 Functional sentence perspective is defined as the distribution of degrees of communicative dynamism (CD) over the elements of a sentence. In written language it is determined by the interplay of three factors, linear modification, semantic structure, and contextual boundness (Firbas 1992: 10–11).

2 In the Prague school treatment of FSP, the theme and the rheme are defined as elements carrying, respectively, a low and a high degree of CD (Firbas 1992: 72–3).

3 Contextual boundness means retrievability of information from the (immediately relevant) preceding context (Firbas 1992: 11).

4 Cf. Firbas's discussion of context-independent objects (1992: 42 if.).

1. The following discussion is based on an analysis of three samples of contemporary fiction (see *Sources*), each providing 500 clauses taken from continuous text, i.e. a total of 1,500 clauses. To eliminate textual diversity, attention was paid only to the authors' monologue, i.e. direct speech was excluded on the ground of the differences between monologue and dialogue on the one hand, and the different role of intonation in speech and writing on the other. In written language the function of intonation as an indicator of FSP is of minor importance insofar as in this medium intonation largely constitutes a concomitant feature of an FSP structure primarily indicated by other means, viz. contextual boundness, syntactico-semantic structure and linear arrangement (Firbas 1992: 10–11, 115; Sgall et al. 1986: 3.10–3.13). In addition, since some of the structures under discussion are not sufficiently represented by the examples excerpted from the three novels, exemplification also includes instances collected variously from other fiction.

1.1 A major syntactic realization of the second participant with the FSP function of theme is found in the passive.

1.1.1 The passive (cf. also the two preceding chapters) is usually described as a device serving to achieve basic distribution of communicative dynamism (CD).[5] This capacity of the passive partly results from the fact that the subject, the second participant, has the FSP function of theme. Equally important is the postverbal section of a passive clause, which usually contains the rheme. In studies of the FSP role of the passive the function of the rheme is mostly described in connection with the *by*-agent (cf. Dušková 1971), the first participant in verbal action, as in (1).

(1) British art has constantly been changed and enriched by contact with European art.

However, the function of the rheme in a passive clause is not confined to the *by*-agent. The rheme can be realized by any context-independent postverbal element, except scene-setting adverbials. In (2) the postverbal adverbial is an adjunct of purpose, in (3) an adjunct of manner, and in (4) the object of a ditransitive passive verb.

(2) The sacrifice has been made for nothing.
(3) The family were now seen to advantage.
(4) We may yet be spared undue publicity.

---

5   Communicative dynamism (CD) is defined as "the relative extent to which a linguistic element contributes towards the further development of the communication" (Firbas 1992: 8); the degree of CD corresponds to "the variation in communicative value" in Quirk et al. (1985: 1356); the degree of CD is also referred to as the information load, or newsworthiness, of a linguistic element in a sentence. By basic distribution of CD is meant a linear arrangement which displays a gradual rise in CD (Firbas 1992: 10), i.e. the order Theme-Transition-Rheme. Basic distribution of CD is comparable to the principle of end focus as presented in Quirk et al. (1985: 1356–57); cf. also the concept of systemic ordering of context-independent participants and circumstants in Sgall et al. (1986: 194–96).

Scene-setting adverbials,[6] whether contextually bound or not, are thematic, as in active clauses, cf. the contextually bound adverbial prepositional phrase in (5) and the context independent temporal setting in (6).

(5) This was accepted between them. (Adams, 18)
(6) He got stuck in the underground last Monday.

In the absence of postverbal elements, the rheme is usually the verb, as in (7).

(7) All our good intentions were forgotten.

Statistical counts (Dušková 1971; Hedviková 1996) show that passives with *by*-agents or quasi-agents[7] almost invariably display the basic distribution of CD, and on this ground the passive is described as a special device of FSP (cf. Mathesius 1975: 101): it serves to rearrange the information structure of the corresponding active clause containing a context-independent subject and a contextually bound object so as to achieve basic distribution of CD.

1.1.2 However, as shown by (8), passives with a thematic *by*-agent are not entirely ruled out.

(8) I am so terribly upset by all this.

Here the *by*-agent is contextually bound and the rheme is constituted by the verb with its intensification. Two points should be noted in this case: first, it is an example taken from speech, which ensures recourse to intonation. And secondly, *upset* is one of the attitudinal verbs which are found more frequently in the passive than in the active, the passive being moreover stative, which endows it with adjectival features.

Another counterexample to the FSP function of the passive is provided by passives with rhematic subjects. Admittedly, they are rare (3 examples out of 127, i.e. 2.4% in my material). A passive clause with a rhematic subject is illustrated by (9).

(9) Near one of the posts, a hammer and a few nails had been left behind. (Adams, 19)

The rhematic function of the subject is due not only to its context-independence, but also to the semantics of the verb, which implies existence/appearance on the scene, and to contextual boundness of the adverbial element. That is, the passive in this case implements the presentation scale.[8]

---

6   Cf. Firbas's setting (1992: 49 ff.).
7   Agents taking lexically determined prepositions other than *by* (*be worried about, interested in*, etc.), cf. (Svart-vik 1966: 102–4).
8   For the concept of the presentation scale, see Firbas (1992: 66–67). This scale typically contains an active intransitive verb of appearance or existence on the scene with the first participant constituting the rheme. The different syntactic forms of the presentation scale and their differentiation are treated in the next chapter.

1.1.3 The FSP function of the passive is also demonstrated by the passive of ditransitive verbs, which normally serves to achieve basic distribution of CD: whichever object in the active is less dynamic becomes the subject of the passive, the more dynamic object preserving its object function, as in (4) and (10).

(10) The ring was left to the eldest daughter.

In (4) the theme is the indirect object of the active, whereas in (10) the theme is constituted by the direct object of the active. However, as shown by (11), this is not always the case.

(11) Strength was given this opposing theory by the meteorological report stating the velocity of the wind.

Here the only contextually bound element is the indirect object, which could be constructed as the subject. The context independent subject (direct object of the active) would then stand in postverbal position before the rheme proper,[9] implemented by the *by*-agent. Cf. (11)'.

(11)' This opposing theory was given strength by the meteorological report stating the velocity of the wind.

A context independent subject in a sentence perspectived to the postverbal part as a rule operates as the diatheme, the most dynamic component of the thematic section. In (11), however, the subject is in fact a component of the predicate, which is here verbo-nominal, cf. *give strength / strengthen*. Accordingly, it is a component of the non-thematic section.

1.2 Since one of the FSP functions of the passive is to achieve initial placement of a thematic element, the object of the corresponding active, it is legitimate to inquire into active clauses with thematic objects, and consider them with respect to passivization. Statistical data from the excerpted material (1,500 clauses) show these two realization structures to be about equally frequent: the passive was represented by 127 and the active with thematic objects by 136 instances, i.e. 8.5% and 9%, respectively. Expectedly, not all active clauses containing a transitive verb and an object lend themselves to passivization. Apart from structural and semantic restrictions, a constraint arises from the FSP structure itself. Significantly, an active clause with a thematic object passivizes primarily where the subject is the rheme. In most active clauses with a thematic object, however, the subject is also contextually bound, often operating as the theme proper.[10] This is reflected in its realization form: half of the subjects of finite clauses with thematic objects are personal pronouns (45 out of 89). On the other hand,

---

9   The most dynamic element in the rhematic section (cf. Firbas, 1992:71–2).
10   The least dynamic element in the thematic section (cf. Firbas, 1992: 80–81, and Svoboda, 1983).

the rare instances of thematic *by*-agents display substantival realization forms, often with modification, which indicates their diathematic function, cf. examples (5) a., (9) a. and (10) in Chapter 9. Accordingly, passivization of clauses containing pronominal thematic subjects and thematic objects appears to be applicable only if the agent can be suppressed, which is usually ruled out by the semantic relevance of the agent. Hence passivization of sentences like (12) and (13), which require expression of the agent, is conceivable only under special contextual conditions.

(12) he greeted them politely[11] (Adams, 23)
(12)' they were greeted politely by him
(13) they followed us all the same (Raverat, 129)
(13)' we were followed by them all the same

　　Passivization is even less likely where the subject is pronominal and the object, though contextually bound, is a noun phrase, the rheme being constituted by a final adverbial, as in (14).

(14) She was evaluating the interview in the light of subsequent events. (James, 352)
(14)' The interview was being evaluated by her in the light of subsequent events.

　　On the other hand, passivization is more feasible where the subject, though contextually bound, is a noun phrase and the object a personal pronoun. It is again the verb that constitutes the rheme, but the subject is diathematic, i.e. it is more dynamic than the object, as in (15).

(15) Her initial testiness had surprised him (James, 350)
(15)' He was surprised by her initial testiness.

　　While (15)' is presumably more acceptable than either (13)' or (14)', owing to the respective forms of realization of the first and the second participant, (16) (cf. (7) a. and b. in Chapter 9) demonstrates an even more important aspect, which presumably also asserts itself in the preceding examples of this group (12)–(15).

(16) ["Are you all right, Blackie? I mean, do you want someone to go home with you?"][12]
　　　The thought appalled Blackie. (James, 195)

　　The action noun realizing the subject resumes the content expressed by the immediately preceding clause, whereas the object refers to an element further to the left in the text. Both noun phrases are again contextually bound, and their form of re-

---

11   The examples preserve the punctuation as found in the source, i.e. where the excerpt is a medial clause of a
　　　sentence it has no final punctuation mark and the first word is not capitalized.
12   The context is added in square brackets.

alization is equally weighty. Their respective positions in the sentence appear to be due to the position of the sentence in the text, specifically to the linear order of their antecedents.

It may be concluded that active clauses with thematic objects do not quality as alternative realization forms of passive clauses with expressed *by*-agent insofar as they lack the second relevant feature of transitive active clauses disposed to passivization, viz. a rhematic subject. Even in the case of the most likely candidates for interchangeability illustrated by (15) and (16), the choice between the two structures is subject to textual factors.

1.3 Although the regular position of thematic objects appears to be postverbal, there are also thematic objects in initial position, as a result of fronting. These should again be considered with respect to passivization, and obviously also with respect to postverbal thematic objects.

Fronted objects are not only thematic, but also rhematic. These two structures should be distinguished because they are motivated by different factors. Consider (17) and (18).

(17) a. [Pen would have liked to have been present at the rendezvous,] but this offer Piers declined.
   b. [A.: "I am the most selfish creature alive. I never do anything to please anyone but myself."]
   B.: "That I know to be untrue."
   c. [A.: "There are things in my life you don't know anything about."
   B.: "Good God, I should hope there were! I've only known you for a month."]
   A.: "And some of them you wouldn't like."
(18) a. Wonderful memory your grandmother has, Miss Smith.
   b. Damn silly names these horses have!
   c. A lot of trust I get around this house, don't I?

Whereas the examples under (17) illustrate fronted objects that are thematic, the preceding context showing them to be contextually bound, the examples in (18) contain context-independent objects constituting the rheme. Both structures are variants of postverbal objects, as illustrated by (17') and (18').

(17)' a. … but Piers declined this offer.
    b. … I know that to be untrue.
    c. … And you wouldn't like some of them.
(18)' a. Your grandmother has a wonderful memory, Miss Smith.
    b. These horses have damn silly names!
    c. I get a lot of trust around this house, don't I?

Neither in (17)' nor in (18)' does the change in the position of the object affect the FSP function of the object. The factor determining the FSP function of the object regardless of its position is its contextual boundness in (17): accordingly, it is thematic; and the context-independence in (18): it is hence the rheme. Fronted objects represent a marked variant which shares one feature in both instances, viz. initial placement makes both thematic and rhematic objects more prominent. Otherwise, the markedness of the two types is of a different kind.

Fronting of a thematic object not only makes the object more prominent, but also allows the rheme to occupy the final position. It thus contributes to basic distribution of CD. At the same time it also serves as a connective link with what precedes—this is amply demostrated in all three examples under (17). Fronted thematic objects thus have not only intrasentential, but also suprasentential function, as a means of cohesion.

A fronted rhematic object, on the other hand, has only intrasentential function. Initial placement makes it not only more emphatic than it would be in its regular postverbal position, but also indicates emotive colouring, expression of an attitude. The emotive aspect of a fronted rhematic object manifests itself in concomitant features such as intensifying imprecations (*damn*), and irony (in (18) c.) *a lot* is used in the opposite sense). Unlike fronting of a thematic object, fronting of a rhematic object results in a deviation from the basic distribution of CD, viz. the rheme precedes the theme. This again testifies to the emotive nature of fronted rhematic objects.

Evidently, it is only the fronted thematic objects that can be considered as a variant of passive structures, and of thematic objects in postverbal position.

As regards the relation between the passive and an active clause with a fronted thematic object, part of what has been said about thematic objects in postverbal position applies even here. The subject is again thematic, but in contrast to clauses with postverbal thematic objects in which it can constitute either the theme proper or the diatheme, with a fronted thematic object it can only serve as the theme proper since the diatheme is implemented by to the fronted object. Apart from the constraints imposed on passivization by the necessity to express the agent, whose FSP function is different in active clauses with thematic objects and in clauses underlying the passives with a *by*-agent, there is also a difference in the FSP function of the fronted thematic object and that of the subject of the passive. As has been pointed out, fronted objects are diathematic, whereas the subject in the passive largely constitutes the theme proper. Accordingly, active clauses with fronted thematic objects do not appear to provide a variant of the FSP structure of the passive.

Nor do sentences with fronted thematic objects provide a variant of active clauses with postverbal thematic objects. As has been noted, fronted thematic objects have a distinctly cohesive function. In contrast to other contextually bound elements, which are also inherently cohesive, the cohesive function of fronted thematic objects consists in "providing direct linkage with what has preceded" (Quirk et al. 1985: 1377).

1.4 Fronted object should also be considered in respect of its relation to the cleft sentence since both fronting and the cleft sentence serve to give prominence to a clause element. As appears from previous studies of the cleft constructions (Dušková 1993; Dvořáková 1988; cf. also Chapter 9, 2.2), *it*-clefts focus both thematic and rhematic elements of the underlying non-cleft clause. In view of the point under discussion, only *it*-clefts focusing thematic elements will be taken into account.

Focusing an element that is thematic in the underlying non-cleft sentence appears to be the primary function of *it*-clefts. Specifically, *it*-clefts most frequently highlight the subject (almost 50%, see Dvořáková 1988: 35–46) and scene-setting adverbials (30%), i.e. elements which appear initially and are mostly context-dependent. Focused objects are the least frequent of the three syntactic functions: they account for 21%. Though thematic in the underlying non-cleft sentence, in the *it*-cleft all these elements operate as the rheme, since the subordinate clause of the *it*-cleft typically presents its content as known, and hence presupposed. Considering these facts, as well as the fact that fronted objects constitute the FSP function of diatheme, not that of the rheme, interchangeability of a fronted thematic object and an object focused by means of an *it*-cleft appears to be unlikely. This is confirmed by the cleft forms of example (17): (17)' a.–c.

(17)' a. Pen would have liked to be present at the rendevous, * but it was this offer that Piers declined.
  b. A: I am the most selfish creature alive. I never do anything to please anyone but myself.
      B: *It is that which I know to be untrue.
  c. A: There are things in my life you don't know anything about.
      B: Good God, I should hope there were! I've only known you for a month!
      A: *And it is some of them that you wouldn't like.

As indicated by the asterisks, the cleft forms are textual misfits. The reason is to be sought in the differences in the FSP structure between the forms with fronted object and the *it*-clefts. In (17) the fronted object constitutes the diatheme, whereas the rheme is implemented by the verb in a. and c, and the object complement in b. On the other hand, in the cleft forms (17'a–c) the diathematic element of the underlying structure becomes the rheme, and the rheme of the underlying structure is backgrounded in the subordinate clause, which presents it as known. Moreover, the cleft constructions involve certain presuppositions which are absent in the particular contexts, and the absence of the presuppositions is reflected in the forms with fronted objects. Thus the cleft form (17'a) presupposes that Piers declined some offer, and the only point in question is which offer. On the other hand the only presupposition of (17a) is that an offer had been made. Similarly in (I7'b–c).

Nevertheless, as shown by example (19), the function to give prominence to an element, which fronting and clefting have in common, may occasionally manifest itself in an appropriate context. It is to be noted, however, that the cleft construction in the last clause of (19) does not represent the more common type with given information in the subordinate clause, reflected in its weak stress, but the informative-presupposition cleft with a normally stressed subordinate clause (Prince 1978).

(19) when I sent that letter, all I was interested in was a leave of absence.
That's still all I'm interested in. I haven't given any thought to the matter of a con-
tract, and I don't think I'm prepared to think about it right now.
A leave of absence I asked for, and it's a leave of absence that I want.

Significantly, all elements in the last sentence are contextually bound: the passage is about a leave of absence, and the context preceding the last sentence implies
that the speaker has asked for it and wants it. The highlighted elements in both
clauses are the verbs. The clause with the fronted object performs its usual function:
it serves to give prominence to a contextually bound element, and at the same time
leaves the final position to the rheme. The *it*-cleft achieves information focus by the
intonation centre on the last word of the subordinate clause. We may even consider
the possibility of interchanging the two constructions.

(19)'a. A leave of absence I asked for, and a leave of absence I want.
b. ?It's a leave of absence that I asked for, and it's a leave of absence that I want.
c. ?It's a leave of absence that I asked for, and a leave of absence I want.

Even though (19) is presumably preferable to (19'a), the latter impairs neither the
FSP structure nor the textual fit. Objections are conceivable on stylistic grounds: repetition of the same structure tends to create a monotonous effect. (19'b, c), as the question marks indicate, appear to be less acceptable. (19'b) tends to be interpreted as an
it-cleft with a presupposed subordinate clause; hence the only element presented as
newsworthy is the focused *leave of absence*, the other relevant component of both the
semantic and the information structure being lost. In (19'c) the more emphatic form
precedes the less emphatic one. As explained above, whereas the fronted object constitutes the diatheme, the focused element, even in the type with new information
in the subordinate clause, implements the rheme, at least within the communicative
subfield of main clause. Hence a focused element is given more prominence than a
fronted one. On the other hand the arrangement in (19), displaying the fronted object
in the first clause and the focused object in the second, achieves an information climax,
which is absent in (19) a. and (19) b., while (19) c. in fact results in an anticlimax.

2. As appears from the foregoing discussion, the FSP structure of the different syntactic realizations of the second participant in verbal action with the FSP function of
theme is more or less differentiated. Consequently, interchangeability is largely ruled
out. Clarification of instances in which it is conceivable calls for further study.

SOURCES

Adams, R. *Watership Down*. Harmondsworth: Penguin Books, 1974.
James, P. D. *Original Sin*. London: Faber and Faber, 1994.
Raverat, G. *Period Piece*. London: Faber and Faber, 1952.

12. SYNTACTIC FORMS OF THE PRESENTATION SCALE AND THEIR DIFFERENTIATION

First published in *Linguistica Pragensia*, Vol. 8/1, 1998, 36–43.

0. This chapter is concerned with the different syntactic constructions in which the first participant in verbal action has the FSP function of rheme. In context-independent sentences this configuration is primarily found in sentences realizing the presentation scale (in Firbas's terminology, cf. 1992: 66–69, 109–110, 134–140), i.e. in sentences with verbs of existence or appearance which present a phenomenon on the scene. There being only one participant in verbal action, it is syntactically construed as the subject. However, expression of this semantic content is not confined to just one realization form in English, which raises the question to what extent the variant realization forms of the presentation scale are interchangeable or differentiated, and, in the latter case, in which respects.

1. The following discussion is based on an analysis of three samples of contemporary fiction (see *Sources*), each providing 500 clauses taken from continuous text, i.e. a total of 1 500 clauses. To obtain a textually homogeneous sample, attention was paid only to the authors' monologue, i.e. direct speech was excluded on account of the differences between monologue and dialogue on the one hand, and the different role of intonation in speech and writing on the other. In written language intonation largely constitutes a concomitant feature of an FSP structure primarily indicated by other means, viz contextual boundness, syntactico-semantic structure and linear arrangement.

The frequency of occurrence of the presentation scale appears to be relatively low: 88 instances within the total of 1 500 clauses, i.e. 5.09%. In the following discussion the relative frequency of occurrence of the different realization forms of the presentation scale is considered within the subset of the 88 instances of the presentation scale.

1.1 The most frequent realization of the presentation scale is the existential construction (39 instances, 43.3%), followed by rhematic subject in preverbal position

(28 instances, 31.7%), inversion with postverbal placement of the subject (12 instances, 13.6%), and the configuration of a semantically adverbial element construed as the subject (the scene) with the phenomenon appearing on the scene construed as the object (9 instances, 10.2%).

The existential construction indicates the rheme by its postverbal placement after existential *be*, preceded by *there*.

(1) There were few alterations (James, 345)

Adverbials as a rule operate as a setting (i.e. an element with a low degree of communicative dynamism (CD)[1] within the thematic section, cf. Firbas 1992: 49–51), whether in initial or final position.

(2) there was nothing alarming there (Adams, 15)
(3) here there was a delay (Adams, 19)

The construction displays the ordering theme–transition–rheme if the scene-setting adverbial appears initially, with a deviation from the gradual rise in CD only within the thematic section, where the initial adverbial constitutes the diatheme[2] and existential *there* the theme proper, as in (3). However, final placement is more frequent, and then the rheme is followed by the diatheme. This is occasionally avoided by a deviation from grammatical word order, as in (4):

(4) There was about the place that dead silence indicative of an untenanted house.

In the material of 1500 clauses, scene-setting adverbials were more frequently found in final position (16 final as against 9 initial adverbials; it is to be noted that while final adverbials were all locative, of the initial adverbials three were conjuncts, five were place adjuncts and one a time adjunct). With one exception, where the final adverbial is given prominence by means of a focalizer,[3] all final adverbials are thematic. Example (5) shows that where the final adverbial belongs to the rheme, it has to be reinforced by a focalizer.

(5) At this height there was no risk of prying eyes even from the top desks of buses (James, 340)

---

1   Communicative dynamism (CD) is defined as "the relative extent to which a linguistic element contributes towards the further development of the communication" (Firbas 1992: 8); the degree of CD corresponds to "the variation in communicative value" in Quirk et al. (1985: 1356); the degree of CD is also referred to as the information load, or newsworthiness, of a linguistic element in a sentence. By basic distribution of CD is meant a linear arrangement which displays a gradual rise in CD (Firbas 1992: 10), i.e. the order theme—transition—rheme, theme and rheme being defined as elements carrying, respectively, a low and a high degree of CD (Firbas 1992: 72–73). Basic distribution of CD is comparable to the principle of end focus as presented in Quirk et al. (1985: 1356–57).

2   The most dynamic element within the thematic section, see Firbas (1992: 79–81) and Svoboda (1981).

3   Focusing subjunct in Quirk et al. (1985: 604–605).

With an initial adverbial *there* is optional, and if omitted, the resulting construction displays the pattern Adv—V—S, as in (6), (7) and (8) a.

(6) Behind the ornaments were two coloured photographs. (James, 341)
(7) At the top of the bank ... was a little group of holes [almost hidden by brambles] (Adams, 15-16)
(8) a. Across the street is a grocery. (Bolinger, 93)
    b. Across the street there's a grocery. (Bolinger, 93)

The two constructions may be used interchangeably as a stylistic device avoiding reiteration of the same structure, as in (9),

(9) In the top drawer of the desk there was a file labelled investments... In another file was a copy of her will. (James, 347)

According to Bolinger (1977: 93-94) "the first [(8) a.] presents something on the immediate stage (brings something literally or figuratively before our presence), whereas the second [(8) b.] presents something to our minds (brings a piece of knowledge into consciousness." According to Quirk et al. (1985: 1410) "the absence of *there* ... is preferred when the final noun phrase is relatively concrete and specific." This difference presumably applies where the existential construction or the construction with inversion is used in isolation, but in a longer description which consists of sentences presenting objects on the scene, different realizations of the presentation scale tend to occur side by side largely as a stylistic device. This is also evident with verbs of appearance or existence on the scene other than *be*.

1.2 In contrast to *there + be*, with verbs other than *be* the use of *there* is distinctly formal (literary) and rare (of the 39 instances altogether 4 occurrences (with *seem, come out, survive* and *exist*), i.e. 10%).

(10) indeed there still survives the unkind saying of one of them ['that little Richards have long ears'.] (Rav, 120)

After integrated initial adverbials it is again optional.

(11) A hundred yards away, at the bottom of the slope, ran the brook, no more than three feet wide... (Adams, 15)

1.3 Apart from sentences with inverted word order, appearance on the scene realized by verbs other than *be* is implemented by clauses with rhematic subject in initial position. This arrangement displays a major deviation from the basic distribution of CD, with the rheme at the beginning and the theme, if there is a scene-setting adverbial, at the end.

(12) [any small concavity in the grass] where moisture may collect (Adams, 29)

Since the incidence of the structures discussed in this section is not sufficiently represented in the excerpted sources, rhematic subjects are also illustrated by examples collected variously from other fiction.

(13) At the bottom of the blackness in front of them a line of light appeared.
(14) A noise, a sort of low growl, came from the waterfall.

As shown by (13) and (14), the position of the scene-setting adverbial is again mobile. Where it stands at the beginning, as in (13), at least this element occupies a position consistent with its degree of CD. On the other hand in final position, as in (14), it contributes to a complete reversal of the basic distribution, the linear arrangement being rheme—transition—theme. Here the FSP is primarily indicated by semantic structure; contextual boundness or non-boundness of a scene-setting adverbial, where present, does not play a role. All instances contain a context-independent subject, and a verb of appearance or existence on the scene (or a verb implying this meaning), which is less dynamic than the context-independent subject. On the whole, final placement of a scene-setting adverbial appears to be the more common (10 as against 3 instances, disregarding 3 adverbials in initial position due to relativization). It is to be noted that the realization of the presentation scale by means of a rhematic subject in initial position + verb of appearance or existence on the scene borders on clauses with rhematic subject and thematic object where the borderline between object and adverbial is not clear-cut. The semantics of the sentence and of the verb, however, tend to override the syntactic aspects. Thus the examples in (15) are regarded as the realization of the presentation scale and so are the examples in (16) despite their clear S–V–O structure on account of the metaphorical meaning of the verb and sentence semantics (cf. Adam 2013: 126–28).

(15) a. A small sigh escaped Fanny here.
  b. A kind of stillness seemed to have fallen on the house.
  c. A chill of horror swept over her.
(16) a. A faint cold hand touched her heart.
  b. An intolerable weight burdened his spirit.
  c. A sensation of vast loneliness possessed him [and this was replaced by a twinge of fear].

1.4 To complete the picture, mention should be made of the presentation scale realized by the passive, both with a rhematic subject alone and with *there* preceding it. Although in this case the subject is not the first, but the second participant in verbal action, the structure as a whole clearly implements the presentation scale in that it introduces a phenomenon on the scene, the nature of the presentation scale being compatible with introducing into discourse phenomena of any semantic role. Cf. (17)–(19).

(17) Near one of the posts, a hammer and a few nails had been left behind. (Adams, 18)

(18) There, a curiosity had been aroused in his mind.

(19) At the moment of his departure a telegram was handed to him.

The rhematic function of the subject is due not only to its context-independence, but also to the semantics of the verb, which implies appearance on the scene, and to contextual boundness of the adverbial element(s).

The passive presentation scale is also found with existential *there*, as in (20), or with subject—verb inversion, as in (21) and (22). Example (21) morever contains a fronted participle, which is the only possible arrangement in the absence of existential *there* or an initial adverbial.

(20) There were exhumed at least a dozen corpses. (Bolinger, 97)

(21) Exhumed were at least a dozen corpses. (Bolinger, 96)

(22) To uneasiness was added a strong sense of guilt.

(23) [What a desk it was ... Its top was a single sheet of heavy glass ...] Under it could be seen posters of films that must have achieved some special honour.

The passive with existential *there* is of special interest in that the two constructions normally indicate different FSP functions: insofar as the passive serves to achieve basic distribution of CD, the subject is thematic. Existential *there*, on the other hand, indicates a rhematic subject, which is moved to postverbal position. Hence the appearance of both the passive and *there* side by side in one clause, as in (20), may at first sight seem contradictory until it is realized that the syntactic form is a mere surface structure implementing a deeper semantic structure—in this case the presentation scale: optional scene—verb of appearance—phenomenon appearing on the scene.

The four variants of the passive presentation scale presumably differ in their degree of markedness. Even though they are all formal and literary, the least marked form appears to be that with the rhematic subject in preverbal position, as in (17)–(19), insofar as it conforms to the rules of English word order. Next comes the variant with *there* (20), the forms with inversion being greatly confined both stylistically (with respect to register) and contextually. These assumptions should be verified by further studies.

1.5 The last construction to be mentioned is the structure illustrated by (24).

(24) a. This road carries a lot of traffic.

    b. There is a lot of traffic on this road.

    c. On this road there is a lot of traffic.

Although the presentation scale is here obscured by a transitive construction with thematic subject and rhematic object, it is revealed both by the semantic role and the FSP function of the subject, as well as by the b. and c. versions, which present the content by means of the existential construction. Here the scene-setting nature of the subject (the theme) finds expression in adverbial construction, while the phenomenon appearing on the scene (the rheme) assumes the syntactic function of subject.

2. In continuous texts the different realization forms of the presentation scale may be found as stylistic variants serving to avoid repetition of the same structure, cf. (25) and (26):

(25) We found ourselves in what had once been a saloon bar. The bar itself was of solid mahogany but sadly stained by bleached rings where *glasses had stood. Round it ran a footrest* apparently made of green verdigris. *There were one or two stools* with legs of uneven length and seats polished by generations of rustic posteriors. Behind the bar *a few shelves held dusty bottles* half full of unlikely liqueurs.
(26) In front of the house *there was a circular drive.* ... *In the centre of this stood a rickety post* from which *an inn sign still swung.*

However, seen from the language system point of view, the different realization forms of the presentation scale appear to be distinguished by their degree of markedness, defined on the one hand by deviation from the word order rules, and on the other by deviation from the basic distribution of CD (or the principle of end focus), which seems to be a general principle of the linear arrangement of the information structure. The unmarked or marked character of a particular structure may be reflected in its stylistic characteristics (stylistically neutral as against carrying stylistic connotations), which evidently also derive from the distribution of the particular structure in different texts.

Two of the active realization forms conform to both the word order rules and the basic distribution of CD: the existential construction (cf. 1.1) and the structure illustrated by (24) a. The former partly deviates from the basic distribution of CD in having the scene-setting adverbial mostly at the end, but then a thematic element in the post-intonation-centre shade (cf. Firbas 1980) is a fairly common feature of Modern English prosody. The actual distribution of these two structures in texts, however, confirms the neutral character of the existential construction alone. The existential construction is found in all kinds of texts, and as shown by the data obtained from the three samples under study, ranks highest among the different realizations of the presentation scale (43.3%). The structure illustrated by (24) a. (10.2%) appears to be more characteristic of written texts, the realization form used in informal speech being again largely the existential construction.

The remaining forms are all more or less marked. The realization form with the rhematic subject in initial position conforms to the word order rules, but the information structure is presented in reversed order: rheme—transition—theme. Nevertheless, according to statistical data (the second most frequent structure, accounting for 31.7% of the realization forms of the presentation scale), English appears to tolerate deviations from the basic distribution of CD more readily than those from the word order rules. Hence with respect to its degree of markedness, this realization form appears to rank next to the existential construction.

The realization form with the subject in final position and inverted word order is marked with respect to the word order rules, even though it conforms to the basic distribution of CD. It carries the stylistic connotation of a descriptive passage included in a longer text. Considering that deviations from the basic distribution of CD are substantially more frequent in English than deviations from the word order rules, this realization form ($Adv{-}V{-}S_{rheme}$) appears to rank higher on the scale of markedness than the form with initial rhematic subject (cf. the respective percentages: 13.6 % and 31.7 %).

The remaining realization forms, the passive presentation scale and *there* with verbs other than *be*, presumably rank at the top of the markedness scale, even though not so much on account of their degree of deviation as owing to their rare occurrence, which assigns them to the periphery of the forms realizing the presentation scale. Stylistically, they connote formal writing, presumably fiction rather than informative prose. However, these conjectures, as well as the conclusions drawn above, call for further research.

SOURCES

Adams, R. *Watership Down*. Harmondsworth: Penguin Books, 1974.
James, P. D. *Original Sin*. London: Faber and Faber, 1994.
Raverat, G. *Period Piece*. London: Faber and Faber, 1952.

13. SYSTEMIC POSSIBILITIES OF VARIABLE WORD ORDER AND THEIR REALIZATION IN TEXT

First published in the *Proceedings of 6th Conference of British, American and Canadian Studies*, Prešov Part. Prešov: Prešov University, 2000, 70–80.

0. The grammatical word order of English in general allows only few changes in the position of sentence elements. Leaving aside different placement of the same element due to transformed structure and emotive and/or emphatic factors, unmarked alternative word order is found with adverbials, whose position is largely mobile, and some verbs with ditransitive complementation. Where the grammatical word order offers more than one choice other factors may come into play, notably the functional sentence perspective (FSP).

Of the permissible unmarked changes in the linear arrangement of postverbal clause elements, this chapter is concerned with the mutual position of the two components of the syntactic structure of a transitive phrasal verb, the object and the particle. Only substantival objects are taken into account, since pronominal objects allow only one position, that before the particle.

The starting point of the following discussion is the position and the realization form of the postverbal elements in the sentences given in (1).

(1) a. He turned down an advantageous offer.
　　b. He turned the offer down.
　　c. He turned it down.

A context independent object is expected to constitute the rheme proper (or a component of the rheme), and hence to be placed after the particle as in (1) a., whereas a contextually bound object, involving the thematic function, is presumed to precede it, as in (1) b. This assumption is strongly supported by the fact that in the case of pronominal objects, which are largely anaphoric, and hence as a rule thematic, the position of the object before the particle is grammaticalized, cf. (1) c. However, rhythm and prosody also play a role here.

1. In order to test this assumption altogether 764 sentences containing a phrasal verb with a substantival object were collected, phrasal verbs being defined as verbs taking an adverbial particle (cf. Quirk et al. 1985: 1153–55). The examples were excerpted from lighter fiction, which was likely to provide a large number of instances: altogether five books were excerpted, see the Sources. To begin with, the 764 examples were considered with respect to whether or not the alternative word order is possible. Obviously only those examples which allow both linear arrangements, particle + object or object + particle, could be taken as the relevant material on which to study the relation between the position of the respective element and its FSP function. On this basis, several groups could be distinguished.

1.1 The first group is constituted by what may be called collocations, i.e. more or less fixed phrases, which are hardly conceivable with the alternative word order (43 instances), cf. (2):

(2) a. the guests had not yet put in an appearance for the meal ...
    b. *the guests had not yet put an/the appearance in ...

Put in an/no appearance occurred in 4 instances, the most frequent collocation being *make up one's mind* (with 17 occurrences), cf. (3):

(3) What do you plan to do now?—I can't make up my mind.

The other collocations found in the material were *get/have the wind up* (6 occurrences), *get someone's back up* (2), *put on an act* (2), *put on weight* (2), *bite someone's head off* (2), the rest displaying only one occurrence: *fill in the time, plague someone's life out, bother someone's life out, eat one's heart out, take up the thread, hand out a raspberry, stick in one's toe.*

The obtained sample of collocations displays both patterns, object + particle, as well as particle + object, on the whole in accordance with the assumption that the two elements will be ordered according to their function in FSP: whichever element comes last completes the meaning, and is hence more dynamic than that which immediately follows the verb: *make up one's mind, put in an appearance, put on an act, put on weight, hand out a raspberry, take up the thread, fill in the time, stick in one's toe* x *get/have the wind up, get someone's back up, bite someone's head off, plague someone's life out, bother someone's life out, eat one's heart out.*

1.2 Another, more numerous group of examples hardly conceivable with the alternative word order involves instances in which the object is postmodified. Postmodified objects as a rule constitute the rheme, which is in accordance with the principle of end weight (cf. Quirk et al. 1985: 1361–62): weighty elements usually carry more information than light ones. Postmodification of the object, especially where realized by a clause, nonfinite verb form or an expanded prepositional phrase, blocks the position of the particle after the object, insofar as the distance between the particle and the verb, whose constitutive semantic component the particle implements, would be too great. The pattern found with postmodified objects is overwhelmingly that of parti-cle—object—postmodification, i.e. a linear arrangement in agreement with a gradual rise in communicative dynamism. Cf. (4)–(6).

(4) You've thrown out a few hints that he was up to no good ...
(5) The staff has not yet cleared away the refreshments intended for the party ...
(6) a taxi ... set down a middle-aged gentleman of lean proportions and expensive tailor-
    ing, who said placidly:

As postmodifying prepositional phrases sometimes border on adverbials, in some instances the prepositional phrase remains indeterminate in this respect. Cf. (7).

(7) ... took up a stance by the table,
    i. what stance?
    ii. a stance where?

The same ambiguity is sometimes found with postmodifying infinitives, cf. (8).

(8) I couldn't bring forward anything to prove I hadn't done it
    i. in order to prove
    ii. that could prove

There were altogether 151 instances with postmodified objects, all of which dis-played the order particle + object + postmodification except five. In two of these cases the particle occurs after the object before the postmodification, which is hence discon-tinuous, cf. (9).

(9) Warrenby liked to find things out about people

Here the ordering is presumably due to the low information load of the noun *things* used as a general substitute for more specific meanings. Expectedly, where it occurs with other verbs, it is also found in this pattern, cf. (10).

(10) a. He is coming up to see me—to talk things over a bit.
     b. We want to clear things up.
     c. I haven't thought things out yet.

In two instances the particle follows after the postmodification, as in (11). Here the postmodifying structure is neither weighty, nor semantically very informative. The remaining example (12) contains multiple postmodification of the object with the particle placed between the postmodifying structures.

(11) Nothing puts the right kind of man off more quickly than a girl who takes too much to drink.
(12) He would be able to put any sort of pressure on that he liked.

In all instances where the particle follows the object, whether before or after the postmodification, this position assigns it a higher degree of communicative dynamism than that carried by the object, even though the latter may itself be a component of the rheme, as in (11) and (12).

In general, the picture presented by postmodified objects supports the assumption of the role of FSP in the ordering of the elements under study. The syntactic structure, notably the principle of end weight, and the information structure here coincide.

1.3 The next group includes instances in which the object is followed by an adverbial prepositional phrase, or a prepositional phrase realizing an optional actant independent of verbal valency. This configuration was registered in 176 instances, out of which 120 (68.2%) displayed the pattern object + particle + prepositional phrase, and 56 (31.8%) particle + object + prepositional phrase. These quantitative data clearly favour the position of the particle after the object, thus suggesting some connection between this position and the following prepositional phrase.

This is indeed the case where the particle *out* is followed by an *of*-phrase, the two elements, *out* and *of* constituting a compound preposition, whose first component cannot be distanced. Nevertheless, the particle is also a constitutive element of the semantic and formal make-up of the verb. Compare (13).

(13) She wrenched her slim body out of the chair.

This use of the particle *out* as a component of both the verb and the compound preposition *out of* was registered in 24 instances (out of 120, i.e. 20%).

A close connection between the particle and the prepositional phrase was also observed in other cases where the prepositional phrase operates as a locative adverbial. Common combinations appeared to be *down on, down to, up to, back from, back in, back to, away from*, and others, cf. (14)–(16).

(14) a. He put his hat down on the table under the gilded mirror.
    b. Presently Marjorie took the tray down to the kitchen.
(15) I went to fetch the cocktail tray up to the drawing-room.
(16) a. Then he swept his hostess back to the studio.
    b. He put the receiver back in its cradle.

Within the group of examples with the order object + particle + prepositional phrase (120 instances), locative adjuncts account for 79 cases, i.e. 65.8% of the entire group. Although the combinations of particles and prepositions illustrated in (14)–(16) do not constitute compound prepositions, the position of the particle before the object is more or less unlikely insofar as there is again close semantic connection between the particle and the preposition: the two elements together specify the particular locative meaning. Expectedly, another reason is found in the FSP structure of all these examples. Although the object is a component of the rheme, it is followed by further specification, implemented by the locative adverbial, which operates as the rheme proper, including the particle and the preposition as relevant components of the locative meaning.

The following example (17) illustrates an instance of a locative adverbial independent of the semantic structure of the verb. Significantly, here the particle can be placed before the object, with the resulting change in the FSP structure, the object thus acquiring the function of the rheme proper.

(17) a. I have to pick my wife up on the way.
      b. I have to pick up my wife on the way.

What has been said largely applies to the examples constituting the smaller group of non-locative prepositional phrases in the pattern object + particle + prepositional phrase (41, 34.2%) with the exception of adverbials with the semantic roles of goal (9 instances) and attendant circumstances (6). Both these roles are frequently realized by personal nouns or pronouns, and show affinity with locative adjuncts in that the alternative position of the particle is again unlikely, cf. (18) and (19). On the other hand, adjuncts with other semantic roles allow it freely: temporal (8 instances), cf. (20), manner (5), cf. (21), means (3), cf. (22), instrument (2), cf. (23) and others.

(18) I sent my resignation in to Dr. Scott.
      *?I sent in my resignation to Dr. Scott.
(19) I brought the parts back with me.
      ?I brought back the parts with me.
(20) I beg you will take that brooch off at once.
      I beg you will take off that brooch at once.
(21) she had switched the current off in disgust
      she had switched off the current in disgust
(22) Don't pick that topee-case up by the handle.
      Don't pick up that topee-case by the handle.
(23) They cut them bits off with a hacksaw.
      They cut off them bits with a hacksaw.

Although in (20)–(23) the particle can be placed before the object, this position is less likely insofar as the object is contextually bound, which is shown by the determiners, and hence less dynamic than the particle. As they are, i.e. with the particle after the object, they support the assumption made in (1).

Proceeding now to the smaller group of examples with the word order particle + object + prepositional phrase (56 instances) we find prepositional phrases with similar syntactic functions and semantic roles as in the previous group: adjuncts of place (20), time (5), means (4), manner (5), attendant circumstances (3), purpose (5), goal (2), source (2), reason (2); beneficiary and recipient (6), apposition (1). Although both positions of the particle are theoretically possible, the placement of the particle after the object mostly appears to be blocked by two factors: besides a change in the FSP, we observe an opposite tendency as compared with the previous group: there, certain particles and prepositions tended to combine to specify a locative meaning, here other particles and prepositions, or other combinations thereof tend to be distanced. This is most noticeable in the case of the particle *up* and prepositional phrases introduced by *from* (5 instances; compare, on the other hand, the frequent occurrence of *back from*):

(24) He picked up their fishing things from the bank.
    ?He picked their fishing things up from the bank.

Here the particle appears to be closely connected with the verb, with its lexical directional meaning somewhat weakened, as against the position after the verb, where the directional meaning retains its full force, which does not fit in the particular context. Other instances of avoiding the adjacency of a particle and preposition by the placement of the particle before the object display *down in*, and *up to*, cf. (25) and (26).

(25) jotting down another note in his notebook
    ?jotting another note down in his notebook
(26) She put up a hand to her brow, pressing it.
    ?She put a hand up to her brow, pressing it.

This tendency is not confined to objects followed by locative adverbials. It is also found with prepositional phrases in other functions and semantic roles, cf. (27) and (28).

(27) reaching out his hand for the beer-jug
    ?reaching his hand out for the beer-jug
(28) to check up his position by a sight of the ground
    *?to check his position up by a sight of the ground

In these instances it is not so much the avoidance of the combined meaning of the two elements as the undesirable prominence of the particle, if placed after the object, which falls within the sphere of FSP. This is the main factor in a number of other instances, compare (29) and (30):

(29) We shall be turning off the main lights in a minute.
    We shall be turning the main lights off in a minute.
(30) I take off my hat to you.
    I take my hat off to you.

The types discussed so far appear to offer little ground for the object and the particle to exchange their position: fixed phrases block the exchange altogether, and so do as a rule objects with postmodification. In clauses with final adverbials or valency-independent participants realized by prepositional phrases the mutual position of the object and the particle is to a large extent influenced by the semantic relations between the particle and the prepositional phrase, especially where the prepositional phrase is locative, which appears to be the most frequent semantic role in this configuration. Nevertheless, the FSP also plays a role insofar as whatever the word order arrangement, it agrees with the gradual increase in communicative dynamism, the final position being occupied by the most dynamic element.

1.4 The role of FSP as a factor in the placement of the object and the particle is best revealed by the last group of examples which display the two elements in clause-final position. In general, the pattern Vb—particle—object was found to be about twice as frequent as the pattern Vb—object—particle, namely 266 (67.5%) as against 128 (32.5%) instances, respectively.

Let us start with the larger group Vb—particle—object (266 instances, 67.5%). According to the assumption made in (1), the object should be context-independent, hence rhematic, and since it is placed in the final position, it should constitute the rheme proper. Objects whose context independence is indicated by overt grammatical means, the type of determiner, account for about 17% (45 instances out of 266, 16.9%), cf. (31):

(31) a. ... replied Jim, pulling forward a chair
    b. You're lazy, that's all that's wrong with you. Why don't take up social work?
    c. They can't throw off unhealthy influences like we can.

A somewhat larger number of objects (57, 21.4%), though context independent, lack an overt indicator of their context independence insofar as they denote unique objects or persons, with no determiner in the case of proper names, and a possessive or the definite article with common nouns. Cf. (32):

(32) a. Why don't you ring up Betty?
    b. I had to stop at Cliff House to pick up my racket
    c. she never entered her bedroom without turning on the radio

A third group of objects may be regarded as derivable from the situation on the ground of constituting an integral component thereof. However, unless they are explicitly mentioned in the immediately preceding context, they behave as new elements. Since contextual boundness is a matter of degree, the quantitative data for this group are to be regarded as an approximate estimate rather than an exact figure (about 50 examples, i.e. 18.7%). Cf. (33).

(33) a. She came back with his coffee and sandwiches. Later she came back and took away the tray.
   b. He stood smoking for several minutes, then he stubbed out the cigarette and walked upstairs to his wife's room.
   c. The telephone rang. Grant picked up the receiver.

Contextual boundness, whether due to previous mention or derivability from the preceding context, may be counteracted by the presence in the context of a contrasting element (some 20 examples, 7.5%). Cf. (34).

(34) a. She raced down the passage to his room, and found to her surprise that it was illuminated only by the moonlight. Switching on the light, ...
   b. Setting aside your own future, you ought to consider Mother, and your father a bit.

The most interesting group of the pattern Vb—particle—object includes objects which overtly display contextual boundness, having been mentioned before as well as being accompanied by anaphoric devices. Some of these objects are thematic, but others appear to operate as the rheme in spite of the absence of a contrasting context. This group accounts for some 30–40 examples (the margin allows for questionable instances).

Since all objects in this group are overtly context dependent, the position of the intonation centre (IC; intonation nucleus, cf. Quirk et al. 1985: 1356), which signals the rheme, is indicated by capital letters. In all preceding examples the IC automatically falls on whichever element (object or particle) is placed last.

About two-thirds of the objects (i.e. some 25 examples) appear to be thematic, despite their position after the particle, cf. (35):

(35) a. Look, I thought you'd shaken OFF that habit.
   b. "I looked in the atlas, but the map's just plain white paper north of Ivanhoe." She pulled OUT the atlas and they studied it together.
   c. If only he could clear UP this thing before he was swamped by the demanding life that was waiting for him on Monday.
   d. There seemed, however, no immediate prospect of being able to follow UP this advice.

Theoretically, we might postulate the position of the particle after the object, which is indeed possible, cf. (35)' b. and c.

(35)' b. She pulled the atlas out and ...
       c. If only he could clear this thing up before ...

In (35) a. and d. the placement of the particle after the object is not likely. Presumably two factors play a role here: as an integral component of both the semantic and the formal make-up of the verb the particle tends to be juxtaposed to the verb. The second factor is the tolerance of English as regards thematic elements in postverbal position, which is connected with the primary grammatical function of English word order (cf. Chapter 10). Since the particle and the verb tend to form one unit and the postverbal position of thematic elements is a systemic feature, the order particle—thematic object falls within the general picture.

The smaller group of examples (about 10) display an overtly context dependent object as the rheme. Here the position of the particle and the object agrees with their respective degrees of communicative dynamism, but calls for an explanation of the fact why a context dependent element complementing a context independent verb is the rheme in the absence of a contrast. Instances of this kind suggest three factors which presumably come into play. The anaphoric object, though presented as known, is distanced from its antecedent, as in (36):

(36) he's carried on, doing everything he can, like starting up THAT GRAVel pit

The notion of the gravel pit is not sufficiently activated because it has not been mentioned in the last few pages.

Where the distance between the antecedent and the anaphoric object is short, a potential factor is found in an additional feature provided by the modification of the object, which may but need not necessarily convey new information, cf. (37) a. and b.

(37) a. [... setting a neat package down on the desk. "I'll be off," Cathercot said,] picking up his TREASured PACKage
       b. [... responded Cynthia, casting off her hat. ... She wrenched her slim body out of the chair] and picked up the disCARDed HAT.

A third factor is found in emotive highlighting of an element presented as known, cf. (38).

(38) I never shall see why people like you and Trixie have to put on that HOLY, HOLY, HOLY, exPRESSion [when anyone so much as mentions Russia].

The last group of examples including clauses with objects followed by the particle is less numerous than clauses with objects placed after the particle, the ratio being approximately 1:2 (128 : 266 [31.8% : 68.2%]). In this group the FSP structure is unequivocally in agreement with the linear arrangement, the object being invariably less dynamic than the particle, which constitutes the rheme proper and carries the IC. Overtly context dependent objects (33 instances, 25.8%), cf. (39), other context dependent objects (22 instances, 17.2%), cf. (40), and semantically weak objects (*things, something* 14 instances, 10.9%), cf. (10) and (41) account for over a half of all examples of this group (53.9%).

(39) a. "Perhaps I had better explain it to you." Jim heard the expiation out, merely interrupting once or twice to put a question.
   b. There was a small rug on the bare boards of the front room ... She took this rug up and fetched a bucket of hot water.
(40) a. [Now you can see what happens if you was to lose the split pin] ... Someone took the split pin out.
   b. [I don't believe that kid's got any right to take Kane's boat out]. He is not precisely in the habit of taking speed-boats out, is he?
(41) a. We can't hide things up.
   b. Wait—you'd better put something on.

On the contrary, context independent objects are few (some 8 examples, 6.25%), cf. (42).

(42) a. remind him that he is holding everyone up
   b. It's time you took some time off to attend to your own affairs.
   c. Let me just slip a few pins in, and you'll be surprised.

The most interesting instances are objects realized by proper names or determined by possessives, which are frequent in both patterns: Vb—object—particle and Vb—particle—object, since here it is the linear arrangement, reflecting contextual boundness or non-boundness, that unequivocally indicates the rheme proper, the element placed last, whichever it may be, cf. (43) and (44).

(43) a. If you're too tired I'll ring Nest up, and ask her ...
   b. I told her how to get to my flat and that I would ring up Shirley
(44) a. i. Timothy drew his knees up and hugged them.
      ii. First I must take my hat off, and have a wash
   b. i. Paul Mansell put up his eyebrows
      ii. he didn't hurry over putting on his coat

In the case of elements derivable from the situation, especially body parts and personal belongings, there appears to be a possibility of subjective choice as to which element should be made the rheme proper, cf. i. in (44) a. and b., and ii. in (44) a. and b. Compare also (45).

(45) a. Shortly before one o'clock Sir Adrian, whose habit it was to read far into the night, laid down his book, and ...
   b. ... laid his book down, and ...

Similarly in the situation of telephoning and turning on/off the light we find both patterns, but the Vb—particle—object predominates, cf. (46) and (47).

(46) a. [I talked to Prendergast for a few minutes more, ...] ... I put the telephone down, wondering if ...
  b. He put down the receiver and stayed a moment lost in thought.
(47) a. He went to bed, and lay wide awake staring at the ceiling. He put the light out and resorted to his own cure for insomnia
  b. she had stopped reading and turned out her light

Another instance offering choice is illustrated by (48) and (49), although here in the a. versions the same FSP structure as in b. may be achieved by placing the IC on the object.

(48) a. he doesn't give anything aWAY / ANYthing away
  b. They won't find out ANYthing.
(49) a. You didn't take anyone IN / ANYone in.
  b. I am not ruling out ANYone yet.

2. A comprehensive account of the mutual position of the object and the particle should also pay attention to the semantic structure of the entire construction Vb—particle—object from the aspect of the semantic content conveyed by each of the three components, but this is beyond the aim of this chapter. We may conclude that the results of the foregoing discussion on the whole confirm the assumption made at the beginning, viz. that the order of the object and the particle is governed by the amount of communicative dynamism carried by these two elements. The high degree of agreement between the linear arrangement and gradual increase in communicative dynamism, however, is largely due to the fact that the FSP structure coincides with the syntactic structure. This has been shown in particular by instances with postmodification. Where the phrasal verb with its object is followed by an adverbial prepositional phrase, the position of the particle is to a considerable extent determined by the semantic relations between the particle and the adverbial, especially the semantics of the preposition in the prepositional phrase. Even in this group there is agreement between the linear arrangement and the gradual increase in CD. FSP as the primary factor asserts itself where the particle or the object stands in the clause-final position. Where the particle is placed at the end, the object is almost invariably presented as less dynamic. In the opposite case of final objects, we find a majority of examples to conform to the gradual increase in CD, the final object constituting the rheme proper. Nevertheless, a small number of instances have a thematic object at the end. Thematic objects are encountered in English in other instances as well, in consequence of the primary grammatical principle of English word order, which is in the case of phrasal verbs supported by the semantic unity of the particle and the verb. Objects derivable from the situation of utterance mostly behave as context independent, but in some instances the mutual position of the object and the particle appears to be a matter of subjective choice.

Collocations	43	5.6%
Object with postmodification	151	19.8%
Particle—object—prepositional phrase	56	7.3%
Object—particle—prepositional phrase	120	15.8%
Verb—particle—object	266	34.8%
Verb—object—particle	128	16.7%
	764	**100.0%**
Particle—object—prepositional phrase	56	31.8%
Object—particle—prepositional phrase	120	68.2%
	176	**100.0%**
Verb—object—particle	128	32.5%
Verb—particle—object	266	67.5%
	394	**100.0%**

SOURCES

Heyer, G. *Detection unlimited.* New York: Bantam Books, 1971.
Heyer, G. *Duplicate death.* London: Panther Books, 1973.
Heyer, G. *They found him dead.* London: Panther Books, 1972.
Shute, N. *No highway.* London: Heinemann, 1951.
Tey, J. *The singing sands.* New York: Collier Books, 1988.

14. NOTE ON A POTENTIAL TEXTUAL FEATURE OF PUTATIVE *SHOULD*

First published in *Linguistica Pragensia*, Vol. 19/2, 2009, 82–88.

0. The subject of this chapter goes back to an observation noted in a book on modal verbs (Nehls 1986: 152)[1] concerning the so-called putative *should* (Quirk et al. 1985: 234–35) which alternates with the indicative in instances like (1):

(1) a. It is regrettable that such books should be printed.
    b. It is regrettable that such books are printed.

This use of *should* is to be distinguished from another use also treated as putative (Quirk et al. *ibid.*), viz. instances of alternation with the subjunctive, as in (2).

(2) a. It is appropriate that this tax should be abolished.
    b. It is appropriate that this tax be abolished.

1. The difference between the two uses appears to be due to the different semantics of the verb in the superordinate clause: while in (1) the verb expresses emotive, attitudinal or modal evaluation, in (2) the *that*-clause is controlled by a directive expression (request, command, recommendation, suggestion, intention and the like). In both cases the controlling expression in the superordinate clause (besides verbs also adjectives and nouns functioning as complements of copular verbs) and the verb form in the dependent clause display semantic concord similar to what Mathesius called negative concord with respect to multiple negation (Mathesius 1937); in Huddleston and Pullum (2002: 179) this feature is referred to as modal harmony.

---

1   Nehls here quotes from F. Behre's *Meditative-Polemic 'Should' in Modern English 'That'-Clauses* (*Gothenburg Studies in English* 4, Stockholm, 1955: 177 ff.).

1.1 The following remarks concern only the first of these two uses, illustrated by (1). In Nehls's study (Nehls 1986: 152) this use of *should* is characterized as an indicator of context dependence of the content being expressed: the proposition in the dependent clause is presented as given, known, mentioned before; on the other hand, the use of the indicative in the dependent clause induces context independent reading of the content being expressed. This observation is presumably connected with the fact that the alternation *should* / indicative is primarily encountered in content clauses in the function of subject, whose extraposition is almost a matter of course irrespective of their context dependence or independence (cf. Biber et al. 1999: 674, "*That*-clauses in subject position are rare in all registers.") If putative *should* can indeed be ascribed this function, English has an explicit device for indicating the distribution of communicative dynamism in sentences with an extraposed subject (mostly a *that*-clause, less often other types of content clauses), i.e. the functional sentence perspective (FSP, cf. Firbas 1992) of the whole sentence, viz. the communicative field constituted by the superordinate and the subordinate clause. Considering this point in the light of some dozens of examples, we find at least partial support for the suggested textual function of *should*.

(3) She gets excited like that from time to time. It's unfortunate it should happen (it has happened) today.

(4) Poor young man! I can't but pity him, though I perfectly appreciate how provoking it is for us all that he should have been born (that he was born).

(5) It was incredible luck, too, that the play should have come (came) into my life just when I had rejected a hundred scripts.

Since the *that*-clause constitutes a communicative subfield with an FSP structure of its own, within this subfield, besides the context-dependent part, there is a novel element operating as the rheme: in (3) two temporal adverbials (*from time to time x today*) are brought into contrast, in (4) existence contrasts with coming into existence (birth), and in (5) the least context-dependent element *into my life* is followed by a clause containing new information. The relatively short context-independent parts of the it-clauses in (3) and (4) suggest only one intonation centre (sentence stress, nuclear tone) on the evaluating adjective implementing the subject complement, which constitutes the rheme of the higher communicative field formed by the *it*- and *that*-clause as a whole.

1.2 Rare instances with a *that*-clause in initial position can be regarded as marked insofar as they appear to be due to specific contextual conditions. In (6) final position of the *that*-clause, though not affecting the FSP structure, would result in a sequence of two almost identical clauses. In addition, the only context-independent element, the rheme (*worried*), would appear in the initial part before a longer thematic section.

(6) "You are giving too many lessons." That she should have to give lessons worried him.

In (7) the initial position of the *that*-clause ensures rhematic interpretation of a short rhematic element, again constituted by the verb (*unnerved*), while extraposition would result in a different FSP structure. Compare (7) a. and b.

(7) a. That such a thought, compounded of fear and unfounded longing, should come into his mind at this moment unnerved him.

b. It unnerved him that such a thought, compounded of fear and unfounded long ing, should come into his mind at this moment,

Examples (8) and (9) are similar: final position of the *that*-clause would obscure the FSP structure.

(8) Recent studies ... have ... shown a disconcerting tendency for natural rules to be replaced by "crazy" rules. Why this should be the case is not clear.[2]

(9) This occurrence (stress on the first member) is often used to test whether a word is lexical or a true compound. *Toothbrush, basketball,* and *mailbox* are lexical. Why *chocolate cake* and *cherry pie* should still have stress on the second part is puzzling.[2]

In (10) the initial subject clause is not only context-dependent, but its extraposition is blocked by the *that*-clause postmodifying the object of the superordinate verb.

(10) That Simone should choose to die so dramatically evoked only surprise that her sister had found the necessary courage.

As in other instances, *should* in initial context-dependent subject clauses is found to alternate with the indicative. In this case the initial position may be the only indicator of the givenness of the subject *that*-clause.

(11) a. That memory is a cognitive process related to language learning is clear in this summary of Neisser's position.[2]

b. In this summary of Neisser's position it is clear that memory is a cognitive process related to language learning.

Here the initial position of the *that*-clause is apparently connected with the fact that the sentence contains only one context-independent element, the adjectival complement of the verb (*is clear*). Since the context-dependence of the subordinate clause lacks overt indication of givenness within the clause itself, its content might not be interpreted as given. The intonation centre on *clear*, which would resolve the interplay of linearity, semantic structure and context-dependence in speech, is in written language only a concomitant feature of an FSP structure determined by the interplay

---

2   For examples with this superscript I am indebted to Smolka (2007).

of the three other FSP factors (cf. Firbas 1992: 51, 108, 110–11). It is to be noted that replacement of the indicative by *should* (+ infinitive) is here inapplicable. A tentative explanation may be sought in the undesirability of any shade of "putative" meaning in a clause whose content is presented as a plain fact. This suggests that even where *should* may be regarded as a textual device, its primary putative meaning partly applies, however weakened.

1.3 In grammars of English the difference between the indicative and putative *should*, if commented upon at all, is subsumed under the use of the term "putative" (Quirk et al. 1985: 1014): "The modal auxiliary *should* is used extensively (esp. in BrE) in *that*-clauses to convey the notion of a 'putative' situation, which is recognized as possibly existing or coming into existence. Contrast

I'm surprised that he should feel lonely. [1]
I'm surprised that he feels lonely. [2]

While [1] questions the loneliness, [2] accepts it as true. Here, as often, the difference is mainly one of nuance, since the factual bias of the matrix clause overrides the doubt otherwise implicit in the *should*-construction."

Huddleston and Pullum (2002: 187) describe *should* in this construction as a use "with little discernible modal meaning of its own," occurring primarily with predicative lexemes indicating surprise or evaluation (*odd, remarkable, surprising, good, bad, a pity,* etc.) (2002: 188). "The *should* clause can generally be replaced by an unmodalised one: *It's surprising that he should be /was so late.* (ibid.)

1.4 Non-factive content of the *that*-clause is in Quirk et al. (1985: 156–57, 1014) primarily illustrated by examples in which *should* alternates with mandative subjunctive, as in the following examples:

The employees have demanded that the manager
$$\left\{ \begin{array}{l} \text{resign (esp. AmE)} \\ \text{should resign} \\ \text{resigns} \end{array} \right\} \text{(esp. BrE)}$$
(Quirk et al. 1985: 157)

In examples falling within this group, the non-realization of the action of the dependent clause is due to its reference to the future. As the action is only assumed to take place, it cannot be presupposed, and hence presented as given.

It is unthinkable that they should deny my request,
It worries me that their children should travel alone, (Quirk et al. 1985: 1014)

Huddleston and Pullum (2002: 188, note 57) point out that in examples of this kind, which involve a potential future situation whose actualisation is unthinkable, an unmodalised form is not possible, but an infinitival construction is, especially with a modalised main clause: *It is unthinkable that she should give up without a fight. / It would be unthinkable for her to give up without a fight.*

1.5 The *should*-clause in examples illustrating an unactualised action appears to be context independent, i.e. it constitutes the rheme. Remarkably, in the adduced examples it has not the function of subject but that of a verbal or adjectival complement. According to the list of expressions that occur with putative *should* or the indicative the least numerous group comprises verbs (*regret, marvel, rejoice, wonder*; Quirk et al. 1985: 1183). Much more numerous are adjectives (*proud, glad, sad, sorry, happy, thankful, angry, amazed, annoyed, astonished, disappointed, pleased, upset*, etc.) and constructions with extraposed subject (*strange, awkward, curious, odd, extraordinary, fortunate, irrational, silly, sad, admirable, deplorable, inconceivable, remarkable, understandable* and *-ing* participles of the verbs adduced above: *upsetting, disappointing, embarrassing* etc. (Quirk et al. 1985: 1223–24). In the case of adjectival and verbal complementation the position of the dependent *that*-clause after its governing expression is in accordance with its syntactic function, which generally blocks initial placement where the clause is context dependent.

2. As shown by (11) and the following examples, the potential textual function of *should* appears to represent a tendency rather than a regular use. Besides *should*, context-dependent *that*-clauses also display the indicative. Whereas in (11) the context-dependence of the *that*-clause is indicated by its initial position, in the following examples there is no such indication insofar as the *that*-clauses occur finally. In the absence of *should*, the only means showing context dependence is the context alone. In the case of the controlling adjective *odd*, the indicative was registered more frequently than *should*, but in some instances the degree of context-dependence may be questioned. In any case, the number of the examples is too small to allow drawing more general conclusions. Compare the following examples:

(12) a. It's odd, isn't it, that she bothered to tell us that?
  b. It's odd, isn't it, that it's a relief just speaking of him to you.
  c. It's odd that my fingers occasionally shake, but not when I am doing calligraphy.
  d. What's odd is that we found no invitations, no evidence she had friends.
(13) a. Only think of our happening to meet him. It was quite a chance ... that he had not gone round by Randalls. ... So very odd we should happen to meet,
  b. I remember thinking it odd that she should be so vehement all of a sudden when she didn't even know the man.

Considering context dependence of the *that*-clauses in these examples, we find that both the examples listed under (12) and under (13) show the same picture: (12) a., b. and (13) a. are clear-cut instances of context-dependence, whereas (12) c., d. and (13) b. display indicators of rhematic function. In (12) c. the *that*-clause contains, besides the context dependent part, novel information in the contrasting adversative section (*but not when I am doing calligraphy*). In (12) d. the rhematic function of the *that*-clause is indicated by the pseudo-cleft construction, a specific syntactic device serving to achieve the order theme—transition—rheme (cf. Dušková 1993). A similar picture appears in (13) b., which contains *should*, but at the same time the focaliser *even*, which assigns the intonation centre to the verb (*know*).

Other controlling expressions found in the collected examples are *wonder, cruel, sorry, fortunate, glad, strange, surprising*, again both with *should* and the indicative, though not after identical controllers.

(14) a. it is surprising that ... Muriel hadn't noticed that one light.
    b. It is strange that Agnes Arbuthnot didn't have it destroyed.
(15) a. It's cruel that all his hopes should come to this.
    b. I can see that it is distressing for you to find him here and I am sorry it should have happened.

The context dependence of the *that*-clauses in all these instances being clearly indicated, the use of textual *should* appears to be optional. Yet however marginal, it is worth considering, even if constituting only one component of a complex function involving grammar, semantics and discourse.

15. ON BOHUMIL TRNKA'S CONCEPT OF NEUTRALIZATION AND ITS NATURE ON THE HIGHER LANGUAGE LEVELS

First published in M. Procházka, M. Malá, and P. Šaldová (eds), *The Prague School and Theories of Structure*, Goettingen: V&R unipress, 2010, 87–103.

0. Bohumil Trnka's concept of neutralization is a recurrent point in his work,[1] closely related to his concept of oppositions. He regards it as a feature of all structural language levels: "The subject of the present paper [Trnka 1982c] is to draw the attention of linguists to two linguistic phenomena called homonymy and neutralization. Both of them operate on all structural levels of language, i. e. on the phonological, morphological, syntactic, and suprasyntactic levels … " (1982c: 356). Trnka himself was mostly concerned with neutralization in phonology and morphology, with a few digressions into syntax, but none—to my knowledge—into the suprasyntactic level.

This chapter is concerned with neutralization on the levels that involve meaning. As a relevant starting point, the first part (Section 1) outlines Trnka's conception of neutralization in morphology and syntax. In the second part (Section 2), neutralization is reconsidered on the level of morphology and elaborated on the syntactic level, with a tentative excursion into the level of utterance.

1. Neutralization is treated as the primary or a major point in two of Trnka's papers: the article from which the above quotation is drawn (Trnka 1982c) and a longer treatise concerned with morphological oppositions (Trnka 1982d). In the former,

---

1   According to the years of the first appearance of his articles included in *Selected Papers in Structural Linguistics* (1982) Trnka's concern with neutralization appears to extend over more than three decades (from 1938 [1982a, 1982i] to 1974 [1982c]; as shown by the years of the first publication of the other papers referred to in the present chapter—1961 [1982h], 1963 [1982f], 1966 [1982g], 1969 [1982e]—his interest in this point was continuous.

neutralization is contrasted with homonymy. The relation between the two concepts is expounded in terms of the phonological identity of the members of a morphological opposition in the case of homonymy, and suppression of the morphological opposition itself in the case of neutralization. Homonymy of lexical and morphemic oppositions is defined here as the identity of their phonological realizations. Pairs of words like *light* ('not heavy') and *light* ('pale'), *to lie* ('be at rest') and *to lie* ('to tell a lie') are homonymous because they are realized by identical phonological formations which do not contrast with each other in spoken English, while their lexical contrast and consequently their contextual distribution show them to be different words (lexical units). As examples of homonymy in the phonological realization of grammatical oppositions Trnka adduces, e.g., Latin inflexional suffixes *-ae:* identical form of the genitive and dative singular of the first declension (e. g. *familiae, agricolae*) in contrast to other declensions in which the two cases are differentiated (e.g. *mulieris : mulieri, dies : diei; -a* (nominative singular feminine—nominative, accusative plural neuter); *-um* (nominative, accusative singular neuter—accusative singular masculine), etc.; the English preterite and past participle suffix *-ed.* On the other hand, the verbal suffix *-ing* is not regarded as a homonymous morpheme, since its participial use differs from the gerundial only on the syntactic level. Similarly the prefix *un-* represents a single non-homonymous morpheme, because its two different senses (*unwise* 'not wise' x *to uncover* opposite of *to cover*) are distributed mechanically according to whether the base morpheme is an adjective or a verb.

Whereas homonymy involves the identity of phonological exponents of a morphological opposition, neutralization is suppression, under specified non-phonological conditions, of the morphological opposition itself. As one of the best known examples, Trnka adduces the suppression of the nominative versus accusative opposition which took place in Indo-European languages in the case of neuter nouns. For example in Latin, nouns like *vinum bonum, vina bona* appear in all syntactic positions in which all masculines or feminines must be put either in the nominative or in the accusative. A case of syntagmatic neutralization of the morphological opposition singular vs. plural is illustrated by the predicative noun, e. g. in *My brothers are merchants.* Here the opposition singular vs. plural in the predicative noun *merchants* is suppressed because it depends on the non-neutralized plural of the subject *my brothers* and does not express the plurality of *merchants.* The example is commented upon as follows:

> the grammatical concord in English and most IE languages is a case of the syntagmatic neutralization of their morphological singular v. plural (or dual) opposition, which is realized by singular or plural in accordance with the number of the governing noun. There is no specific form of a noun available which would be neither singular nor plural and which could be used in this syntagmatic position which requires a noun devoid of numerical qualification.
>
> (Trnka 1982c: 359)

A similar case of neutralization is found in negative sentences, since in his view negation is incompatible with a meaningful distinction between singular and plural in a sentence like *he has no child = he has no children* (Trnka 1982g: 343).[2] The most clear-cut formulation of the distinction is found in the treatise on morphological oppositions:

> The neutralization of morphological oppositions is fundamentally different from homonymy. In neutralization the opposition meaning of the members of the morphological pair disappears under certain non-phonological conditions and the whole opposition is represented by either one or the other member. Homonymy, on the other hand, does not have the function of the semantic suppression of the opposition, but only represents the identity of its phonological realization under certain phonological conditions. For example, the opposition of genitive singular vs. dative singular in the Czech feminine paradigm *kost* (bone) is realized by the same exponent (i, with occasional alternation of the final dental plosive), whereas in other Czech feminine paradigms the distinction of the two cases is upheld; the identity of genitive and dative singular *kosti* cannot be explained by stating semantic reasons, we must interpret this identity as a case of homonymy.
>
> (Trnka 1982d: 313)

Among other examples of homonymy of morphological exponents in Czech Trnka adduces nominative singular and nominative plural in neuter nouns *znamení* 'signal, sign', *moře* 'sea, ocean'—*znamení* 'signals, signs'—*moře* 'seas, oceans'. These instances are regarded as homonymous on the basis of the existence of other neuter paradigms, viz. *slovo* 'word', pl. *slova* 'words', *ptáče* 'young bird', pl. *ptáčata* 'young birds', *sémě* 'seed', pl. *semena* 'seeds'. If the Czech system of neuter nouns did not include these paradigms, the opposition of singular/plural in the nominative of all neuter nouns would be neutralized in Czech.

Neutralization plays an important role in the classification of morphological oppositions, which can be grouped according to whether they are relevant in the whole language system or whether they are suppressed (neutralized) under certain conditions. Neutralization of morphological oppositions is illustrated by gender in German, where gender distinctions are found in the singular but not in the plural. Similarly the morphological opposition nominative/accusative in the plural of animate masculines is neutralized in Slovak and Russian. According to whether neutralization depends on the base of the word, on the interplay with other morphological oppositions or on the syntactic context, Trnka distinguishes three types of neutralization:

(1) The neutralization of a morphological opposition is caused by the meaning of the base. For example the opposition of degrees of comparison, which characterizes adjectives, is neutralized in all adjectives that do not participate in the opposition of antonymy: *heavy, heavier, heaviest* against *metallic, Praguean*, etc. Only adjectives

---

2   The distinction between neutralization and homonymy is also expounded elsewhere, cf. "On morphemic homonymy" (Trnka 1982f) and "On some problems of neutralization" (Trnka 1982b).
"… morphemic homonymy must be strictly distinguished from neutralization of morphological oppositions. Whereas the former consists in the identity of the phonemic implementation of a morphological opposition, the latter is the suppression, under specific non-phonemic conditions, of the morphological opposition itself. Thus in Latin the identical form of the genitive singular and the dative singular of the first declension (e.g. *familiae, agricolae*) is an example of homonymy of both cases that are differentiated in other declensions (e. g. *mulieris : mulieri, dies : diei* …), the endings *-um* in *vinum* and *-a* in *verba* is a phonemic implementation of the neutralized opposition nominative/accusative. The neutralization of this opposition consists in the structural incompatibility of all neuters to take part in it." (Trnka 1982f: 336; similarly in Trnka 1982b: 153–54)

like *heavy* (x *light*), *poor* (x *rich*), *quick* (x *slow*), *healthy* (x *ill*) take the degrees of comparison.

(2) Neutralization is due to the participation of members of an opposition in another morphological opposition. Here Trnka adduces many examples, some of which have been mentioned above: the opposition of gender in nouns in the plural in German, Dutch and Scandinavian languages; the opposition nominative vs. accusative in the plural of animate masculine nouns in Slovak and Russian; the opposition nominative vs. accusative in the singular of neuter and inanimate masculine nouns in Slavonic languages; in Latin the opposition dative/ablative in all nouns in the plural; in Czech, Slovak and Russian the opposition nominative vs. accusative in inanimate masculine, all feminine and neuter nouns is neutralized in the plural.

In German the opposition of gender in nouns is neutralized in the plural: *der Knabe/er, die Frau / sie, das Kind / es—die Knaben / sie, die Frauen / sie, die Kinder / sie.*

(3) Neutralization is due to participation of the opposition members in syntactic oppositions. This type of neutralization is illustrated by concord in number between the subject and the predicative noun in a classifying predication, already adduced above, viz. *Moji bratři jsou rolníci* [my brothers are peasants]. The noun *peasants* does not express the opposition of plurality, because the plural form is only used to express concord in number with the subject, the actual number of peasants not being our concern. In other words, the neutralization of the opposition singular/plural is realized by the singular or by the plural form according to the grammatical number of the subject. Agreement with the number of the subject is further illustrated by instances like *The men had high hats on their heads*, where the forms *heads* and *hats* are used as a realization of the suppressed opposition of plurality. A fairly general case of neutralization of the singular/plural distinction is found in generic sentences. The realization form of this opposition is, according to Trnka, usually the singular *The swallow is a bird, An island is a piece of land surrounded by water*, or sometimes the plural *Dogs are useful animals*. Generic nouns displaying neutralization of the number opposition occur especially in negative and interrogative sentences.

Trnka also asks the question what is the cause of morphological neutralization. The answer seems easier for type one and three than for type two. Neutralization of the first type manifests itself as incompatibility of the particular opposition with the meaning of the word base. There is no point in comparing an adjective like *ferrous* if we refer to the substance. As for the third type of neutralization, it results from the fact that every word participating in a morphological opposition must also participate in its phonological realization either as the marked or the unmarked member of the opposition, even if this opposition is not desirable or even pointless in signalling the meaning of the particular syntactic context. Thus in the sentence *The dog is a domestic animal* the singular does not signal the opposition singular/plural, but refers to dogs in general. Since a language usually does not have nominal forms which are neither singular nor plural, it must use one of the two forms. Trnka points out that such a structure of morphological oppositions has certain disadvantages, of which a language like Chinese is free.

The causes of the second type of neutralization, the participation of an opposition in another morphological opposition, are less evident. According to Trnka they are to be sought neither in the phonological realization of the morphemes, nor in the operation of morpho(no)logical analogy, but in the needs of the sentence structure, and in the sphere of structural morphology in which the members of morphological oppositions are grouped along the syntagmatic axis.

The last point of importance with respect to neutralization in morphology concerns the number of features by which the members of an opposition pair are distinguished. The examples discussed so far all differ only in one feature. However, there are far more morphological oppositions whose members differ by several features and still correlate, e.g. the instrumental singular *otcem* in Czech: dative plural *otcům*. Can these oppositions be neutralized? According to Trnka, evidence for the existence of this type is provided, e. g., by Czech feminine nouns, all of which have identical form in the genitive singular and the nominative and accusative of the plural: *ženy* 'of a woman', 'women' (nominative and accusative plural); similarly in all the other feminine paradigms. This would appear to be a specific feature of morphology (or possibly of all higher levels), distinctly contrasting with the situation in phonology, where neutralization is found only between members of oppositions differing in one distinctive feature.

2. The extension of the phonological notion of neutralization to the higher language levels introduces a dual aspect into it: the loss of a distinction applies at the same time to form and meaning. As noted above, of the higher levels Trnka's treatment of neutralization mostly concerns morphology. Neutralization of morphological oppositions is explicitly defined in Trnka (1982d: 306):

> As any other morphological element, all these oppositions [=morphological oppositions] must consist of meaning and the phonological implementation of this meaning. The determination of the morphemic meaning is often very difficult—recall the problem of Russian case inflection which was examined by R. Jakobson (1936: 240–248). Let us therefore choose a less complex opposition: the opposition singular/plural in Present-day English. Its morphological (or general, classifying) meaning is 'plurality' vs. 'non-plurality' [...]. The marker of plurality is manifested with countable nouns as a number larger than one. [...] In the morphological analysis we are only interested in the basic semantic opposition of both members [...].

What follows from these formulations is that neutralization in morphology concerns the loss of distinction between the members of an opposition both in form and basic meaning (morphological, general, classifying), as demonstrated by plurality vs. non-plurality in the case of nouns.

2.1 Reconsidering the three types of neutralization of morphological oppositions specified above, we find that the aspect of meaning (Trnka's concept of the basic or morphological/ general/ classifying meaning) is fully operative in Types 1 and 3. In Type 1 the basic meaning involves the distinction between degrees of comparison: positive vs. comparative: vs. superlative. In the case of non-gradable adjectives, this distinction is blocked by the lexical meaning of the base morpheme. Accordingly, both prerequisites of morphological neutralization, neutralization of form (the opposition is expressed by one form, the positive) and meaning (loss of the capacity to distinguish degrees) are satisfied.

This type of morphological neutralization appears to be fairly common not only in the case of adjectives (and adverbs, for that matter, cf. *soon, sooner, soonest* x *now, then,* etc.), but also with nouns and verbs. For example, the opposition between generic and non-generic reference is incompatible with nouns that have unique reference (proper names), and the opposition singular vs. plural is blocked by the uncountable nature of uncountable nouns. As regards the verb, in Slavonic languages the opposition perfectivity vs. imperfectivity is incompatible with atelic verbs;[3] in English the opposition simple vs. progressive conjugation is annulled in the case of non-dynamic, stative verbs. A general constraint on verbal categories is due to the basic meaning of the categories themselves: thus the basic meaning of the imperative mood excludes reference to the past, and the basic meaning of the present conditional blocks the distinction between reference to the future and reference to the present.

Type 3 involves interaction between morphology and syntax. Significantly, all examples illustrating this type display neutralization of the singular/plural distinction. This is presumably not incidental, but rather reflects the fact that the meaning distinction between the singular and the plural is relatively easy to determine. In the case of concord between subject and subject complement in copular sentences

(1) My brothers are merchants.

the suppression of the singular/plural distinction in the subject complement primarily results from the semantics of the respective sentence type: the subject and the predicative noun are co-referential, the latter merely assigning the subject to a class. As shown by instances of discord, co-referentiality of the subject and the subject complement is a relevant feature of the sentence semantics. Compare examples adduced by Leech and Lu Li (1995):

(2) a. The successes of the Labour Party are good evidence of this.
    b. Mushrooms are a very risky crop.
    c. His achievements were just a part of a magnificent year.
    d. They are now a threat.

Here the subject complements lack the feature of co-referentiality. Although they also assign the subject to a class, they are closer to qualification than classification. Leech and Lu explain the discord by the adjective-like character of the predicative

---

3   Panevová (1981: 88) regards this type of neutralization as semantic defectiveness.

nouns,[4] basing their arguments on the prototype theory. The definitional core of the category of NPs consists in (a) being referring expressions, (b) beginning with a determiner, and (c) containing a head noun of variable number. Noun phrases in the discussed sentence type resemble the prototypical adjective phrase in being (a) property ascribing, (b) abstract, (c) gradable and (d) invariable.

The other instance of neutralization of the singular/plural distinction due to the interaction of syntax is even more illustrative:

(3) The men had high hats on their heads.

In this type the loss of the semantic distinction sometimes overrides the concord principle: the member representing the neutralized opposition may take either form, i.e. also the discordant one. Quirk et al. (1985: 768) treat this type of concord as distributive number, with the following comment and examples after the prototypical example (4) a.: "While the distributive plural is the norm, the distributive singular may also be used to focus on individual instances."

(4) a. Have you all brought your cameras? ['Each has a camera']
    b. The students raised their hand(s).
    c. Some children have understanding fathers / an understanding father.
    d. We all have good appetites / a good appetite.
    e. Pronouns agree with their antecedent(s).

Besides concord, this type of neutralization is illustrated by the loss of number distinction in generic sentences.

(5) a. The swallow is a bird.

The suppression of the singular/plural distinction between both form and meaning is easily demonstrated here by the potential alternation of singular and plural forms in many of these instances:

(5) b. Swallows are birds.

There is even orthographic evidence for the loss of both the formal and the meaning distinction between the singular and the plural of generic nouns, found in some instances of the possessive case. Instances listed under (6) (drawn from Quirk et al. 1985: 327–28) show vacillation between the singular and the plural even in writing.

---

4   Among other adjectival features of noun phrases in the function of subject complement they noted their restricted occurrence with copulas other than *be*, the tendency of singular count nouns to omit the article, facile coordination of nouns and adjectives in this function, occurrence of nouns with the semantic feature of gradability, the dummy noun phenomenon, e.g. *our departure was a hurried one*. (Leech and Lu Li 1995)

(6) a. There were ten farmer's / farmers' wives at the meeting,
    b. a girl's school / a girls' school.[5]

Yet another example of neutralization of the singular/plural opposition is demon-strated by negative sentences of the type

(7) a. He has no brother / no brothers.

A set that is empty remains empty whatever number of potential members is de-nied. It is worth noting that this type represents the only instance referred to under neutralization in the index of *The Cambridge Grammar of the English Language* (Hud-dleston and Pullum 2002: 389). In the adduced example, here listed as (7) b., the two forms are described as semantically equivalent with little pragmatic difference.

(7) b. No juvenile was admitted. / No juveniles were admitted.

In other instances, the pragmatic difference may play a role: one of the forms may be preferred or required.

(7) c. He has no father. / *He has no fathers.
    d. He has no child. / He has no children.

In (7) c. the singular is required because one does not have more than one (bio-logical) father. In (7) d., on the other hand, the plural may be preferred as reflecting the more usual case.[6]

The realization form of a neutralized morphological opposition appears to play a role only in the respective pragmatic implications. As is known from phonology, neutralization of an opposition is formally implemented by either member in depen-dence on the environments; e. g. in Czech the neutralization of voice in paired con-sonants is realized by the voiceless member at the end of words (cf. *led* [let] 'ice' and *let* [let] 'flight'), but by the voiced member before a paired voiced consonant (cf. *prosba* [prozba] and *hrozba* [hrozba]). There are also instances where the neutralization form is identical with neither member, e. g. *comfort* [kaɱfət], containing a variant of the phoneme /m/, which represents all nasal phonemes in English before labials.

---

5 Quirk et al. (1985: 328, note [a]) point out the tendency of the genitive of generic nouns (descriptive genitive in their terminology) to have an idiomatic connection with the head noun, which may eventually result in the formation of a compound.

6 On the basis of these examples the authors argue for the plural as the default choice: in (7) c. the singular is re-quired because one does not have more than one (biological) father; in (7) d. the plural would be normally used because it is more usual to have two or more children than just one. One may wonder whether the comment on (7) d. still applies, and what the pragmatic choice would be in (7) a. and in instances with a fixed number of the members of a set like *He has no grandmother / grandmothers*.

The second type of neutralization, neutralization due to the participation of members of an opposition in another morphological opposition, is illustrated by many examples, most of which are drawn from the declension of nouns. Specifically, neutralization is postulated for cases for which none of the respective paradigms displays distinctive forms: the opposition nominative vs. accusative in the plural of animate masculine nouns in Slovak and Russian; the opposition nominative vs. accusative in the singular of neuter and inanimate masculine nouns in Slavonic languages; in Latin the opposition dative/ablative in all nouns in the plural, the opposition of nominative/accusative in both the singular and plural of all neuter nouns, etc.

(8) *vinum bonum* nominative/accusative singular
     vina bona nominative/accusative plural
(9) *feminīs, servīs, puerīs, victōribus, rēbus …*
     dative/ablative plural

Yet this type appears deficient in meeting the second criterion of neutralization, the suppression of meaning; cf. the formulation quoted above, "[=morphological oppositions] must consist of meaning and the phonological implementation of this meaning." What is here identical is only the form. The basic meaning of the cases is different, however difficult to determine it may be, especially as regards the nominative and the accusative (cf. the definition of the ablative and dative in Pyles and Algeo (1993: 338, 343): Ablative A case typically showing separation and source, but also instrument and cause; Dative A case typically marking the indirect object or recipient.) In the above quotation, Trnka himself refers to Jakobson's *Kasuslehre* (1936), where cases are treated as forms involving invariant meaning.

As shown by (10) a. and b., the semantic relations between the undifferentiated nominative and accusative forms of neuter nouns are identical to those between the differentiated nominative and accusative forms in other genders: the nominative is here the agent and the accusative the patient.

(10) a. House kloflo kachně. The gosling$_{nom}$ pecked the duckling$_{acc}$
         x Kachně kloflo house. The duckling$_{nom}$ pecked the gosling$_{acc}$
     b. Husa klofla kachnu. The goose$_{nom}$ pecked the duck$_{acc}$
         x Kachna klofla husu. The duck$_{nom}$ pecked the goose$_{acc}$

All examples of neutralization discussed so far, including types 1 and 3, involve neutralization of morphological oppositions. Even in the two types that involve the syntactic aspect, neutralization again affects morphological oppositions, not syntactic ones.

2.2 Looking for potential candidates of neutralization in syntax, we need to specify the features on the basis of which they can be identified. On the analogy of morphological oppositions we seek related syntactic structures which differ in one syntactic feature and alternate with each other; in other words, syntactically related structures whose semantic distinction has been suppressed. As an instance of this kind we may consider the non-agentive passive which alternates with the active without appreciable difference in meaning. Compare the examples under (11).

(11) a. Atoms are formed / form if the ions are diatomic
  b. In ion-ion recombination the electron transfers / is transferred from the negative ion to the positive ion.[7]
  c. The word derives / is derived from Latin.

Here we have two related syntactic structures differing in the feature active vs. passive, which normally contrast with each other semantically, but which appear to be more or less in free variation.

Another instance of syntactic neutralization within the English verb system is found in the infinitive operating as a postmodifier of a noun. Compare (12) a. and b. While in (12) a. the active and the passive convey their respective meanings, in (12) b. the formal distinction becomes irrelevant since both forms express passive meaning.

(12) a. his wish to teach ≠ his wish to be taught (is sincere)
  b. The only thing to do / to be done (is to deny everything).

In the sphere of sentences and clauses, potential neutralization can be exemplified by two contrasting structures: positive vs. negative polarity and locative vs. existential sentences.

Theoretically, sentence polarity appears to be irrelevant in *yes-no* questions, whose primary function is to ascertain in which polarity the content being expressed applies; this function can be served by either polarity. The only systemic constraint is the marked nature of the negative form. In language use this constraint appears to be a powerful one, alternation of positive and negative polarity being found only in rare cases. One type is encountered in Czech: either a positive or negative question can be used in the same situation with hardly any semantic distinction. What differences there are consist in the pragmatic aspects, the negative form being less direct, and hence more tentative. Compare examples (13) a. and b.:

(13) a. Máš / nemáš známku? (literally: Have you / not-have you stamp?)
  b. Znáš / neznáš jeho adresu? (literally: Know you / not-know you his address?)

In English this use of negative *yes-no* questions does not occur. Nevertheless, a marginal case of alternating polarity may be found in *yes-no* questions operating in the secondary function of expressing invitation, offer, suggestion, as in (14).

---

7   Examples (11) a. and b. are shortened versions of examples adduced in Dušková (1971: 124), where this point is treated at more length.

(14) Will / won't you join us ?

As in (13), the difference between the two forms is here of a pragmatic nature: the negative form gives the addressee more freedom in responding according to his/ her choice.

As regards locative and existential sentences, their structures and contrasting meaning are nearly always fully operative. Instances of blurred structure and meaning are even more marginal than in the preceding cases. It is to be noted that here neutralization requires very special contextual conditions. Compare (15) a. and b.

(15) a. There is cheese and ham in the fridge. / In the fridge there is cheese and ham.
        ≠ The ham and cheese are in the fridge.
     b. He seemed to see the appeal in her eyes, *as there surely was*, for she was thinking, If his mother comes ..., ... it will be someone else to talk to.

The *there*-clause in (15) b. appears as a case of suppression of the locative vs. existential distinction in that *there* in this clause merges both the locative *(there= in her eyes)* and the existential function *(as there surely was there=in her eyes)*.

The last two points to be discussed are two types of subordinate clauses which do not lend themselves to facile classification.

The first is the subordinate clause in the cleft sentence. Although resembling the relative clause, it also differs from it in several relevant points.[8] In the case of some antecedents the deviation from the relative clause is so essential that the subordinator *that*, which is the only choice here, is to be regarded as the conjunction and not a relative pronoun. Compare the first two examples in (16) with those given under c. a d.: while in (16) a. and b. the subordinate clause bears all features of a relative clause, in c. and d. relative interpretation fails to apply.

(16) a. Those who are faithful know only the trivial side of love. It's the faithless who know love's tragedies.
     b. It was the girl whom/that/zero they blamed (not the boy).
     c. It was with great misgivings that he looked at the strange food on his plate.
     d. Why is it that you dislike her so much?

As shown by these instances, the contrast between the relative clause vs. content clause is here suppressed, the neutralized form being identifiable with neither; the subordinate clause of the cleft sentence represents a structure sui generis, which is doubtless a consequence of the relationship between the cleft and the underlying non-cleft form: a sentence expressing one propositional content is syntactically dissociated into two clauses.

---

8   For a more detailed discussion of this point and references to the literature, see Dušková (1993: 73–77).

The other type of clause that can be regarded as a neutralized form of two distinct types of subordinate clauses is found in the case of an *if*-clause in the position of an extraposed subject content clause, as in (17). Compare a. and b.

(17) a. It is understandable that they feel threatened.
    b. It is understandable if they feel threatened.
    c. If they feel threatened, it is understandable. x That they feel threatened is understandable.

Leaving aside the interpretation of the *if*-clause in (17) b. as a straightforward adverbial clause of condition, which presupposes anaphoric function of the initial *it*, we get an entirely analogous structure as in (17) a.: initial *it* has an anticipatory function and the *if*-clause occurs in the position of extraposed subject. The only difference here consists in the presentation of the content of the subordinate clause: whereas in (17) a. it is presented as a fact, in (17) b. its truth value is conditional.[9] As shown by (17) c., the subject interpretation of (17) b. applies only to the linear arrangement with the *if*-clause in final position. When placed initially, the *if*-clause is again clearly adverbial, its only special feature being the co-referentiality of *it* and the content of the entire *if*-clause.

Considering the examples under discussion with respect to their character, they appear to differ from instances of morphological neutralization in two respects: the first is inherent in the syntactic level as such, and the second is connected with it. While in morphology, neutralization involves form and meaning, in syntax it involves another additional aspect: apart from form (structure) and semantic roles and/or sentence semantics, it also comprises syntactic function. Consequently, the conditions giving rise to neutralization are more complex. Even though more examples of syntactic neutralization can doubtless be found, they will hardly substantially differ from those that have been presented. The complexity of the neutralizing conditions rules out the central functions and uses of most structures, so that potential instances have to be looked for on the periphery of syntactic categories. This circumstance determines the characteristics of the adduced examples of neutralization: all types are (1) rare, (2) marginal (within the range from very marginal to more or less marginal), and (3) involve special, in some cases marked, uses. These characteristics will presumably remain true even for a larger collection.

2.3 The last point to be considered is neutralization on the suprasentential level. As stated in the introductory quotation, Trnka postulated neutralization for all levels, including the highest. His conception of this level was very broad insofar as it covered not only functional sentence perspective, but also stylistics and some pragmatic aspects such as illocutionary force and conversational implicatures (cf. Trnka 1990: 23).

---

9   This point is treated at more length in the doctoral dissertation of Vladislav Smolka (Smolka 2007: 19). Clauses like (17) b. are regarded as "a combination of a subject clause and a conditional clause which have merged and where the subject clause is meaningful only if the condition expressed in the *if*-clause is true."

However, the highest level is not elaborated in his work. According to his brief outline, functional sentence perspective appears to play a major role insofar as the basic units of the suprasentential level are identified with the theme and the rheme. Hence instances of neutralization are to be sought in the suppression of the distinction between the FSP functions.

Here the first problem that arises is the system of the FSP functions themselves. Although most theories of information structure recognize only two, the theme and the rheme (whatever terms may be used), the theoretical framework elaborated by Jan Firbas (1992), the most widely used theory among Czech anglicists, works with a third function, transition, implemented by the verb. In general, the FSP structure is regarded as a gradient which in the interpretative arrangement displays a gradual rise in communicative dynamism. Nevertheless, since the only poles in this arrangement are the theme and the rheme, even this framework offers only these two functions as potential candidates for neutralization.

Another problem arises in connection with the realization form of these units. In contrast to the units of the lower levels, the realization forms of the theme and the rheme fail to provide a distinctive formal criterion. The theme and the rheme are largely realized in the same way, by noun phrases and adverbial phrases. A different realization form is found only in the case of the verb where one constituent of the verb phrase, usually the lexical element, may operate as the rheme. This also applies to the verbo-nominal predication when the subject complement, which as rule constitutes the rheme, is implemented by an adjective phrase.

Altogether, the problem appears to be approachable only on the basis of the distinctive features of the FSP functions. These are to be sought in the FSP factors: linearity, context, semantics, and intonation in speech.

Starting with linearity, the theme is by definition the least dynamic and the rheme the most dynamic element, irrespective of position. Still, though not invariably, position as the indicator of an FSP function applies in a majority of instances: the theme is mostly found at the beginning of the sentence or in preverbal position and the rheme at the end or in postverbal position. To this extent it might be argued that where the rheme occurs at the beginning and the theme at the end, the (limited) distinctiveness of linearity is neutralized. This might be illustrated by rhematic subjects in initial position, as in (18):

(18) A car pulled up at the curb.

Compare the Czech equivalent *U chodníku zastavilo auto* [At the curb pulled up a car] in which the rheme occurs at the end.

Context dependence/independence is of a similar nature. Although given (context-dependent) elements mostly constitute the theme and new (context-independent) elements the rheme, both these functions often display a composite structure containing both given and new elements. Moreover, even given elements function as rhemes and new elements as themes, the FSP structure being ultimately determined by the interplay of all factors. Only an FSP configuration displaying an entirely new theme and an entirely given rheme might be regarded as neutralization of the contextual factor, but such a configuration is hard to conceive.

Within the FSP theory the semantic factor is treated in terms of dual semantics, static and dynamic, the latter being represented by the dynamic semantic functions constituting the presentation scale and the quality scale. Since the distinction between the two basically depends on the dynamic semantics of the verb in conjunction with the context independence of the subject, instances of the neutralization of this factor might be sought where the verb fails to indicate presentation or quality, which is regarded as an instance of potentiality by Firbas (1992: 108–110), "which occurs when the interplay of FSP factors permit of more than one interpretation." Compare his example:

(19) as great crowds gathered to him, [he entered a boat and sat down]

While the potential interpretation of the FSP structure in (19) either as the presentation of a phenomenon (*great crowds*) on the scene, or as ascribing a quality (*gathered*) to a quality bearer (*great crowds*) is an instance of homonymy, it might be argued that the distinctive function of the semantic factor is neutralized insofar as it fails to operate.

The last factor, intonation, primarily operates in speech, while in writing the FSP structure as a rule results from the interplay of the other three factors. Even so it appears to qualify as a neutralizable feature best in that the rheme generally bears the intonation centre (the nucleus). Hence it may be said that where the intonation centre falls on an element other than the rheme, the distinctive potential of this feature is neutralized. Such instances are rarely found where the automated pattern of falling intonation with the intonation centre at the end overrides the rhematic function of the initial subject, illustrated in (18).

To conclude, this tentative discussion of neutralization on the level of FSP has confirmed what was found about neutralization in syntax: the more variables are involved, the less favourable the conditions for neutralization become. Even more than in syntax, the instances of neutralization found on the level of FSP, if accepted as such, are peripheral or even non-existent.

ACKNOWLEDGEMENTS

The research reported in this chapter has been supported by the Czech government grant MSM-0021620825.

16. SOME THOUGHTS ON POTENTIALITY
IN SYNTACTIC AND FSP STRUCTURE

First published in V. Smolka (ed.), *The Dynamics of the Language System. South Bohemian Anglo-American Studies*, No. 2, České Budějovice: University of South Bohemia, 2008, 3–13.

0. The term potentiality has been introduced by Mathesius in his seminal paper "On the potentiality of the phenomena of language" (Mathesius 1911). Potentiality is here defined as static vacillation at a particular period of time, 'static' being used in the sense of 'synchronic' (changeability at one point of the temporal axis), in contrast to 'dynamic', i.e. 'diachronic': changeability in the course of time (along the temporal axis). The concept is clarified by a discussion of points from different language levels: vowel quantity in dependence on the position and the following consonant(s); identifiability of the word within the flow of speech, potential distinction of word classes according to the degree of the word stress they carry, vacillation of intellectual and expressive elements in the semantic structure of a large majority of naming units, and finally the relationship between linguistics and stylistics (stylistic aspects in pronunciation, vocabulary and syntax). The point at issue appears to be the delimitation of two adjacent categories, such as the boundary between short and long English vowels, determination of the function of a diminutive suffix (small size, attitudinal connotation or both), etc. This view closely coincides with the concepts of centre and periphery, developed some fifty years later by the adherents of the Prague school (cf. *Travaux linguistiques de Prague* 2, 1966). In particular, Mathesius' potentiality and the peripheral sphere of a linguistic category share the feature of indeterminacy with respect to the assignment of a point to one or two or even more categories. Where a linguistic item is only weakly marked as regards the prototypical features of its category and there is no other competing category to which the item can be assigned, it still belongs in the periphery of the former; however, it fails to constitute a case of potentiality. This distinction clearly follows from the treatment of non-thematic subjects by Firbas (1966), as will appear from the part concerned with potentiality in FSP.

In the second volume of *Travaux linguistiques de Prague*, which is as a whole devoted to the question of centre and periphery (it bears the subtitle *Les problèmes du centre et de la périphérie du système de la langue*), the criteria for distinguishing central from peripheral phenomena are specified in the opening article by Daneš (1966). He adduces two criteria established by Vachek (1964: Chapter 2: 9–21), relevant on the phonological level: the degree of integration within the respective phonological system and the functional load. That is, a peripheral phoneme is not fully integrated and/or has a low functional load. To these criteria, Daneš adds a third, the frequency of occurrence of the given language unit. This criterion is demonstrated by the verb *be / být / esse*, which has a very low degree of integration in the verb system, but is functionally highly versatile and has a high frequency of occurrence. Accordingly, it cannot be regarded as peripheral. As an example of a peripheral element Vachek (1966: 28) adduces the ModE phoneme /h/: "... the Present-Day Standard English /h/ constitutes an example of ... a heterogeneous, non-integrated element of the ModE phonological system, an element not bound by any paradigmatic relations with any other member of the pattern." Explicitly, ModE /h/ lacks a voiced counterpart and its position is greatly limited in that it occurs only before vowels. This peripheral phoneme can well serve as an example of an element whose peripheral status does not involve potentiality: its phonemic status remains indisputable. On the other hand instances of potentiality need not invariably belong in the very periphery of a category, but may rank somewhat higher. For example, there are numerous words in English whose morphemic structure remains indeterminate in respect of their assignment to affixation or compounding. "Constituents in complex words are sometimes identical in form with bases but yet resemble affixes in certain respects so that it is not always easy to justify regarding the resultant words as compounds. For example, *input, output, sit-in* (n), *drop-out* (n), *childlike* have components formally and functionally resembling separate items in corresponding phrases ('they put the data in', 'he dropped out of college', 'he is like a child') that make them like compounds. On the other hand, the items *in-, -like*, etc., have the type of wide distribution and nonlexical character that is typical of affixes. Given the historical fact that *–like* is cognate with the indisputably affixal *–ly* ..., it seems clear that the distinction is gradient rather than absolute." (Quirk et al.1985: 1520).

In linguistic literature the centre/periphery aspect of linguistic phenomena is dealt with under diverse terms. Neústupný (1966: 39) treats the problem in terms of linguistic vagueness, which he regards as synonymous with a number of other terms: "complexity and indeterminacy" (Kruševskij), "potentiality" (Mathesius), "border-line cases" (Bloomfield), "Klarheit der Differenziation" (Skalička), "asymmetry" (Skalička), "des nuances plutôt que des oppositions" and "oppositions phonologiques de stabilité différante" (Malmberg), "open systems" (Milewski), "complexity" (Skalička), "continuities," "differences of degree" (Wells), "degrees of relevance" (Jensen), "generality and gradience" (Bolinger), "vagueness of linguistic structure," "asymmetry" (Neústupný), "Zentrum, Peripherie, Übergang" (Daneš), "peripheral elements" (Vachek) and the like. Of the large recent grammars of English this concept, referred to as "gradience," is widely employed by Quirk et al. (1985; e.g. gradience between modal and main verbs, 147–48); gradience between complex prepositions and free noun-phrase sequences, 671–72; gradience and multiple analysis, 732–38; ellipsis defined in terms of gradience, 888–89).

In what follows potentiality is conceived as assignability of a linguistic element to two different categories, whether or not it can be classed as strictly peripheral. It is demonstrated on two language levels, in syntax and on the level of functional sentence perspective. A comparison of the two language levels from this viewpoint shows the different nature of the respective factors potentiality is due to, thus displaying their specificity.

1. In syntax, potentiality is met with as a consequence of asymmetry between form and function. English is systemically predisposed in this respect insofar as its analytic nature involves a limited inventory of formal distinctions. Of the many points that might be adduced to demonstrate this feature, two will be considered: potentiality due to polyfunctional syntactic position(s) and potentiality resulting from the counteraction of purely formal syntactic and functional/semantic criteria.

1.1 Polyfunctional syntactic positions as such do not as a rule result in potentiality since the valency of the verb determines both the obligatory clause elements and their semantic roles, and sentence semantics. Thus the postverbal position which may contain an object, a subject complement or an adverbial rarely involves potentiality, only one of these functions being allowed by the respective syntactico-semantic relations. Compare the examples given under (1).

(1) a. He has a good teacher. (transitive verb: object)
    b. He is a good teacher. (copular verb: subject complement)
    c. He looked angrily (at the mess). (full verb < adverb as modifier: adverbial of manner)
    d. He looked angry. (copular verb < adjective as complement: subject complement)
(2) a. He kept turning from side to side. (copula if *turning* is a participle; transitive verb if *turning* is a gerund)
    b. He looked hard. (copula if *hard* is an adjective; intransitive verb if *hard* is an adverb)

As shown by (2), potentiality is here peripheral in that it arises only under specific conditions: in both a. and b. the verb belongs in several valency classes and the complement or modifier lacks formal categorial (verb-form or word-class) distinctions; in b., moreover, the verb is used in a minimal context.

Another instance of potentiality is found where the verb is followed by two elements: NP + NP, NP + PrepP, or NP + infinitive. Again, the structure is as rule unequivocal owing to the valency of the verb and sentence semantics (including semantic roles of the nominal elements.) Compare the examples listed under (3).

(3) a. He gave the class difficult homework. (ditransitive verb, personal referent of the first NP, inanimate referent of the second NP: indirect object + direct object)
   b. They appointed Mr. Brown chairman. (complex transitive verb, personal referent of the first NP, second NP coreferential with the first: direct object + object complement)
   c. Have you read the book everybody praises so much? (the sequence of the post-verbal nominal elements, inanimate participant before the animate personal, rules out ditransitive interpretation of *read*; two finite verbs, two clauses: first NP object of the first verb, second NP subject in the second clause)

Potentiality due to this configuration is mostly found with the verbs *make*, *find* and *call* occurring in minimal contexts, which is again rare, cf. (4)

(4) I found him a good teacher. (ditransitive verb, indirect object, direct object: 'I found a good teacher for him'; complex transitive verb, direct object, object complement: 'I found that he was a good teacher.')

Nor is potentiality frequent in the case of verb complementation by NP + PrepP. In spite of being polysemous, the lexical component of the preposition governing the second element indicates explicitly, though on occasion not unequivocally, the underlying semantic relations. Here the PrepP may function as postmodification of the object or as a separate clause element, an adverbial, as shown in (5) a. and (5) b. Example (5) c., presenting an instance of potentiality, shows that the contextual conditions which allow assignment of the prepositional phrase to two categories are very specific, viz. definite reference in both nouns. Indefinite reference of the noun in the prepositional phrase, cf. (5) d., would preferably indicate adverbial function, unless the context is contrastive.

(5) a. a. They hired a room with mahogany furniture. ('a room furnished with mahogany furniture'; postmodification)
   b. They furnished the room with mahogany furniture. ('How did they furnish the room?'; adverbial)
   c. He hit the man with the cane. ('the man who carried the cane': postmodification; or 'the act was performed with a cane': adverbial)
   d. He hit the man with a cane. ('the act was performed with a cane'; ?'the man who had a cane' < 'he hit the man who carried a cane, not the man with the crutch')

Similarly (5)':

(5)'a. He wrote a book about ancient myths. ('what kind of book?' postmodification)
   b. He walked hundreds of miles about these parts. ('where did he walk?' 'about these parts he walked hundreds of miles; adverbial of place)
   c. English cathedrals have open spaces about them.

('English cathedrals have open spaces surrounding them / which are about them'; postmodification)
('Where do English cathedrals have open spaces?' 'About them, English cathedrals have open spaces'; adverbial of place)

Where the second element is expressed by an infinitive, there is usually no explicit indication of the syntactic function since adverbial infinitives of purpose mostly occur without their markers *in order* or *so as*. Nor does *for* serve as a means of distinction because it merely introduces the subject of the infinitival clause; this applies not only to the adverbial and the postmodifying function, but also to all the other syntactic functions of the infinitive. Of the three adduced realization forms, potentiality in this type is met with most frequently. Compare (6) a., b. and c.

(6) a. He could think of nothing to say. ('nothing that he could say' / 'that could be said'; postmodification)
   b. I sent that letter to ask for a leave of absence. ('in order to ask'; adverbial of purpose)
   c. He gave his staff time to return to their offices. ('time in which they could return', postmodification; or 'so that they could return', adverbial of purpose)

Similarly (6'):

(6)'I know you have some theory to make sense of it all.
   ('a theory that makes sense of it all'; postmodification)
   ('I know you have some theory in order to make sense of it all;' adverbial infinitive of purpose).

Another type of potentiality displayed by an infinitive in the position after a nominal element is illustrated by (7).

(7) He wants her to have kids.
   a. 'he wants that she should have kids'
   b. 'he wants her in order to have kids / so that he can have kids'.

Here the infinitive is either a complex object which has a subject different from that of the superordinate verb, cf. (7) a.; or the object is the nominal element alone, and the infinitive is a regular infinitive of purpose with a subject identical with that of the superordinate verb whose semantic structure includes the feature of intentionality, as in (7) b. Jespersen (1940: 286–87) notes yet another type of potentiality shown by the verb *want*, viz. between complex object [NP + inf.] and postmodified substantival object: "such a man wants a wife to look after him = either 'wants that a wife looks after him', or (rather) 'wants a wife that may ...'" He adduces another example of this kind: "I wanted a woman to save me." (*ibid.*)

1.2 The second instance of syntactic potentiality to be mentioned involves the counteraction of formal syntactic and functional semantic criteria. This problem was encountered in the chapters dealing with syntactic constancy of clause elements between English and Czech. Here the first step required to establish the measure of syntactic constancy was identification of syntactically corresponding and non-corresponding counterparts in the other language. This appeared to be problematic in the case of the subject complement and the verb, cf. Chapters 4 (2., 2.1, 2.2), 5 (1., 2.) and 7 (1.2, 1.4).

In the case of the subject complement the problem arose where a subject complement in the original appeared as a dependent component of a subject complement in the translation. This happened in the case of subject complements reflected in modifiers of subject complements realized by nouns. On purely formal grounds such instances qualify for inclusion among non-identical instances. From the semantic point of view, however, there is the question how to treat qualifying predications rendered in the other language as a qualification by non-genuine classification (to use the term coined by Mathesius 1975: 114).The point is illustrated by examples from Chapters 4 and 5, cf. (8).[1]

(8) a. náš odjezd byl velmi kvapný [our departure was very hurried]
     our departure was a hurried one
  b. She was the first person to see the bones ...
     Byla první, kdo spatřil kosti ... [She was first who saw ...]
  c. Věda je vznešená a krásná. [science is sublime and beautiful]
     Science ... was a sublime and beautiful thing
  d. bylo to hrozné [it was awful]
     It was something awful

None of the heads of the subject complements introduces a distinctive element into the semantic structure of the sentence. In a. the head is an anaphoric proform of the noun realizing the subject; in b. the subject complement repeats the semantic features of the personal pronoun implementing the subject; and in c. and d. the heads of the subject complements are, respectively, a general noun and an indefinite pronoun, both referring generally to unspecified inanimate entities. Assignment of these sentences to the classifying or the qualifying predication represents an instance of potentiality.

Problems of this kind appear to be connected with the clause elements constituting the predicative act. This is even more evident from the translation counterparts of the finite verb (cf. Chapter 7, 1.2, 1.4), which range on a gradient from fully corresponding to fully non-corresponding. The gradient nature of the equivalents appears to be due

---

1   In the study by Leech and Lu Li (1995), who demonstrated the adjectival features of nouns functioning as subject complements in copular predications displaying disagreement in number between the subject complement and the subject (cf. Chapter 15, 2.1) there was one example qualifying as an instance of potentiality *Father Harry was a pro, brother Phil turned pro on the same date as Danny* (1995: 188), where the word-class status of *pro* in the second clause is indeterminate.

to the asymmetry between verbal categories and the syntactic function of the finite verb. However, since variation in the verbal categories of the finite verb does not affect its syntactic function, non-correspondence in this respect may be disregarded. Accordingly, finite verbs deviating in tense and/or mood were classed as identical, cf. (9) a. and b.:

(9) a. Mrs Poulteney thought she *had been* the subject of a sarcasm. (FL, 83)
       Paní Poulteneyová zatrnula, že *je* [is] obětí sarkasmu. (Ž, 84)
   b. To the ignorant it *may* seem that ... (FL, 58)
       Nezasvěceným lidem *by* se *mohlo* [might] zdát, že ... (Ž, 58)

Presumably lower on the gradient from correspondence to non-correspondence rank predicates which differ in modal or phasal modification, as in (10) a. and b.

(10) a. But in a way the matter ... worried her less than it *might* a modern girl. (FL, 68)
       V určitém smyslu ji otázka ... znepokojovala méně než *by* tomu *bylo* [would be] ... u moderního děvčete. (Ž, 68)
    b. Mrs Poulteney *began to change* her tack. (FL, 83)
       Paní Poulteneyová *změnila* [*changed* perfective] taktiku. (Ž, 83)

Since neither of these components constitutes a separate clause element but functions only within the verb phrase, i.e. together with the lexical component they realize one syntactic unit, verb phrases showing shifts of this kind again quality as corresponding rather than non-corresponding.

Proceeding still lower on the gradient we arrive at shifts in polarity, and finally to shifts from verbal to verbonominal predicates and vice versa, which are primarily treated as instances subsumable under the constancy of the subject complement. This gradient may serve as an example of full coincidence between the concept of centre/periphery and that of potentiality.

2. Proceeding to potentiality on the level of functional sentence perspective, we again find the second volume of *Travaux linguistiques de Prague* to be instrumental in this respect.

2.1 In his treatise on non-thematic subjects Firbas (1966) considers their status within the system of FSP in order to verify Mathesius' pronouncement stating (in Firbas's translation, p. 239) that "English differs from Czech in being so little susceptible to the requirements of FSP as to frequently disregard them altogether." This view was based on Mathesius' conception of word order as the only factor of FSP, which cannot explain non-thematic subjects in initial position. By demonstrating that FSP is the result of an interplay of several factors, viz. semantic structure and context in/dependence in addition to word order, with intonation as a fourth factor operating in speech, Firbas shows two things: first, that non-thematic subjects do not testify to the insusceptibility of English to FSP because their FSP function is clearly indicated by the same means as that of thematic subjects; and second, "Although they may not belong to the very centre of the language system, they are, together with the thematic subjects, fully integrated in it, and cannot be regarded as peripheral phenomena." (1966: 253) What he regards as peripheral FSP phenomena are instances of multifunctionality, i.e. instances which do not allow unequivocal assignment of an FSP structure. The term potentiality is not employed here but its application to cases of the same kind in later works (esp. Firbas 1992: 108–110, 129–30, 165–66, 180–82, 183–86, 221–22) shows that these two terms are used as synonyms.

As regards the causes of multifunctionality, the adduced examples show indeterminacy in the semantic classification of the verb, cf. (11) a. and b. "... *hospitable people and the scribes and elders* ... will be rhematic ... if the verbs *waiting* and *gathered* are understood to distinctly express the notion of 'appearance or existence on the scene'. ... On the other hand, the two verbs can be understood fully to express the notions of 'waiting' and 'gathering' respectively, the subjects becoming thematic. ... the English versions would lose their multifunctional character only in the spoken language, which has at its disposal another important means of FSP—that of intonation." (Firbas 1966: 250–51).

(11) a. [... and then, another half-hour, and you are outside the greatest city in the world; you alight at a small station] where hospitable people are *waiting* for you, [and you are in the English country]
      b. [but those who had seized Jesus took him away to the house of Caiaphas the high priest,] where the scribes and elders had *gathered*. (Firbas1966: 250)

In later works (1992, 1994, 1995) Firbas adds two more factors that may give rise to potentiality: the graded nature of givenness and the length of the retrievability span.

The graded nature of givenness is expounded in connection with co-referentiality, which in the case of mere re-expression of the same element signals fully retrievable information. Here the co-referential element is homogeneous with respect to retrievability, and hence unequivocally signals givenness, which is—apart from contrastive contexts—a mark of thematicity. But where re-expression of the same referent contains additional, irretrievable information, the co-referential element is heterogeneous in regard to ir/retrievability and may acquire different FSP functions. As an example of homogeneous and heterogeneous means of re-expression Firbas (1995: 20–21) adduces the following co-referential string: *a general, this general, the general, he, [ellipsis]*—homogeneous co-referents; *the brave old soldier, the frail old-timer*—heterogeneous co-referents. In (12) the heterogeneous co-referential expressions occur in postverbal position, which may, together with their heterogeneous character, conduce to potentiality. In the given example, this is not the case, the semantic structure of the sentence, due to the semantics of the verbs, being such as to assign the sentence unequivocally to the quality scale.

(12) There was *a general* at the party. *He* fought both in World War One and in World War Two and [ellipsis] had many a story to tell. Everybody <u>took to</u> the brave old soldier. I must say I could not help <u>admiring</u> the frail veteran. (Firbas 1995: 21)

Here the retrievable information in the heterogeneous co-referent expressions *the brave old soldier* and *the frail old-timer* appears to predominate, which allows the fully irretrievable information conveyed by the verbs *took to* and *admiring*, together with their semantics—they express quality, not presentation—to become the focal point, involving the FSP function of rheme.

The multifunctionality of expressions heterogeneous with respect to ir/retrievability is demonstrated in Firbas (1992: 32–33), where the same expressions are shown to be unequivocal with respect to their FSP function in one context, but involve potentiality in another.

(13) a. In the introduction the author characterizes the personality of *Ernest Heming-way*. *This admirer, adorer* and *worshipper of Africa, hunter, fighter* and *writer* is here presented as ... (Firbas 1992: 32)

b. In the introduction the author characterizes the personality of *Ernest Heming-way*. And who would not like to read something about *this admirer, adorer* and *worshipper of Africa, hunter, fighter* and *writer*. (Firbas 1992: 33)

In both a. and b. the expressions *this admirer ... writer*, though co-referential with Ernest Hemingway, convey a considerable amount of irretrievable information. However, they differ in that in a. the communication is perspectived away from them, hence they acquire, in spite of containing mostly irretrievable information, the FSP function of theme (having the dynamic semantic function of quality bearer). On the other hand b., unlike a., permits two interpretations: either the additional information in the co-referential expressions asserts itself to such an extent as to constitute the element to which the communication is perspectived, i.e. *this admirer ... writer* acquires the FSP function of rheme (the dynamic semantic function of specification); or it is the co-referential nature of these expressions that prevails and then the sentence is perspectived to the notion of 'reading', which hence becomes the rheme. Firbas concludes "The two interpretations point to potentiality. Under the contextual conditions intonation would decide which way the sentence is perspectived. In an overwhelming majority of cases, however, it is without the disambiguating aid of intonation that either the retrievable or the irretrievable feature predominates for one reason or another." (1992: 33)

Potentiality due to the fuzziness (variability) of the retrievability span is demonstrated by four English translations of a passage from Victor Hugo's *Les Misérables* (Firbas 1994: 120–121), cf. (14).

(14) Il y a ... sous un grand if, auquel grimpent ... les liserons, une pierre. ... [7 intervening sentences] ... Au printemps, les fauvettes chantent dans l'arbre.

a. beneath *a big yew tree*, surrounded by mosses and dandelions, there is a stone. ... [5 intervening sentences] ... and birds sing *in the tree*.
b. beneath *a great yew tree* over which climbs the wild convolvulus, there lies a stone. ... [7 intervening sentences] ... In the spring, linnets warble *in the trees*.
c. There is ... under *a yew*, upon which bind-weed climbs ... a tombstone. ... [7 intervening sentences] ... and in the spring linnets sing *on the trees*.
d. There is ... under *a lofty yew*, upon which bindweed climbs ... a tombstone. ... [6 intervening sentences] ... and in the spring linnets sing *on the trees*.

The retrievability span of an element without its re-expression has been found to cover a stretch of seven clauses (Firbas 1994:121, 1992: 23–24). However, in three of the four translations this span appears to be long enough to weaken the co-referential link between 'if/yew' and its re-expression 'arbre/tree'. Firbas concludes that "obliteration of retrievability is a gradual process which operates over a very brief stretch of text, [and] the Victor Hugo versions indicate the impossibility of making a generally valid exact statement as to how many intervening sentences it takes to completely obliterate retrievability. Though playing the most important role in the process of obliteration, the distance between an expression and its re-expression does not operate quite independently of other features in the text, such as the length of the intervening sentences and the character of their semantic content." (Firbas 1994: 121).

2.2 Returning at this point to the first factor that may induce potentiality, viz. indeterminate semantics of the verb with respect to the expression of presentation or quality, illustrated by (11) a. and b., other instances of equivocal FSP structure suggest that potentiality may arise not only from indeterminacy between the presentation and the quality function of a verb, but from indeterminacy in the componential structure of a lexical element (cf. Chapter 10, 3.). Example (15) (example (36) in Chapter 10) illustrates this point on a deverbal noun, but potential semantic indeterminacy presumably applies to words of any word class. Unlike semantic indeterminacy in the expression of existence or appearance on the scene on the one hand, or quality on the other, which is not related to ir/retrievability, here the indeterminacy consists in potential obliteration of a link to a notion that would be retrievable if the given element contains or implies a certain semantic feature.

(15) [she had nothing on which to spend her ... energy except the *management* of her house and her husband;] and she could have ruled a kingdom *with success*.

Here the potentiality of the FSP structure concerns the last element 'with success', whose interpretation depends on whether *manage(ment)* implies success (as in *I can manage*) or not. If it does, then 'with success' is retrievable and the focal element is the object 'a kingdom.' If it does not, 'with success' is irretrievable, hence a component of the rheme and carries together with 'a kingdom' the sentence stress. As pointed out above by Firbas, the potentiality is removed in speech by the assignment of stress.

Example (16) (discussed in connection with thematic objects in Chapter 10, 1.3.1) shows yet another type of indeterminacy in the meaning of a lexical unit, resulting from a pragmatic aspect rather than from the semantic structure.

(16) ['Lord, let me know mine end, and the number of my days: that I may be certified how long I have to live.'] Surely few people could pray that prayer *with any sincerity.*

Here the context suggests that people can pray insincerely, but basically prayer does involve sincerity. If it does, the only focal element in the sentence is the subject with the rheme proper being constituted by its quantifier; on the other hand if prayer is conceived as a mere form, 'with sincerity' acquires a second intonation centre and becomes a component of the rheme.

The second factor of potential indeterminacy in FSP structure, the graded nature of givenness, demonstrated by the homogeneous vs. heterogeneous make-up of co-referential expressions, also extends to instances of partial co-referentiality, displayed in particular by inalienable possessions such as the body parts and functions, when related to their antecedents by means of the possessives. Compare (17).

(17) she noticed that there was a gap *between his front teeth* (B, 50)

The final adverbial contains irretrievable information except for the possessive which is co-referential with an antecedent established in the preceding text; obviously the irretrievable components greatly predominate. Nevertheless the semantic structure of the sentence, the existential construction, perspectives the communication to the subject, which is here entirely context-independent. The adverbial may thus be regarded a scene and acquire the FSP function of diatheme (cf. the Czech translation 'všimla si, že má mezi předními zuby mezeru' [she-noticed that he-has between front teeth gap]). However, owing to its position and the specific character of the prevailing irretrievable information, the adverbial can also be regarded as a component of the rheme (specification), the sentence then qualifying as an extended presentation scale (cf. Chamonikolasová and Adam 2005), cf. 'všimla si, že má mezeru mezi předními zuby' (the rendition chosen in the Czech translation BB: 50).

As regards the retrievability span, example (18) again raises the question of its length, which is here decisive in determining whether or not a repeated utterance represents a second instance.

(18) ["The game-keeper, Mellors, is a curious kind of person," she said to Clifford; "he might almost be a gentleman."
"Might he?" said Clifford. "I hadn't noticed."
"But isn't there something special about him?" Connie insisted.
"I think he is quite a nice fellow, but I know very little about him. He only came out of the army last year less than a year ago. From India, I rather think. He may

have picked up certain tricks up there, perhaps he was an officer's servant, and improved on his position. Some of the men were like that. But it does them no good, they have to fall back into their old place when they get home again."
Connie gazed at Clifford contemplatively. She saw in him the peculiar tight rebuff against anyone who might be really climbing up, which she knew was characteristic of his breed.
"But don't you think there is something special about him?" she asked.
a. But don't you think there IS something special about him?
b. But don't you think there is something SPECial about him? (L, 71)

Here the intervening stretch of text, given in full, consists of 8 sentences containing 16 clauses; the intervening stretch of text in (14) (given in full in Firbas 1992: 3) comprises 5 sentences made up of 10 clauses. Nevertheless, the final sentence, which repeats what was said before this stretch, allows a second-instance interpretation with a single focal element, the positive polarity (indicated by upper case in (18) a.) Alternatively, presentation of the content as a response to the interlocutor's immediately preceding utterance without recall of what has been said before is also possible, cf. (18) b.

The following example (19) is even more suggestive of the complex nature of the factors determining the length of the intervening text conceivable as the retrievability span. The scene of the event presented in (19) is described at page 12, and is re-introduced without re-expression as given after twenty-three pages.

(19) [The vehicle, a delivery van of sorts, was disappearing into Capricorn Place. A group of three youths outside *a garage* stared at the cat which lay like a blot of ink on the pavement. (M, 12)] ...
He opened an account, left the shop and continued his explorations. He arrived at the scene of his encounter with the black cat. A large van was backing into *the garage*. (M, 35)

Examples (15)–(19) suggest that each of the factors conducive to potentiality, revealed and expounded in Firbas's studies, may be further fruitfully explored and the concept of potentiality in FSP elaborated.

3. The last point to be briefly mentioned is potentiality in the light of deviant FSP structures in translated texts. As shown by (14), indeterminacy in ir/retrievability may result in differing translation equivalents (the same applies to indeterminacy in expressing presentation or quality, cf. (11)); however investigation of this point presupposes the availability of more than one translation of the same text. In any case, translations differing in the rendition of a potentially indeterminate FSP structure cannot be regarded as deviant (cf. (17)) unless the deviation fails to capture one of the potential interpretations. As regards actual instances, in the chapters dealing with syntactic constancy potentiality as the cause of a deviant FSP structure in the translation has not been attested. A marginal instance is illustrated by (20), for which it can be argued that if despite the Czech demonstrative inducing retrievability of 'from the road' is indeterminate with respect to context dependence, the translation selects the other alternative.

(20) Uvědomí si, že má od té dlažby kabát *plný prachu.* (F, 30) [... that he-has from that pavement coat full of-dust]
I realized his coat was covered in dust *from the road.* (U, 33)

Truly deviant FSP structures appear to be of a different kind. On the one hand, there are instances of misrepresentation: in the parallel texts the sentence content appears to be perspectived in a different way, cf. (21).

(21) Zase bylo jednotvárné *ticho.* [Again was uneventful silence]
The uneventful *silence* returned. (Cf. Chapter 14, example (17))

While instances of this kind do not point to a more general tendency, other deviations appear to display a certain patterning which suggests partial differences between the two languages in the syntactico-semantic and/or FSP subsystems. Two subgroups of examples may be distinguished here. The first includes instances displaying a partly deviant FSP structure in connection with the employment of *be/být* against *have/mít* and vice versa:

(22) a. *měla* vzteklou tvář [she-had livid face] (K, 134)
her face *was* livid (H, 125)
 b. The Snout's eyes *were* rheumy. (J, 23]
Drban *měl* uslzené oči. [Drban had rheumy eyes.] (S, 423)

Here the difference consists in the composition of the rheme. In a. the rheme in the original is the object realized by a modified noun. In the translation it is dissociated into the subject and the subject complement. The subject occupies initial position, hence has the function of theme. The subject complement corresponds to the modification of the object and constitutes the rheme. Since the modifier in a noun phrase is usually more dynamic than the head noun, the rheme proper remains preserved (cf. Firbas 1992: 84, 95). In b. it is the other way round: a component of the subject, the theme (*the eyes*), appears as a component of the object, the rheme. The deviation itself appears to be due to differences in the use of possessive, copular and locative predications between Czech and English. However, it is to be noted that instances of this kind, deviating in the type of predication, also display corresponding FSP structures, cf. (23).

(23) Her face was pale and long. (J, 27)
Tvář měla bledou a podlouhlou. (S, 435)

The second subgroup suggests differences between English and Czech in the system of FSP. Consider (24) a. and b.:

(24) a. [Trhne rukou] a začne mu tuhnout šíje. ... [and begins to-him stiffen neck]
   (F, 9)
   [He snatched his hand back] and his *neck* felt stiff. (U, 4)
   b. Poklesne *v ramenou* [He-droops in shoulders] (F, 23)
   His shoulders drooped (U, 20)

Instances of this kind contain verbs of the semantic class describing body movements and overt reflexes of internal states independent of the will of the experiencer, such as *tremble, quiver, falter*, generally construable only with the body part/organ as the subject, which conduces to its thematic function, while the verb functions as the rheme. On the other hand in Czech both perspectives are possible, cf. *Hlas se mu zlomil / Zlomil se mu hlas* [voice to-him faltered / faltered to-him voice]—*His voice faltered, nohy se mu třásly / třásly se mu nohy* [legs to-him shook / shook to-him legs]—*his legs shook, Hořely mu tváře / tváře mu hořely* [burned to-him cheeks / cheeks to-him burned]—*his cheeks were burning*. However, the unmarked perspective in Czech appears to be that with the nominal element as the rheme at the end, cf. (24) a. and b. English, on the other hand, shows the opposite FSP structure. These instances represent a narrower concept of potentiality in that they are peripheral without displaying indeterminacy.

4. Summing up, we find two points recurrently appearing in the foregoing discussion: first, potentiality appears to be much more elusive and involved on the FSP level than in syntax. Secondly, although some of the noted instances do not belong to the very periphery of the respective categories, potential indeterminacy in general appears to belong in this sphere.

SOURCES

B   Bainbridge, B. *The Bottle Factory Outing*. Glasgow: Duckworth,1974.
BB Bainbridgeová, B. *Podnikový výlet*. Translated by Hana Bělohradská. Prague: Odeon, 1981.
F   Fuks, L. *Pan Theodor Munstock*. Prague: Československý spisovatel, 1985.
U   Fuks, L. *Mr. Theodor Mundstock*. Translated by Iris Urwin Lewit. New York: Ballantine Books, 1969.
FL Fowles, J. *The French Lieutenant's Woman*. London: Triad-Granada, 1983 (1st ed. 1969).
Ž   Fowles, J. *Francouzova milenka*. Translated by Hana Žantovská. Prague: Mladá fronta–Smena–Naše vojsko, 1976.
J   James, P. D. *An Unsuitable Job for a Woman*. New York: Warner Books, 1972.
S   Jamesová, P. D. *Povolání pro ženu nevhodné*. Translated by Josef Schwarz. In *3× Adam Dalgliesh*, Prague: Odeon, 1986.
K   Kundera, M. *Kniha smíchu a zapomnění*. Toronto: Sixty-Eight Publishers, 1981.
H   Kundera, M. *The Book of Laughter and Forgetting*. Translated by Michael Henry Heim. New York: Penguin Books, 1981.
L   Lawrence, D. H. *Lady Chatterley's Lover*. Harmondsworth: Penguin Books, 1967 (1st ed. 1960).
M   Marsh, N. *Black As He's Painted*. Glasgow: Fontana Books, 1975 (1st ed. 1973).

III. FSP
AND SEMANTICS

17. THE RELATIONS BETWEEN SEMANTICS AND FSP AS SEEN BY ANGLICIST MEMBERS OF THE PRAGUE LINGUISTIC CIRCLE

First published in Czech under the title "Vztahy mezi sémantikou a aktuálním členěním z pohledu anglistických členů Pražského lingvistického kroužku", *Slovo a slovesnost* 69/1–2, 2008, 67–77. Revised.

0. This chapter discusses the relationship between semantics and functional sentence perspective as treated in the works of Vilém Mathesius, Bohumil Trnka and the representatives of the Brno approach to FSP.[1] As can be expected, the extent to which the semantic aspects of this question are elaborated in the works of different authors varies, and so does the degree of relevance of the particular treatments for the clarification of the relationship between semantics and FSP. The aspects involved cover sentence semantics, semantic roles of clause elements and even lexical semantics, especially in the case of the verb. Recent studies concerned with these questions show a need for closer examination, to which this paper attempts to contribute by suggesting possible lines of further research.

1. Of the Anglicist members of the Prague Linguistic Circle the relationship between semantics and FSP has been treated by Vilém Mathesius, in a general outline by Bohu-

---

[1] As follows from this delimitation, the approaches discussed here cover only the conceptions of Czech scholars concerned with English studies. A comparison with the theories developed by Czech general and formal linguists and Bohemicists, some of whom also include English in their research work, remains outside the scope of treatment. Cf. Hajičová 1993, 1994; Hajičová, Partee and Sgall 1998; Daneš 1964, 1986; for a comparison of the Brno and the Lesser Town conception (functional sentence perspective and topic-focus articulation, respectively), see Sgall 2002.

mil Trnka, and fundamentally by Brno Anglicists, above all Jan Firbas and currently by his successors of the younger generations.

1.1 Mathesius describes language phenomena on the basis of the encoding and decoding processes, the former being the primary concern of his *Functional Analysis of Present Day English* (1975). He divides the encoding process into two stages: functional onomatology, the study of the naming units, and functional syntax, the study of the means serving to bring the naming units into mutual relations. Functional syntax starts from the definition of the sentence, based on the use of the sentence in a communicative situation, i.e. the sentence defined as an utterance. Functional sentence perspective is included in the primary classification of the sentence structure into the FSP and formal structure. The basic units of the FSP structure of the sentence are the basis (theme) and the nucleus (the rheme), the basic units of the formal structure are the subject and the verb (1975: 79–86). As regards the semantics of clause elements, which are dealt with in considerable detail (cf., e.g., the treatment of the objects (1975: 120–128), the most relevant point for the present topic is Mathesius' view of the subject (1947a). The agent role of the subject and its FSP function appeared to him as features of the same level: "The original Indo-European sentence seems to have been built on the concepts of agent—action. This original conception was departed from in connection with the gradual development of the passive ... and began to express, at least in some instances, the theme of the utterance, not directly involved in the action expressed by the verb. ... In Czech [this development] has not proceeded so far as in Modern English; the Czech subject still very often expresses the agent and does not coincide with the theme of the utterance."[2] (1947a: 284–85; translation L. D.; see also Mathesius 1975: 100–101).

Sentence semantics is described in the treatment of predication, conceived as the nucleus of the utterance (rheme). Mathesius' conception of the theme appears from the quotation "an overwhelming majority of sentences [is shown] to contain two basic content elements: a statement and an element about which the statement is made. The element about which something is stated may be said to be the basis of the utterance, and what is stated about the basis is the nucleus of the utterance or the rheme." (1975: 81). It can be illustrated by his well-known passage about John and his progress at school, presented in Czech and in English translation for comparison. (1961: 115–118; 1975: 101–103):

(1) [1]Jan velmi dobře prospíval. [2]Ve škole horlivě naslouchal každému slovu svých učitelů a [3]doma mu pomáhal otec [at home to-him helped father], [4]kdykoliv mu byla nějaká úloha příliš těžká [whenever to-him was any task too difficult]. [5]Práce všeho druhu se mu velice dařila [Work of all kind to-him very succeeded] a [6]říkalo

---

2   „Původní věta indoevropská byla, jak se zdá, formálně vybudována na pojetí konatel-konání. Od tohoto původního pojetí se jazyky indoevropské uchýlily již vytvořením počátků pasivní predikace, ... a [subjekt] stával se alespoň někdy vyjádřením výpovědního thematu na ději predikátem vyjádřeném aktivně nezúčastněného. ... V češtině [tento vývoj] nedospěl ani přibližně tak daleko jako v moderní angličtině, a podmět v české větě je ještě velmi často vyjádřením konatele a neshoduje se s výpovědním thematem."

se o něm [it-was-said of him], ⁷že pracuje stejně přirozeně jako dýchá [that he works equally naturally as he-breathes].

(1)' ¹John prospered very well. ²At school he eagerly listened to every word of his teachers. ³At home he was helped by his father ⁴whenever he found his task too difficult. ⁵He was successful in any kind of work. ⁶He was said ⁷to be working as naturally as he was breathing.

Mathesius here points out that while in English the subject remains the same, in Czech it changes five times, and explains this difference by the thematic function of the English subject, a consequence of the fixed character of English word order. As shown by the Czech version, the theme need not be expressed only by the subject, while the English translation shows that retaining the same subject in successive sentences gives rise to thematic progressions with constant theme. As follows from this example and the foregoing quotations, in Mathesius' conception the level of information structure (FSP) and the semantic level are not distinguished: they are merged in one level. In the works of his Brno followers the semantic level is treated separately and within a different hierarchical framework in which FSP constitutes a separate higher, superordinate level: FSP (the theme—rheme structure) as the result of an interplay of four factors, context, semantics, linearity and intonation, as will be discussed below.

1.2 Trnka, Mathesius' pupil and successor, was also both a founding and prominent member of the Circle, and a foremost personality of Prague English studies. His conception of the language system has been described in many of his numerous studies, but its elaboration remained long preserved only as a mimeographed university text. A re-edition of the three parts of the university text appeared in 2014 thanks to the editorial efforts of Jan Čermák (Trnka 2014). Although even here the highest level of the language system is not elaborated, its constitutive part in the composition of the language system is apparent from Trnka's overall conception of it. The language system is regarded as a whole formed by four levels defined by their basic units and realized by the units of the immediately lower level. The three lower levels, phonological, morphological and syntactic were each treated in a separate volume (1954, 1956, 1967). The highest level was characterized as the utterance level primarily conceived as the domain of style. An idea of Trnka's conception of this level may be gained from its basic units, the theme and the rheme, and the following quotation: "The sentence is not an entity of the highest language level. The unit of this level is a concrete utterance that presupposes the relation between a concrete speaker and hearer, a certain situation and a certain context. This unit is not constituted by linking the subject with the predicate, but by connecting a theme known to the hearer with the core of the utterance, which communicates something new to the hearer. It is a higher unit than a word or the unit formed by the subject and predicate: this is presupposed and modified. Subjects, verbs and other clause elements remain in the utterance, but differ or may differ only in the modification of their function and meaning due to their subordination to the relation theme / rheme. In many instances this modification of function/meaning may not differ from the written sentence by any formal means. If someone says 'it's cold' it can have a vast number of meanings, such as 'it's time to go inside' or 'help me to put on my coat' or 'your talking bores me' or even 'come and sit closer to me,' etc., according to the actual situation and concrete speakers. However, it can also be a straightforward statement of the temperature of the air without any implications."[3] (1990: 23; translation L. D.). Obviously Trnka's functional and meaning modification resulting from the division of the utterance into the theme and the rheme is broader than the current conception of the theme and rheme in including the illocutionary force and conversation implicatures.

Trnka's concern with semantics covered word semantics (1990: Chapter XIII; 1982: Words, Semantemes and Sememes, 97–101), the semantics of morphological oppositions and clause elements (1956). The meanings of morphological oppositions and word meanings are treated under two headings: contextual meanings of morphological oppositions and words are dealt with in syntax, whereas the basic meanings of words and morphological oppositions are assigned, respectively, to semantics and morphology.

1.3 The third approach to be discussed is the theory of functional sentence perspective, conceived and elaborated into a consistent theoretical framework by Firbas. Within this theory the semantic aspects are shown to play a decisive part in determining the FSP structure. Treatment of the semantic aspects, apart from substantial contributions to other aspects of the FSP theory, is also found in the works of Firbas's closest co-worker Aleš Svoboda (1989; 2005); in the works of their pupils and successors Jana Chamonikolasová and Martin Adam this aspect represents one of the major lines of further research (Chamonikolasová and Adam 2005; Adam 2003).

1.3.1 Firbas (1992; 1991; for his other studies, see the bibliography in 1992, 1991) deals with the semantic component of FSP in connection with the four factors that determine the FSP structure: contextual, semantic, linear modification and intonation in speech. The term "factor" has been substituted for the earlier term "means", which is conceived as a signal in Firbas's later works. He explains the difference between the two terms in the following way: "The phenomena that serve as simple signals or that co-constitute complex signals are the means of FSP. This raises the question of the relationship between FSP factors and FSP means/signals (prompted to me by Daneš in a private communication). By 'factors' (linear modification, the contextual factor and the semantic factor, and in addition intonation in the spoken language) I mean the

---

3   „Věta ovšem není entitou nejvyššího jazykového plánu. Tou je aktuální promluva, která předpokládá vztah ak-
      tuálního mluvčího a posluchače i jistou situaci a jistý kontext. Je konstituována ne spojením subjektu a pre-
      dikátu, nýbrž spojením posluchači známého tématu s jádrem výpovědi, sdělujícím něco nového posluchači.
      Toto spojení je vyšší jednotka než slovo a než větné spojení podmětu a predikátu, které předpokládá a modifiku-
      je. Podměty, predikáty a jiné členy věty v promluvě zůstávají, ale liší se nebo se mohou lišit jen svým funkčním
      zaměřením významovým tím, že se ve výpovědi podřizují vztahu téma/jádro výpovědi. Mnohdy toto zaměření
      nemusí se nijak lišit od psané věty formálně. Jestliže např. někdo poznamená ‚Je chladno', může to znamenat
      nekonečně mnoho věcí, jako ‚je čas jít dovnitř' nebo ‚pomozte mi obléci plášť' nebo ‚vaše povídání mě už nudí'
      nebo dokonce ‚sedněte si trochu blíže' atd., podle konkrétní situace a konkrétních mluvčích. Může to ovšem
      znamenat také jen prosté konstatování teploty vzduchu bez jakýchkoli implikací." (1990: Chapter III, Jazykové
      roviny a jejich strategie, 23)

formative forces co-implementing the distribution of degrees of CD. Particularizing the operations of a factor, I specify the phenomena involved (e.g., the position in the actual linear arrangement, the objective presence of a piece of information within the immediately relevant context, a definite semantic character linked with a grammatical form, and a prosodic feature in the spoken language). These phenomena become the means/signals of FSP." (1992: 115). The terms factor and means/signal thus appear to denote an aspect of the same nature, but at different levels, factor being superordinate to means/signal.

In the Brno conception of the role of semantics in FSP, a distinction is made between two types of semantics, static and dynamic. An explicit formulation of this conception is found in Firbas (1991): "The static meaning is not yet modified by the process of functional syntactic structuration. It is conveyed by the naming units (implemented as words or word groups) before they are subjected to this process. Participating in the process, FSP modifies the meanings of the naming units, which come to co-constitute communicative units. Through the interplay of FSP factors, FSP determines the positions of communicative units, i.e. their degrees of CD, in the development of the communication that takes place within the sentence. It is in this manner that meaning acquires a dynamic aspect—that they becomes dynamic." (89)

The most important dynamic semantic function (DSF) for sentence semantics is the DSF of the verb in that it perspectives the communication either to a context-independent subject or the verb complementation or, in the absence of verb complementation, to the verb. Accordingly, the verb performs the DSF of presentation or quality. For a verb to perform the presentation function, the subject must be context-independent: it then has the DSF of a phenomenon presented on the scene. Verbs with the DSF of quality perspecting communication from the subject to their complementation or themselves assign to subjects the DSF of quality bearer. Quality bearers have the FSP function of theme irrespective of their context dependence or independence. The concept of quality is conceived very broadly: "Quality is to be understood here in a wide sense, covering an action or a state, permanent or transitory, concrete or abstract" (Firbas 1992: 5). As regards objects and adverbials, according to their context independence or dependence they have the DSF of specification or setting (some types of adverbials may moreover be transition-proper oriented). Considered from the viewpoint of their semantic content, some elements performing the DSF of setting may show disagreement between their static and dynamic semantics. This especially applies to context-dependent objects with other than adverbial semantic roles (such as patient, agent, experiencer).

Static semantics is taken into account in the case of verbs in connection with their dual DSF, presentation and quality. Attention has so far been paid to verbs that express the presentation function. They are primarily defined on the basis of their static semantics as verbs expressing existence or appearance on the scene explicitly or with sufficient implicitness. In the case of context-independent subjects, it is this semantic content of the verb that actuates the presentation semantics of the sentence, the so-called presentation scale. Compared with the quality scale, implemented by sentences in which the verb has the DSF of quality, the textual occurrence of the presentation scale is far less frequent than that of the quality scale (the adduced quantitative data for the presentation scale are, depending on the text sort, 8–12%, cf. Adam 2013). This raises the question whether the static semantics and semantic role(s) of the complement(s) of multiple valency verbs are compatible with the DSF setting in the case of their context dependence. If so, then the disagreement between lexical semantics and semantic roles on one hand and the DSF function of setting on the other acquires considerable proportions, considering that the syntactic and semantic sentence structure is here much more complex. In the prototypical realization form of the presentation scale the verb is intransitive and the adverbials, if any, are of the scene-setting type, temporal and/or locative. Static and dynamic semantics, as well as sentence semantics, are here in full agreement with the respective dynamic semantic functions. The adverbials moreover need not be context-dependent, their scene-setting function being semantically based. On the other hand, in sentences with context-dependent complements of multiple valency verbs the FSP function of setting is entirely determined by context and appears to require a very broad interpretation virtually independent of the respective lexical meanings and semantic roles.

Problems are also encountered in presentation sentences with context-independent adverbials with full-fledged semantics that do not lend themselves to scene-setting interpretation.

Proposals for solutions of such instances have been advanced by Firbas's pupils and successors (cf. (20)–(22)).

As follows from what has been said, the relationship between the dynamic semantic functions of nominal and adverbials elements and their respective FSP functions is straightforward in that a dynamic semantic function invariably has only one FSP function: phenomena and specifications are rhemes, quality bearers and settings are themes. FSP functions involving more than one element are further differentiated according to the degree of communicative dynamism carried by each element, e.g. the thematic section may be divided into the theme proper and the diatheme and contain further elements, theme proper and diatheme oriented.

Sentence semantics in the Brno approach is thus regarded as a dichotomy between the presentation scale and the quality scale and the need for the two types of semantics is demonstrated by sentences like (2) and (3), where identical elements have different dynamic semantic functions, and hence different FSP functions.

(2) A girl came into the room. (Firbas 1966: 243)
(3) The girl came in. (ibid.: 245)

In (2) the subject has the DSF of a phenomenon presented on the scene, the verb the DSF of presentation and the adverbial constitutes the setting (cf. in Czech *Do místnosti vešla (nějaká) dívka* [Into the room came (some) girl]). In (3) the subject is the bearer of quality, the verb has the DSF of quality and the adverbial implements the setting.

The quality scale has two modifications, the combined scale, cf. (4), and the scale with a copular verb, cf. (5) (Firbas 1992: 66–69).

(4) Ages ago a young king ruled his country capriciously and despotically. (p. 67)

This configuration represents a telescopic realization of both scales, the presentation scale introducing a phenomenon (*There was a young king*) that in the quality scale acts as the quality bearer (*who ruled his country ...*).

(5) A writer felt despondent and disillusioned. (p. 68)

In (5) the DSF of quality, implemented by a verb in the quality scale, is divided into two components, categorial, realized by the copula (ascription of quality) and notional, implemented by the nominal component constituting the quality.

These two modifications have been subjected to further study ((13) and (14) below).

The more detailed delimitation and classification of verbs disposed to perform the presentation function on the basis of static (lexical) semantics is presumably connected with their simpler identification: they are primarily intransitive verbs with a generally definable meaning. The basic realization form of the presentation scale is the existential construction *there + be* (*es gibt* in German, *il y a* in French).

Verbs explicitly expressing existence or appearance on the scene are represented by (2) and further include verbs like *exist, be in existence, be in sight, be within view, obtain, appear, arrive, become plain, begin, come forth, come forward, come into sight, come into view, come up, commence, crop up, develop, emerge, ensue, evolve, grow out of, happen, issue, loom, materialize, occur, recur, rise, set in, show up, spring up, stand out, start, surface, take place, turn up, unfold* (Firbas 1992: 60).

Verbs expressing existence or appearance on the scene with sufficient implicitness are illustrated not only by intransitive verbs like *hover, settle, steal over, fly, gleam*, cf. (6).

(6) a. A haze hovered over the prospect.
   b. A fly settled on his hair.
   c. A wave of the azalea scent drifted into June's face, ...
   d. A goldfinch flew over the shepherd´s head ... (Firbas 1992: 60)

Here a relevant feature appears to be semantic affinity between the verb and the subject (as in (6) c. and d.).

The presentation function can also be ascribed to transitive verbs in instances like (7).

(7) a. A cold blue light filled the window panes.
   b. grey light flooded the dull room.

    c. For a moment or two big tears brimmed her eyes.

    d. A dumb and grumbling anger swelled his bosom.

    e. Grey curls banded her forehead, ... (Firbas 1992: 61)

Support for conceiving the DSF of these verbs as presentation is found in synonymous expressions with an explicit verb of existence or appearance on the scene and a locative adverbial in place of the object, cf. *Grey light dawned into the room, big tears appeared / sprang up in her eyes.*[4]

Interpretation of transitive verbs as capable of performing the presentation function suggests the possibility of expressing presentation by a passive verb. Examples of presentation sentences with verbs in the passive so far adduced display transitive verbs of several semantic classes, primarily verba efficiendi in agentless passives. Instances presented by Firbas (1992: 62) show configurations of context-independent subjects with context-dependent postverbal adverbials, if present, with the intonation centre on the subjects. The Czech translation counterparts of these sentences would all have the subject in the typical rhematic final position.

(8) a. Quite a number of new houses have been built in our town.

    b. Powerful machines have been constructed.

    c. An uncanny impression is thereby created.

    d. A new method has been developed. Ingenious new schemes were devised in various institutes.

    e. Monuments will be erected in the centre of the city.

    f. Printing was then invented in Germany.

    g. A new daily will be launched next week.

    h. An unnecessary mistake was made.

    i. Important discoveries were made towards the end of the nineteenth century.

    j. Shoes are manufactured there.

    k. More food must be produced this year.

Also in these instances there is agreement between the static and dynamic semantics as the subject of these verbs, the object of the active, comes into existence in the course of the verbs' action. Being employed in agentless passives with the presentation function, these verbs display similarity with intransitive verbs of appearance on the scene. Both these classes express appearance of a phenomenon on the scene, with the difference that in the case of verba efficiendi this happens through some external agency.

Passives of other verb classes are demonstrated by the following two examples.

(9) a. Then a blind and dumb demoniac was brought to him. (Firbas 1992: 63)

---

4   For a complex monographic treatment of presentation verbs with respect to determining the syntactic and semantic features that enable a verb to perform the DSF of presentation, see Adam (2013).

b. Sometimes a terrible cry was to be heard [when the doctor was pulling out the teeth of some little boy] (Firbas 1966: 244)

Example (9) a. is another instance of a phenomenon appearing on the scene through some (unexpressed) external agency. Here the verb is ditransitive, and as shown by (10), which presents another verb of this class, the passives of these verbs are also semantically disposed to perform the DSF of presentation. The goal of the action, the expression of which is required by the ditransitive nature of these verbs, is conceivable as the scene and the passive verb as appearance of a phenomenon on it through some (unexpressed) external agency.

(10) At the moment of his departure a telegram was handed to him.

Example (9) b. suggests another semantic class of verbs whose passive is conceivable as presentation of a phenomenon on a scene: verbs of sensory perception do so through the respective sense / means of the respective sense, cf. (11):

(11) Sometimes a faint tremor of the ground could be felt in this place.

The absence of an expressed agent appears to be a relevant features of these constructions insofar as expressed agents are as a rule context-independent, and hence perform the FSP function of the rheme or (one of) its components. However, in the rare case of agentive passives with context-dependent agents, the presentation function of the passive is not excluded, cf. (12).

(12) In the six years 1956–61, a total of 81,079 applications for disablement benefit were made by coal miners.

The preceding context of this sentence deals with applications of miners for benefits, and since the miners are not contrasted with other groups of applicants, the only new element, apart from the initial temporal setting, appears in the quantifying expressions within the subject noun phrase (cf. Chapter 9, example (5) a.).

1.3.2 In further research (Chamonikolasová, Adam 2005; Adam 2003) the prototypical types of the two scales and their modifications, illustrated by (2)–(5), were found to be inadequate for determining the FSP structure of sentences containing more context-independent elements, such as (13) and (14).

(13) a. In these days came John the Baptist, preaching in the wilderness of Judea.
(14) a. Blessed are the poor in spirit for theirs is the kingdom of heaven.

In Adam's first interpretation (2003) these instances were analysed as structures containing two rhemes, with a considerable degree of potentiality (Chamonikolasová, Adam 2005). In further elaboration Chamonikolasová proposed a modification of the original tripartite scheme of the scales—presentation, quality, combined scale, based on the different dominant DSF function of the subject in the original combined scale, cf. (4), and in instances illustrated by (13) and (14). Whereas in (4) the dominant DSF of the subject is the quality bearer, in (13) and (14) it is the presented phenomenon. Hence she proposed to classify (13) and (14) as the extended presentation scale (viz. presentation scale extended by adverbial specification) and to incorporate the type represented by (4) in the quality scale. As a result, the category of the combined scale has been dispensed with (Chamonikolasová, Adam 2005).

2. The extended presentation scale covers instances of existential constructions containing, in addition to the context-independent subject, a context-independent adverbial with the FSP of rheme, viz. a final context-independent adverbial that cannot be moved to the initial position. This has been pointed out by Grzegorek (1984: 78) in connection with the two types of intonation: two intonation centres, on the subject and the adverbial, in (15) a., as against one intonation centre on the subject in (15) b. (cf. Chapter 9, (33) a. and b.).

(15) a. There's a strange looking WOMan in the HOUSe.
    b. There's a strange looking WOMan in the house. / In the house, there's a strange looking WOMan.

These sentences are of contrastive interest in that the configuration illustrated by (15) a. has no existential counterpart in Czech (at least in the declarative form), cf.

(16) a. ?Je divně vypadající žena v domě. [Is strangely looking woman in house.]
    b. Nějaká divně vypadající žena je v domě.
      [Some strangely looking woman is in house.]

This Czech counterpart corresponds to the English non-existential counterpart of the existential construction, viz. (15) c. (cf. Huddleston and Pullum 2002: 1396–97).

(15) c. A strange woman is in the house.

Here the indefinite article does not indicate the introduction of a new referent into discourse, but "a new token of a previously known type" (according to Huddleston and Pullum 2002: 1397). Specifically in (15) c., the indefinite article signals the indeterminate status of referential identity / non-identity, i.e. non-specific indefinite reference, with respect to the preceding context, such as *They are looking for a strange woman.*— *There is a strange woman in the house / A strange woman* (viz. *some woman matching this description*) *is in the house.* As the term "non-existential counterpart of the existential" (Huddleston and Pullum, *ibid.*) suggests, the sentence is not existential, but locative. In Czech, the context-dependence of the subject is overtly indicated by the word order (the corresponding existential sentence has the subject at the end: *V domě je nějaká divně vypadající žena.* [In house is some strangely looking woman.]. On the other hand, the situation in English is not straightforward insofar as the existential construction is a specific syntactic device for the expression of existence / appearance of a phenomenon and retains this function even if the subject is context-dependent, whatever the character of the context-dependence may be. The configuration with a context-dependent subject thus results in a conflict between the syntactic structure of the sentence, indicating the presentation function, and its assignment to the DSF of quality.

However, what has been said about the existential construction does not apply to the instances that led to the concept of the extended presentation scale, viz. (13) and (14). They represent other realization forms of the presentation sentence and the rhematic adverbials have other than locative or temporal semantic roles. The question arising here is the specification of the realization form of both the presentation sentence and the adverbial, in particular in respect of the non-clausal, non-finite and clausal realization and the semantic role of the latter, considered from the viewpoint of the respective communicative subfield.

Example(14) b. moreover raises another question. Here the context-independence of the subject also leads to presentational conception of copular sentences with context-dependent subject complements. Example (14) a., which is followed by sentences reiterating its beginning, cf. (14) b., contains a context-dependent subject complement in initial position and a postverbal rhematic subject. Hence they are classified as presentation sentences, extended by the reason adjunct with the DSF of specification.

(14) b. Blessed are the poor in spirit, for theirs is the kingdom of heaven.
Blessed are those who mourn, for they will be comforted.
Blessed are the meek, for they will inherit the earth. (Chamonikolasová and Adam 2005: 62)

The presentational interpretation of copular sentences with a context-dependent subject complement is presumably based on Firbas's treatment of examples taken over from Quirk et al. (1985: 1380–81). Although they are not explicitly denoted as presentation sentences, it more or less follows from Firbas's comment: "Let us note that the examples arrange the elements in what may be termed presentation order, in which the initial element is followed by an intransitive verb and a context-independent subject. This presentation order reflects linear modification and strengthens the perspective of the communication towards the context-independent subject, occurring in end position." (1992: 47).

(17) a. [His answer was a disgrace;] equally regrettable was his departure immediately afterwards.
b. [Her face was stony] and even stonier was the tone of her voice.
c. Especially remarkable was her oval face.
d. Faint grew the sound of the bell. (Firbas 1992: 47)

Examples (17) b. and c. contain focalizers, viz. *even, especially*, which usually signal the rheme, but here, like *equally* in (17) a., they appear as components of the theme in connective function.[5] Hence not only the immediately preceding context and initial placement, but also cohesive lexical means show the subject complements to be context-dependent. Example (17) d. is described as poetic in Quirk et al. (1985: 1380). However, as regards the semantic structure of these instances, the verbonominal predicates *be regrettable, be remarkable, be stony, grow faint* do not lend themselves to presentational interpretation understood in its literal sense since copular sentences with adjectival subject complements basically express qualification: they ascribe a feature to the subject: hence the sentence semantics, based on the syntactic structure and its lexical realization, and the FPS dynamic semantics are once again brought into conflict.

The last point to be discussed concerns instances described as special cases of presentation sentences (Chamonikolasová and Adam 2005: 64–65).

(18) A v tom údolí   si postavil chatu   jeden můj bývalý spolužák.
      Set [seting]   Pr [presentation] ?   Ph [presented phenomenon]
      [And in that valley   for-himself built cottage   one my former schoomate.]

(19) V zítřejším zápase Sparty proti Slavii   nastoupí do brány   uzdravený Petr Čech.
      Set [setting]   Pr [presentation] ?   Ph [phenomenon]
      [In tomorrow's match Sparta against Slavia   appears in goal   recovered Petr Čech.]

(20) A pak přes dvůr   tryskem   přeběhl   nějaký kluk.
      Set [setting]   Set [setting] ?   Pr [presentation]   Ph [phenomenon]
      [And then across courtyard   at-a-gallop   ran   some boy.]

The question marks under the object *cottage* in (18) and the adverbials *in the goal, at a gallop* in (19) and (20) indicate the problems involved in the assignment of a dynamic semantic function. These elements cannot be classed as specifications since their scope is confined to the content of the presentational verb. Neither does the DSF of setting offer an adequate solution since the semantic roles of the object and the adverbials do not fall within the usual scene-setting semantics.

Adam proposed two solutions: a special kind of specification or a component of the presentational element. His second solution is based on Svoboda's conception of some verbs + their object or adverbial modifiers as one communicative (FSP) unit: *vyjádřit souhlas* [express agreement] (=*souhlasit* [agree]) (Svoboda 1989: 79–80). This interpretation appears to be plausible in that *nastoupit do brány* [appear in the goal] in (19) indicates the function of the goalman. Similarly, typical use of the manner adjunct is analogous to nouns modified by adjectives, cf. *grow slowly / slow growth*, which constitute one FSP unit.

However, this solution does not apply to (18) insofar as *postavit si chatu* [build a cottage] is not a verbonominal predicate like *vyjádřit souhlas* [express agreement]. As

---

5   For the function of focalizers in FSP, see Hajičová, Partee and Sgall (1998: 151 ff.).

regards presentation of a phenomenon on the scene, what appears on it is primarily the cottage which comes into existence as a result of verbal action.

Sgall, Hajičová and Buráňová (1980: 42) adduce (21), which also contains an action verb with an object with the commentary "from the viewpoint of the content and the context-nonboundness of the agent even sentences with an action verb can be denoted as appearance on the scene"[6] (translation L. D.), which also speaks for the assignment of these instances to the presentation scale.

(21) U nás pečou housky pekaři [Here bake rolls bakers]

However, (18) and (21) differ not only in the scope of context dependence—the object in (21) is context-dependent, whereas in (18) context-independent, but also in the semantic relationship between the subject and the verb, cf. *pekaři—péci* [bakers—bake] x *spolužák—postavit* [schoolmate—build]. Semantic affinity, a significant feature of verbs implicitly expressing appearance / existence on the scene, is lacking in the latter. Consequently, classification of sentences like (18) as presentation scales remains problematic. Clarification is to be sought in further research based on representative material comprising all types of verb complementation and modification with differing scopes of context dependence.

In general, the discussion of examples (13)–(21) suggests that further study of the relationship between semantics and functional sentence perspective may be sought in the areas of verbs with complex complementation, copular sentences with context-dependent subject complements and existential sentences signalled by specific syntactic-semantic means containing a context-dependent subject with a view to agreement between the semantic roles of the complements, sentence semantics and the conception as a presentation or quality scale.

---

6   „obsahově a z hlediska kontextové nezapojenosti konatele lze za vstup na scénu označit i věty se slovesem akčním"

18. EXPRESSING INDEFINITENESS
IN ENGLISH

First published in *Prague Studies in English* 22, *Acta Universitatis Carolinae, Philologica* 5, 1997 (issued 2000), 33–50.

0. In the extensive work of Jiří Nosek the category of definiteness received attention in several treatises written about the turn of the last decade (cf. Nosek 1989, 1990, 1991). As in many other studies, his interest in this question is general linguistic, embracing the relation of definiteness to other function words and to linguistic typology.

The aim of this chapter is to contribute to a partial aspect of the question, viz. the means expressing nongeneric indefinite reference within the English determiner system, their semantic differentiation, and their role in functional sentence perspective.

Of the vast literature dealing with the category of definiteness (Christophersen 1939, Hawkins 1978, Hewson 1972, Yotsukura 1970, among others), the most relevant to the present study is the treatment in Quirk et al. (1985), Chesterman (1991), Sahlin (1979), and Mráz (1998).

1. The first question to be considered is the repertory of indefinite determiners. Besides the indefinite and zero article, most descriptions include unstressed *some* in the article system. Thus Quirk et al. (1972: 150) speak of *some* as the "light quantitative article," and Quirk et al. (1985: 274; *CGEL* henceforth) include the "unstressed determiner *some*" among the uses of the zero article, since it is sometimes the plural or non-count equivalent of *a/an*. Similarly Yotsukura (1970: 53) includes unstressed *some* as an article, on the grounds that most informants give *There are some boys there* as the most obvious plural equivalent of *There is a boy there*.

2. Accordingly, three exponents of nongeneric indefinite reference will be considered to begin with: the indefinite article, the zero article, and unstressed *some*. In addition, attention will also be paid to *some* with countable singulars.

2.1 The article status of *a/an* is established to the extent that if discussed at all, then only from the historical point of view. Its origin in the numeral *one*, apart from petrified uses, such as *in a word*, *at a blow*, is reflected on the one hand in its incompatibility with other than singular countable nouns, and on the other hand in its basic function, viz. denoting one member of a set composed of more than one. The former feature, being a matter of form, applies equally to the numeral and the article. Where *a/an* determines a plural noun, as in *a barracks of a house*, or *a crossroads*, the noun is a notional singular. Unlike this basically general formal correspondence between the numeral and the article, the functional correspondence 'one of a set of more than one' necessarily represents only one of the uses of the indefinite article. In generic use, which constitutes the criterion of the article status of any potential article-like element, the indefinite article refers to the whole class, the opposition between the singular and the plural being neutralized. In nongeneric use, the meaning 'one of a set of more than one' combines with the function of introducing a non-unique referent into discourse (a first mention of an entity). Compare

(1) They were received by an official (situationally non-unique referent).

    as against

(2) They were received by the Mayor (situationally unique referent).

The aspect of a first mention overrides the aspect of situational uniqueness of an otherwise non-unique entity in instances like

(3) I have sent him a letter

where the entire correspondence between sender and sendee may involve no more than one single letter. The predominance of the first-mention aspect is due to the fact that the determiner consistent with the notion of uniqueness, the definite article, would at the same time present the referent as having been mentioned before. What we are faced with is the interaction between the semantics of the articles and their role in functional sentence perspective.

A similar case is encountered where the uniqueness of the referent is due to cataphoric definiteness, which may again be overridden by the aspect of a first mention.

(4) He mentioned *an accident* he met with as a boy.
(5) I had *an impression* that they had just had an argument.

In (4) the accident involved may be the only one that the person concerned has ever had, the situational uniqueness of the impression in (5) being self-evident. However, while (4) follows the pattern of (3) in that the replacement of *an accident* by *the accident* again changes the presentation of the accident, respectively, from a first mention to anaphoric reference, no such change results from a corresponding replacement in (5). Example (5)' presents the object as an entity first introduced into discourse.

(5)' I had the impression that they had just had an argument.

Here the difference presumably involves a subjective view of the speaker. In general, where the use of the definite article does not produce anaphoric reading, the difference between *a/an* and *the* with cataphorically determined nouns appears to conform to the indication of uniqueness by the definite article, cf. (6), as against the indication of 'one of a set of more than one' by the indefinite article, cf. (6)'.

(6) We took *the bus* that runs only on Sundays.
(6)' We took *a bus* that runs only on Sundays.

Whereas in (6) there is only one bus, in (6)' there may be one or more buses, the indefinite article being neutral in this respect.

A similar distinction presumably applies to (5) and (5)'. While in (5) the impression is presented as a member of a large set including all impressions, in (5)' the impression suggests a set with one member. This question is discussed in Chesterman (1991),[1] but even here we do not find an answer to the question why the cataphoric definite article sometimes induces anaphoric reading of the given noun phrase, and in others is consistent with the NP's first mention.

Indication of uniqueness being the domain of the definite article, of special interest are instances in which *a/an* determines a noun with a unique referent, such as a body part, against cases of unique reference where indefinite determination is impossible. Compare the following examples, taken over from *CGEL* (273): examples (7) and (8), and Chesterman (1991: 22–23): examples (9), (10), (12) and (13).

(7)   He's broken a leg.
(8)   *Roger has hurt a nose.
(9)   *Fred lost a head during the war.
(10) Fred lost a leg/a finger during the war.
(11) *Fred lost a right leg in the war.
(12) I have a head.
(13) There is a head on my body.
(14) There is no doubt that he has a shrewd head on his shoulders.
(15) She has a sweet voice.
(16) He is growing a beard.

---

1   Cf. Chesterman's explanation of the difference between *We heard the/a cry of a jackal* (1991: 13–14 and 82). He points out that although the contrast between *the man I met* and *a man I met* can be explained in terms of the presence or absence of previous knowledge, the same is not true of examples like *Fred has come to the conclusion that articles are a pseudo-category*, which are possible first mentions, not implying any necessary previous knowledge (13–14).

Examples (7) and (8) are explained as follows: "The indefinite article ... is sometimes used with body parts: Sally has sprained *an ankle*, He's broken *a leg*. BUT NOT:
*Roger has hurt *a nose*. *A/an* cannot be used unless the body has more than one of the
body parts mentioned; hence (8)[2] is absurd in implying that Roger has more than
one nose. (*CGEL*: 273, Note). Chesterman (1991: 22–23) explains the oddness of (9) by
Hawkins' opposition of 'inclusiveness' vs. 'exclusiveness': when using *the* the speaker
"refers to the totality of the objects or mass within this [i.e. the shared] set which
satisfy the referring expression" (1978: 167); and when using an indefinite article the
speaker "refers to a proper subset, i.e. not-all, of the potential referents of the referring expression" (1978: 187). Since Fred has only one head, the exclusiveness of a *head is*
odd, implying that there were also other heads (which Fred did not lose). "If anything,
this would have to mean that there were a number of other people's heads involved,
which Fred was responsible for, and that he lost one of these. On the other hand, (10)[3]
... is grammatical because it is possible to refer to 'not-all' the legs or fingers of a person: there exists at least one leg or finger which the speaker excludes from the reference." (Chesterman 1991: 22–23). In contrast to *a leg* in (10), **a right leg* in (11) denotes
a unique body part just as *head*, and conveys an analogous meaning to (9), which is so
odd as to relegate this use of the indefinite article to the sphere of ungrammaticality.

Examples (12) and (13) are exceptions to the exclusiveness condition of indefinite
reference, which Hawkins (1978: 221) explains by the meaning of the verbs involved:
in contexts with *have* and *be* and other 'set-existential' verbs, which define existence
within a set, the exclusiveness condition of indefinite reference does not hold. Chesterman (1991: 23) presents these examples without suggesting any contexts in which
they would sound natural, and hence presumably regards them as natural even out of
context. Yet they sound odd on account of the trivial nature of the information being
conveyed. The information structure of these examples lacks a focus insofar as the relationship between the nominal elements representing the theme (*I, on my body*) and
the rheme (*a head*), expressed by the verb, is pragmatically given, known. The fact that
a person has a head is known to everyone, and need hardly be stated unless invoked
by a special context (for example, enumeration by a child of the body parts that it can
name: *I have a head, a nose, a chin, a neck, arms and legs ...*).[4]

The fact that the oddness of (12) and (13) is entirely due to the trivial nature of
the content being expressed (to the lack of irretrievable information in the focus) is
demonstrated by (14), in which the same noun *head*, constituting the rheme, is modified, the modification representing new information. Hence the information structure contains a new, irretrievable element in the focus part, and conforms to the usual
configuration of a given, or more given, theme and a new, or less given element in the
rheme. As regards the combination of a given and a new item in the rheme (*head*

---

2 In *CGEL* the numbering of the examples is [4] and [5], hence (8) corresponds to [5].
3 (34) in Chesterman's numbering.
4 In this connection, a well-known instance comes to mind, viz Olivia's inventory of her charms (*Twelfth Night*,
   Act I, Scene IV).

and *shrewd*, respectively), this type of composite rheme has been found to be the most common (cf. Dušková 1985).

What has been said about (14) applies to (15), with a minor difference consisting in the greater acceptability of *She has a voice* even without overt modification of the object since it would be understood as implying a voice of superior quality even without explicit qualification.

As shown by (16), the appropriateness of indefinite determination of a unique body part increases if the part in question ceases to be a universal feature. Since beards are worn only by some men, the information structure of (16) conveys irretrievable information in the focus even without modification of the object noun phrase, and hence avoids the deficiency of (12) and (13). The use of the indefinite article with a unique object can be ascribed to the particular meaning of the verb *grow*, which, in the sense conveyed by (16), allows to be classed with 'set-existential' verbs in that it brings into existence the entity referred to by its complement, cf. *he has a beard*. However, classing a verb with 'set-existential' verbs still fails to explain why these verbs behave differently from others, specifically why (17) a. is grammatical, while (17) b. is not.

(17) a. He grew/had a beard.
  b. *He shaved off a beard.
  c. He shaved off his beard.

The verb *have*, which may serve to illustrate the category,[5] expresses the possessive relationship between the possessor and the thing possessed, and hence makes other means indicating this relationship, most importantly the possessives, redundant. In consequence, the determiner of the thing possessed can be selected according to the type of reference and function in the information structure (functional sentence perspective), as in (17) a. However, in (17) b. there is no indication of the fact that *a beard* is a thing possessed by the subject. In the absence of a verb indicating the possessive relationship the use of the possessive becomes obligatory, cf. (17) c. A determiner other than the possessive suggests a possessor different from the subject, cf. a sentence like *Can you shave off a beard now?* said by a barber to his assistant. A similar interpretation applies to the definite article, cf. *he broke a/the neck, he hurt a/the nose, she lost a/the head*. The difference between *the* and *a/an* consists in suggesting, in the case of the indefinite article, the presence of several objects with necks, noses and heads, whereas in the case of the definite article, which here indicates associative anaphoric relationship to an antecedent, some such context as *the neck of the bottle, the head of the doll*.[6]

---

5   As shown by Lyons (1971: 389–393), existential, locative and possessive sentences are to some extent parallel. Among other things, this parallelism manifests itself in the transformational relations between *have* and existential sentences, as illustrated e.g. by (14) and *There is a shrewd head on his shoulders*.

6   For a more detailed discussion of the role of the possessives in the English determiner system, see Dušková (1986b).

The discussion of the indefinite article may be concluded by pointing out that the degree of grammaticality of the indefinite article with unique body parts depends not only on the semantics of the indefinite article ('one of a set of more than one'), but also on its role in functional sentence perspective, as well as on the semantic structure and functional sentence perspective of the sentence as a whole.[7]

2.2 The assumption of a zero form of the indefinite article is based on two facts, both connected with the existence of two other noun categories in English, number and countability. The overt form of the indefinite article *a/an* being found with countable singulars, plurals[8] and uncountable nouns are assumed to be determined by its zero form because the types of determination expressed by *a/an* with countable singulars appear to be denoted by plurals and uncountable nouns without an overt determiner. Compare the expression of generic reference by the indefinite article in (18) a., as against indication of the same type of determination in (18) b. and c. by zero:

(18) a. A dog is a mammal.
　　b. Dogs are mammals.
　　c. Salt is soluble in water.

An analogous situation is found where the indefinite article determining a countable singular expresses nongeneric indefinite reference. Plurals and uncountable nouns again appear without an overt determiner, cf. (19) a., b. and c.

(19) a. There is a watchdog there.
　　b. There are watchdogs there.
　　c. Remember to buy salt.

Another reason for assuming a zero form of the indefinite article with plurals and uncountable nouns is the alternation, in some cases, of zero with unstressed *some*, as in (20) a. and b.

(20) a. I've been writing *(some) letters* this morning,
　　b. Would you like *(some) coffee* or *(some) tea?*[9]

Although there is a minor difference in meaning between the two forms ("The variant without *some* will focus on the category as a whole; ... But when *some* is added, the focus changes to whatever quantities of tea and coffee, or of letters, that the speaker has in mind." (*CGEL*: 275–276), in the given contexts they are more or less interchange-

---

7　For a treatment of the indefinite article with body parts, see Vaňková (2014).
8　Plurals as a rule correspond to countable singulars, and are themselves countable. Uncountable uses of plural nouns such as *vegetables, potatoes, cornflakes, soap suds* differ only in the choice of quantifiers (cf. *a little vegetables*), not in article usage. The latter follows the pattern of other plurals, identical with that of uncountable singulars.
9　Examples given in *CGEL* (275).

able. In (19) a., b., c. the variant with *some* is less likely because the meaning here is categorial, rather than quantitative. Nevertheless, instances which allow the choice between *some* and zero support the assumption that the indefinite article has a zero form, occurring in complementary distribution with *a/an*,[10] and in alternation with *some*. The zero article thus aligns itself with other zero exponents of grammatical categories, such as zero plurals and zero exponents of the preterite and past participle.

2.3 However, plurals and uncountable singulars are not the only noun categories that are found without an overt determiner.

CGEL (276–281) presents a section on the zero article with definite meaning, listing different classes and uses of countable singulars. The introductory formulation (5.41: 276) includes proper names, but in the sections treating proper names in detail this category is presented as having no article (cf. the section Proper names, 288–297). In the section on Noun classes (5.2: 246) an explicit distinction is made between no article in cases like *I like Sid* and zero article as in *I like music*.

The zero article with definite meaning is illustrated by the following eleven groups of examples ((21)–(31)) in CGEL (276–281).

The zero article with a singular count noun as complement (or an equivalent appositive noun phrase), naming a unique role or task:

(21) Maureen is *(the) captain of the team.*
(22) *As (the) chairman of the committee,* I declare this meeting closed.

The zero article with noun phrases with 'sporadic' definite reference (comparable with definite noun phrases such *the radio, the theatre*).

(23) be in/go to *town, bed, hospital, prison*
          be at/go to *school, sea*
          be in/at *church,* go to *college*

      as against

(23)' *The* town is very old, lie down on *the* bed, admire *the* church, walk around *the* prison

      Means of transport and communication

(24) travel/leave/come/go by *bicycle, bus, car, boat, train, plane*

      as against

---

10   The view that the zero article is the plural and non-count equivalent of the indefinite article *a/an*, alternating in many contexts with unstressed *some*, has not gone unchallenged; see Chesterman's discussion of Carlson's counterexamples (Chesterman 1991: 29–32).

(24)' take *the* bicycle, be on *the* bus, prefer *the* car, choose *the* boat, take *a/the* train, be on *the* plane

(25) communicate/communication by *radio, telephone, telex, post, mail, satellite*

as against

(25)'a talk on *the* radio, Jill is on *the* telephone, put a letter in *the* post, send it through *the* mail, etc.

Times of day and night

(26) at *dawn/daybreak*, when *day breaks, at sunrise/sunset, at/around noon/midnight, at dusk/twilight, at/by night, (by) day and night, before morning came, evening approached, after nightfall/dark* etc.

as against

(26)' watch *the* dawn, during *the* day, we admired *the* sunset, in *the* afternoon, see nothing in *the* dusk, etc.

Seasons, meals, illnesses

(27) in (the) spring/summer
(28) stay for/have *breakfast, tea, lunch, dinner, supper*
before/after/at/for *breakfast, tea, lunch, dinner* ...
(29) *anaemia, appendicitis, diabetes, influenza* ...
(the) flu, (the) measles, (the) mumps, (the) chickenpox

Parallel structures

(30) *arm in arm, face to face, eye to eye, day by day* ...
from father to son, husband and wife, from (the) beginning to (the) end, etc.

Fixed phrases involving prepositions

(31) *at home, by hand, on foot, in turn*, etc.

Compare also proper names:

(32) *Paris x The Hague, Crete x the Crimea*
(33) *Lake Michigan, Mount Everest x the River Thames, the Suez Canal*

Of these, most attention has been paid to contrasting instances like (34) and (35).

(34) I like cheese.
(35) I like London.

It is argued that the overt absence of a determiner in the two cases is of a different kind. Yotsukura (1970: 68) distinguishes between the zero article in (34) and no article in (35), basing the distinction on the possibility of using the definite article in (34) (*I like the cheese* 'a particular kind of cheese that is present'), which is not possible in (35) *I like the London,* unless the proper name is modified. Similarly Chesterman (1991: 45-47) differentiates between the overt absence of a determiner with a plural or an uncountable singular (*olives, cheese*), for which he retains the term 'zero' article, and the overt absence of a determiner with proper names in the singular (*John, Helsinki*). He moreover distinguishes a third group represented by some count singular common nouns in certain 'idiomatic' structures (*at church, hand in hand, What about question seven? Breakfast is ready,* etc.). For the latter two groups he coins the term 'null'. In contrast to Yotsukura, Chesterman bases the distinction between zero and null on the type of reference indicated by the overt absence of a determiner in the two cases: whereas the nouns with zero are indefinite, those with null are definite.

A virtually identical standpoint was adopted in Dušková et al. (1988: 75-81). The type of determination expressed by proper names is here conceived as identical with that denoted by common nouns having nongeneric definite reference, in particular definite reference due to the presence in the situation of utterance of only one possible referent (cf. *George Washington* and *the first President of the United States*). Besides the absence of an overt determiner, even with proper names this type of reference is expressed by the definite article, i.e. by the same means as in the case of common nouns (cf. *Crete, Hampton Court* x *the Crimea, the Parthenon*). The absence of an article (here called *bezčlennost* 'articlelessness') is distinguished from the zero article on the basis of their distribution and the respective type of determination: whereas the former is found with countable singulars and expresses nongeneric definite reference (situational uniqueness), the latter occurs with plurals and uncountable singulars and denotes either nongeneric indefinite or generic reference.

The uses illustrating 'the zero article with definite meaning' represent instances of different kinds. A noun can be classed as having no (or 'null') article only if it is a countable singular expressing nongeneric definite reference, against the background of, or potential alternation with, the definite article. Of examples (21) to (31) only some meet the conditions for 'no article'.

Apart from univerbal proper names such as *John, Helsinki,* the clearest case of the 'null' article is presented by appositional constructions which are partly found among proper names, both personal and geographical, cf. *Dr Brown, Professor Smith, Captain Cook;* (33) *Lake Michigan, Mount Everest,* and analogous instances like *the Emperor Napoleon, (the) Czar Alexander, (the) Archduke Ferdinand, (the) Reverend John Smith* (examples from *CGEL*: 292, Note [d]); *the River Thames, the Suez Canal.* However, the construction is not confined to proper names. As shown by (36) and (36)', it also occurs with common nouns, which again here display both types of determiner: 'null' alongside the definite article.

(36) What about question seven? Open your books at page 10.
        Figure 3, line five, Part 2, Example (36), Chapter 6, Section 8, Table 1, Type A, etc.
(36)' the letter A, the word *bizzare*, the year 2000, the plural *brethren*, etc.

Other structures that satisfy the conditions for the 'null' article may be found among instances illustrated by (30) and (31). In *They were walking arm in arm, talking face to face* and the like, the nouns *arm* and *face* can be regarded as referring to the particular arms and faces, but on the other hand, apart from being set phrases, the constructions have acquired an adverbial function, hence coming close to adverbs. This interpretation is presented in *CGEL*: "Phrases with the noun repeated typically have an adverbial function ... It can be argued that the nouns have no article because they have largely lost their independent nominal status." (280). Yet some of these instances, especially those where 'null' alternates with *the*, can be classed with the use illustrated by (36) and (36)', cf. *from (the) right to (the) left, from (the) west to (the) east, from (the) beginning to (the) end.*
        A similar case is illustrated by (27), which shows alternation between 'null' and *the* not only in the function of a temporal adverbial, but also in other functions. Where the reference is deictic the use satisfies the condition of unique reference, cf. *(The) winter is coming* (*CGEL*: 278). Presumably also *I look forward to (the) spring.*
        Of special interest in this connection is the behaviour of other temporal nouns, illustrated by (26) and (26)'. All uses displaying 'null' are either adverbial with certain prepositions (*at dawn/daybreak, at dusk, at/by night*) or the temporal noun is the subject (when *day breaks, dusk was falling, before morning came, evening approached*). On the other hand, *the* is found with the object, cf. *watch the dawn, we admired the sunset*, and in adverbial prepositional phrases involving other prepositions. As regards the adverbial function, the choice between 'null' and *the* appears to depend on which preposition is used (cf. *at/by night* as against *during the night, all through the night*). The adverbial use of nouns of this group not only satisfies the condition of alternation between 'null' and *the*, but since they mostly refer to the respective time of a particular day or night, they also fulfil the condition of definite reference (as (27)).
        However, the distribution of 'null' and *the* in the case of other syntactic functions, in particular the subject, appears to follow a different pattern. We are still mostly concerned with unique reference (*we watched the dawn* [on a particular day], *Evening came* [of a particular day]. Owing to their semantics, determiners signalling reference to a unique object are as a rule excluded from playing a role in functional sentence perspective insofar as noun phrases with this type of determination occur both in the theme and the rheme, their FSP function being determined by the interplay of the other FSP factors (see 3.). However, in instances like (37) the use of the 'null' form tends to conform to the pattern found with the nongeneric zero article indicating contextual independence of its head noun, in this case the subject, and together with the

semantic structure of the sentence (presentation of a new phenomenon on the scene by means of a verb of existence or appearance on the scene), it signals the rheme.

(37) before morning came; evening approached;
    dusk was falling

For this reason temporal nouns in this use may be regarded as uncountable rather than countable.

Proceeding to (24) and (25), we again find the uses displaying 'null' to have a distinctly adverbial function, that of the adverbial of means. Significantly, as shown by (24)', and (25)', it is only in the adverbial function that the 'null' is found with these nouns. It can hardly be claimed that the nouns as used in (24) and (25) express unique reference. When saying *I'll go by train* the speaker is more likely to be referring to the means of transport rather than to a particular train. Or at least the two notions are merged. Consequently, this use might be classed with (30) and (31): the determiner is neither 'zero' nor 'null', the noun in this adverbial use having lost its independent nominal status, and consequently the noun categories. This interpretation is supported by the situation in Czech, where this adverbial function is expressed not only by noun phrases, but also by adverbs, cf. *letecky* [*flying* + adverbial suffix] 'by air', *pěšky* [*walk* + adverbial suffix] 'on foot', *koňmo* [*horse* + adverbial suffix] 'on horseback', *telefonicky* [*telephone* + adverbial suffix] 'by telephone', etc.

Examples (21) and (22) are interesting in that the nouns in predicative and appositive function are nonreferential. Otherwise, both conditions for 'null' are satisfied: 'null' actually alternates with *the*, and at the same time indicates that the predicative/appositive noun, albeit nonreferential, denotes a set with only one member.

The uses listed under (23) and (23)' display semantic differentiation, which is at variance with the concept of 'null' as an alternative form of nongeneric *the*. This also applies to the meals as an institution, cf. (28), but where 'null' with a noun of this group alternates with *the* in reference to a particular meal, as in (38), the concept of 'null' is applicable.

(38) That day, *(the) lunch* was served at the terrace.[11]

Names of illnesses, as illustrated by (29), display alternation of 'null' with *the*, thus resembling proper names, but are not confined to unique reference, and might thus be regarded as a transitional category between proper and common nouns.

Although concerned with a type of reference other than indefinite, the foregoing discussion has been necessary insofar as it shows that the overtly unrealized determiner, usually described as the zero article, involves instances of different kinds: the zero article with plurals and uncountable singulars, which corresponds to the indefi-

---

11   An example from *CGEL* (279).

nite article with countable singulars and expresses generic and nongeneric indefinite reference; in the latter function it alternates with unstressed *some*; the null article with countable singulars, which alternates with the definite article and expresses nongeneric definite reference; and no article in adverbial prepositional phrases in which the noun has lost its independent nominal status, and hence its noun categories. As regards proper names, their type of reference shows them to be determined by null.

2.4 Unstressed *some* has been included in the article system on the grounds that it is found as an alternative form of the zero article with uncountable nouns and plurals where countable singulars are determined by the indefinite article expressing nongeneric reference (see 2.2). Although the interchangeability of the zero article and unstressed *some* is restricted to contexts in which the difference between the categorial meaning of the former and the quantitative meaning of the latter is not relevant, yet unstressed *some* appears to fit the article system better than it does the quantifier system. Not only does its prosodic structure conform to that of the articles, but also its quantitative meaning is weakened. This is what makes alternation with zero possible. Conversely, quantifiers are stressed, as a consequence of the full force of their quantitative meaning. Compare:

(39) a. She has made (*some*) films abroad.
     b. *Some* people don't like it. x People don't like it.

However, within the article system unstressed *some* has a special position insofar as it is the only member that fails to express generic reference. Admittedly, Chesterman (1991: 37) does adduce examples of generic *some*, which becomes acceptable 'if a subspecies reading is possible', cf. (40), but this use of *some* involves the quantifier, not the article, and is marginal in any case.

(40) Continued destruction of the rainforest will lead to the extermination of *some rare insects*.

On the other hand, it may be claimed that the incapacity of *some* to express generic reference is no argument against its article status since this property is inherent in the very nature of a partitive article.

While the semantics of unstressed *some* often prevents its use where the zero article is appropriate, there are also instances in which *some* is a closer equivalent of *a/an* than zero. In discussing Carlson's arguments against treating the zero article as the plural and non-count equivalent of *a/an*, Chesterman (1991: 29-32) presents examples with quantifiers whose scope is ambiguous in the singular and equally ambiguous in the plural with *some*, but unambiguous in the plural with the zero article. Compare (41) a., b. and c.:

(41) a. Everyone read *a book* on caterpillars, (ambiguous as to whether the universal or the existential quantifier has the wider scope)

b. Everyone read *some* books on caterpillars, (ambiguous in the same way as (41) a.)

c. Everyone read *books* on caterpillars, (only the universal quantifier has the wider scope)

Another difference involves the specific/nonspecific reference of both *a/an* and *some*, as compared with only nonspecific reference of the zero article, cf. (42) a., b. and c.:

(42) a. Minnie wishes to talk with *a young psychiatrist*, (specific or nonspecific)

b. Minnie wishes to talk with *some young psychiatrists*, (specific or nonspecific)

c. Minnie wishes to talk with *young psychiatrists*, (only nonspecific)

Obviously, this difference is connected with the categorial meaning of the zero article as against the quantitative meaning of *some*. The two plural forms of the indefinite article thus appear to be partly specialized, the zero form corresponding to both the generic and nongeneric *a/an*, while *some* only to the latter. On the whole, the semantic relations between *a/an* and *some*, illustrated by (41) and (42), testify to the integration of *some* into the English article system.

2.5 Two forms of indefinite determination are found not only with plurals and uncountable nouns, but also with countable singulars, cf. *a man* and *some man*. *Some* with countable singulars is as a rule excluded from the article system because it is stressed, according to *CGEL* (257, Note [a]) even strongly stressed, especially with temporal nouns; according to Sahlin (1979: 13),[12] "*some* + Sg Count has some degree of stress-prominence in the majority of cases." Hence it is classed with the quantifier *some*, which also occurs with plurals and uncountable nouns.

In a study by Mráz (1998), *some* determining a countable singular is treated comprehensively on the basis of a corpus of 352 occurrences of determinative *some*,[13] out of which *some* + countable singular accounts for 100 (29%) instances.[14] In this study, Mráz is mainly concerned with verifying the presentation of *some* + countable singular in *CGEL*, which describes it as occurring especially with temporal nouns, less usually with other singular nouns, in the latter case with the meaning 'a certain' or 'some ... or other' (384, and 257 Note [a]). Mraz's results (1998: 51, Table 10) show the use of *some* with temporal nouns (*Some day he'll get his scholarship*) to be represented by 15%. A comparable number of his examples (14%) illustrates expressive *some*, which carries emotive loading, mostly that of disparagement (*some wild wag of an oculist*). By far the largest group of *some* + countable singular is represented by what he calls 'alternative' ('alternative' because it alternates with other determiners), or neutral *some* (*... restricted in some way*) 69%, while the least frequent use (2%) is found in instances

---

12   Sahlin's spoken material is based on the Survey of English Usage (University College London).
13   The sources of Mráz's corpus were fiction (the concordance to *Great Gatsby*), a linguistic text (Crystal and Davy's *Investigating English Style*) and a spoken sports commentary
14   In the two written sources the percentage is even higher: 38% in Crystal and Davy, and 34% in *Great Gatsby* (Mráz 1998: 43).

in which strongly stressed *some* means 'remarkable', 'extraordinary' (*Look at that coat. Some coat!*).

As a means of expressing indefinite reference, *some* + countable singular has to be included in the present discussion, and considered with respect, on the one hand, to *some* with plurals and uncountable singulars, and on the other hand, to the indefinite article.

Unlike unstressed *some* with plurals and uncountable singulars, which, as was explained in 2.4, fits the article system, *some* + countable singular qualifies as a quantifier, on account of being stressed and expressing specialized indefinite meaning (qualitative rather than quantitative, the term 'quantifier' being here used in contrast to 'article'). Accordingly, the relation between *some* determining a countable singular and the indefinite article can be compared to the relation between stressed (quantifying) *some* and unstressed *some* (article) with plurals and uncountable singulars, rather than to the relation between unstressed *some* and zero with these two noun categories.

In contrast to the indefinite article, *some* presents the identity of the referent as unknown both to the speaker and to the hearer, and is nonspecific. In both these respects the indefinite article is more neutral: the referent of the noun phrase with *a/an* may be unknown only to the hearer, and besides nonspecific reference, the indefinite article also expresses indefinite specific reference. Of the two types of reference, the specific is presumably the more usual. It might be expected that the specific indefinite article cannot be replaced by *some*, and this is indeed the case in (43).

(43) a. He is growing a beard.
 b. *He is growing some beard.

The only interpretation of (43) b. in which *some* is acceptable is to assign *some* strong stress and the meaning 'extraordinary', 'remarkable'. However, as shown by (44), this seems to apply only to 'set-existential' verbs:

(44) a. He has written a book about it.
 b. He has written some book about it.

While the actual state of the speaker's knowledge about the book may be the same in both (44) a. and b., the indefinite article is noncommittal in this respect. On the other hand, the use of *some* makes the speaker's lack of knowledge explicit; admittedly, the speaker may merely lack an interest in the referent, and only pretend a lack of knowledge.

As was shown by Mráz (1998: 25–28), the nonspecificity of *some* shows different degrees, which he classifies into two types, referential and nonreferential. However, *some* is inherently referential.[15] The distinction that Mráz draws between the examples

---

15 "A referential NP ... involves, roughly the speaker's intent to 'refer to' or 'mean' a nominal expression to have non-empty references—i.e. to 'exist'—within a particular universe of discourse. All uses of *some* fulfil this condition, at least in assertive clauses" (Sahlin 1979: 29, quoting Givón).

listed under (45), and those under (46), which he regards, respectively, as nonreferential and referential, does not consist in non/referentiality, but in a smaller or larger degree of locatability.

(45) a. I want to invite *some actress*. Can you suggest *any*?
    b. *Some day* he'll get his scholarship.
    c. Tom's got *some woman* in New York
    d. *Some rare animal* has escaped from the zoo.
(46) a. *Some man* was talking to him in a low voice ...
    b. He was saying *some last word* to her ...

The least locatable referents appear to be in (45) a. and b., which is reflected in the proform *any* (or *one*) in (45) a., and the replaceability of *some* by *one* in (45) b. In neither case does the noun phrase with *some* refer to a particular, albeit unspecified referent, replacement of *some* by *a certain* being thus inapplicable. In (45) c. and d., the referent is a particular unspecified person or animal, but non-locatable within the particular situation of utterance, whereas in (46) a. and b., the referents are present in the situation of utterance, and only presented as unspecified. These aspects do not appear to affect the replaceability of *some* by *a certain* insofar as in (46) b. *a certain* is again inapplicable, whereas in (45) a., b., and in (46) a., the use of *a certain* indicates the speaker's ability, as against his/her inability if s/he uses *some*, to identify the referent. The distinctions suggested between the three uses, (45) a. b., as against (45) c., d., as against (46) a. b., are obviously due to the context, reference to no particular objects being favoured by nonfactive ones. Compare (45) b. and (45)' b. In the latter, only *one* can be used.

(45)' b. *Some day he got his scholarship. / One day he got his scholarship.

It thus appears that even an extensive monographic study of *some* + countable singular, such as Mráz's diploma dissertation, leaves a number of questions open, and calls for further research.

3. The last point to be briefly discussed is the role of indefiniteness in functional sentence perspective (FSP). The relevance of FSP has already been mentioned in connection with the functions of the indefinite and the zero article. What remains to be surveyed here is the FSP role of indefiniteness in general.

The FSP aspect of indefiniteness, in particular of *some*, is discussed by Sahlin in terms of contextual non/boundness (contextual in/dependence) (1979: 37–41). *Some* + countable singular, as well as non-selective *some* with plurals and uncountable singulars, is always contextually independent, and as such introduces new information. On the other hand, contextually bound *some* is found in what Sahlin calls the selective use, cf. *Some of them could have done it, Some people think so* (37–38). Presenting givenness as a natural property of the theme, since given items make a natural starting point for the sentence, Sahlin points out that noun phrases with *some*, except the selective uses, are rare in the subject, whereas selective *some*, being closely connected with definiteness, abounds in this function (46). "Moreover, non-selective *some*, whether article or quantifier, is usually found with types of VPs held to favour new information in the subject, notably those indicating 'appearance or existence on the scene'" (ibid.). Sahlin's examples, however, support the claims made in the foregoing passage only where the sentence contains a verb of existence or appearance on the scene, as in (47).

(47) a. A tavern, …, or *some other business* may go up near enough to hurt your home or to hurt its value.
   b. When *some question* arises in the medical field concerning cancer, for instance, we do not … (p. 47)

On the other hand, the examples here listed under (48) (p. 49 in Sahlin) are presented as "difficult to classify" and providing "compelling evidence in favour of the grammatical principle" (i.e. new information, which should appear at the end, is found in the subject).

(48) a. We found *some owls* had built a nest in the chimney …
   b. At the rear of the auditorium, upstairs, *some men* tried to push open the door to the box corridor.
   c. We are worried …—that *some crazy fool* may push the button.
   d. She felt as if *some dark, totally unfamiliar shape* would clutch at her arm, …

In (47) both a. and b. realize the presentation scale (cf. Firbas 1992: 66–69, 134–140), that is, a contextually independent phenomenon (the subject) is introduced on the scene (the adverbial) by means of a verb of appearance on the scene. Although the grammatical word order operates counter to the basic distribution of communicative dynamism (cf. Firbas 1992: 10 and 118), the order theme—transition—rheme being here replaced by rheme—transition—theme, the FSP structure of the sentences is clearly indicated by the other FSP factors, the semantic and contextual (in speech an additional factor is intonation) (cf. Firbas 1992: 10–11, 107–108, 147–148).

Interpretation in terms of the presentation scale may also be ascribed to (48) d., which, though not containing a verb of appearance or existence in the narrow sense, semantically implies appearance of a phenomenon (the subject) on a contextually bound scene (*at her arm*). However, this reading depends on the classification of the verb, which is not unequivocal.

In (48) a., b., and c. the communication focuses on verbal complementation, the verbs being outside the category of existence or appearance on the scene, cf. Firbas's quality scale (1992: 66–69, 109–110, 134–140). As in general, the FSP structure is determined by the interplay of all FSP factors: contextual, semantic, and linear modification, including intonation in speech. In writing the latter is as a rule indicated by the other three factors. Given and new items, even though disposed to operate, respectively, within the theme and the rheme, are not necessarily thematic in the case of given, and rhematic in the case of new. The theme and the rheme being defined, respectively, as the least and the most dynamic element, new items, as well as given items, may be found in both the theme and the rheme.[16]

Indefiniteness as a means of indicating new, contextually independent items, appertains to the semantic factor, but as such is subordinated to the higher level of semantic structure, i.e. whether the particular sentence realizes the presentation scale or the quality scale, and ultimately acquires the respective amount of communicative dynamism from the interplay of all the FSP factors, semantic structure, contextual boundness and linear modification.

Taking into account these facts, as well as conceivable preceding contexts, Sahlin's examples being presented without context, we may interpret the FSP structure of (48) a. as having thematic subject (*some owls*) and rhematic object (*a nest*), which are both contextually independent, as indicated by the determiners. The FSP function of the prepositional phrase depends on the preceding context since the definite article, which indicates a situationally unique object, may determine either a new or a given item. A likely interpretation is to regard it as derivable from the situation of utterance, and hence belonging to the thematic section.

In (48) b. the thematic nature of the locative adverbial is indicated even by its initial position. The determiner of the subject involves contextual independence, but the semantic structure of the sentence (the quality scale) assigns it the function of theme. The determiners in the object noun phrase play no FSP role since they again denote situationally unique objects, presumably mentioned for the first time and hence context independent. As a result of the interplay of all these factors, the object constitutes the rheme.

As regards (48) c., the most relevant factor appears to be the preceding context. According to the semantic structure of the sentence (the quality scale) the subject (*some crazy fool*) is again thematic. The FSP of the object (*the button*) depends on whether it is contextually dependent or not. In the former case, the rheme is constituted by the verb, in the latter by the object, the intonation centre (the nucleus) being placed correspondingly.

This brief discussion of Sahlin's examples will have shown that the role of indefiniteness in functional sentence perspective cannot be considered in isolation, but in connection with all participating factors, which determine the FSP structure through their interplay. The disposition of indefinite determiners to operate in the rheme is subject to the semantic structure of the sentence as a whole, and to the effect of linear modification and contextual dependence or independence of all elements constituting the sentence.

---

16   For the realization of themes and rhemes with respect to given and new items, see Dušková (1985).

4. The main points emerging from the foregoing discussion may be summed up as follows.

The means serving to express indefiniteness comprise both articles and quantifiers, the two categories in determinative function being basically distinguished by their prosodic structure and semantics. Articles are unstressed, and whatever their source, the original meaning is weakened in favour of indicating primarily the type of reference. On the other hand, quantifiers are stressed, and retain the full force of their quantitative meaning.

As regards the indefinite article, of special interest are instances of reference to a situationally unique object, which are considered with respect to the semantic and FSP structure of the sentence as a whole, as well as with respect to the function of the indefinite article in functional sentence perspective.

The zero article is conceived as a counterpart of the indefinite article, since it expresses the same types of reference with plurals and uncountable singulars as the indefinite article with countable singulars. Although in nongeneric indefinite reference it is sometimes a less fitting counterpart of the indefinite article than unstressed *some*, the zero article appears to be an established member of the article system on account of both its distribution and alternative means of expression. Unstressed *some* as an alternative form of the nongeneric zero article with plurals and uncountable singulars is included in the article system owing to its prosodic structure, weakened quantitative meaning, and close semantic relations to the indefinite article in certain uses.

Where overt absence of an article is found with a countable singular, it is distinguished from the zero article as 'null' or 'no article' on the basis of alternating with the nongeneric definite article, and expressing nongeneric definite reference (situational uniqueness). The term 'no article' is reserved for those instances in which the noun loses its independent nominal status.

Unlike unstressed *some* with plurals and uncountable singulars, *some* with countable singulars is a quantifier outside the article system. In comparison with the indefinite article, its reference is confined to indefinite nonspecific, different degrees of nonspecificity, being reflected in the respective proforms and replaceability by *a certain*.

As regards the role of indefinite determiners in functional sentence perspective, owing to their semantics, which indicates contextual nonboundness, they are disposed to determine noun phrases in the rheme. However, this disposition is subject to the semantic structure of the sentence as a whole, as well as to the effect of the other FSP factors, contextual boundness or nonboundness of the other sentence elements, linear modification, and intonation (in speech). Consequently, in dependence on the interplay of all FSP factors, indefinite determiners appear not only in the rheme, but also in the theme.

IV. SYNTAX, FSP, TEXT

19. THEME MOVEMENT
IN ACADEMIC DISCOURSE[1]

First published in M. Procházka and J. Čermák (eds), *Shakespeare between the Middle Ages and Modernism. From Translator's Art to Academic Discourse.* A Tribute to Professor Martin Hilský, OBE. Prague: Charles University / Faculty of Arts, 2008, 221–247.

0. This chapter examines the tendency of English to retain the same subject in successive clauses with regard to its largely prevalent function of theme. Both these properties of the English subject were first pointed out by Vilém Mathesius (1975: 100–103; 1947a) and confirmed in further studies (Dušková 1986a) especially with regard to the subject's thematic function. The other property of the English subject, the disposition to remain the same in successive clauses, suggested a promising line of research in connection with the concept of thematic progressions proposed by František Daneš (1974).

1. The concept of theme is based on Jan Firbas's theory of functional sentence perspective (FSP, i.e., information structure) (Firbas 1992). The FSP theory works with four FSP factors: semantic structure, context dependence/independence (cf. discourse old and discourse new) (Huddleston and Pullum 2002: 1370), linearity and intonation in speech. The interplay of these four factors determines the FSP functions (theme, transition, rheme) of the clause elements. In the deep (interpretative) word order the clause elements are arranged according to gradual increase in the information load (i.e., the degree of communicative dynamism). This arrangement constitutes the basic distribution of communicative dynamism, and basically corresponds to what is called the principle of end focus in British grammar (Quirk et al. 1985, esp. 1361–62; cf. also the general tendencies regarding information structure in Huddleston and Pullum 2002: 1372). The theme and the rheme are defined, respectively, as the ele-

---

1   A shortened version of this chapter was presented at the Lund Conference of the International Association of University Professors of English (IAUPE) in 2007.

ments carrying the lowest and the highest degree of communicative dynamism irrespective of sentence position. This is the meaning in which the term "theme" is used henceforth. In the more general sense "the subject matter" the term employed is the "hypertheme."

As regards thematic progressions (TP), the following analysis draws on Daneš (1974: 118–20), who proposed the following major types: (1) Simple linear TP (= TP with linear thematization of rhemes): each rheme becomes the theme of the next utterance. (2) TP with a continuous (constant) theme: successive utterances contain the same theme to which different rhemes are added. (3) TP with derived themes: the utterance themes are derived from a "hypertheme" (of a paragraph, or another text section). Of the various combinations into which these types of thematic progressions may enter, Daneš mentions (4) the progression with a split rheme: a rheme composed of more than one (mostly coordinated) component provides successive themes constituted by each component treated separately.

Considering these types of theme development in connection with the tendency of English to preserve the same subject in successive clauses and the subject's largely thematic function, it can be assumed that a prominent role in the text build-up will be played by the second type of thematic progression, viz. the progression with a constant theme.

2. This assumption was tested on a section of text on a natural science topic comprising 100 clauses (both finite and non-finite).[2] The results are given in Table 1 (see Appendix); items with identical superscripts denote recurrent subjects, items without superscripts denote subjects with one occurrence (different subjects) and subjects due to syntactic construction (*it* and *that* as components of a cleft sentence, and *it* anticipating extraposed infinitives).[3] Where discussed, these subjects are referred to by the number of the respective clause.

As a prerequisite of arriving at the data presented in Table 1, it was necessary to determine which subjects were to be regarded as identical (recurrent) and which as different. This appeared to be a matter of degree rather than a clear-cut division. As shown by columns 2 and 3, which list identical subjects, i.e. subjects with more than one occurrence, apart from instances displaying full identity, denoted by numbers alone, these columns also include subjects whose identity is only partial, which are marked by the respective number + a letter. Six items are found here: *label*[1], *black-footed squirrel*[2], *time*[3], general *we*[4], *the zoologist*[5], and *human species*[6].

The figures in Table 2 show that among the six recurrent items, two display a much higher frequency of occurrence than the rest: item [2], *the black-footed squirrel*, the hypertheme of a greater part of the examined text section (30 instances); and item [4], general *we*, represented by 31 occurrences. Item [6], *the human species*, shows less than a half of this frequency of occurrence (12 instances). However, this is due to the lim-

---

2   Source text: Desmond Morris, *The Naked Ape* (1967) (London: Triad Grafton Books, 1986) 13–15. See Appendix.
3   Cf. information packaging constructions in Huddleston and Pullum (2002: 1366, v and viii).

Table 2: Subjects with More Than One Occurrence

Item	Number of Occurrences
Label[1]	2
Black-footed squirrel[2]	30
Time[3]	2
General subject we[4]	31
The zoologist[5]	3
Human species[6]	12
Total	80

ited length of the text: this item appears in the last part of the examined section, and reflects a shift to a new hypertheme, which is the global theme of the entire text. Items[1],[3], each with two occurrences, are of interest in that they denote the local and temporal scene on which the first hypertheme is discussed. In this respect they are inherent components of the content build-up, their low frequency of occurrence indicating their background, scene-setting nature.

The four recurrent items with the highest frequencies of occurrence—*black-footed* squirrel[2], general we[4], *the zoologist*[5], *human species*[6]—may be divided into two groups: the two hyperthemes *black-footed squirrel* and *human species* on the one hand, and general *we* and *the zoologist* on the other. Even here, the dividing line is not quite clear-cut: *the zoologist* is associated with both hyperthemes, but like the general *we* and unlike the two hyperthemes, does not represent 'what is spoken about', and in that sense both *we* and *the zoologist* are external to the text and can be classed together.

The distinction between the two groups moreover appears in their realization forms. As shown in Table 1 (see Appendix), the superscripts [2] and [6], which denote the two hyperthemes, are in a number of instances followed, respectively, by the letters [a-f] and [a-d]. These indicate partly identical subjects, and are specific to the hyperthemes; the items forming the other group, the general *we* and *the zoologist*, do not display them. In the case of the two hyperthemes both fully and partly identical subjects are realized by three forms: anaphoric pronouns (personal, relative and demonstrative), zero (ellipsis in finite clauses and structural deletion in nonfinite clauses) and referentially identical noun phrases. General *we* and *the zoologist* have only pronominal and zero forms of realization (which is accidental in the case of the latter).

2.1 Examining the two hyperthemes in more detail we arrive at the following findings.

2.1.1 The hypertheme *black-footed squirrel* is realized by pronouns and zero both in the case of fully and partly identical subjects. Fully identical subjects have pronominal realization in 9 instances (in clauses 5, 6, 9, 10, 13, 20, 22, 28, 42); the zero form occurred in one instance (in clause 23); in total 10 instances. See Table 1, items with the superscript [2] in columns 2 and 3. In the case of partly identical subjects anaphoric pronouns are found in three instances (cf. clauses 35 *they* [*mating calls and displays*], 43 *these* [*the markings of its fur—its black feet*], 58 *it* [*every aspect of its behaviour*]); and zero in 5 clauses (15, 30, 32, 34, 59); altogether 8 instances.

The distinction between fully and partly identical subjects results from the differences between the objects being referred to, which are primarily denoted by nouns (antecedents of the pronominal and zero realization forms). Fully identical subjects are found among referentially identical noun phrases reiterating the same head noun (clauses 4, 7, 19, 25; altogether 4 instances). A group of 3 designations by a more general, superordinate term (hypernym) is again a border line case assignable to either fully or partly identical subjects: clause 3 *this animal*, clause 21 *the new form*, clause 36 *a new species*. Superordinate terms have been classed as fully identical. Clause 14 *the ancestors of this animal*, where the head noun denotes a subclass, is connected with this group through its postmodification, and is hence included in this group (accordingly, 4 instances in total).

Partly identical subjects are characterized by a distinctive semantic feature, mostly the relationship of part/whole with respect to the hypertheme, which may also involve an inalienable characteristic (4 instances): *social and sexual behaviour* [*of black-footed squirrels*] in clause 29, *their anatomy* in clause 31, *mating calls and displays* [*of black-footed squirrels*] in clause 33 and *the markings of its feet* in clause 41. See Table 1, items with the superscripts [2, 2a-f] in columns 2 and 3.

2.1.2 The hypertheme *human species* presents a similar picture. Pronominal and NP realization is found in both fully and partly identical subjects: pronouns in clauses 77, 83, 89, 92 and 99 (*that* referring to a partly identical subject *skin*), altogether 5 instances; noun phrases: hypernyms classed as fully identical in clauses 78 (*a strange form of life*) and 96 (*this species*). Partly identical noun phrases (e.g., *legs, arms*) occurred in clauses 93, 94, 95, 98 and 100. In total the hypertheme *human species* is represented by 6 fully identical subjects and an equal number of partly identical subjects, altogether 12 instances. See Table 1, items with the superscripts [6, 6a-d] in columns 2 and 3.

2.2 Recurrent subjects of the second group, general *we* and *the zoologist*, differ not only from the hyperthemes, but partly also from each other.

2.2.1 As noted in Section 2, the distinctive features of general *we* consist of the form of realization, semantics and the FSP aspect. Its two realization forms (pronominal—18 instances, and zero—13 instances [3 ellipses and 10 deletions]; in total 31 instances) entail the full identity of all occurrences. The semantics of general *we*— designation of the general human agent, here people interested in zoology, including the text producer and text recipient—is reflected in the different FSP nature of this recurrent subject. Whereas the two hyperthemes in the subject function largely represent the theme both in the sense of the least dynamic element within the respective clause, i.e., the theme as defined in the FSP theory, they also denote what is being spoken about. On the other hand, general *we* complies with only one of these aspects: it does not constitute what is spoken about, but merely the least dynamic element of the sentence. This distinction is closely connected with the other FSP feature of general *we*, viz. its non-occurrence as the rheme. On the other hand both hyperthemes, representing what is spoken about, first appear as rhemes, mostly in syntactic functions constituting the verb complementation, but also as the subject. Where they operate as themes in a thematic section composed of several elements, the two aspects of the theme (the theme as the carrier of the lowest degree of communicative dynamism, and the 'aboutness' aspect) are realized by two separate elements, theme proper and diatheme (the most dynamic element within the thematic section; cf. Svoboda 1981). What is spoken about then represents one of the components of the thematic section. The distinction between different thematic elements can be found even in Mathesius' initial general outline of the FSP theory: themes like general *we* would be classed as the starting point of an utterance (*východiště výpovědi*) (Mathesius 1947b: 234–35).

2.2.2 The recurrent subject *the zoologist* is most similar to general *we* in the last respect, i.e., in the text under study it does not convey what is spoken about, but represents the starting point for statements about the hyperthemes. However, its more specific meaning does not exclude it from what might be spoken about in another context, which presupposes previous occurrence in the rheme. The more specific semantic structure is moreover reflected in a narrower scope of inclusiveness. While it may (and virtually does) include the T (the producer) of the text (a non-specialist could not write it), it is non-inclusive with respect to the text recipient (the addressee).

The zoologist has three occurrences in the text, one pronominal (clause 70) and two zero realizations (clauses 71 and 73).

3. Proceeding to the non-recurrent (different) subjects, the eight items in the right-hand column of Table 3 include four clauses constituting *it*-clefts and two instances of *it* anticipating extraposed infinitives (their subjects are listed in the third column of Table 1). Both constructions are derived from underlying simpler structures, from which they differ in their FSP. The two *it*-clefts represent the more frequent type (called stressed-focus *it*-clefts by Prince (1978); discourse-old presupposition *it*-clefts in Huddleston and Pullum 2002:1424), in which the *that*-clause conveys context-dependent, given information.[4] The focused element is in both cases the interrogative pronoun *what*, which in the underlying non-cleft clause—in the absence of the prosodic factor, operating in speech—implements a thematic subject, cf.

Clauses 11, 12: (7 No black-footed squirrel has ever been found in that continent before. 8 Nothing is known about it. 9 It has no name. 10 For the zoologist it presents an immediate challenge.) 11 What is it about its way of life 12 that has made it unique? < What has made it unique?

Clauses 16, 17: (14 the ancestors of this animal must have split off from the rest and 15 established themselves as an independent breeding population.) 16 What was it

---

4   In the less frequent type the *that*-clause contains new, context-independent information. For a more detailed treatment, see Dušková (2003).

Table 3

Noun Phrases	Clausal Subjects and Constituents of Syntactic Constructions
8 nothing	11 it (in *it*-cleft)
18 the new trend	12 that (in *it*-cleft)
39 all	16 it (in *it*-cleft)
44 (the rash) that	17 that (in *it*-cleft)
47 (the starting point) telling us	27 it (anticipatory S>S=infinitive)
48 something	51 that (clausal proform)
61 The great advantage	72 it (anticipatory S>S=infinitive)
65 (a fact) which	84 just how odd (S=verbless clause)
66 (humility) that	
67 things	
82 (other species) that	
97 (locomotion) which	
Total 12	8

in the environment 17 that made possible their isolation as a new form of life? < What made possible their isolation as a new form of life?

Whereas in the non-cleft forms the subject interrogative pronoun is thematic, in the clefts it becomes the rheme owing to the splitting of the propositional content into two clauses.

In the case of subject infinitives the extraposed construction appears to be the basic structure, since it is the extraposed component that usually contains new information. The principle of end focus here as a rule operates jointly with the principle of end weight. On the other hand, initial placement of a subject infinitive, regardless of the degree of the subject's weightiness, assigns it thematic function. Hence the FSP structures of the extraposed and non-extraposed construction usually differ in that both constructions have the rhematic component at the end, cf. *to become isolated from possible contamination by their neighbours* in clause 27 but *advantageous* in the non-extraposed form, added for comparison; and similarly in clauses 72–73.

Clauses 27, 28: 27 it would be advantageous for them 28 to become isolated from possible contamination by their neighbours, x To become isolated from possible contamination by their neighbours would be advantageous for them.

Clauses 72, 73: 72 Even for the zoologist [...] it is difficult 73 to avoid the arrogance of subjective involvement, x Even for the zoologist [...] to avoid the arrogance of subjective involvement is difficult.

Of more immediate relevance to the present discussion, however, appear to be the subjects realized by noun phrases. Four of these are general categorial expressions (indefinite pronouns 8, 39, 48, and 67 *things*), which are not specific to any one type of text or any subject matter.

Six subjects of this group are anaphoric pronouns or zero (44, 47, 65, 66, 82, 97) constituting the second component of a simple linear progression, whose rhematic component occurs in the preceding clause as a context-independent complement of the verb (object, subject complement, adverbial), cf. 4.2.

4. Before proceeding to discuss the types of thematic progressions that occur in the text, all subjects need to be considered with respect to their FSP function. While Types 2 and 3 (progressions with a constant and derived theme) involve thematic subjects, Type 1 (simple linear progression) may have a subject with the FSP function of rheme. This is due to the configuration of the FSP functions required by this type: the thematic subject is preceded by a rhematic antecedent, which may appear in any syntactic function. Such configurations may also occur in Type 4 (progression with split rheme).

Both the largely thematic character of the English subject and its tendency not to vary in successive clauses suggest that thematic subjects are primarily to be sought among recurrent subjects.

4.1 Considered from the viewpoint of their realization form, all recurrent (identical) subjects implemented by anaphoric pronouns are, unless given prominence prosodically, by a focalizer or a syntactic construction (esp. a cleft sentence) inherently thematic; in the case of zero subjects the thematic function is the only possible one. Accordingly, when occurring in succession, these subjects induce Type 2 of thematic progression, progression with a constant theme. Fully identical subjects realized by noun phrases, whether by identical nouns or a more general term, may have either thematic or rhematic function. The former again give rise to progressions with a constant theme, but where the subject has rhematic function and is followed by a thematic one, the resulting configuration constitutes Type 1, simple linear progression.

Partly identical subjects present a similar picture: anaphoric pronouns (except for the instances specified above) and zero form basically induce Type 3 of TP, progression with derived themes. This type of progression appears to serve as a major device of thematic ramification. Partly identical subjects expressed by nouns, like fully identical substantival subjects, induce two types of thematic progressions. Where they have thematic function, they form Type 3 of TP, progression with derived theme, while subjects with rhematic function again give rise to Type 1 of TP, simple linear progression (see 4.3).

Apart from the FSP function of the subject, a relevant factor of thematic progression is the distance between clauses, i.e., the section of the text across which the notion denoted by the subject remains activated. In Daneš's framework of thematic progressions this question is not explicitly discussed. However, from his formulation

> TPs are often complicated by various insertions (supplements, explanatory notes) or asides. They may also occur in an incomplete or somewhat modified form. [...] Our types of TPs are to be considered as abstract principles, models, or constructs, (Daneš 1974: 121)

immediate succession does not appear to be a necessary condition. Moreover, unspecified distances between clauses are indicated in some of his examples by dots [...] (*ibid.*).

Nevertheless, the distance between clauses is relevant from the viewpoint of the retrievability span (Firbas 1992: 23–24), i.e., the length of text within which individual components of the text build-up remain derivable from the preceding context. The retrievability span of thematic elements has been shown to extend, in general, to seven clauses.[5] Obviously, the retrievability of an item derives from all its occurrences in any syntactic function, not just from its being construed as the subject. In the case of *the black-footed squirrel* the retrievability span of seven clauses applies even when restricted to the subject: here all distances except one fall well within this span, the majority of clauses with identical subjects occurring in direct contact. In terms of the intervening clauses the distance was 1 to 4; the sole exception to the seven-clause retrievability span was reiteration of this identical subject after a gap of 15 clauses (43, 58). However, this has no effect on the retrievability span since this hypertheme remains activated by occurring in other syntactic functions.

4.1.1 As stated above, the hypertheme *black-footed squirrel* has the thematic function in all instances of pronominal and zero realization, e.g.:

Clauses 5, 6: 5 **It** [Th] has black feet and 6 **it** [Th] comes from Africa.

Clauses 22, 23: 22 **it** [Th] would be no more than a race of the basic species and 23 [**zero**/Th] could be swamped out, reabsorbed into the mainstream at any point.

Among the 12 instances realized by noun phrases seven are thematic (in clauses 3, 14, 19, 21, 25, 29, 41) and five rhematic (in clauses 4, 7, 31, 33, 36), e.g.:

Clause 3: **This animal** [Th] is new to science.

Clause 4: Inside the cage there sits **a small squirrel** [Rh].

On the whole among the 30 instances of this hypertheme there are 25 thematic and 5 rhematic subjects.

4.1.2 A similar picture is presented by the hypertheme *human species:* all pronominal and zero realizations serve as themes, cf.

Clauses 77, 78: [76 by approaching the human being] 77 as if **he** [Th] were another species, a strange form of life on the dissecting table, 78 [**zero**/Th] awaiting analysis.

Thematic subjects also prevail, even more prominently, among substantival subjects (in clauses 93, 94, 95, 96, 100); the only rhematic subject occurs in clause 98 (five and one instances, respectively). For example:

Clauses 93–96: 93 **The legs** [Th] are too long, 94 **the arms** [Th] are too short and 95 **the feet** [Th] are rather strange. 96 Clearly **this species** of primate [Th] has developed a special kind of locomotion ...

---

5   The retrievability span as determined so far is subject to special contextual configurations which may extend it to much longer distances. Cf. Firbas 1994, 1995 and Chapter 16, 2.2.

Clause 98: There is yet **another characteristic** [Rh] (99 that [Th] cries out...)

Altogether, among the 12 instances of this hypertheme in the subject function 11 subjects are thematic and one subject is rhematic.

4.1.3 Both recurrent subjects conveying the local and temporal scene, *label* and *time*, have two occurrences each, one of which is thematic and the other rhematic:

Clauses 1, 2: 1 There is **a label** [Rh] on a cage at a certain zoo 2 **that** [Th] states simply

Clauses 24, 26: If, 24 as **time** [Th] passed, (25 the squirrels became more and more perfectly tuned-in to their particular environment,) 26 **the moment** [Rh] would eventually arrive [27 when it would be advantageous for them 28 to become ...].

4.1.4 The recurrent subjects, the general *we* and *the zoologist* are all thematic as a result of their pronominal or zero form and initial position.

Clauses 37–38: 37 When **we** [Th] look at our unidentified squirrel in its zoo cage, 38 **we** [Th] can only guess about these things.

Clauses 70, 71, 73: Even for the zoologist 70 **who** [Th] is used 71 [zero/Th] to calling an animal an animal (72 it is difficult) 73 [zero/Th] to avoid the arrogance of subjective involvement.

4.1.5 As regards non-recurrent (different) subjects, although the feature of continuous recurrence is lacking, even these subjects have been found to be largely thematic (cf. Dušková 1986a). As follows from Table 3 and the attached comment, the subjects relevant with respect to thematic progressions are the twelve subjects realized by noun phrases. Of these, ten are thematic and two rhematic. Apart from anaphoric pronouns (in clauses 44, 65, 66, 82, 97; five instances) and one zero realization (clause 47), thematic subjects are also realized by nouns and an indefinite pronoun (clauses 18 *the new trend*, 39 *all*, 61 *the great advantage*, 67 *things*). Indefinite pronouns are also the realization forms of the two non-recurrent subjects with the rhematic function (*nothing* in clause 8 and *something* in clause 48). Compare:

Clause 44: ... the rash **that** [Th] gives a doctor a clue

Clause 47: ... starting point [**zero/**Th] telling us

Clause 18: **The new trend** [Th] must have started out in a small way

Clause 8: **Nothing** [Rh] is known about it.

Clause 48: there is **something** [Rh] worth pursuing.

4.1.6 As noted in Section 1, the assignment of the FSP functions is based on the three factors operating in written language: linearity (word order), context in/dependence and semantics. In the case of thematic subjects the FSP function is largely indicated by the initial position and context dependence signalled by anaphoric devices (pronouns and zero).

In the case of rhematic subjects, whether recurrent or nonrecurrent (ten in total), final or postverbal position is found only where they appear after existential *there*—a special device for moving a rhematic subject to the postverbal part of the sentence. This was found in four instances:

Clause 1: There is **a label** [Rh] on cage at a certain zoo

Clause 4: Inside the cage there sits **a small squirrel** [Rh].

Clause 48: there is **something** [Rh] worth pursuing
Clause 98: there is **another characteristic** [Rh]

The six other rhematic subjects occur in the initial or a preverbal position. Here linearity is counteracted by semantic structure and context in/dependence. Let us first consider the fairly straightforward instances in clauses 26, 36 and 31, 33.

Clause 26: **the moment** [Rh] would eventually arrive (27—when it would be …)
Clause 36: At last, **a new species** [Rh] would have evolved, separate and discrete, …

Here an important role is played by the semantics of the verb which expresses appearance on the scene. The subject in clause 26 (*the moment*) is partly context-independent in that it adds a specifying feature to the preceding concept of *time*, which assigns it a higher degree of communicative dynamism than is conveyed by a verb of this semantic class. In this configuration the subject acquires the function of rheme, but preserving its regular preverbal position, it displays a discontinuous structure as regards its postmodification, the *when*-clause, which constitutes the most dynamic part of the rheme, the rheme proper.[6] Clause 36 also contains a verb of appearance on the scene, and the novel aspect of the recurrent item *species* is indicated by the nongeneric indefinite article.

In contrast to clauses 26 and 36, the verbs in clauses 31 and 33 do not express existence or appearance on the scene; hence determination of the FSP functions of the clause elements rests on their degree of context in/dependence. The verbs in both clauses, *change* and *differ*, are derivable from *undergo special modifications* in clause 29. Clause 33 moreover contains a context-dependence indicator *also*. Although the subjects are partly context-dependent in being derived from the hypertheme *black-footed squirrel*, they contain novel features defining a particular aspect, which contrast with the preceding derived theme *their social and sexual behaviour* in clause 29, and are consequently more dynamic than the fully context-dependent verb.

Clause 31: At first **their anatomy** [Rh] may have changed
Clause 33: later **their mating calls and displays** [Rh] would also differ.

Clauses 7 and 8 have been classed as having rhematic subjects owing to the universal negator which constitutes, or is a component of, the subject. Negators as such largely act as rhematizers.

Clause 7: **No black-footed squirrel** [Rh] has ever been found in that continent before.

Clause 8: **Nothing** [Rh] is known about it.

The subject in clause 7 constitutes the rheme only potentially. The negator implements the determiner of a context-dependent (recurrent) head noun, i.e., the subject is a composite element heterogeneous with respect to context-in/dependence. Having clausal scope, the negative determiner negates verbal polarity, which is in fact the most important novel feature, the rheme proper, of this clause. If we resort to prosody for indication of the carrier of the main intonation centre (nuclear tone), which as

---

6   Discontinuous postmodification may serve as a device for reconciling the conflict between the grammatical principle and the principle of end focus (cf. Dušková 1995).

a rule falls on the rheme, we find three potential candidates: the subject, the lexical component of the verb *found* and the final adverbial *before*). As in other instances of potentiality (cf. Chapter 16), in writing the FSP structure of the clause remains ambiguous.

Clause 8 is similar in that *Nothing*, having clausal scope, again negates the verb, the rheme proper being negative polarity. However, this subject is entirely context-independent and will in speech carry a stronger stress than the verb.

As regards the percentage of thematic and rhematic subjects in the group of recurrent subjects on the one hand, and in the group of different subjects on the other, it appears that recurrent thematic subjects are more frequent, viz. out of 80 recurrent subjects, 8 (10%) are rhematic and 72 (90%) thematic. (If the subject in clause 7 is assigned thematic function, the percentage of thematic subjects rises to 91.2.) In the case of different subjects, out of the 12 relevant for the present discussion (see Table 3 and Section 4.1.5), 2 (16.7%) are rhematic and 10 (83.3%) thematic. This result appears to confirm the assumption of a close relationship between recurrence and thematicity as well as of the thematic character of the English subject.

4.2 As a final point the foregoing findings are considered with respect to the assumed connection between the tendency of the English subject not to vary and Type 2 of thematic progression.

4.2.1 In the examined text section clauses with identical subjects were found to form three types of thematic progression: progressions with a constant theme, progressions with a derived theme and simple linear progressions.

4.2.1.1 The most frequent type is the progression with a constant theme. In the case of the general *we* and *the zoologist* it is the only type of progression registered. This is not accidental, since the absence of progressions with a derived theme follows from the full identity of these subjects in all their occurrences. The non-occurrence of the simple linear progression, on the other hand, is consequent only in the case of general *we*, whose rhematic function, required as a constituent of this progression, is virtually ruled out by its semantics. This does not apply to *the zoologist*, whose more specific meaning allows it to appear in contrastive contexts, conducive to rhematic function.[7] Thematic progressions with a constant theme containing general *we* and *the zoologist* account, respectively, for 31 and 3 clauses (*we* in clauses 37, 38, 40, 45, 46, 49, 50, 52, 53, 54, 55, 56, 57, 60, 62, 63, 64, 68, 69, 74, 75, 76, 79, 80, 81, 85, 86, 87, 88, 90, 91; *the zoologist* in clauses 70, 71, 73).

The two hyperthemes form, apart from progressions with a constant theme, also progressions with a derived theme and simple linear progressions. In the case of *black-footed squirrel*, progressions with a constant theme are again the most frequent; they are found in 13 clauses (clauses 3, 5, 6, 9, 10, 13, 19, 20, 21, 22, 23, 25, 28). As regards *the human species*, progressions with a constant theme are as frequent as progres-

---

7   The difference in this respect between the two notions is shown by the in/applicability of a focalizer, cf. *even a zoologist*, but **even we* (applicable only to 1st person plural, in contrast to other persons, cf. *even I*; but not to the general sense 'one').

sions with a derived theme, each accounting for 4 clauses, the former in clauses 77, 78, 83, 96.

Accordingly, the total number of clauses forming thematic progressions with a constant theme is 51. For example:

Clauses 45, 46, 49, 50, 52, 53, 54: 45 To really [**zero**/Th] understand this new species, 46 **we** [Th] must use these clues only as a starting point [47 telling us 48 there is something worth pursuing]. 49 **We** [Th] might try 50 [**zero**/Th] to guess at the animal's history [51 but that would be presumptuous and dangerous]. 52 Instead **we** [Th] will start humbly 53 by [**zero**/Th] giving it a simple and obvious label: **we** [Th] will call it the African black-footed squirrel.

Clauses 70, 71, 73: 70 (for the zoologist) **who** [Th] is used 71 to [**zero**/Th] calling an animal an animal, [72 it is difficult] 73 [**zero**/Th] to avoid the arrogance of subjective involvement.

Clauses 9, 10: 9 **It** (= *the black-footed squirrel*) [Th] has no name. 10 For the zoologist **it** [Th] presents an immediate challenge.

Clauses 77, 78, 83, 96: 77 as if **he** (= *the human species*) [Th] were another species, a strange form of life on the dissecting table, 78 [**zero** Th] awaiting analysis. ... 83 **he** [Th] is obviously a primate of some sort. ... Clearly **this species of primate** [Th] has developed a special kind of locomotion.

4.2.1.2 Progressions with a derived theme rank second in the frequency of occurrence among the clauses with recurrent subjects. Being based on partly identical subjects, they are found only with the two hyperthemes, *the black-footed squirrel* in 7 instances (in clauses 14, 15, 29, 30, 43, 58, 59; within these clauses the derived themes form progressions with constant theme); and *the human species* in 4 clauses (93, 94, 95, 100). Altogether, progressions with a derived theme account for 11 clauses. For example:

Clauses 29, 30: 29 At this stage **their** (= *the black-footed squirrels'*) **social and sexual behaviour** [derived Th] 30 would undergo special modifications, [**zero**/derived Th] making interbreeding with other kinds of squirrels unlikely and eventually impossible.

Clauses 93, 94, 95, 100: 93 **The legs** (= of *the human species*) [derived Th] are too long, 94 **the arms** [derived Th] are too short 95 and **the feet** [derived Th] are rather strange. ... 100 **the skin** [derived Th] is virtually naked.

4.2.1.3 As regards simple linear progression, apart from the two hyperthemes (*the black-footed squirrel* in clauses 4, 5 (6); 31, 32; 33, 34 (35); *the human species* in clauses 98,99) it is also found with the scene-setting subject *label* (in clauses 1, 2); altogether in 10 clauses. In the group of identical subjects it appears to have a comparable frequency of occurrence to the progressions with a derived theme (11 clauses, cf. 4.2.1.2). For example:

Clauses 4, 5 (6): 4 Inside the case there sits *a small squirrel* [Rh]. 5 **It** [Th] has black feet (and 6 **it** [Th] comes from Africa).

Clauses 33, 34 (35): 33 **their mating calls and displays** [Rh] would also differ, 34 [**zero**/ Th] ensuring (that 35 **they** [Th] attract only mates of the other type).

Clauses 98, 99: 98 But there is **another characteristic** [Rh], 99 **that** [Th] cries out for attention:

Clauses 1, 2: 1 There is **a label** [Rh] on a cage at a certain zoo 2 **that** [Th] states simply

As shown by examples with a clause number in brackets, the simple linear progressions often open progressions with a constant theme.

4.2.2 Clauses with different subjects (cf. Table 3) provide favourable conditions for thematic progressions only where the subjects have non-subject identical antecedents (the other potential configuration with non-subject identical postcedents does not occur in the text section under study). Sequences of different subjects with non-subject antecedents are found in clauses 43, 44; 46, 47; 64, 65, 66; 81, 82; 96, 97. In all these clauses the subjects are anaphoric devices (pronouns or zero) with the thematic function whereas their non-subject antecedents occur in the rheme. Accordingly, the resulting sequences constitute simple linear progressions, cf.

Clauses 43, 44: 43 But these are only the symptoms, **the rash** [Cs=Rh] 44 **that** [S=Th] gives a doctor a clue about his patient's disease.

Clauses 46, 47: 46 we must use these clues only **as a starting point** [Co=Rh] 47 [S/**zero**=Th] telling us ...

Clauses 64, 65, 66: 64 we ourselves are not black-footed squirrels—**a fact** [appositive of Cs=Rh] 65 **which** [S=Th] forces us **into an attitude of humility** [O_{prep} = Rh] 66 **that** [S=Th] is becoming to proper scientific investigation.

Clauses 81, 82: 81 by comparing him **with other species** [O_{prep}=Rh] 82 **that** [S=Th] appear to be most closely related.

Clauses 96–97: 96 this species of primate has developed **a special kind of locomotion** [O=Rh] 97 **which** [S=Th] has modified its basic form.

It should be noted that while simple linear progressions mostly terminate with the second component or open progressions with a constant theme, clause 65, whose subject forms the second (thematic) component of the simple linear progressions 64, 65, contains a rhematic prepositional object with a thematic subject postcedent in clause 66, so that the three clauses give rise to a sequence of two simple linear progressions.

These instances (11 clauses in total) do not in principle differ from simple linear progressions found among recurrent subjects in that both types comply with the required sequence of FSP functions: a rhematic element is followed by a co-referential thematic one. As a result, the total number of clauses forming simple linear progressions amounts to 21.

Considering the frequency of occurrence of thematic progressions on this basis and taking clauses with both identical and different subjects together, the first place on the frequency scale belongs to progressions with a constant theme (owing to the prevalence of identical subjects; 51 clauses), with simple linear progressions ranking second (21 clauses), and progressions with a derived theme in the last position (11 clauses). This leaves 17 clauses to be accounted for.

4.2.3 This group contains clauses with both identical and different subjects.

4.2.3.1 The group of identical subjects displays three clauses that appear to stand outside thematic progressions: clauses 36 and 24, 26.

Clause 36: At last, **a new species** would have evolved, separate and discrete, a unique form of life, a three hundred and sixty-seventh kind of squirrel

Clauses 24, 26: If, as **time** [Th] passed, (25 the new squirrels became more and more perfectly tuned-in to their particular environment,) **the moment** [Rh] would eventually arrive when ...

Clause 36 is a clear instance of a presentation scale, with a verb of appearance on the scene and a rhematic subject, within a progression of derived themes. Consequently, it stands outside the progression.

Clauses 24, 26 form a sequence of two partly identical subjects, the first having the function of theme, while the second constitutes the rheme, again in a clear case of a presentation scale. A configuration of this kind fails to align itself with a thematic progression.

4.2.3.2 As in the foregoing section, out of all the different and excluded subjects, listed in Table 3, only those in the first column are considered here. The excluded clauses in the second column comprise, besides those constituting parts of syntactic constructions (discussed in Section 3) two clauses (51 and 84) whose subjects are clause equivalents. The role of all these devices in the text build-up and theme development remains to be studied.

The clauses containing anaphoric subjects with non-subject rhematic antecedents have been added to simple linear progressions (cf. 4.2.2). The remaining nonrecurrent subjects, those realized by nouns and indefinite pronouns (in clauses 8, 18, 39, 48, 61, 67) appear to stand outside thematic progressions. It should be noted that except clause 67 the clauses with different thematic subjects, which considerably prevail over the different rhematic ones, are the most informative because they contain a novel item even in the subject.

Clause 8: **Nothing** [Rh] is known about it.

Clause 18: **The new trend** [Th] must have started out in a small way, ...

Clause 39: **All** [Th] (we can be sure about) is that...

Clause 48: ... there is **something** [Rh] worth pursuing.

Clause 61: **The great advantage** [Th] ... is that...

Clause 67: How different **things** [Th] are, how depressingly different (68 when we attempt to study the human animal.)

The textual role of these instances also calls for further study.

4.2.4 The relative frequency of occurrence of the thematic progressions found in the text under study has been given in terms of clauses for two reasons. First, as appears from some of the examples, progressions with derived themes and simple linear progressions often combine with progressions with constant themes. Secondly, in strings of progressions with a constant theme it may be difficult to determine the terminal component where the clauses containing identical subjects cease to stand in immediate succession.

Another point to be noted in respect of the quantitative data is that since thematic progressions also occur among clauses with different subjects, there is no correlation between the number of clauses with identical and different subjects on the one hand, and the number of clauses forming thematic progressions on the other.

5. In sum the ascertained quantitative data appear to confirm the assumption that the tendency of English to preserve the same subject in successive clauses, together with its largely thematic character, provides favourable conditions for thematic progressions with a constant theme. However, this is largely due to the recurrence of general *we*, which has been characterized as external to the subject matter dealt with in the text. Moreover, it is at variance with a prominent feature of formal academic writing—frequent use of the passive voice. As shown in previous studies of the passive voice and *man-Sätze* (cf. Dušková 1971, 1973), the active with general *we* as the subject and the passive are often interchangeable. In the text under study, general *we* is used as a starting point partly owing to its inclusive meaning, but more importantly because it allows context-independent, rhematic elements, construed in the active as a verbal complement, to stand in the regular postverbal position, and thus to comply with the principle of end focus. It is in this clausal position that the subject matter—in our text the two hyperthemes *the black-footed squirrel* and *the human species*—is developed. In this respect, the use of general *we* appears to be an important device in the text build-up.

However, the results obtained from one text of limited length cannot be generalized. A cursory glance at another text that could not be included for considerations of space has displayed frequent occurrence of Type 4 of thematic progression, progression with split rheme. This suggests that the strategy and devices employed in the text build-up depend both on the subject matter and the author's approach to it.

Nevertheless, some general points about thematic progressions have emerged even from this limited probe: simple linear progressions appear to suit the opening part of a text or smaller textual units, which introduces the subject matter to be dealt with. For this reason, these progressions mostly consist of only two members, the first rhematic and the second thematic. Elaboration of the subject matter largely depends on its nature, which may favour any one of the other thematic progressions: with a constant or derived theme, with split rheme, or their combinations. Of these, progressions allowing the largest number of members are to be sought among progressions with a constant theme. Overall, a complete picture of the role of thematic progressions in the text build-up calls for an analogous examination of the concluding part that closes the text.

APPENDIX

Table 1

Clause	Subjects with More Than One Occurrence		Subjects with One Occurrence	
	Finite	Nonfinite	Finite	Nonfinite
1 there is	label[1]			
2 states	that[1]			
3 is	this animal[2]			
4 there sits	A small squirrel[2]			
5 has	it[2]			
6 comes	it[2]			
7 has been found	no blackfooted squirrel[2]			
8 is known			Nothing	
9 has	it[2]			
10 presents	it[2]			
11 is	it (it-cleft)			
12 has made	that (it-cleft)			
13 does it differ	it[2]			
14 must have split	the ancestors of this animal[2a]			
15 and established	zero (ellipsis)[2a]			
16 was	it (it-cleft)			
17 made	that (it-cleft)			
18 must have started			the new trend	
19 becoming		with a group of squirrels[2]		
20 would be	they[2]			
21 would be	the new form[2]			
22 would be	it[2]			
23 could be	zero (ellipsis)[2]			
24 passed	Time[3]			
25 became	the new squirrels[2]			

Clause	Subjects with More Than One Occurrence		Subjects with One Occurrence	
	Finite	Nonfinite	Finite	Nonfinite
26 would arrive	the moment[3]			
27 would be	It (anticipatory)			
28 to become		for them[2]		
29 would undergo	Their social and sexual behaviour[2b]			
30 making		zero[2b]		
31 may have changed	Their anatomy[2c]			
32 at coping		zero[2c]		
33 would differ	Their mating calls and displays[2d]			
34 ensuring		zero[2d]		
35 attract	they[2d]			
36 would have evolved	A new species[2]			
37 look	we[4]			
38 can guess	we[4]			
39 is			All	
40 can be	we[4]			
41 indicate	the markings of its fur—its black feet[2e]			
42 is	it[2]			
43 are	These[2e]			
44 gives			(the rash) that	
45 to understand		zero[4]		
46 must use	we[4]			
47 telling				(starting point) zero
48 there is			something	
49 might try	we[4]			
50 to guess		zero[4]		
51 would be			that (clausal preform)	

Clause	Subjects with More Than One Occurrence		Subjects with One Occurrence	
	Finite	Nonfinite	Finite	Nonfinite
52 will start	we[4]			
53 by giving		zero[4]		
54 will call	we[4]			
55 must observe	we[4]			
56 (must) record		zero[4] (ellipsis)		
57 (must) see		zero[4] (ellipsis)		
58 differs	it[2f] (every aspect of its behaviour			
59 is		zero[2f] (ellipsis)		
60 can piece	we[4]			
61 is			the great advantage	
62 have	we[4]			
63 studying		zero[4]		
64 are not	we[4]			
65 forces			(a fact) which	
66 is becoming			(humility) that	
67 are			things	
68 attempt	we[4]			
69 to study		zero[4]		
70 is used	(the zoologist) who[5]			
71 to calling		zero[5]		
72 is	It (anticipatory)			
73 to avoid		zero[5]		
74 can try	we[4]			
75 to overcome		zero[4]		
76 by approaching		zero[4]		
77 as if were	he[6] (the human being)			
78 awaiting	zero[6] (a strange form of life			

Clause	Subjects with More Than One Occurrence		Subjects with One Occurrence	
	Finite	Nonfinite	Finite	Nonfinite
79 can begin	we[4]			
80 can start	we[4]			
81 by comparing		zero[4]		
82 appear to be			(other species) that	
83 is	he[6] (the human being)			
84 becomes			just how odd (subject clause)	
85 lay out	we[4]			
86 try	zero (ellipsis)[4]			
87 to insert		zero[4]		
88 put	we[4]			
89 looks	(the human pelt) it[6a]			
90 are driven	we[4]			
91 to position		zero[4]		
92 is	it[6]			
93 are	the legs[6b]			
94 are	the arms[6c]			
95 are	the feet[6d]			
96 has developed	this species[6]			
97 has modified			locomotion (which)	
98 there is	Another characteristic[6a]			
99 cries out	that[6a]			
100 is	the skin[6a] (= another characteristic)			

Desmond Morris, *The Naked Ape*, pp. 13–15

There (1) is a label on a cage at a certain zoo that (2) states simply, 'This animal (3) **is** new to science.' Inside the cage there (4) **sits** a small squirrel. It (5) **has** black feet and it (**6**) **comes** from Africa. No black-footed squirrel (**7**) **has** ever **been found** in that continent before. Nothing (**8**) **is known** about it. It (**9**) **has** no name.

For the zoologist it (**10**) **presents** an immediate challenge. What (**11**) **is** it about its way of life that (**12**) **has made** it unique? How (**13**) **does** it **differ** from the three hundred and sixty-six other living species of squirrels already known and described? Somehow, at some point in the evolution of the squirrel family, the ancestors of this animal (**14**) **must have split off** from the rest and (**15**) **established** themselves as an independent breeding population. What (**16**) **was** it in the environment that (**17**) **made** possible their isolation as a new form of life? The new trend (**18**) **must have started out** in a small way, with a group of squirrels in one area (**19**) **becoming** slightly changed and better adapted to the particular conditions there. But at this stage they (**20**) **would** still **be** able to inter-breed with their relatives nearby. The new form (**21**) **would be** at a slight advantage in its special region, but it (**22**) **would be** no more than a race of the basic species and (**23**) **could be swamped out,** reabsorbed into the mainstream at any point. If, as time (**24**) **passed,** the new squirrels (**25**) **became** more and more perfectly tuned-in to their particular environment, the moment (**26**) **would** eventually **arrive** when it (**27**) **would be** advantageous for them (**28**) **to become** isolated from possible contamination by their neighbours. At this stage their social and sexual behaviour (**29**) **would undergo** special modifications, (**30**) **making** inter-breeding with other kinds of squirrels unlikely and eventually impossible. At first, their anatomy (**31**) **may have changed and become** better at (**32**) **coping** with the special food of the district, but later their mating calls and displays (**33**) **would** also **differ,** (**34**) **ensuring** that they (**35**) **attract** only mates of the new type. At last, a new species (**36**) **would have evolved,** separate and discrete, a unique form of life, a three hundred and sixty-seventh kind of squirrel.

When we (**37**) **look** at our unidentified squirrel in its zoo cage, we (**38**) **can** only **guess** about these things. All we (**40**) **can be** certain about (**39**) **is** that the markings of its fur—its black feet—(**41**) **indicate** that it (**42**) **is** a new form. But these (**43**) **are** only the symptoms, the rash that (**44**) **gives** a doctor a clue about his patient's disease. (**45**) **To** really **understand** this new species, we (**46**) **must use** these clues only as a starting point, (**47**) **telling** us there (**48**) **is** something worth pursuing. We (**49**) **might try** (**50**) **to guess** at the animal's history, but that (**51**) **would be** presumptuous and dangerous. Instead we (**52**) **will start** humbly by (**53**) **giving** it a simple and obvious label: we (**54**) **will call** it the African black-footed squirrel. Now we (**55**) **must observe** and (**56**) **record** every aspect of its behaviour and structure and (**57**) **see** how it (**58**) **differs** from, or (**59**) **is** similar to, other squirrels. Then, little by little, we (**60**) **can piece** together its story.

The great advantage we (**62**) **have** when (**63**) **studying** such animals (**61**) **is** that we ourselves (**64**) **are not** black-footed squirrels—a fact which (**65**) **forces** us into an attitude of humility that (**66**) **is** becoming to proper scientific investigation. How different things (**67**) **are,** how depressingly different, when we (**68**) **attempt** (**69**) **to study** the human animal. Even for the zoologist, who (**70**) **is used** (**71**) **to calling** an animal an animal, it (**72**) **is** difficult (**73**) **to avoid** the arrogance of subjective involvement. We (**74**) **can try** (**75**) **to overcome** this to some extent by deliberately and rather coyly (**76**) **ap-**

proaching the human being as if he (77) **were** another species, a strange form of life on the dissecting table, (78) **awaiting** analysis. How (79) **can** we **begin**?

As with the new squirrel, we (80) **can start** by (81) **comparing** him with other species that (82) **appear to be** most closely related. From his teeth, his hands, his eyes and various other anatomical features, he (83) **is** obviously a primate of some sort, but of a very odd kind. Just how odd (84) **becomes** clear when we (85) **lay out** in a long row the skins of the one hundred and ninety-two living species of monkeys and apes, and then (86) **try** (89) **to insert** a human pelt at a suitable point somewhere in this long series. Wherever we (88) **put** it, it (89) **looks** out of place. Eventually we (90) **are driven** (91) **to position** it right at one end of the row of skins, next to the hides of the tailless great apes such as the chimpanzee and the gorilla. Even here it (92) **is** obtrusively different. The legs (93) **are** too long, the arms (94) **are** too short and the feet (95) **are** rather strange. Clearly this species of primate (96) **has developed** a special kind of locomotion which (97) **has modified** its basic form. But there (98) **is** another characteristic that (99) **cries out** for attention: the skin (100) **is** virtually naked.

20. THEME DEVELOPMENT
IN ACADEMIC AND NARRATIVE TEXT

First published in Czech under the title "Rozvíjení tématu v akademickém a narativním textu," in S. Čmejrková, J. Hoffmannová, and E. Havlová (eds), *Užívání a prožívání jazyka. K 90. narozeninám Františka Daneše.* Prague: Karolinum, 2010, 253–260.

0. Like the preceding chapter, this chapter has been inspired by František Daneš's seminal treatise "Functional sentence perspective and the organization of the text" (Daneš 1974). The subject matter of both chapters is theme development as shown by thematic progressions. While in the foregoing chapter the topic is treated on the basis of an academic text, this chapter, following up the former findings, elaborates it in another text sort, viz. fiction.[1] The aim of this follow-up is to compare the use of thematic progressions in the two text sorts with a view to finding out to what extent, if at all, the representation of the different types of progressions is specific to the respective text sort and its subject matter.

1. To exclude variables other than those inherent in the respective text sort and its subject matter, the analysis was carried out on a narrative passage of the fiction source, i.e. on the author's monologue. Again with a view to the comparative aim, the same theoretical framework was employed as in Chapter 19. The term theme is used in two senses, viz. as a term in the theory of functional sentence perspective (cf. Firbas 1992), where it is defined as the element carrying the lowest amount of communicative dynamism (information load); and as a textual theme, i.e. what a text or part of a text is about. To distinguish the two senses, Daneš's term hypertheme is here used for the latter. The two texts under comparison display a major difference in this respect in that the subjects of most clauses in the fiction sample express both the FSP theme

---

1   P. D. James, *Original Sin* (1994) (London: Faber and Faber), 6-8. See Appendix. The academic text (Morris) is here reprinted because of the more detailed notation.

and the hypertheme, whereas in the academic sample most subjects constitute only the FSP theme.

The treatment also reiterates the methodology applied in Chapter 19. The analysis is based on a hundred instances of finite and non-finite clauses whose subjects are classified into (a) identical (pronominal, zero realization, noun phrase reiteration and substitution by synonyms or hypernyms): (b) non-identical (subjects with one occurrence) and (c) partly identical (subjects sharing only certain features, most frequently subjects related by meronymy, and instances of inalienable attributes). The results obtained from the academic sample are given in Sections 2.1, 2.2 and 3. of Chapter 19.

2. The fiction sample contained four recurrent identical subjects, viz. *Mandy*[1]: 1, 2, 3, 4, 5, 6, 8, 9, 10, 11, 12, 14, 15, 16, 19, 20, 21, 22, 24, 25, 26, 29, 32, 34, 41, 54, 56, 57, 58, 61, 64, 67, 69, 72, 73, 74, 79, 87, 88, 91, 92, 93, 94, 95, 96, 98, 99, 100 (48); *possibility*[4]: 48, 49 (2); *Tuesday*[5] : 50, 51 (2) a *Innocent Passage*[7]: 76, 77 (2); in total 54.

Non-identical subjects in fiction (8 instances) essentially form the same groups as in the academic sample (cf. Section 3 in Chapter 19): non-recurrent noun phrases *little point* (13), *obvious advantages* (23) *the ride* (53); anaphoric pronouns or zero realization of subjects constituting the second component of simple thematic progressions whose rhematic component is contained in the preceding clause as a context-independent complement of the verb (31, 36, 40, 52, 59). There were also two occurrences of *it* in the cleft sentence (90, 97). Reference by anaphoric pronouns in fiction included instances with antecedents referring to parts of the preceding text (7, 43) and one subject was specific to this sample, viz. empty *it* (55) in a sentence giving the time of day.

The subjects treated as partly identical were of two kinds: derived subjects as in the academic sample: *Mandy*: *her literacy*[1a] (17, 18), *her fidelity*[1b] (33); *Mrs Crealey*[2b]: *Mrs Crealey's troubles*[2b/i] (35), *her life*[2b/ii] (38), *Mrs Crealey's love life*[2b/iii] (42); *some of them*[3a] (46), *elderly unprepossessing males*[3] (47); *the gate*[7a] (*of Innocent Passage*) (78); *proportions*[6a/i] (*of Innocent House*[6a]) (65); *the front door*[6a/ii] (*of Innocent House*[6a]) (68). In total 11.

The second type of partly identical subjects included split subjects whose antecedents were hypernyms: *employers*[2a] (27, 28), *some of them* (30); employer *Mrs Crealey*[2b] (37, 39, 44, 45); *three houses*[6] (60): *Innocent House*[6a] (62, 63, 66), *a smaller house*[6b,c] (*on either side*) (70, 71), *first smaller house*[6b] (75), *the second of these smaller houses*[6c] (89); *three men*[8] (80, 81), *one*[8a] (*of the three men*) (82, 83, 84), *the other two*[8b] (85, 86). Altogether 22 instances. One of the partly identical subjects of the first group (*her literacy*[1a] 17, 18) and all partly identical subjects of the second group were recurrent. These instances raised the overall number of recurrent subjects in the fiction sample by 23 (23+54), i.e. 77.

2.1 As regards the distribution, semantics and textual role of the recurrent subjects, the two texts display considerable differences. The academic text contains two recurrent identical subjects with a high frequency of occurrence, the hypertheme *black-footed squirrel*[2] (17 occurrences) and the general human agent *we*[4] (31 occurrences), the two accounting together for 80%, respectively, for 28.3% and 51.7%, of all recurrent identical subjects in this text (60 instances), cf. Sections 2.1.1 and 2.2 in Chapter 19. The fiction sample contains only one frequently recurrent identical subject, the hypertheme of a longer passage, *Mandy*[1] with 48 occurrences, reaching nearly 89% of all recurrent identical subjects in this sample (54). As regards the semantics of these subjects, the most prominent difference is found in the case of the general human agent, the most frequent recurrent identical subject in academic prose with 31 occurrences, while in fiction a general subject occurs only once and significantly in a different realization form, general *one*. Moreover, *one* does not refer to the general human agent as such but to the hypertheme of the passage, the girl Mandy, thus performing its secondary function of deconcretization of the agent, cf. sentence 25.

While the hyperthemes *black-footed squirrel*, *human species* and *Mandy* represent textual themes and reflect the content of the two texts, viz. what the respective passages are about / deal with, the general human agent *we*, considered as a device of text built-up in the academic sample, stands apart in that it is not a textual theme, the concern of the texts being specific agents, treated generically in academic prose and as an individual in fiction. The difference between the hyperthemes and the general human agent is also evident from the respective realization forms: while the former pronominalize and are referred to by synonyms and hypernyms, in the case of general *we* the only realization form is pronominal. Synonymous expression is found only in agentless passives, whose implied agent is mostly general, apart from instances of authorial passives.

Another, albeit minor difference between the two samples was found in fiction, which in contrast to the academic sample displays two types of partly identical subjects, derived and split subjects. Potential significance of this feature as an indicator of the text sort calls for further study.

2.2 The high representation of identical subjects denoting the general human agent in academic prose raises the question of what is the cause of it, considering that it contradicts a generally observed feature of academic texts, the frequent use of passives implying this agent (cf. Dušková 1971, 1973). In the academic sample under study, general *we* is partly used to refer to the author in the inclusive sense (I, author + you, readers), but more importantly it appears to be used as a device of the linear arrangement of the content being conveyed. Clauses with general *we* in the subject display verbs with context-independent elements in their complementation. By means of this device and the concomitant active voice these elements are placed in the postverbal, rhematic position in which the content of the passage is further developed. From this point of view, the subject realized by general *we* appears to be an important device of the build-up of academic text, serving as the starting point of the sentence, i.e. exclusively as the theme of the FSP structure, which makes possible the achievement of the basic distribution of communicative dynamism with the theme at the beginning and the rhematic part at the end.

3. Proceeding to the relationship between identical subjects and thematic progressions, rhematic identical subjects induce simple thematic progressions and progressions with split rheme. Thematic identical subjects give rise to progressions with constant theme.

3.1 Rhematic subjects had a higher frequency of occurrence in the academic sample, cf. 4.1.6 in Chapter 19. There were altogether ten of them, four in the existential construction (sentences 1, 4, 48, 98), four in presentation sentences with rhematic subjects in the initial position (sentences 26, 36, 31, 33) and two rhematic subjects were realized by negative quantifiers (sentences 7 and 8). Two of these (8 a 48) were non-recurrent, non-identical subjects standing outside the thematic progressions. Accordingly, the percentage of rhematic subjects participating in thematic progressions was 13.3 (8 out of 60). Fiction displayed only three rhematic subjects: two in existential constructions (sentences 13 a 23) and one in a sentence with subject-verb inversion after an initial adverbial (70). Of these, only (70) induced a thematic progression, the two other rhematic subjects being non-recurrent: 1.8% (1 out of 54).

As follows from these figures and from the entailment of thematicity of identical recurrent subjects, with the exception of the rhematic subjects mentioned above, all identical subjects were thematic and participated in the formation of thematic progressions, either as the second member of a simple thematic progression (e.g. sentences 1, 2) or as a member of a progression with constant theme (e.g. sentences 77, 78).

Accordingly, in the academic sample the respective percentages of thematic and rhematic subjects included in thematic progressions were 86.7 and 13.3. The role of thematic subjects in the formation of thematic progressions appears to be even more prominent when thematic progressions based on the derived subjects (cf. 3.1), which were all thematic, are taken into account: their percentage rises from 86.7 (52 out of 60) to 93.7 (75 out of 80).

In fiction, the single rhematic subject participating in the formation of thematic progressions, when considered with respect to the total of thematic subjects, both identical, and derived + split, which gave rise to thematic progressions, represents 1.03% (1 out of 77) as compared with 1.8% (1 out of 54).

3.2 The difference between the examined samples of academic prose and fiction consists not only in the number of rhematic subjects and their inclusion or non-inclusion in thematic progressions; there are also differences in the realization form of the presentation sentence (cf. Chapter 12). While the existential construction is shown to be non-specific, inherently neutral in regard to the text sort, the realization form with a rhematic subject in the initial position appears to be a feature of academic prose rather than of fiction. On the other hand, the form with subject-verb inversion after an initial adverbial appears to be characteristic of narrative and descriptive[2] passages in fiction. Being based on small samples, these findings, especially those concerning the distribution of presentation sentences with rhematic subject in the initial position, cannot claim general validity and call for further studies treating more extensive and varied samples of both academic prose and fiction.

---

2   Cf. the account of this presentation sentence type in Dušková (1998), illustrated by examples (6) Behind the ornaments were two coloured photographs. (7) At the top of the bank ... was a little group of holes /almost hidden by brambles/ and (9) In the top drawer of the desk there was a file labelled investments ... In another file was a copy of her will.

3.3 As regards the relationship between identical thematic and identical rhematic subjects on the one hand and the distribution of the types of thematic progressions on the other, as shown by the following findings, no significant interconnections have been observed.

3.3.1 The academic sample contained three types of thematic progressions (cf. 4.2.1 in Chapter 19), the most frequent type of which was constituted by thematic progressions with constant theme. In the case of the identical subjects *we* and *the zoologist* it was the only type, accounting for all 31 and 3 (70, 71, 73) instances, respectively. For an example, see sentences 52–53–54.

The hypertheme *black-footed squirrel* and *the human species* moreover formed simple thematic progressions and progressions with derived theme. In the case of *black-footed squirrel*, the most frequent of type of thematic progressions was again found in thematic progressions with constant theme, cf. sentences 3, 6, 9, 10, 13, 19, 20, 21, 22, 23, 25, 28, 42 (altogether 13 sentences). Progressions with derived themes were formed by 8 sentences (14, 15, 29, 30, 41, 43, 58, 59). As regards the hypertheme *the human species*, progressions with constant theme and with derived themes were equally frequent, each represented by five sentences, respectively 77, 78, 83, 92, 96 and 89, 93, 94, 95, 100). They are illustrated e.g. by sentences 9–10 and 93–94–95–100.

Simple thematic progressions were formed by 11 sentences: *the black-footed squirrel* (4,5 [6]; 31, 32; 33, 34, 35; *the human species* (98, 99); *label* (1, 2). In some cases, they open thematic progressions with constant theme. In these instances only the first sentence or clause after the rhematic antecedent is counted as a component of a simple thematic progression, the following sentence(s) or clause(s) (in square brackets) being counted among thematic progressions with constant theme. In addition to the simple thematic progressions formed by the hyperthemes, the academic sample contained 7 sentences in which a non-recurrent thematic subject had an antecedent in the rhematic section (context-independent verb complementation) of the preceding clause, specifically in the case of subjects realized by anaphoric pronouns and subjects with zero realization: [43] 44; [46] 47; [50] 51, [64] 65, [65] 66; [81] 82; [96] 97). For an example of a simple thematic progression opening a progression with constant theme, see sentences 4–5–6. Sentences 64, 65, 66 form a sequence of two simple thematic progressions in succession.

Including the last mentioned type of simple thematic progressions, the academic sample shows the following overall frequency of occurrence of thematic progressions: the largest number of sentences, viz. 52 (*we* 31, *the zoologist* 3, *black-footed squirrel* 13, *human species* 5) formed progressions with constant theme. Simple thematic progressions ranked second, the respective number of sentences being 18. The lowest place on the scale of the frequency of occurrence was taken by thematic progressions with derived theme: altogether 13 sentences (*black-footed squirrel* 8, *human species* 5).

Outside the sentences that formed thematic progressions, there remained 17 sentences: syntactic constructions 11, 12, 16, 17, 27, 72, sentences with non-recurrent subjects 8, 18, 39, 48, 61, 67, 84 and sentences 7, 24, 26, 36.

3.3.2 Comparing the distribution of thematic progressions in the academic text with their frequency of occurrence in the fiction sample, a similar distribution was found in the case of the most frequent type, which was again constituted by thematic progressions with constant theme. This type accounted for 58 sentences: *Mandy* in all 48 sentences, the other recurrent subjects forming altogether 10 sentences, with each subject contributing two sentences: employers 27, 28; the employer *Mrs Crealey* 44, 45; *possibility* 48, 49; *Tuesday* 50, 51; *Innocent House* 63, 66. This progression type was formed by both progressions with identical subjects (*Mandy, possibility, Tuesday* and subjects treated as partly identical (employers, *Innocent House*).

Simple thematic progressions were found in 11 sentences of the fiction sample: [4, 5, 6] 7, [30] 31, [35] 36, [39] 40, [41] 43, [51] 52, [58] 59, [59] 60, [61] 62, [75] 76, 77 (the sentences in square brackets are components of other types of thematic progression).

The same representation was shown by progressions with derived subject, which also comprised 11 sentences: with subjects derived from *Mandy* (17, 18, 33), *Mrs Crealey* (35, 38, 42), *elderly unprepossessing men* (46, 47), *Innocent House* (65, 68) and *Innocent Passage* (78). Some of these further form progressions with constant theme (*Mandy's literacy* 17, 18).

Thematic progressions with split rheme were found in 12 sentences: three houses ([60], *Innocent House* 62, 66, *the first of the smaller houses* 70, 71, 75; *the second of the smaller houses* 89); three men ([79] 80, 81, *one of the three men* 82, 83, 84; *the other two* 85, 86); *some of the male employers* (30). The first two of the split hyperthemes moreover form a simple thematic progression.

Outside the sentences that formed thematic progressions, there remained 8 sentences: 13, 23, 53 (sentences with non-recurrent subjects), sentences with subjects due to the respective syntactic construction: 55, 90, 97, and sentences 37, 39.

The clauses forming thematic progressions mostly occurred in succession (in contact); discontinuous progressions formed by non-contact clauses appeared to be rarer.

3.3.3 Considering the findings about the occurrence of the different types of thematic progressions in the two texts, we find that from the aspect of theme development the simpler text of the two is academic prose in that its structure is more clear-cut. Albeit the lack of progressions with split rheme in this text is most likely accidental, the fiction sample displays more varied and complicated combinations of the different types of thematic progressions. On the other hand, the academic text is more complex from the syntactic point of view, which is shown by the number and types of sentences that remained outside thematic progressions owing to their syntactic structure. The cleft sentences, even though found in both samples, are of a different kind. The two registered in fiction represent the type which in this text sort and in journalistic writing serves as a stylistic device of presenting new content in the subordinate clause while the main clause, whose function is to highlight an item, focuses an anaphoric element, a locative / temporal adverbial forming the scene of the action / event being described. This contrasts with the primary function of the cleft sentence to serve as an unequivocal device of indicating the information structure: the main clause focuses the most important content element, whereas the subordinate clause contains context-dependent, presupposed elements. This configuration is found in both cleft sentences drawn from the academic text.

Another syntactic difference characteristic of the two texts is the function of non-anaphoric *it* in the subject. The fiction sample displays a sentence with an empty *it*, expressing the temporal location of the action (sentence 55), whereas the academic sample contains two instances of extraposed subjects anticipated by anticipatory *it* (sentences 27, 72). This difference presumably reflects only a different frequency of occurrence insofar as constructions with extraposed clausal or infinitival subjects also occur in other text sorts. The occurrence of empty *it* in fiction, however, appears to be a specific feature of this text sort.

The greatest difference between the build-up of the two texts was found in the character of the progressions with constant theme. While in the academic text progressions of this type prevalently displayed the non-textual, FSP theme constituted by the general human agent *we*, these progressions in the fiction sample were constituted only by textual themes and textual subthemes involved in the narrative.

4. The foregoing quantitative findings appear to confirm the initial assumption of the connection between recurrent thematic subjects and the incidence of thematic progressions with constant theme. Whether this is a specific feature of English, as follows from Mathesius' treatment, remains to be shown by contrastive studies.

As regards other findings of relevance to text build-up, this probe has shown that it is not only thematic, but also rhematic subjects that appear to play a role. In contrast to thematic subjects, rhematic subjects give rise to another type of thematic progressions, viz. simple thematic progressions, whose role in the text-build is significantly different. They introduce novel textual themes and subthemes, while in progressions with constant theme textual themes and subthemes are further developed. It is to be noted, however, that simple thematic progressions based on rhematic subjects are considerably less frequent than simple thematic progressions based on rhematic elements contained in the verbal complementation of a previous clause, viz. a clause element other than the subject. Accordingly, while the different textual roles of simple thematic progressions, based on a configuration of rheme and theme, and progressions with constant theme, based on configurations of themes alone, account for the much higher frequency of the latter, the much lower frequency in the text of simple thematic progressions is only partly due to the low representation of rhematic subjects. Further lines of research into thematic progressions may also be sought in theme development by means of progressions with derived themes and split rhemes.

SOURCE TEXTS

MORRIS

There **(1) is** a **label**[1] on a cage at a certain zoo **that**[1] **(2) states** simply, 'This animal[2] **(3) is** new to science'. Inside the cage there **(4) sits a small squirrel**[2]. **It**[2] **(5) has** black feet and **it**[2] **(6) comes** from Africa. **No black-footed squirrel**[2] **(7) has** ever **been found** in that continent before. **Nothing (8) is known** about it. **It**[2] **(9) has** no name.

For the zoologist **it**[2] **(10) presents** an immediate challenge. What **(11) is it** about its way of life **that (12) has made** it unique? How **(13) does it**[2] **differ** from the three hundred and sixty-six other living species of squirrels already known and described? Somehow, at some point in the evolution of the squirrel family, **the ancestors of this animal**[2a] **(14) must have split off** from the rest and **(15) established**[2a] themselves as an independent breeding population. What **(16) was it** in the environment **that (17) made** possible their isolation as a new form of life? **The new trend (18) must have started out** in a small way, **with a group of squirrels**[2a] in one area **(19) becoming** slightly changed and better adapted to the particular conditions there. But at this stage **they**[2a] **(20) would** still **be** able to inter-breed with their relatives nearby. **The new form**[2] **(21) would be** at a slight advantage in its special region, but **it**[2] **(22) would be** no more than a race of the basic species and **(23) could be swamped out**[2], reabsorbed into the mainstream at any point. If, as **time**[3] **(24) passed**, the new **squirrels**[2] **(25) became** more and more perfectly tuned-in to their particular environment, **the moment**[3] **(26) would** eventually **arrive** when it **(27) would be** advantageous for them **(28) to become**[2] isolated from possible contamination by their neighbours. At this stage **their social and sexual behaviour**[2b] **(29) would undergo** special modifications, **(30) making**[2b] inter-breeding with other kinds of squirrels unlikely and eventually impossible. At first, **their anatomy**[2c] **(31) may have changed and become** better at **(32) coping**[2c] with the special food of the district, but later **their mating calls and displays**[2d] **(33) would** also **differ**, **(34) ensuring**[2d] that **they**[2] **(35) attract** only mates of the new type. At last, **a new species**[2] **(36) would have evolved**, separate and discrete, a unique form of life, a three hundred and sixty-seventh kind of squirrel.

When **we**[4] **(37) look** at our unidentified squirrel in its zoo cage, **we**[4] **(38) can** only **guess** about these things. All **we**[4] **(40) can be** certain about **(39) is** that **the markings of its fur—its black feet**[2e]**—(41) indicate** that **it**[2] **(42) is** a new form. But **these**[2e] **(43) are** only the symptoms, the rash **that (44) gives** a doctor a clue about his patient's disease. **(45) To** really **understand**[4] this new species, **we**[4] **(46) must use** these clues only as a starting point, **(47) telling** us there **(48) is** something worth pursuing. **We**[4] **(49) might try (50) to guess**[4] at the animal's history, but **that (51) would be** presumptuous and dangerous. Instead **we**[4] **(52) will start** humbly by **(53) giving**[4] it a simple and obvious label: **we**[4] **(54) will call** it the African black-footed squirrel. Now **we**[4] **(55) must observe** and **(56) record**[4] every aspect of its behaviour and structure and **(57) see**[4] how **it**[2f] **(58) differs** from, or **(59) is**[2f] similar to, other squirrels. Then, little by little, **we**[4] **(60) can piece** together its story.

The great advantage we[4] **(62) have** when **(63) studying**[4] such animals **(61) is** that **we**[4] ourselves **(64) are not** black-footed squirrels–a fact **which (65) forces** us into an attitude of humility **that (66) is** becoming to proper scientific investigation. How different **things (67) are**, how depressingly different, when **we**[4] **(68) attempt (69) to study**[4] the human animal. Even for the zoologist, **who**[5] **(70) is used (71) to calling**[5] an animal an animal, **it (72) is** difficult **(73) to avoid**[5] the arrogance of subjective involvement. **We**[4] **(74) can try (75) to overcome**[4] this to some extent by deliberately and rather coyly **(76) approaching**[4] the human being as if **he**[6] **(77) were** another species, a strange form of life on the dissecting table, **(78) awaiting**[6] analysis. How **(79) can we**[4] **begin?**

As with the new squirrel, **we**[4] **(80) can start** by **(81) comparing**[4] him with other species **that (82) appear to be** most closely related. From his teeth, his hands, his eyes and various other anatomical features, **he**[6] **(83) is** obviously a primate of some sort, but of a very odd kind. **Just how odd (84) becomes** clear when **we**[4] **(85) lay out** in a long row the skins of the one hundred and ninety-two living species of monkeys and apes, and then **(86) try**[4] **(87) to insert**[4] a human pelt at a suitable point somewhere in this long series. Wherever **we**[4] **(88) put** it, **it**[6a] **(89) looks** out of place. Eventually **we**[4] **(90) are driven (91) to position**[4] it right at one end of the row of skins, next to the hides of the tailless great apes such as the chimpanzee and the gorilla. Even here **it**[6a] **(92) is** obtrusively different. **The legs**[6b] **(93) are** too long, **the arms**[6c] **(94) are** too short and **the feet**[6d] **(95) are** rather strange. Clearly **this species**[6] of primate **(96) has developed** a special kind of locomotion **which (97) has modified** its basic form. But there **(98) is another characteristic**[6e] **that**[6e] **(99) cries out** for attention: **the skin**[6a] **(100) is** virtually naked.

JAMES

Mandy[1] **(1) could never decide** whether **she**[1] **(2) hated or admired** Mrs Chilcroft, but under her inspired if unconventional teaching **she**[1] **(3) had learned (4) to speak**[1] English, **(5) to write, to spell**[1] and **(6) to use it**[1] confidently and with some grace. Most of the time **this (7) was** an accomplishment which **she**[1] **(8) preferred (9) to pretend**[1] **she**[1] **(10) hadn't achieved. She**[1] **(11) thought**, although **she**[1] never **(12) articulated** the heresy, that there **(13) was** little point **(14) in being**[1] at home in Mrs Chilcroft's world if **she**[1] **(15) ceased (16) to be accepted**[1] in her own. **Her literacy**[1a] **(17) was** there **(18) to be used**[1a] when necessary, a commercial and occasionally a social asset, to which **Mandy**[1] **(19) added** high shorthand-typing speeds and a facility with various types of word processor. **Mandy**[1] **(20) knew** herself **(21) to be**[1] highly employable, but **(22) remained**[1] faithful to Mrs Crealey. Apart from the cosy there **(23) were** obvious advantages **(24) in being regarded**[1] as indispensable; **one**[1] **(25) could be sure (26) of getting**[1] the pick of the jobs. **Her male employers**[2a] occasionally **(27) tried (28) to persuade**[2a] her **(29) to take**[1] a permanent post, **some of them**[2a] **(30) offering** inducements **which (31) had** little to do with annual increments, luncheon vouchers or generous pension contributions. **Mandy**[1] **(32) remained** with the Nonesuch Agency, **her**

fidelity[1b] (33) **rooted** in more than material considerations. **She**[1] occasionally (34) **felt** for her employer an almost adult compassion. **Mrs Crealey's troubles**[2b/i] principally (35) **arose** from her conviction of the perfidy of men (36) **combined**[2b/i] with an inability (37) **to do**[2b] without them. Apart from this uncomfortable dichotomy **her life**[2b/ii] (38) **was dominated** by a fight (39) **to retain**[2b] the few girls in her stable **who** (40) **were** employable, and her war of attrition with her ex-husband, the tax-inspector, her bank manager and her office landlord. In all these traumas **Mandy**[1] (41) **was** ally, confidante and sympathizer. Where **Mrs Crealey's love life**[2b/iii] (42) **was concerned this** (43) was more from an easy goodwill than from any understanding since to Mandy's nineteen-year-old mind the **possibility**[4] that her **employer**[2b] (44) **could actually wish** (45) **to have**[2b] sex with the elderly—**some of them**[3a] (46) **must be** at least fifty—and unprepossessing males **who**[3a] occasionally (47) **haunted** the office (48) **was** too bizarre (49) **to warrant**[4] serious contemplation.

After a week of almost continuous rain **Tuesday**[5] (50) **promised** (51) **to be**[5] a fine day with gleams of fitful sunshine (52) **shafting** through the low clusters of cloud. **The ride** from Stratford East (53) **wasn't** long, but **Mandy**[1] (54) **left** plenty of time and **it** (55) **was** only a quarter to ten when **she**[1] (56) **turned off** The Highway, down Garnet Street and along Wapping Wall, then right into Innocent Walk. (57) **Reducing**[1] speed to a walking pace, **she**[1] (58) **bumped** along a wide cobbled cul-de-sac (59) **bounded** on the north by a ten-foot wall of grey brick and on the south by the three houses **which**[6] (60) **comprised** the Peverell Press.

At first sight **she**[1] (61) **thought** Innocent House (62) **disappointing**[6a]. **It**[6a] (63) **was** an imposing but unremarkable Georgian house with proportions[6a/i] which **she**[1] (64) **knew rather than felt** (65) **to be**[6a/i] graceful, and **it**[6a] (66) **looked** little different from the many others **she**[1] (67) **had seen** in London's squares or terraces. **The front door**[6a/ii] (68) **was closed** and **she**[1] (69) **saw** no sign of activity behind the four storeys of eight-paned windows, the two lowest one each with an elegant wrought-iron balcony. On either side (70) **was a smaller, less ostentatious house**[6b,c], (71) **standing**[6b,c] a little distanced and detached like a pair of deferential poor relations. She[1] (72) **was** now opposite the first of these, number 10, although **she**[1] (73) **could see** no sign of numbers 1 to 9, and (74) **saw**[1] that **it**[6b] (75) **was separated** from the main building by Innocent Passage, (76) **barred**[7] from the road by a wrought-iron gate, and obviously (77) **used**[7] as a parking space for staff cars. But now the gate[7a] (78) **was** open and **Mandy**[1] (79) **saw** three men (80) **bringing**[8] down large cardboard cartons by a hoist from an upper floor and (81) **loading**[8] them into a small van. **One of the three**[8a], a swarthy under-sized man (82) **wearing**[8a] a battered bush-ranger's hat, (83) **took** it off and (84) **swept**[8a] Mandy a low ironic bow. **The other two**[8b] (85) **glanced up** from their work (86) **to regard**[8b] her with obvious curiosity. **Mandy**[1], (87) **pushing up**[1] her visor, (88) **bestowed** on all three of them a long discouraging stare.

The second of these smaller houses[6c] (89) **was separated** from Innocent House by Innocent Lane. **It** (90) **was** here, according to Mrs Crealey's instructions, that **she**[1] (91) **would find** the entrance. **She**[1] (92) **switched off** the engine, (93) **dismounted**[1], and (94) **wheeled**[1] the bike over the cobbles, (95) **looking**[1] for the most unobtrusive place in which **(96) to park**[1]. **It (97) was** then that **she**[1] **(98) had** her first glimpse of the river, a narrow glitter of shivering water under the lightening sky. **(99) Parking**[1] the Yamaha, **she**[1] **(100) took off** her crash helmet, **rummaged** for her hat in the side pannier and **put it on**, and then, with the helmet under her arm, and **carrying** her tote bag, she **walked** towards the water as if physically **drawn** by the strong tug of the tide, the faint evocative sea smell.

21. SYNTACTIC CONSTRUCTION, INFORMATION STRUCTURE AND TEXTUAL ROLE: AN INTERFACE VIEW OF THE CLEFT SENTENCE

First published in *Brno Studies in English*, Vol. 36/1, 2010, 29–45.

0. This chapter elaborates an outcome of the foregoing chapter, which examined thematic progressions with constant theme in two sorts of text, academic prose and fiction. The study suggested, among other things, differences between the two text sorts in the type of the cleft sentence on the one hand, and in the function of the cleft sentence in the text build-up on the other. While in fiction the cleft sentence appeared to serve as a stylistic device of achieving narrative tension by presenting the informative part of the proposition in the subordinate clause and by focusing an anaphoric locative or temporal element which sets the scene of the event, academic prose displayed the cleft construction in what is usually regarded as its primary function: the focused element constituted the most important informational item, cf. examples (1) and (2), respectively:

(1) a. It was here, according to Mrs Crealey, that she would find the entrance. (James 7)
    b. It was then that she had her first glimpse of the river, a narrow glitter of shivering water under the lightening sky. (James 8)
(2) a. What is it about its way of life that has made it unique? (Morris 13)
    b. What was it in the environment that made possible their isolation as a new form of life? (Morris 13)

1. The FSP structure and the textual functions of the cleft sentence are examined on 54 examples drawn almost equally from fiction (James) and academic prose (Matthews, see *Sources*). The number of examples was determined by excerpts obtained from equally long samples of each text, with the lower limit of 25 instances in whichever of the two texts they might have been found. In this way equally long samples of academic prose and fiction (112 and 124 pages)[1] supplied, respectively, 25[2] and 29 instances of the cleft sentence. The inconsequential difference in the quantitative data disproves any assumptions about this aspect, and calls for seeking distinctions elsewhere, viz. in the FSP structure of the construction, and its distribution and role in the text build-up.

1.1 As a first step the examples were examined from the viewpoint of context dependence/independence of the content expressed by the two constitutive clauses, the *it*-clause and the subordinate clause.[3] This involved the basic distinction, in Prince's terms (1978), between stressed-focus *it*-clefts, i.e. cleft sentences with context-dependent information in the subordinate clause which is hence weakly stressed; and informative-presupposition *it*-clefts, whose subordinate clauses are context-independent and stressed accordingly. The same distinction is made by Huddleston and Pullum (2002: 1424) in terms of discourse-old and discourse new-presupposition. Compare (3) and (4):

(3) Inexperienced dancers often have difficulty in ending the Natural Turn in the correct alignment... *it is usually the man who is at fault*. (Huddleston and Pullum 2002: 1424)

(4) The Indians were helpful in many ways. *It was they who taught the settlers how to plant and harvest crops successfully in the New World*. (Huddleston and Pullum 2002: 1424)

While in (3) having difficulty implies the possibility of being at fault, and hence is derivable from the preceding context, the content of the subordinate clause in (4) is irretrievable. The type illustrated by example (3) is largely regarded as prototypical. The examples listed under (1) represent informative presupposition clefts, while those listed under (2) contain predominantly context-independent information in both clauses.

In the case of informative presupposition *it*-clefts Quirk et al. (1985: 1384, Note b.) draw attention to a use illustrated in (5):

(5) It was late last night that a group of terrorists attacked an army post.
(5)' Late last night a group of terrorists attacked an army post.

---

1   The difference in the number of pages between the two samples is due to the fact that the fiction sample contains half-full pages and pages with only a few lines, whereas in the academic text nearly all pages contain a full number of lines, i.e. pages without vacant space.

2   The academic text in fact contained 26 cleft sentences, but the last cleft sentence on page 112 is an example illustrating Bloomfield's concept of emotional relations: "Bloomfield added ... 'emotional relations', in which one element, like the pronoun *me* in *It's me they beat* is 'dominant'." This example was excluded insofar as it occurs in a specific context outside the types of context relevant for the present study.

3   The term relative clause is avoided because the subordinate clause in the cleft sentence differs in several relevant formal, syntactico-semantic and functional features (cf. Dušková 1993 and Section 2 in Chapter 9).

Instances of this kind (met with especially in BrE radio and television news, and sometimes objected to) are commented upon as "using the cleft sentence structure with an item that might be less obtrusive with simple fronting," viz. (5)'. The cleft sentence "conveys unwarrantably the impression that the fact of the attack was known to the hearer, but not the time at which it had taken place. The habit can be defended in that an adjunct (especially of time or place) is a fitting scene-setting and that it is this function that the cleft structure emphasizes" (Quirk et al. 1985: 1384, Note b.). It is to be noted that here the focused element conveys irretrievable information so that the cleft construction presents context-independent content in both clauses.[4]

Since context dependence/independence is a crucial point in assigning cleft sentences to one or the other type, and context itself is a phenomenon of a graded nature (cf. Firbas 1992: 32–35; 1994), a significant role is played by the factors through which a given element becomes disengaged from context dependence. According to Firbas (1995: 22), these factors involve (a) selection, (b) contrast, (c) identification, (d) purposeful repetition and (e) the summarizing effect. Considering that context is inherently a textual feature, all these factors play a textual role. This is most prominent in the last, the summarizing effect, in that it is related to a longer stretch of text whereas the other factors mostly involve a single element referred to in the closely preceding shorter context. With respect to the cleft sentence, in the texts under study all these factors except purposeful repetition were found to be operative. In other approaches to the textual function of the cleft sentence (Hasselgård 2004) two more functions have been added, viz. topic linking and topic launching, the term topic being used in the sense of textual theme.

1.2 Textual functions related to longer stretches of text, viz. summarization, topic launching and topic linking, involve textual units higher than the sentence, in particular paragraphs. Accordingly, in addition to the aspects discussed so far, attention was also paid to the position of cleft sentences in paragraphs. In this respect, three groups were distinguished, paragraph initial, paragraph internal, and paragraph final on the assumption of potential connection between the position in the paragraph build-up and the textual function of the cleft sentence, viz. a correlation between the three paragraph positions and topic launching, topic linking and the summarizing function, respectively.

2. Classification of the examples according to context dependence/independence of the content of the two clauses showed a prominent prevalence of informative presupposition clefts, i.e. cleft sentences with context-independent information in the subordinate clause. This rather disproves the largely held view of stressed focus *it*-clefts as the prototypical type. The prominence of context-independent subordinate clauses

---

4   Stylistic clichés like *It was a very troubled wife that greeted Henry on his return that night* (Quirk et al. 1985: 1384, Note b) and the proverbial type, e.g. *It is an ill bird that fouls its nest*, were not registered in the texts under study (for their status with respect to cleft structure, see Dušková 1993).

was even more marked in the academic text, viz. 20 instances out of 25, i.e. 80%. In fiction this ratio was 18 out of 29, i.e. 62%. As for the type of context independence/dependence of the two clauses and the textual position of the cleft sentence, the analysis brought the following findings.

2.1 Academic prose displayed several configurations of context dependent/independent elements in the two clauses.

2.1.1 Informative presupposition clefts most frequently contained an anaphoric, given item, not disengaged from context dependence, in the *it*-clause and new information in the subordinate clause (11 instances, i.e. 45%), cf. the examples listed under (6).

(6) a. is it not possible to start from a more comprehensive view, in which the whole stick, at both ends, is grasped at once? On my reading of Bloomfield's *Language*, that is precisely what he did, and *it is from that that the complexity of his treatment, which has struck most serious readers and commentators, largely springs*. (Matthews 52, end of paragraph and end of section)

b. We do not trace linguistic usage act by act, but assume that, once individuals have 'acquired the habit of using a certain linguistic form', they will continue to utter it in similar circumstances. But, for psychology itself, the hypothesis implies the postulates of behaviorism.

It is against this background that Bloomfield reshaped the theory of grammar, first in his 'Set of postulates' of the previous year (1926) and then in *Language*.

(Matthews 64, end of first and beginning of second paragraph, opening a new topic)

In (6) a. the cleft sentence occurs at the end of a paragraph, and at the same time closes a section, thus serving the summarizing function in the paragraph build-up and closing function on the higher level of sections. On the other hand in (6) b. the cleft sentence occurs paragraph initially and opens a new topic. Both instances show agreement between paragraph position and textual function. Of these two positions the final position, correlating with the summarizing and/or concluding function, largely prevails. Within the configuration of anaphoric given, not disengaged items in the *it*-clause and new information in the subordinate clause (11 instances) final or near-final position of the cleft sentence was found in 5 instances, i.e. 20%, whereas the initial position only once (4%). In the total of 25 instances drawn from academic prose, the final position was the most frequent, viz. 12 instances (48%), while the initial position with three occurrences ranked lowest (12%), see Table 2.

2.1.2 To this group may be added 3 examples in which the focusing by the *it*-cleft of an anaphoric item not disengaged from context dependence is reinforced by a focalizer, cf. (7).

(7) The rules of morphology then generate a 'dictionary' which will have to contain, among other things, the word *write*. But we are later told that *it is only in this dictionary that we will find* 'such crucial information as', for example, 'that *arrive* is a verb'.

This is not wholly clear. Does *arrive* not also include a root *arrive?* If so, we can surely say …
(Matthews 103–104, paragraph internal)

All three examples represent informative presupposition clefts, i.e. they contain context-independent information in the subordinate clause.

The group of examples with a focalizer in the *it*-clause included three other examples in which the focused element was a context independent or context disengaged item, cf. (8) a. and b.

(8) a. In Harris's own words, his critique is directed 'against the present treatment of morphemes' … He does not say 'the present treatment of morphology'. For *it is only if we assume* that all forms which are grammatically equivalent must be a single unit at the level of the morpheme *that the 'contradiction'* which he finds in Bloomfield's criterion *can arise.*
   Why was this assumed? The reasons lie deep and it is not easy … (Matthews 79–80, paragraph final)

b. But in principle, and above all in the techniques of describing formal structure, the fields are as distinct as they are in the other works which stand in the nineteenth-century German tradition. *It is only in the 1920s that what many scholars might see as the implication of such remarks began to be thought through.* (Matthews 62, end of paragraph and end of section)

Example (8) a. is the only one of those discussed so far that represents the stressed-focus *it*-cleft, i.e. a cleft sentence with context independent information in the *it*-clause and context-dependent in the subordinate clause. The other two instances contain predominantly context-independent information in the subordinate clause, cf. (8) b.

In the case of cleft sentences with a focalizer in the *it*-clause only two positions were registered: paragraph final or near final (in 4 instances, cf. (8) a. and b.) and paragraph internal (2 instances, cf. (7)). In the final position the cleft sentences of this group again have the summarizing or concluding function, whereas in paragraph internal position they serve to elaborate an argument or further explicate a point.

A notable feature about paragraph final *it*-clefts appears in (8) a., for here the cleft sentence not only concludes an argument, but also opens a new topic constituted by the context-independent focused part of the *it*-clause. In addition to the concluding function it thus at the same time forms a link to a new topic. This dual function was also noted in the group of cleft sentences with anaphoric items in the *it*-clause without context-disengaging factors or focalizers, cf. (9).

(9) each solution now has its proponents, as we will see in part §2.5. But such a critique of Bloomfield's *Language*, whether fair or not, is clearly only similar in part to the critique which underlies the work of his immediate successors, in what is

widely known as the 'Bloomfieldian' school. Their solution was also radically different, and *it is this that we must explore now.*
(Matthews 75, paragraph final, end of section)

2.1.3 Focused items disengaged from context dependence by contrast, identification or selection alone, i.e. without a focalizer, were found in 4 examples. It is in this group that three of the five stressed-focus *it*-clefts were found. Compare examples (10) a., b. and (12) with (11), which is the only one in this group with new information in the subordinate clause.

(10) a. It is therefore a remarkable tribute to the inertia of ideas that, when these scholars together addressed the phonology of English, *it was the other, morpheme-based solution that they adopted.*
(Matthews 92–93, near-initial paragraph position)
   b. ... in the 1920s and 1930s ... the inherited 'Word and Paradigm' model was supplanted, especially in America, by models based on the morpheme. ... But three generations later what were at that time innovations are among the elementary things that students of linguistics are first taught. *It is the advocate of a word-based model who now has to argue against an inherited tradition.* The most obvious influence is in and through textbooks. (Matthews 98, end of paragraph)
(11) We have seen in chapter 2 how Bloomfield's concept of the morpheme was transformed by his immediate successors. But we have yet to consider contemporary developments in syntax. ... From the late 1940s syntax had basically two tasks, one to establish the hierarchical structure of sentences and the other to sort out the units of this hierarchy into classes with equal distribution. For the same period also saw the firm adoption of distributional criteria. Not merely did the study of language start from form rather than from meaning; but the investigation of form was separated strictly from that of meaning, and necessarily preceded it. *It was in syntax that this programme was particularly attractive* and met with the fewest doubts and criticisms.
(Matthews 111, end of paragraph and section)

The last example of this group occurs in paragraph-internal position, cf. (12).

(12) If such an approach had also been pursued in inflectional morphology, it would have led ... to the form of word-based treatment that is now advocated by Anderson (1992). But in the work directly inspired by Halle's article, *it was in fact the other solution that tended to prevail.* It does not follow again that morphemes must be minimal signs. But a feature like plural ...
(Matthews 105, paragraph internal)

Neither the group of *it*-clefts containing in the *it*-clause a focalizer or an item disengaged from context dependence by contrast or another context-disengaging factor shows any correlation with the textual function. It is the position in paragraphs that appears to be relevant in this respect. While paragraph-final clefts serve the concluding or summarizing function, sometimes connected with linking the point being concluded with a new one, paragraph internal clefts serve elaboration of an argument or further explication of a point, just as was the case in the previous groups.

2.1.4 The last group of informative presupposition clefts contains predominantly context independent information in both clauses, without focalizers or context-disengaging factors in the *it*-clause (3 instances). As in the previous group, this configuration of content does not show any correlation with the textual function, each cleft sentence appearing in a different paragraph position, cf. (13) a., b. and c.

(13) a. *It was not until well after the war that Language ceased to be a major vehicle* for philological papers.
(Matthews 11, paragraph near-final)

   b. Of the alternants in *duke* and *duchess*, [djuwk] was basic because 'it has a much wider range than the other'. *It is presumably for that reason that Chomsky and Halle took [d] as a basic form for 'past'.*
(Matthews 94, paragraph internal)

   c. This chain of argument has been set out without direct quotations, both because the individual points are well known and because we will return to Chomsky's work in later chapters. *But it was in these radical reversals of priorities that its impact was first felt.*
(Matthews 32–33, paragraph near-initial)

2.1.5 As regards the group of cleft sentences with context-dependent information in the subordinate clause (5 instances), most of them have been noted in the previous sections, cf. (8) a., (10) a., (10) b. and (12).

The last example of this group contains context dependent items in the *it*-clause (in this respect it is similar to instances with an anaphoric item, treated in 2.1.1) which are disengaged from context dependence by being brought into a new relationship. This feature in turn groups them with focused items disengaged from context dependence, i.e. with instances treated in 2.1.3. Compare (14):

(14) The second phase is 'semantics', and grammar, as Bloomfield saw it, was only one of two parts into which semantics was 'ordinarily divided'. The other was the lexicon. *It was then between grammar and lexicon, as we have seen, that Bloomfield's parallels had been drawn.*
(Matthews, 82, paragraph near-final)

2.1.6 The main findings from academic prose show lack of correlation between the type of context dependence/independence of the content expressed by the two clauses of the cleft sentence and the textual functions involving larger stretches of text; and correlation of textual functions of the cleft sentence with the position in paragraphs.

The quantitative data are summarized in Tables 1 and 2.

Table 1: Focused element: academic prose

Focused element in *it*-clause	Context independent information in subordinate clause	Context dependent information in subordinate clause	Number of cleft sentences
Anaphoric item	11	1	12 (48%)
Reinforcement by focalizer	5	1	6 (24%)
Disengaged from context dependence	1	3	4 (16%)
Predominantly context-independent information in both clauses	3		3 (12%)
Total	20	5	25 (100%)

Table 2: Position in paragraph: academic prose

Position in paragraph	Number of occurrences
Final	12 (48%)
Internal	10 (40%)
Initial	3 (12%)
Total	25 (100%)

2.2 An analogous analysis of the fiction sample brought the following findings. As noted in 2., classification of the examples according to the context dependence/independence of the content expressed by the two clauses showed a prominent prevalence of the informative presupposition clefts, i.e. cleft sentences with context-independent information in the subordinate clause. However, in fiction this prominence was less marked than in the academic sample, viz. 18 instances out of 29, i.e. 62%, as against 20 instances out of 25, i.e. 80%, respectively.

2.2.1 The most frequent configuration of the context dependent/independent information in the *it*-clause and the subordinate clause was a given item disengaged from context dependence by being contrastive, or serving identification or selection in the *it*-clause (15 instances) and retrievable or irretrievable information in the subordinate clause (10 and 5 instances respectively, see Table 3), illustrated in (15) a. and b., and (16), respectively:

(15) a. George Copeland ... heard the clatter of the feet on the cobbles with relief. ... Lord Stilgoe halted his angry pacing and they both turned to the door. Mr de Witt gave one look at George's worried face and asked quickly: 'What's wrong, George?'

It was lord Stilgoe who answered. Without greeting de Witt he said grimly: (James 110, paragraph initial)

    b. Miss Etienne seemed to Mandy expensive, ... But the physical closeness of her companion and her heightened senses ... told her something more; that Miss Etienne wasn't at ease. *It was she, Mandy, who should have been nervous.* Instead she was aware that the air of the claustrophobic lift, jerking upwards with such maddening slowness, was quivering with tension.
(James 12, end of paragraph)

(16) Miss Blackett ... for the past nineteen years ... had lived with her older widowed cousin, Joan Willoughby. ... early in these nineteen years of shared life a routine had established itself ... which satisfied them both. *It was Joan who managed the house* and was responsible for the garden, *Blackie, who on Sundays cooked the main meal of the day* which was always eaten promptly at one o'clock, ...
(James 45, paragraph internal)

In this point the two text sorts under study considerably differ: whereas in fiction this is the prevalent type, found in 51.7% of all instances (15 out of 29), in academic prose it accounts for 4 (out of 25) instances, i.e. 16%, see Tables 1 and 3. The prevalence of this type, as shown by (16), is presumably connected with the character of fiction in that the narrated events often involve several participants that alternate as the event/description develops, and hence need to be identified, selected or contrasted.

This is evident from the underlying syntactic functions of the focused elements. In academic prose a large majority of the underlying elements brought into focus are adverbials, whereas underlying subjects and objects occur in 2 and 3 instances, respectively. On the other hand in fiction the focused elements prevalently involve underlying subjects (19 instances),[5] adverbials being focused in 7 instances and objects in 3 (as in the academic text), see Table 5.

As regards the position in paragraphs, most cleft sentences of this type occurred paragraph internally, as in example (16) (9 instances), the other two positions being each found in 3 instances (see (15) a. and b.). These positions again correspond with the three textual functions connected with larger stretches of text: the clefts in initial position launch new topics, in final (or near-final) position serve the concluding/summative function, and in internal position shift the narrative to a different participant in the evolvement of the story. This differs from the textual function of paragraph-internal clefts in academic prose in that here they served to elaborate an argument or further explicate a point.

The only other instance with context-dependent subordinate clause has context independent information in the *it*-clause in the absence of a focalizer or a factor disengaging it from context dependence, see (20) a. in 2.2.4.

---

5   For the textual roles of *it*-clefts rhematizing subjects of the underlying clauses, compared with the textual roles of initial rhematic subjects in presentation sentences, see Dušková (2015).

2.2.2 The configuration of the context dependent/independent information in the *it*-clause and the subordinate clause that ranked second in the frequency of occurrence displayed an anaphoric item in the *it*-clause, focused by the cleft alone (7 instances, i.e. 24.1%). As shown in Table 3, all instances display context independent information in the subordinate clause, cf. (17):

(17) a. She referred to her room as the 'cosy', and Mandy was one of the few girls who was admitted to its privacies.
It was probably the cosy that kept Mandy faithful to the agency, ...
(James 3–4, paragraph initial)

b. She switched off the engine, dismounted, and wheeled the bike over the cobbles, looking for the most unobtrusive place in which to park. *It was then that she had her first glimpse of the river*, a narrow glitter of shivering water under the lightening sky. Parking the Yamaha, she took off her crash helmet, rummaged for her hat in the side pannier and put it on, and then, with the helmet under her arm, and carrying her tote bag, she walked towards the water as if physically drawn by the strong tug of the tide, the faint evocative sea smell.
(James 7–8, paragraph internal)

As regards the position in paragraphs, 5 instances were found in the initial position, cf. (17) a., and 2 in the internal position, cf. (17) b. While the clefts in initial position launch a new topic, as in all the other instances discussed so far, the two clefts in internal position introduce a deviation whereupon the narrative resumes the previous topic which is the main paragraph topic. In (17) b. the topic introduced by the deviation appears to be relevant in that it reappears in interaction with the main paragraph topic. However, as shown by (18), the cleft presenting a deviation may have other functions. In (18) it serves as a link to reintroduce the main paragraph topic.

(18) He got up from the table and moved over to the window. As he watched a cruise ship suddenly and silently blocked his view, so close that for a moment he could look into a lighted porthole and see, in the half-circle of brightness, the head of a woman, delicate as a cameo, pale arms raised, running her fingers through an aureole of hair, and could imagine that their eyes met in a surprised and fleeting intimacy. He wondered briefly, and with no real curiosity, *who it was who shared her cabin*—husband, lover, friend—and *what plans they had for the evening*. He had none. By established habit he worked late on Thursday night. He wouldn't see Lucinda until Friday ...
(James 85, paragraph internal)

2.2.3 The only other configuration of the context in/dependent information in the *it*-clause and the subordinate clause registered with more than one occurrence is represented by instances containing more or less predominant context-independent information in both clauses (5 instances, see Table 3).

(19) a. They left together in silence. *It wasn't until Kate was double-locking the front door* after them *that he spoke* again. He said: 'Shall I see you again before I leave next Wednesday?'
(James 123, paragraph internal: the example forms the whole paragraph)
   b. It's said that Sir Francis went mad with remorse in his old age and used to go out alone at night trying to get rid of that tell-tale spot. *It's his ghost that people claim to see*, still scrubbing away at the stain.
(James 32, paragraph near-final)

Example (19) a. was included in this group on account of containing the adverbial *again*, which operates as a context disengaging factor. It carries the second intonation centre in speech. In example (19) b. a similar role is played by *still* in the subordinate clause, while the *it*-clause contains the irretrievable element *ghost*. Admittedly, the context dependence/independence of the clauses constituting the clefts of this group is hard to classify, which leaves ground for assigning them to other types. Since they did not show any patterning relevant for the present discussion, they were left for possible future consideration.

2.2.4 The remaining configurations occurred only once: context-independent information (in the absence of a focalizer or a factor disengaging given items from context-dependence) in the *it*-clause in combination with context-dependent subordinate clause, cf. (20) a., and a focused item reinforced by a focalizer with a context-independent subordinate clause, cf. (20) b.:

(20) a. The advertised star of the evening was Gabriel Dauntsey. He had asked to go on early but most of the poets before him had overstepped their limits, the amateurs in particular being insusceptible to Colin's muttered hints, and *it was nearly 9.30 before Dauntsey made his slow progress to the rostrum*. He was listened to in a respectful silence and loudly applauded ...
(James 106, paragraph internal)
   b. They had moved to number 12 in 1983 when the firm was expanding ... Her father had accepted the need to move philosophically, had indeed seemed almost to welcome it, and she suspected that *it was only after she joined him in 1985* on leaving Oxford *that he began to find the flat restrictive*, almost claustrophobic.
(James 70–71, paragraph final)

In these instances the focused elements are not only new but also contrastive, especially in (20) b., where the temporal adjunct sets the scene for a contrasting situation.

The different types of configuration of the context dependent/independent information in the *it*-clause and the subordinate clause are summarized in Table 3. The positions in paragraphs are given in Table 4.

Table 3: Focused element: fiction

Focused element in it-clause	Context independent information in subordinate clause	Context dependent information in subordinate clause	Number of cleft sentences
Anaphoric item	7	–	7 (24.14%)
Reinforcement by focalizer	1	–	1 (3.45%)
Disengaged from context dependence	5	10	15 (51.72%)
New information	–	1	1 (3.45%)
Predominantly context-independent information in both clauses	5		5 (17.24%)
Total	18	11	29 (100%)

Table 4: Position in paragraph: fiction

Position in paragraph	Number of occurrences
Final	9 (31%)
Internal	13 (45%)
Initial	7 (24%)
Total	29 (100%)

Table 5: Underlying syntactic functions of focused elements

Syntactic function	Academic prose	Fiction
Subject	2 (8%)	19 (65.5%)
Object	3 (12%)	3 (10.3%)
Adverbial	20 (80%)	7 (24.2%)
Total	25 (100%)	29 (100.0%)

2.3 Comparing the two text samples under study with respect to the paragraph positions in which the clefts occur, we find differences in all three positions. The initial position, though showing agreement in ranking lowest in both samples, is twice as frequent in academic prose as in fiction, cf., respectively, 7 instances out of 29, i.e. 24%, against

3 instances out of 25, i.e. 12%. Another prominent difference was found in the representation of the final position: academic prose 12 out of 25, i.e. 48% against 9 out of 29, i.e. 31% in fiction; the internal position was represented near-equally in the two samples: 10 out of 25, i.e. 40% in academic prose, against 13 out of 29, i.e. 45% in fiction. As regards paragraphs as such, it should be noted that fiction contained a much larger number of them than academic prose. The paragraphs in fiction varied in length, most of them being short, while the paragraphs in the academic sample were in general very long. However, the different representation of paragraphs in the two texts is not supposed to be relevant to the obtained findings since the present concern is not the frequency of occurrence of cleft sentences measured by the number of paragraphs.

As regards differentiation of the two samples with respect to the textual functions of clefts in the three positions, agreement was essentially found in the function of clefts in paragraph final and paragraph initial positions. In both text samples cleft sentences in these positions serve, respectively, the summarizing / concluding and topic launching function. A minor difference was found here in the function of clefts in the final position insofar as the summarizing or concluding function was more frequently connected with the linking function in academic prose than in fiction.

Prominent functional differentiation was displayed by clefts in the paragraph internal position. Here clefts in academic prose served to elaborate an argument or further explicate a point, whereas in fiction they shifted the narrative to a different participant in the event/situation being described, or introduced a deviation, relevant for further evolvement of the story, or self-contained.

3. Summarizing the points treated in the foregoing sections, we find that the assumption of differences in the textual functions of *it*-clefts according to the type of text, which motivated the writing of this chapter, has been confirmed, but on the basis of aspects other than those displayed by the examples that served as a starting point. According to these examples fiction appeared to favour clefts with an anaphoric scene-setting adverbial in the *it*-clause and new content in the subordinate clause, whereas academic prose was supposed to display context-independent information in both clauses. None of these examples could be classed with one of the two principal types of clefts described in the literature, the prototypical stressed focus *it*-cleft and the informative presupposition *it*-cleft. Consequently, the first criterion of classification was sought in the representation of these two types.

Since context dependence/independence is a crucial point in assigning cleft sentences to one or the other type, and context itself is a phenomenon of a graded nature, a further classification criterion was found in the factors through which a given element becomes disengaged from context dependence: (a) selection, (b) contrast (c) identification, and (d) the summarizing effect. The textual role of these factors is most prominent in the case of the summarizing effect in that it is related to a longer stretch of text, whereas the other factors mostly involve single elements referred to in short contexts. The textual approach called for the inclusion of other textual functions involving larger stretches of text, topic linking and topic launching. Concern with longer stretches of text then led to the inclusion of a third classification criterion, the position of clefts in paragraphs.

Classification of the examples according to the context dependence/independence of the content of the two clauses constituting cleft sentences showed a prominent prevalence of the informative presupposition clefts, i.e. cleft sentences with context-independent information in the subordinate clause. This rather disproves the largely held view of stressed focus *it*-clefts as the prototypical type.

An analysis of the texts with respect to the factors disengaging a given item from context dependence did not show any correlation with the textual functions involving larger stretches of text. These functions were found to correlate with the position of clefts in paragraphs.

Particular differences between the academic and the fiction sample were found in the following points.

Clefts with context-independent information prevailed in both text sorts, but the prevalence was more prominent in academic prose (80% and 62%, respectively). Another difference was found in the character of the focused element in the *it*-clause. While in fiction the most frequently focused element was a given item disengaged from context dependence by contrast, identification or selection (51%), in academic prose this type accounts for only 16%. The prevalence of this type in fiction is presumably connected with the character of this genre in that the narrated events often involve several participants that alternate as the event/description develops, and hence need to be identified, selected or contrasted. This is evident from the underlying syntactic functions of the focused elements. Whereas in academic prose a large majority of the underlying elements brought into focus are adverbials (80%), in fiction the focused elements prevalently involve underlying subjects (65%).

Other differences were found in the case of focused items reinforced by a focalizer which were considerably more frequent in academic prose than in fiction (24% and 3.45%, respectively), and in the case of focused anaphoric/given items which prevailed in academic prose (48% as against 24%).

The textual functions involving longer stretches of text largely correlate with the position of clefts in paragraphs in both text sorts: clefts in initial position serve the topic launching function. In final position they correlate with the summarizing/concluding function, sometimes displaying a dual function: in addition to concluding a point they operate as a bridge to another topic. This dual function was more frequent in academic prose. As regards clefts occupying the paragraph internal position, in academic prose they serve to elaborate an argument or further explicate a point, whereas in fiction they achieve a shift in the narrative to a different participant in the event/situation being described, or introduce a deviation which may be relevant for further evolvement of the story, or self-contained.

These findings are to be regarded as a mere probe of limited validity. They are based on small samples, and moreover represent only one type of text in the respective text sort, the chosen text sorts as such being internally further differentiated. Nevertheless it may suggest some points worth further study.

SOURCES

James, P. D. *Original Sin*. London: Faber and Faber, 1994.

Matthews, P. H. *Grammatical Theory in the United States from Bloomfield to Chomsky*. Cambridge: Cambridge University Press, 1994 (1st ed. 1993).

Morris, D. *The Naked Ape*. London: Triad Grafton Books, 1986 (1st ed. 1967).

22. A TEXTUAL VIEW
OF NOUN MODIFICATION

First published in M. Černý, J. Chamonikolasová, S. Kavka, and E. Klímová (eds), *New Chapters in Functional Syntax*. Spis Ostravské univerzity v Ostravě, No. 236, Ostrava: Universitas Ostraviensis / Facultas Philosophica, 2011, 18–30.

0. Drawing on Aleš Svoboda's analyses of the distributional field of the noun phrase, this chapter examines the relations between the FSP structure of a modified NP and the NP's position in the text with the aim of ascertaining the role that modified NPs play in the text build-up. According to the FSP structure of the NP the following discussion is divided into two parts. The first part is concerned with NPs in which both the head noun and the modifier are context-independent. The second part deals with the varying FPS structure of modified NPs as they move through sections of the text, a further division being made according to whether the recurrent NPs under observation reiterate both components or whether a recurrent lexico-semantic element is found in the realization form of only one of them.

1. The FSP structure of context-independent modified noun phrases is best illustrated by book titles. The context independence of a book title rests on its being the first component of a whole text which introduces the text's hypertheme. As such it has no antecedents and contains only novel elements.

This type of context-independent NP is presented on a contrastive Czech-English and English-Czech basis, which makes a suitable starting point for demonstrating the relevant points by bringing into relief the differing systemic possibilities of modification structure in an analytic and an inflecting language. Two book titles have been chosen, Mark Corner's translation of the title of Vladislav Vančura's *Rozmarné léto*, and Martin Hilský's translation of the title of D. H. Lawrence's *Women in Love*.

1.1 Starting with Mark Corner's translation of the book title *Rozmarné léto*, literally 'A Capricious Summer', we find it rendered as *A Summer of Caprice*.

(1) Rozmarné léto / A Summer of Caprice

From the FSP point of view this appears to be a felicitous counterpart, although possibly due not so much to the translator's choice as to semantic (collocational) factors, and thus may have nothing to do with what appears to be a salient FSP point. The semantic aspect of the chosen equivalent is involved in the collocational propensities of the adjective *capricious*, which usually modifies personal activities and features. The only inanimate entity commonly described as capricious, unrelated to personal behaviour, acts and mental processes, is the weather. In the case of other inanimate nouns without personal associative ties the use of the adjective involves a certain degree of personification. This may have led to the choice of a less marked structure in English, viz. a prepositional phrase containing the respective cognate noun instead of its adjectival derivative. The assignment of a quality to the referent of a head noun by means of an *of*-phrase is looser than direct modification by the respective adjective, hence the assignee remains more or less vague.

However, it is not the semantic aspect that primarily draws attention to the English counterpart of the Czech title. More importantly in the present context, it is the linear arrangement of its information structure. According to Aleš Svoboda's initial conception of the distributional field of a noun phrase (Svoboda 1968), the modifier, unless context dependent, is more dynamic than the head noun, irrespective of the latter's context dependence or independence. In terms of FSP functions, if both the modifier and the head noun are context independent, the modifier constitutes the rheme, the head serving as the theme. This appears to be due to the modifier's semantics which is as a rule more specific than that of the head noun. In the case of premodifiers the importance of semantics and context independence for their rhematic function in the communicative subfield of a noun phrase stands out especially when these factors are considered in connection with the other two FSP factors, intonation and linearity. Both these factors here operate counter to semantics and context independence. The more dynamic element, which in the basic distribution of communicative dynamism follows the less dynamic one(s), is here preposed, and as regards the prosodic factor, not only the premodifier, but also the noun carries the word stress, which contradicts the usual placement of the intonation centre on the rheme.

Svoboda's later conception (Svoboda 1987, 1989, esp. 101–104) is based on his drawing a parallel between the communicative function of the verb in a clause and that of the head noun in a complex noun phrase, which led him to assign the notional component of the head noun to an extensive transitional section: "... in the complex noun phrase, the function of the head is that of nominal transition, which—together with the nominal transition proper [the case and number]—belongs to the transitional sphere of the nominal distributional field," cf. (2) (Svoboda 1987: 76, 77). In the present paper the FSP analysis of the noun phrase is based on Svoboda's earlier thematic interpretation of the head and rhematic interpretation of the modifier if context-independent[1] because of the relations between the NP's distributional field and its syntactic structure. In the underlying predicative construction the head noun represents the subject and as such has thematic function, cf. *the girl is (standing) in the corner.*

(2) *Can you see the girl* [quality bearer, nominal transition] *(standing) in the corner* [specification, rheme proper].

The Czech form of the title of Vančura's novel, cf. (1), represents the most frequent type of noun modification, viz. modification of a noun by an adjective (cf. the Tables in Section 3), the basic ordering in both languages: adjective—noun, irrespective of the information structure. In English this order is largely obligatory for lack of inflections, cf. (3) a. This is in agreement with the primary grammatical function of English word order which often acts counter to the principle of end focus. In contrast, inflectional Czech, whose primary word order principle is the functional sentence perspective, allows both positions[2], cf. (3) b. Looked at from this viewpoint, the placement of a more dynamic element before a less dynamic one is a certain anomaly: Czech word order normally follows the basic distribution of CD, i.e. thematic elements precede the rheme. Nevertheless, even in Czech the order adjective—noun is the basic arrangement, the unmarked, usual order, whereas postposition of an adjective in the noun phrase is a marked order emphasizing the importance of the attributed quality (cf. Daneš et al. 1987, 161–162). This is evident in the translation of the title of D. H. Lawrence's book in (4):

(3) a. *he was a handsome fellow* vs. **he was a fellow handsome*
    b. *byl to hezký člověk / byl to člověk hezký*
(4) *Women in Love / Ženy milující*

In this light, of the two versions of the title *Rozmarné léto* vs. *A Summer of Caprice*, cf. (1), the English rendition appears to be more consistent with the respective FSP functions. While in Czech the more dynamic adjective precedes the less dynamic noun, the English realization form of the counterpart of the Czech adjective, a prepositional phrase, whatever its motivation, has brought the two major word order principles, grammatical structure and information structure, into agreement: both operate in the same direction.

In the case of the second title, *Women in Love / Ženy milující*, cf. (4), agreement between grammatical structure and gradual increase in CD is found in both languages. However, here the English original and its Czech counterpart differ in the respective degrees of markedness. Whereas the English construction is neutral, the postposition of the adjective in Czech is marked in that it intensifies the importance of the attributed quality.

---

1   This is also the view taken by Firbas (1992: 84, 94–95).
2   Grammatical anteposition applies only to adjectives lacking inflectional endings.

1.2 In English the grammatical status of the position of adjectives with respect to nouns, generally applicable to anteposition, is in some instances also found in the case of adjectival modifiers in postposition. The word order head—adjectival modifier is displayed by noun phrases with pronominal heads realized by indefinite pronouns, cf. (5). In Firbas's formulation "the unqualified indefinite pronoun *something...* usually acts as a semantic slot filler" (1992: 45). Here the position of an adjectival modifier and its head, which is a general categorial concept semantically endowed with a low degree of CD, is again in agreement both with the grammatical structure, the postposition of the adjective being obligatory, and with the placement of the focal element at the end.

(5) He said something strange. Did you see anything interesting?

Another instance of this kind occurs in modified noun phrases of French origin, such as *notary public, heir apparent,* cf. (6). However, these phrases—unproductive, mostly fixed legal terms—have been taken over as wholes from French, and their linear arrangement is due to the French order noun—adjective.

(6) notary public, heir apparent

As shown by the adduced examples, in some instances English displays more agreement between the grammatical and the FSP structure of a modified noun phrase than Czech[3]. This may be found not only on the level of attributive modification within the noun phrase structure, but also on the level of clauses where the modifier is construed predicatively as the complement of a copula. Consider the following examples:

(7) *Her face was pale, yellowish,* with a clear, transparent skin, she leaned forward rather, *her features were strongly marked,* handsome, with a tense, unseeing predative look. (Lawrence, 27)
Měla bledý, zežloutlý obličej, s čistou, téměř průsvitnou pletí, neustále se držela v mírném předklonu, *měla nápadné, výrazné, hezké rysy* a napjatý, nevšímavý, trochu dravčí pohled. (Hilský, 15)
(8) *Měl vůbec humor* nepřijatelného druhu. (Jirotka, 17)
His sense of humour was really almost beyond the pale. (Corner, 18)

---

3   In the case of modified indefinite pronouns such as *něco zajímavého, něco divného* the postposition of the modifier is due to its non-congruent form, the genitive case of the modifying adjective. This construction is also an instance of grammatical postposition, but due to the non-congruent form, not to the head. In the congruent form the adjective would be preposed: *to zvláštní neidentifikovatelné něco v jejím půvabu* 'that strange unidentifiable something in her charm'. However, as shown by the English counterpart, which also displays the adjective in premodification, the pronoun is here used as a lexical item and behaves as an ordinary noun.

Here the Czech noun phrases, in (7) a translation equivalent, in (8) the Czech original, are heterogeneous with respect to context in/dependence (cf. Firbas 1992: 32–37). In both examples the modifiers carry a high degree of CD, being irretrievable from the context, hence fully context independent, and moreover semantically loaded. The head nouns, on the other hand, are less dynamic: in (7) they are partly derivable from the pragmatic (associative) context, 'face' and 'features' being in the relation of parts to the whole 'person' (*she*); in (8) the notion of a sense of humour is implied by the preceding context. While in Czech these heterogeneous elements are contained in one postverbal clause element which constitutes the rheme, in English the structure is decomposed into its less and more dynamic part, the thematic component, the head noun, being construed as the subject in initial position, and the rhematic modifier in the function of subject complement after a copula as the only element in the postverbal focus position.

Also these instances, frequently found in parallel English-Czech and Czech-English texts, lend support to the interpretation of modified noun phrases which assigns to the head the function of the theme and to the modifier that of the rheme. The validation or disproval of correspondences of this kind needs further testing on sufficient data.

2. Although the FSP structure of a modified noun phrase (or for that matter, of any noun phrase) is intrinsically a textual feature deriving from the context dependence/independence of its components, its role in the text fully manifests itself in its movement through the text as a device of its build-up.

2.1 An illustrative example is presented by recurrent noun phrases whose modifier has two alternative realization forms, one in premodification and another in postmodification. Prototypically, this is found where the premodifier is a converted noun functioning as a syntactic adjective, or a morphologically derived adjective, whose substantival base constitutes the nominal component of a prepositional phrase in postmodification. Compare the two English counterparts of the Czech word *klouzačka* in the English translation of Zdeněk Jirotka's novel *Saturnin:*

(9) I was like someone who upon descending from a snow-covered hill steps onto a *patch of ice* hidden beneath the snow … Only a person with no knowledge of what it is to engage in a desperate battle to keep one's balance would say that I could have left *the ice patch* at any moment … (Corner, 9)

Example (10) comes from expository prose:

(10) *The process of charging a capacitor* consists of transferring a charge from the plate at lower potential to the plate with higher potential. *The charging process* therefore requires the expenditure of energy. (Daneš's example, 1979)

On the assumption that of the two text sorts exemplified by (9) and (10), the nature of academic prose provides more favourable conditions for the occurrence of stretches

of text displaying variation of this kind[4]—the treatment of textual topics and subtopics calls for frequent reference to them—the following tentative probe is based on the
exposition of two topics (textual subthemes), *the work/theories of Basil Bernstein* and
urban speech, drawn from M. A. K. Halliday's book *Language as a Social Semiotic*, parts
of Chapters 5 (*The significance of Bernstein's work for sociolinguistic theory*, 101–103) and
Chapter 8 (*Language in urban society*, 154–157).

The length of the two text samples was determined by the occurrence in each of approximately one hundred modified noun phrases. The number is approximate because
both in the case of the heads and of the modifiers the inclusion or exclusion of some
forms is questionable. Basically, the included structures have a noun as the head and
a modifier realized by a syntactic adjective. Noun phrases realized by pronouns were
left out of account. A borderline category was found in the case of quantifiers (*some,
enough*, etc.) as potential heads or as potential modifiers. When construed with a noun,
quantifiers structurally function as determiners, but semantically specify their head,
and thus operate as modifiers. Moreover, quantifiers like *a number of*, though formally
constituting the head, are surface realization forms of the same category as dependent quantifiers (whether these are regarded as modifiers or determiners), cf. *a number of books, some/many books*. In addition to some quantifiers (like *enough, many*) the
importance of the linear arrangement of the NP's two components led to including
among modifiers the determinative possessive case of nouns (on the basis of the alternation *the theories of Bernstein / Bernstein's theories*).

2.2 Among the noun phrases registered in the section on this topic, modified NPs
and simple noun phrases were represented almost equally. In the group of modified
noun phrases fourteen contain different recurrent heads: *work* (or its contextual synonym), *process, education, system, failure, problem, children, language, vocabulary, term,
people, years, version* and *variant*. However, not all of them also contain identical modifiers. The point at issue is best illustrated by the first of these noun phrases, *Bernstein's work*.

(11) *The work of Basil Bernstein*$_{a1}$ has sometimes been referred to as '*a theory of educational failure*'$_{b1}$. This seems to me misleading … because *Bernstein's theory*$_{a2}$ is *a theory about society*$_{b2}$ … Nevertheless, it is perhaps inevitable that *Bernstein's work*$_{a3}$
should be best known through its application to educational problems … Something has gone wrong … with the language; and the source of it is to be found *in
Bernstein's work*$_{a4}$—even though the various forms in which it is mooted often bear
little relation to *Bernstein's ideas*$_{a5}$ (101–102).
[… If language is the key factor, the primary channel, in socialization, and if the
form taken by the socialization process is (in part) responsible for educational

---

4   As shown in Chapter 24, one of the constraints on noun modification in fiction is the frequent occurrence of
    noun phrases whose heads are proper nouns (personal names), i.e. a class of head nouns that generally do not
    favour modification. This also applies to another frequent realization form of noun phrases in fiction, personal
    pronouns.

failure, then language is to blame.] … The language failure theory is sometimes referred to *Bernstein's work*$_{a6}$ … language failure is offered both as an interpretation of *Bernstein's theories*$_{a7}$ and as an alternative to them (102).

The head word *work* recurs in 4 instances (11_{a1}, 11_{a3}, 11_{a4}, 11_{a6}); 3 instances contain a referential (contextual) synonym: *ideas* (11_{a5}), *theory* (11_{a2}), *theories* (11_{a7}). This noun phrase is the global theme of Chapter 5 *The significance of Bernstein's work for sociolinguistic theory*. Within the chapter it constitutes the hypertheme of the introductory part (first two pages: 101–102). The middle part of the chapter is concerned with the theory of language failure, a notion sometimes referred to Bernstein's work. Through this connection the language failure theory constitutes a derived theme of the global theme. In the concluding part (105–107) it is reconsidered in the light of Bernstein's work (ideas), which is reflected in the recurrence of noun phrases reiterating both components of the global theme.

(12) But, reconsidering in the light of *Bernstein's work*$_{1}$, especially his more recent thinking, we can see that the question 'deficit or difference?' is the wrong question. (105)…What *Bernstein's work*$_{2}$ suggests is that there may be differences in the relative orientation of different social groups towards the various functions of language in given contexts … There is evidence in *Bernstein's work*$_{3}$ that different social groups or subcultures place a high value on different orders of meaning. (106) … Language is central to *Bernstein's theory*$_{4}$; (107)

Considering the FSP structure of the noun phrase from the viewpoint of context-dependence/ independence, both components are given since the phrase denotes the global theme of the chapter, presented in the chapter's title, *The significance of Bernstein's work for sociolinguistic theory*. However, as the global theme *Bernstein's work* moves through the text, its distributional field changes. Although basically the relative degree of communicative dynamism of context-dependent elements is determined by the semantic factor, as in the case of context-independent structures, other factors also play a role. In general, the semantic factor assigns a higher degree of communicative dynamism to the modifying element, in this case to the possessive determiner, since it specifies (narrows) the meaning of the head noun. This is reflected in the realization form of the noun phrase when it occurs for the first time in the body of the text. The specifying component appears in the form of a prepositional phrase in postmodification, in accordance with the final placement of the focal element within the noun phrase. It is to be noted that it contains an additional novel feature, Bernstein's first name, which is not derivable from the preceding linguistic context: *The work of Basil Bernstein* (11_{a1}). Once a textual theme denoted by a modified noun phrase is introduced in the form that reflects its FSP structure, i.e. with the modifier in postposition, in the subsequent occurrences its givenness is indicated by a shift from the postmodifying to the premodifying form. In other words, the structure with premodification functions as a textual indicator of the givenness of the concept; it signals its occurrence in the previous context, cf. (11) *Bernstein's theory*$_{a2}$, *Bernstein's work*$_{a3}$, etc., (12) *Bernstein's work*$_1$, *Bernstein's theory*$_4$, etc. However, in the successive occurrences of the global theme *Bernstein's work* the degree of CD carried by the two components displays a shift from the possessive case to the head noun reflected in stronger word stress on the latter (*work/ theory, theories/ ideas*). This is presumably due to a higher degree of activation of the referent of the possessive case, the name of Bernstein naturally also occurring elsewhere throughout the text. Moreover, the denominations of the global theme *work/theory, theories/ideas*, though broadly synonymous, present the notion from different points of view, and may acquire semantic significance resulting in contrast, cf. (11) *Bernstein's work*$_{a4}$ and *Bernstein's ideas*$_{a5}$.

As regards the role of the distributional subfield of the noun phrase within the higher distributional field of the clause, the FSP function of the noun phrase is determined by the factors operating on the higher clausal level, its own distributional subfield being in this respect only a potentially contributive factor.[5] Accordingly, the noun phrase occurs both in the theme, cf. e.g. (11$_{a2}$), (11$_{a3}$), (12$_2$); (12$_4$) in sentence-final position; and in the rheme (11$_{a4}$), (12$_1$); the only form with postposition occurs in the theme, cf. (11$_{a1}$). There is one instance of potentiality due to the extent of synonymy of the head nouns in *Bernstein's work* (11$_{a4}$) and *Bernstein's ideas* (11$_{a5}$). If *ideas* in (11$_{a5}$) are interpreted as contrasting with *work* in (11$_{a4}$), they are disengaged from context dependence and acquire rhematic function (if regarded as a separate element at the clause level); however, if regarded as synonymous, i.e. as reiterating the concept, they belong to the theme.[6]

This only confirms the subordinate status of the FSP structure of the noun phrase in the higher, clausal communicative field where the NP's FSP function is determined by the interplay of all the FSP factors. On the level of the noun phrase the configuration of postposition of the modifier at its first occurrence and anteposition in the subsequent occurrence(s), which reflects, respectively, its context independence and dependence, resembles the simple thematic progression at the clause level. In the clausal distributional field simple thematic progressions are characterized by the occurrence of the same item as the rheme in one clause and as the theme in the clause that follows (cf. Daneš 1974: 118–19), the sentence position of the items being largely in agreement with the respective FSP function. On the phrasal level a parallel may be seen in the first occurrence of a context-independent modifier in postmodifcation signalling its rhematic function, and subsequently in pre-modification which indicates its thematization.

Apart from the noun phrase *Bernstein's work*, recurrence of a noun phrase in which the same modifier appears with the same head both in pre- and postmodification, the

---

5   Cf. Firbas (1992: 32–33), who demonstrates the subordinate role of the distributional subfield of the noun phrase in the FSP structure of the higher clausal field, but also draws attention to the potential role of complex and heterogeneous NP structure in causing ambiguous assignment of FSP functions to the clause elements (instances of potentiality).

6   This also being a case of syntactic potentiality, the noun phrase *to Bernstein's ideas* (11$_{a5}$) can be interpreted as postmodification of the preceding NP *little relation*, in which case it is a component of the rheme whether disengaged from context dependence or context-dependent.

first text sample displayed only one other example, *process of transmission/transmission process*. Its realization form follows the pattern outlined above, cf.

(13) it is a theory of the nature and *processes of cultural transmission*, and of the essential part that is played by language therein. Education is one of the forms taken by *the transmission process* (101)

Though retrievable from the immediately preceding context, *the transmission process* is disengaged from context dependence by the factor of selection: the theory is concerned with two aspects of cultural transmission, the processes through which cultural transmission takes place and its nature. Nevertheless, the modification structure *transmission process* indicates that the concept has occurred before.

To these examples may be added (14) in which the heads are related by the relationship of a part (*channel*) to the whole (*process*). Also this example follows the pattern outlined above.

(14) If language is the key factor, *the primary channel, in socialization*, and if the form taken by *the socialization process* is (in part) responsible for educational failure, then language is to blame; (102)

This pattern, which indicates the shift from context independence to context dependence by a different realization form of a recurrent modifier, is a different and more general case insofar as context dependence results from previous occurrence of the same element as a component of another syntactic structure. In general, any element in any syntactic function induces context dependence through being reiterated in whatever form or function, cf. (15):

(15) *Education* is one of the forms taken by the transmission process, and must inevitably be a major channel for persistence and change; but there are other channels—and *the education system itself* is shaped by the social structure. (101)

Context dependence resulting from the content of a whole stretch of text, rather than from previous occurrence of a particular item, can be demonstrated by an instance of a rare realization form, a complex premodifier. As shown by all preceding examples, premodifiers mostly have a simple, univerbal structure. Example (16) displays a complex premodifier constituted by a noun that is itself premodified, i.e. the premodification structure involves two dependency levels:

(16) [If language is the key factor, the primary channel in socialization, and if the form taken by the socialization process is (in part) responsible for educational failure, then language is to blame; *there must be something wrong about the language of the children who fail in school.* So the reasoning goes. Either their language is deficient in some way, or, if not, then it is so different from the 'received' language of the

school (and by implication, of the community) that it is as if it was deficient—it acts as a barrier to successful learning and teaching.] So we find *two main versions of the 'language failure' theory*, a 'deficit' version and a 'difference' version. *The language failure theory* is sometimes referred to Bernstein's work... (102)

Example (16) contains the complex premodifier *language failure* twice, first in inverted commas. The concept of educational failure due to language is built up by the preceding context, but is not yet established as a term. This presumably motivates the use of inverted commas at its first occurrence. At the second occurrence the concept is presented as fully established. It may not be incidental that at the clause level it first occurs as a component of the rheme, whereas in the second occurrence it constitutes the theme.

However, it is to be noted that even a modifier structurally construable both in pre- and postmodification may not follow the pattern demonstrated above. In (17) *failure*, though context dependent, appears in postmodification.

(17) Bernstein does not claim to be providing a total explanation of the causes *of educational failure*: he is offering an interpretation of one aspect of it, the fact that *the distribution of failure* is not random but follows certain known and sadly predicable patterns ... (101)

The discussion in this section may be concluded by characterizing the examined pattern as a textual device which within the given constraints and with the status of a tendency rather than that of a consistently applied principle serves to develop textual topics and subtopics through its changing form.

2.3 This tendency is also shown in the second source text, drawn from Chapter 8, *Language in urban society*. Example (18) duplicates the pattern illustrated by (11).

(18) The modern development of urban dialectology is due largely to *the innovations of one linguist William Labov*, who first took linguistics into the streets of New York ... Labov very soon found that the inhabitants of a metropolis are united much more by their linguistic attitudes and prejudices, ... than by their own speech habits, ... *Labov's subjects* showed striking agreement in their ratings of recorded utterances... (155)

More importantly, the second source text was chosen to demonstrate the changing FSP function of a recurrent modifier, due to its being disengaged from context dependence by one of the context-disengaging factors (Firbas, 1995)[7]. From this viewpoint, of special interest is the treatment of the global theme of the chapter, urban speech, which upon being resumed in the middle of the examined section displays the modi-

---

7   Specified as selection, contrast, identification, purposeful repetition and summarizing effect (Firbas 1995: 22).

fier, disengaged from context dependence by contrast, in postmodification indicating its context-independence. In the successive occurrences the modifier follows the described pattern and moves in adjectival form to anteposition.

(19) [... by the time dialects began to be systematically studied, this trend towards linguistic divergence has been replaced in these rural communities by a trend towards convergence. The younger speakers no longer focused on the village, and so in their speech they were already moving away from the more highly differentiated forms of the village dialect.] (155)
It was not until the 1960s that serious interest came to be directed towards *the speech of the cities*. The modern development of *urban dialectology* is due largely to the innovations of one linguist ... *In an urban context* the classical speech community model soon breaks down. (155)

Here the disengagement from context dependence follows from the content of the preceding paragraphs which deal with rural speech as the closest approximation to the concept of a speech community. In this context *speech community* also appears as a complex premodifier, its context dependence persevering through a retrievability span of 24 clauses (cf. *speech community model* on p. 155 ← *speech community notion* on p. 154). In the case of *speech community notion* the retrievability span of the complex premodier does not exceed eight clauses (cf. *a speech community* [154] → *this* [154] → *the speech community notion* [154]).

Premodification by the adjective *urban* in the successive occurrences raises the question why the noun *city* is not used here, as it is in the opening paragraph, though construed with other head nouns, cf. (20).

(20) *A city* is a place *of talk* ... If one listens to *city talk*, one hears constant reference to the institutions, the times and the places ...characteristic of *city life*. (154)

Two factors appear to be at play here, semantics and style. In (19) in the case of *urban dialectology* premodification by *city* is ruled out not only semantically but also by the terminological status of the whole noun phrase. In the case of *urban context*, which is a free combination, *city* is conceivable, but semantically vaguer than *urban*, which moreover better fits the tenor of this part of the text. The operation of the stylistic factor is most noticeable at the beginning of the chapter. When first introduced in the opening paragraph, cf. (20), the topic of the chapter is presented in non-technical language, but as the concept is being elaborated, the discussion becomes more technical and the tenor shifts to strictly academic, which involves the use of terms and more precise formal synonyms.

The opening paragraph of the chapter is of interest for another point, viz. the relation between the title and the opening sentence of the chapter. Both deal with the concepts of *language* and *city*, but the functional perspective is reversed, cf. (21). In the nominal field of the title *language* constitutes the theme, its postmodifier operates as the rheme and the most dynamic element of the whole phrase is the premodifier of the noun in the postmodifying prepositional phrase, the adjective *urban*. In the clausal field of the first two sentences the concept of the *city* is the starting point, the theme, and the information structure is perspective to *language*, which constitutes the rheme. In the first sentence this is achieved with the aid of an added locative element, *place*. In the second sentence *language* is disengaged from context dependence through the factor of purposeful repetition.

(21) Language in urban society.
   A city is a place of talk. It is built and held together by language. (154)

This reversal again evokes the pattern of a simple thematic progression in that the rheme of the communicative field of the title becomes the theme of the opening sentence, and as is frequently the case, launches a progression with constant theme. The only special feature here is that the theme of the title constitutes the rheme proper of both sentences, which in both occurs in the final position.

The last example to be discussed in this section illustrates the shifts in the nominal distributional field reflecting the contextual status of the modifier in its realization form.

(22) If we think of the inhabitants of an old-established European village, they probably did form some sort of communication network: in Littleby$_1$, or Kleinstadt or Malgorod, strangers were rare ... in a rural context *the 'speech community' notion* works reasonably well. *'The dialect of Littleby$_2$'* can be taken, and by consent is taken, to refer to the highly differentiated form *of Littleby speech$_3$*, that which is most clearly set apart from *the speech of the neighbouring villages$_4$*. (154)

Here although *Littleby* is mentioned in the immediately preceding relevant context (22)$_1$, it appears as context-independent in the postmodification of the head *dialect* (22)$_2$, which is also retrievable from the preceding sentence. While *Littleby* is disengaged from context dependence by the factor of selection (cf. *Littleby*, or *Kleinstadt* or *Malgorod*), the whole noun phrase introduces a novel feature by bringing the two elements into relation in construing them as one unit. The second occurrence of the noun phrase, with the coreferential head noun *speech* (*speech* (22)$_3$ ↔ *dialect* (22)$_2$), displays the now familiar pattern, while the last occurrence in this passage (22)$_4$ demonstrates a prototypical correspondence between the basic distribution of CD and the grammatical order. The whole noun phrase is disengaged from context dependence by contrast, with the most dynamic element conveying a novel feature presented in postmodification.

A point that emerges from this section is the role of the decontextualizing factors in the development of textual subtopics.

3. In conclusion the registered types of nominal distributional fields and their realization forms are considered with respect to their respective representation in the two text samples.

According to the account of the nominal distributional field given in 1.1, in general the more dynamic element is the modifier. This applies to instances where both components of the modification structure are context-independent irrespective of the realization form. In the case of premodification, the linear arrangement acts counter to the increasing degree of communicative dynamism. As premodification accounts for about a half of all modification structures (cf. the figures for the adjective in the two Tables), the most frequent modification structure displays disagreement with the FSP structure. In the case of postmodification, linearity and final position of the rhematic element are in agreement. Here the relevant realization form is the prepositional phrase, whose representation shows it to be the second basic type. This configuration of the nominal distributional field can be changed only by the contextual factor, where the modifier is context-dependent and the head noun context-independent. Then the head noun becomes the rheme and the modifier is thematicized. If both components are context-dependent, the semantic factor acts in favour of the modifier, as in the case of context independence.

As was shown in 2.1, the realization form appears to come into a play in the case of recurrent modified noun phrases where the modifier has alternative forms for pre- and postmodification. In this case there is a tendency for the modifier to occur in postmodification at the first occurrence of the noun phrase and shift to premodification when the modified noun phrase is reiterated. The respective FSP functions of the modifier and the head noun remain the same insofar as a higher degree of CD is carried by the modifier, but the role of the noun phrase in the text build-up is shown to have changed, the shift to the premodifying form of the modification structure indicating the NP's previous occurrence, and hence its context dependence.

In 2.2 the realization form and FSP structure was observed also in the case of modified NPs with only one recurrent component. A novel point noted here was the role

Table 1: Bernstein's work

	Adjective	39
Premodification	Noun	7
	Possessive case	5
	Prepositional phrase	18
Postmodification	Finite clause	19
	Nonfinite clause	3
Post- and premodification		19
Total		**110**

Table 2: Language in urban society*

	Adjective	40
Premodification	Noun	6
	Possessive case	1
	Prepositional phrase	21
Postmodification	Finite clause	20
	Nonfinite clause	5
Post- and premodification		19
Total		**112**

*In this text the count includes the noun phrases on pages 155–156.

of factors disengaging recurrent items from context dependence, thus serving to develop textual subtopics.

As regards changes in the basic distributional nominal field due to the contextual factor, they were found to be rare: a configuration of a context-dependent thematic modifier and a context-independent rhematic head noun was observed in less than ten instances. Compare (17), noted before, and the followings examples:

(23) So we find two main versions *of the 'language failure' theory*$_1$, a 'deficit' version and a 'difference' version; ... The language failure theory is sometimes referred to Bernstein's work and he has even been held responsible for *the deficit version of the theory*$_2$. ... The fact that language failure is offered both as an interpretation of *Bernstein's theories*$_3$ and as *an alternative to them*$_4$ shows how complex the issues are and how easily they become clouded. (102)

The context inducing the context dependence of the postmodifier *the 'language failure' theory* in (23)$_1$ is given in (16). The head noun *two main versions*, though derivable from the immediately preceding context, is disengaged from context dependence by the factor of the summarizing effect. Similarly, the head noun in (23)$_2$, *the deficit version*, though present in the preceding context, is decontextualized through the contrast with respect to *a difference version*; the context dependence of the postmodifier *of the theory* is here so highly activated that it appears in a reduced form: *theory = language failure theory*. In the case of (23)$_3$ the context dependence of the postmodifier *Bernstein's theories*, in the absence of decontextualizing factors, follows from its constituting the hypertheme of the whole chapter; in (23)$_4$ its context dependence results from the immediately preceding context and is reflected in its pronominal form. The head nouns *interpretation* and *alternative* are not only irretrievable from the context, but moreover contrast with each other.

The only other example of a rhematic head and thematic postmodifier is very similar, cf.

(24) ... there are *two variants of the theory* and possibly *a third* ... (102)

Here the postmodifier *of the theory* represents the same use as in (23)$_2$, i.e. it is co-referential with *language failure theory*, this relationship being again indicated by the anaphoric definite article and the high degree of activation by the NP's reduced form.

The only instance of a context dependent premodifier (if *enough* is classed as one) was found in (25):

(25) ... not *enough vocabulary*, not *enough grammar*, and ... not *enough meanings*... (102)

It can thus be concluded that even as it moves through a text, the modified noun phrase largely preserves its basic distributional field with a rhematic modifier and a thematic head, irrespective of the form of realization. The rare distributional field containing a thematic modifier and a rhematic head appears to be due to the configuration of a context-dependent modifier with a novel head or a head disengaged from context dependence by one of the decontextualizing factors. The realization form appears to play a role in the case of recurrent modified noun phrases whose modifier has both a premodifying and a postmodifying form. In this case there is a tendency for the noun phrase to be construed with postmodification at the first occurrence and premodification when reiterated. Being based on a small sample, these findings are only a first probe and need to be tested by further study.

SOURCES

Halliday, M. A. K. *Language as a Social Semiotic*. London: Edward Arnold, 1978.
Jirotka, Z. *Saturnin*. Prague: František Borový, 1943.
Jirotka, Z. *Saturnin*. Translated by Mark Corner. Prague: Karolinum Press, 2003.
Lawrence, D. H. *Women in Love*. London: Penguin Popular Classics, 1996 (1st ed. 1921).
Lawrence, D. H. *Ženy milující*. Translated by Martin Hilský. Prague: Odeon, 1982.
Vančura, V. *Rozmarné léto*. Translated by Mark Corner, *A Summer of Caprice*. Prague: Karolinum Press, 2006.

V. STYLE

23. TEXTUAL LINKS AS INDICATORS
OF DIFFERENT FUNCTIONAL STYLES

First published in *Prague Studies in English* 21, *Acta Universitatis Carolinae, Philologica* 2, 1996 (issued 1997), 113–123.

0. This chapter deals with overt devices of textual cohesion in regard to their capacity for acting as stylistic markers.[1] It aims at showing that textual links differ not only in the representation of the basic types in different functional styles, but that there are also differences in particular items and uses where different styles display comparable representation of the same type of textual link.

1. Of the different textual links attention is paid to those which are usually treated in hypersyntax, i.e. intersentential ties of a grammatical character.[2] These include devices of coreference and pronominalization (which largely coincide), ellipsis and conjunction, the last being on the borderline between grammar and lexis. All these points also occur within the sentence, but here they contribute not to textual but to internal sentence cohesion, and hence are left out of account.

1.1 The conception of grammatical devices of textual cohesion is in general based on Halliday and Hasan (1976), although no distinction is made between what they call reference, viz. coreference and substitution. The reason for treating the two points together is that in practice they largely overlap: both involve a relation between two items, mostly anaphoric between an antecedent and an expression replacing it, prevalently a proform (in the case of coreference the proform may also occur first and point cataphorically forward in the text). They differ mainly in that coreference, apart from proforms, also makes use of definite determiners with noun phrases which may be related to the antecedent only semantically or pragmatically and expressed by differ-

---

1   For the concept of stylistic markers, see Enkvist (1964: 41–43 and 1973: 122–126).
2   For a contrastive treatment of this point in English and Czech, see Dušková (1984).

ent lexical means, whereas substitution invariably involves pronominalization[3] and need not necessarily be coreferential. There is also a difference in the possibility of repeating the antecedent, which is largely confined to substitution, while in the case of coreference it is an exception rather than the rule (especially within the sentence, cf. Quirk et al., 1985: 863–864).

1.1.1 Accordingly, the first stylistic marker under study is found in endophoric uses of personal pronouns and other substantival proforms (*one, the former, the latter*), possessives, demonstratives (both as determiners and as pronouns), other determiners (the definite article, *such*) and verbal, predicative, clausal and adverbial proforms (*do; do/be so; this, that, it; there, then, here*).

1.1.2 The second stylistic marker is constituted by ellipsis, which is conceived as an incomplete structure derived from a complete structure according to language-specific rules. In other words, ellipsis arises by rule-governed omission of certain elements which are present in the context and can be uniquely recovered. The underlying complete structure coexists alongside the elliptical one.[4] For example, [M: *Did you sleep well?*] X: *Would you expect me to* (sleep well)?[5] (Bond, 8)

Ellipsis is to be distinguished on the one hand from unfinished fragmentary sentences like [A: *I warn you.*] *I'll* … [N: *Go on. Go on.*] (Ayckbourn, 30–31), which are not subject to linguistic rules, being due to extraneous factors such as strong emotion, interruption, etc.; the other hand from utterances lacking regular sentence structure but complete in themselves, without the possibility of being uniquely "filled in" by some missing elements, e.g., *yes, no, all right*, vocatives, greetings, interjections, as well as instances like [S: *Norman.*] N: *What?* [… S: *Will you try … not to start any more scenes or arguments?*] N: *Me?*[6] (Ayckbourn, 32).

1.1.3 As regards the third stylistic marker, conjunction, the present analysis is restricted to what is termed conjuncts in Quirk et al. (1972: 520–523; 1985: 631–647). Conjuncts represent a class of sentence adverbials with the function of conjoining different independent units, in this case sentences or larger stretches of the text. At the same time they explicate the semantic relation obtaining between the two units. Syntactically, conjuncts are distinguished from other (sometimes homonymous) adverbial elements of the sentence by standing outside its structure (i.e. they are not integrated into the syntactic relations of the sentence).

---

3   In Halliday and Hasan (1976: 310) the term pronominalization is confined to personal reference within the sentence, which is the usual conception of pronominalization in generative transformational studies. Pronominalization is here regarded as an obligatory process, which presumably hinders the use of the term from referring to the same process across sentence boundaries, where it becomes optional. In textlinguistic literature pronominalization is largely included among the points treated within the framework of a text grammar (cf., e.g., Rieser 1978; Kuno 1978).

4   This conception essentially corresponds to what is termed standard ellipsis in Quirk et al. (1985: 885–889). Another clear type of ellipsis, represented by instances like (I) *Can't find either of them* (Ayckbourn, 38). (Did) *Somebody call?* (Ayckbourn, 37), does not fall within the scope of the examined suject matter, since it is confined to intrasentential structure.

5   The context of the point being demonstrated is presented in square brackets. The omitted elements in an elliptical sentence are added, unitalicized, in round brackets.

6   For a more detailed treatment of irregular sentences and nonsentences, see Dušková (1991).

1.2 The three stylistic markers were investigated in four samples of text representing two functional styles, informal conversation (samples C_1 and C_2) as reflected in two contemporary plays, and scientific writing (S_1 linguistics and S_2 psychology) (see Sources). The temporal span of the samples does not exceed ten years, all four having first appeared between 1972 and 1982.

As regards the measure of length for obtaining comparable stretches of text, a measure that readily presented itself was the number of sentences. However, even a cursory glance at the two kinds of samples shows that the units constituting conversation and scientific writing are very different. While the latter consists almost exclusively of regular sentences, the former contains a considerable number of what Quirk et al. (1985: 838–853) call irregular sentences and nonsentences, of the kind illustrated in 1.1.2 Consequently, recourse was taken to the number of words, determined so as to provide at least a hundred sentences, which resulted in samples of 3,500 words each.

2. The distribution of regular sentences, irregular sentences and nonsentences is shown in Table 1. The column "regular sentences" presents the number of sentences with regular sentence structure, delimited by an initial capital letter and final full stop. That is, colons and semicolons were regarded as intrasentential punctuation marks. It is worth noting that in scientific writing semicolons are fairly common (21 in S_1 and 19 in S_2, the respective number of colons being 4 and 2). On the other hand in the two conversation samples these punctuation marks are almost entirely lacking (there is only 1 colon in C_1).

The conception of ellipsis, unfinished sentences and nonelliptical irregular or nonsentence structures has been explained in 1.1.2.

2.1 The figures in Table 1 show that scientific writing and conversation differ both in sentence length and in sentence structure. The former is characterized by a much greater sentence length, the average number of words per sentence in S_1 being 33.9 and in S_2 26.1 as compared with 6.9 in C_1 and 6.0 in C_2. As regards sentence structure, scientific writing appears to be much more homogeneous insofar as it is composed almost exclusively of regular sentences; the eight nonsentence structures are found only in headings of sections (e.g., *Introduction, Iconic Memory, Text and Meaning*, etc.). In conversation, on the other hand, the percentage of irregular sentences and nonsentences appears to be considerable (14.5 in C_1 and 35.3 in C_2).

2.2 Table 2 shows the overall distribution of the three stylistic markers in the four samples. In both functional styles the most frequent cohesive tie is coreference and substitution (76.1% in scientific writing and 69.3% in conversation). Ellipsis ranks second in conversation (20.9%) but last in scientific writing (1.5%), the order of conjuncts being also reversed: 22.4% in scientific writing and 9.8% in conversation.

2.2.1 The greatest difference is found in the representation of ellipsis, which appears to be characteristic of conversation, all occurrences except 4 (i.e. 95.7%) being provided by the conversation samples. Moreover, there is a basic difference in the type of ellipsis found in S_1 on the one hand and in C_1 and C_2 on the other. All instances of ellipsis in scientific writing represent ellipsis within the noun phrase of the following kind:

[... *selections in these three areas of meaning potential.*] *The ideational* (area of meaning potential) *represents the potential of the system for the speaker as an observer* (Halliday, 127). Apart from the elliptical noun phrase, the four sentences listed under ellipsis in Table 2 have regular sentence structure; therefore, they do not appear in the column of elliptical sentences in Table 1. On the contrary, in the instances of ellipsis in conversation elliptical construction mostly results in irregular sentence structure, regardless of whether the ellipsis occurs in the utterance of the same speaker or in the response of his interlocutor, cf. [*I'll be glad when you've all gone home.*] *I really will* (Ayckbourn, 30). [R: *It's not your back, is it?*] S: *Not at the moment* (Ayckbourn, 34). On the whole, ellipsis in conversation is slightly more frequent in responses than in the utterances of the same speaker (47 as against 41 instances).

2.2.2 The devices of coreference and substitution are presented in Table 3.

The figures for verbal and adverbial proforms are too low to allow generalization, but even so, the occurrence of *here* in scientific writing alone is presumably not incidental. It should be pointed out that *here* is listed among adverbial proforms on formal grounds, its typical function in scientific writing being to refer summarizingly to a stretch of text, e.g., [*Consider a traditional story as it is told by a mother to her child at bedtime.*] *Here the context of situation is on two levels* (Halliday, 125). Similarly the occurrence of verbal proforms only in conversation appears to indicate at least a tendency for this point to characterize conversation rather than scientific writing.

A major difference between conversation and scientific writing concerns exophoric vs. endophoric use of forms that have both these functions. Although exophoric uses have not been registered because of having no cohesive force, each item had to be considered with respect to qualifying or not qualifying as a textual link. In conversation many exophoric uses are found among demonstratives and adverbs with primary deictic function, e.g., *You want these mats?* (Ayckbourn, 34) *You go up the end there* (Ayckbourn, 38). *She lives down here now* (Bond, 6). Similarly *this evening, this house,* etc. There is also exophoric reference by personal pronouns,[7] e.g., [*Norman goes to the door and passes Reg coming in. 'Evening, Reg, old sport.' Norman slaps Reg on the back and exits.*] Reg: *What's up with him?* (Ayckbourn, 33) Here *him* refers exophorically to Norman.

In scientific writing, on the other hand, exophoric reference is rare. Apart from instances like *This chapter* (Coltheart, 64) there is exophoric use of *one* referring to the general human agent: *... if one is focussing attention on the text* (Halliday, 127).

Moreover, there are also differences in endophoric uses of pronouns and determiners. In scientific writing *he* and *his* are often used to refer to a generic person regardless of sex, e.g., to nouns like *subject, speaker, child.*

Another typical feature of scientific writing is clausal reference by *this* (25 occur-

---

7   The correctness of the exophora/endophora distinction drawn by Halliday and Hasan has been (at least partly) questioned by Brown and Yule (1987: 199–201), who suggest that "the processor establishes a referent in his mental representation of the discourse and relates subsequent references to that referent back to his mental representation, rather than to the original verbal expression in the text" (200–201). The complexity of the endophora/exophora distinction in the material of this Chapter appeared mainly in instances which are vague in this respect.

rences in S_1 and S_2 as against 2 in C_1 and C_2), e.g., *Nevertheless, they could report virtually all the items in the indicated row. This showed conclusively that ...* (Coltheart, 65). Where the same stretch of text is referred to twice, the first reference is made by *this*, the second by *it: What may be happening is that the subject begins to process all the material as soon as possible, but when the cue occurs he switches to the cued material and selectively processes it. This is not consistent with von Wright's observation, but it is consistent with the results of ...* (Coltheart, 67).

A similar pattern is found in consecutive reference to a noun phrase: *Are these* (= Hymes' categories) *to be thought of as descriptive categories ...? Or are they predictive concepts providing a means for ...?* (Halliday, 129) This pattern shows the increasing degree of activation of the concept being referred to by a 'stronger' form of the first referring expression and a 'weaker' one of the second.

On the contrary, in conversation clausal reference is predominantly realized by *that* and *it* (38 and 41 occurrences, respectively), cf. S: *No, I don't hate you, Norman.* N: *Thank you. Thank you for that, at least* (Ayckbourn, 32). *You've resigned yourself as if you were meeting fate. It's not like you* (Bond, 10).

The reference of *it* is occasionally vague: it is not clear what exactly is being referred to, whether the preceding context, or a part of it, or the situation of utterance, e.g., [R: *You've not got the shakes again, have you?* S: *You ought to know me by now, Reg. I can't bear these sort of atmospheres ...* R: *Well, sit down. Have a rest for a second. ...* S: *How can I possibly sit down?* R: *All right, stand up. Suit yourself. ...* S: *We're going to need two more chairs. ...* R: *All right, I'll look for chairs. Don't worry, keep calm.*] *It'll be all right* (Ayckbourn, 34).

Compare also the explicit enquiry (used for comical effect) about what is being referred to: [A: *Oh, yes, they* (= the chairs) *fell to bits ... Everything does that in this house. Wood worm or old age.* R: *You should get that treated.*] A: *Old age, you mean?* (Ayckbourn, 34) The following example again illustrates vague reference [R: *Somebody's saucepan seems to be getting rather agitated out there.*] S: *Did you turn it down?* (Ayckbourn, 35) The second speaker obviously refers to the burner of the gas ring on which the contents of the saucepan are cooking.

Almost all examples of coreference in the four samples represent anaphoric relation. An example of cataphora occurs in C_2: *It was rather unfortunate. Believe it or not, I was attempting unsuccessfully to give him lessons on how to woo you* (Ayckbourn, 36). Another appears in S_2 after a colon.

2.2.3 The last point under discussion is summarized in Table 4. With a few exceptions the figures for particular conjuncts are too low to provide conclusive evidence. The occurrence of a particular conjunct only in one sample is largely incidental (e.g., *consequently* in S_2 and not in S_1, *hence* in S_1 and not in S_2, *otherwise* only in C_1, but there are 4 occurrences in S_2 after a semicolon, etc.).

The only safe conclusion to be drawn is that conjuncts are more characteristic of scientific writing than of conversation, which is due to the character of scientific communication: the need for clarity and unambiguousness calls for explicit expression of all relevant semantic relations, including intersentential ones.

The distribution of conjuncts in the four samples presented in Table 4 largely confirms the stylistic characteristics assigned to particular conjuncts in grammars and dictionaries (e.g. *nevertheless, hence, consequently* formal, *anyway, well, on top of everything* informal; *so* and *also* appear in both sets of material).

The most frequent conjunct in conversation *well* (16 occurrences) is a polyfunctional device whose conjunctive function awaits detailed investigation. In Quirk et al. (1972) it is treated as an initiator distinguished from, and hence not included among, conjuncts (274). In Quirk et al. (1985), however, it does receive the status of conjunct (635–636, 1469–1470). Similarly *of course* is presented only as an attitudinal disjunct in Quirk et al. (1972: 675).

2.2.4 As regards the density of the cohesive ties under study, the absolute figures are higher for conversation than for scientific writing (420 and 264, respectively). However, if we consider the number of sentences in the four samples, even if limited to that of regular sentences, we find higher density in the two scientific samples. Table 5 shows the density of cohesive ties to be more than twice higher in scientific writing than in conversation (1.15 as against 0.52 cohesive ties per sentence). This is again a consequence of the character of scientific communication.

In both sets of samples a cohesive tie usually refers to the sentence that immediately precedes (in conversation it may also involve a change of the speaker). Occasionally, however, there are one or two intervening sentences, e.g., ... *you may not even care for the man. You've never really said one way or the other. We've always assumed you and Tom, Tom and you. Presumably you wouldn't have him round here at all if you didn't* (care for him) (Ayckbourn, 36).

The distribution of the ties is partly uneven in that a sentence may have more than one tie, e.g., *However, in attempting to find such an explanation ...* (Coltheart, 65). [X: *Are the telephones working? D: Yes.*] X: *They didn't two years ago* (Bond, 6). On the other hand all samples contain passages without the grammatical cohesive ties under consideration. For example:

A: *Where am I sitting? S: You're here, Tom. Sit here. R: Annie, you should be sitting here. You are the hostess* (Ayckbourn, 38).

It is characteristic of the adult language system that the text it engenders is not tied to the immediate scenario as its relevant environment. The context of situation of a text may be entirely remote from what is happening around the act of speaking or writing (Halliday, 125).

3. Summarizing the foregoing findings, grammatical cohesive ties, coreference and substitution, ellipsis, conjuncts, appear to have considerable capacity for indicating functional style. While ellipsis appears to characterize conversation, conjuncts are more frequent in scientific writing. Coreference and substitution display differences mainly in the means of clausal reference and in the treatment of sex distinctions. The density of cohesive ties appears to be significantly higher in scientific writing, which is presumably due to the character of scientific communication. The lower density of grammatical cohesive ties in conversation is in turn probably connected with frequent occasion for exophoric reference.

SOURCES

Ayckbourn, A. *The Norman Conquests, Table Manners* (Act II, pp. 29–40). London: French, 1975.

Bond, E. *Summer and Fables, Summer* (Act I, pp. 1–14). London: Methuen, 1982.

Coltheart, M. Visual information processing. In: *New Horizons in Psychology* 2. Harmondsworth: Penguin Books, 1980 (1st ed. 1972), 64–72.

Halliday, M. A. K. *Learning How to Mean—Explorations in the Development of Language.* London: Arnold, 1975, 123–131.

Table 1

| | Regular sentences | | Irregular sentences ad nonsentences | | | | | | | | Total | |
| | | | elliptical sentences | | unfinished sentences | | other irregular or non-sentence structures | | total | | | |
	abs.	%	abs.	%	abs.	%	abs.	%	abs.	%	abs.	%
S_1	100	97.1	–	–	–	–	3	2.9	3	2.9	103	100
S_2	129	96.3	–	–	–	–	5	3.7	5	3.7	134	100
total	229	96.6	–	–	–	–	8	3.4	8	3.4	237	100
C_1	430	85.5	28	5.6	2	0.4	43	8.5	73	14.5	503	100
C_2	372	64.7	60	10.4	16	2.8	127	22.1	203	35.3	575	100
total	802	74.4	88	8.1	18	1.7	170	15.8	276	25.6	1,078	100
total	1,031	78.4	88	6.7	18	1.7	178	13.5	284	21.6	1,315	100

Table 2

| | Coreference and substitution | | Ellipsis | | Conjuncts | | Total | |
	abs.	%	abs.	%	abs.	%	abs.	%
S_1	85	73.9	4	3.5	26	22.6	115	100
S_2	116	77.9	–	–	33	22.1	149	100
total	201	76.1	4	1.5	59	22.4	264	100
C_1	178	80.5	28	12.7	15	6.8	221	100
C_2	113	56.8	60	30.2	26	13.0	199	100
total	291	69.3	88	20.9	41	9.8	420	100

Table 3: Coreference and substitution

		S₁		S₂		total		C₁		C₂		total		total	
		abs.	%	abs.	%	abs.	%	abs.	%	abs.	%	abs.	%	abs.	%
substantival proforms	personal pronouns	21	4.3	12	2.4	33	6.7	105	21.4	50	10.1	155	31.5	188	38.2
	possessive pronouns	-	-	-	-	-	-	1	0.2	-	-	1	0.2	1	0.2
	demonstrative pronouns	8	1.6	1	0.2	9	1.8	1	0.2	6	1.3	7	1.5	16	3.3
	one	1	0.2	-	-	1	0.2	4	0.8	-	-	4	0.8	5	1.0
	the former the latter	2	0.4	-	-	2	0.4	-	-	-	-	-	-	2	0.4
coreferential determiners	demonstrative	14	2.9	33	6.7	47	9.6	4	0.8	2	0.4	6	1.2	53	10.8
	definite article	8	1.6	54	11.0	62	12.6	10	2.0	2	0.4	12	2.4	74	15.0
	possessive	5	1.0	2	0.4	7	1.4	11	2.2	1	0.2	12	2.4	19	3.8
	such	5	1.0	2	0.4	7	1.4	1	0.2	-	-	1	0.2	8	1.6
clausal proforms	this	16	3.3	9	1.8	25	5.1	1	0.2	1	0.2	2	0.4	27	5.5
	that	-	-	-	-	-	-	15	3.1	23	4.7	38	7.8	38	7.8
	it	2	0.4	1	0.2	3	0.6	17	3.5	24	4.9	41	8.4	44	9.0
verbal proforms	do	-	-	-	-	-	-	1	0.2	4	0.8	5	1.0	5	1.0
	be /do so	-	-	-	-	-	-	2	0.4	-	-	2	0.4	2	0.4
adverbial proforms	here	3	0.6	2	0.4	5	1.0	-	-	-	-	-	-	5	1.0
	there	-	-	-	-	-	-	3	0.6	-	-	3	0.6	3	0.6
	then	-	-	-	-	-	-	2	0.4	-	-	2	0.4	2	0.4
total		85	17.3	116	23.5	201	40.8	178	36.2	113	23.0	291	59.2	492	100.0

Table 4: Conjuncts

		S₁	S₂	total	C₁	C₂	total	total
concessive	however	3	9	12	–	–	–	1
	on the other hand	–	2	2	–	–	–	2
	nevertheless	–	1	1	–	–	–	1
	yet	–	–	–	1	–	1	1
	in any case	1	–	1	–	–	–	1
	anyway	–	–	–	2	1	3	3
resultive	thus	–	8	8	–	–	–	8
	consequently	–	1	1	–	–	–	1
	therefore	1	2	3	–	–	–	3
	hence	1	–	1	–	–	–	1
	so	3	–	3	2	2	4	7
	now	–	1	1	–	–	–	1
	of course	–	–	–	1	–	1	1
appositional	in other words	3	–	3	–	–	–	3
	for example	1	–	1	1	–	1	2
	that is to say	–	–	–	1	–	1	1
	in particular	–	1	1	–	–	–	1
enumerative	first of all	1	1	2	–	–	–	2
	firstly	–	1	1	–	–	–	1
	at first	1	–	1	1	–	1	2
	in the first place	2	–	2	–	1	1	3
	secondly	1	2	3	–	–	–	3
	in the second place	1	–	1	–	–	–	1
	thirdly	–	1	1	–	–	–	1
	later	1	–	1	–	–	–	1
reinforcing	also	2	1	3	1	1	2	5
	furthermore	–	1	1	–	–	–	1
	on top of everything	–	–	–	1	–	1	1
	inferential then	–	1	1	1	4	5	6
	otherwise	–	–	–	1	–	1	1

		S_1	S_2	total	C_1	C_2	total	total
transitional	well	–	–	–	2	14	16	16
	now	–	–	–	–	2	2	2
temporal transition	meanwhile	1	–	1	–	–	–	1
equative antithetic	in the same way	1	–	1	–	–	–	1
	on the one hand	1	–	1	–	–	–	1
	on the other hand	1	–	1	–	–	–	1

Table 5

	Number of regular sentences	Number of cohesive ties	Average number of cohesive ties per sentence
S_1	100	115	1.15
S_2	129	149	1.15
total	229	264	1.15
C_1	430	221	0.51
C_2	372	199	0.53
total	802	420	0.52

24. NOUN MODIFICATION IN FICTION AND ACADEMIC PROSE

First published in *Brno Studies in English. Discourse as Function*, Vol. 35/2, 2009, 29–51.

0. The last topic treated in this book is the occurrence, structural variety and semantics of modification of complex noun phrases, defined as NPs containing, in addition to a determiner and a head noun, one or more modifiers. Two sorts of texts were examined from these aspects, a sample of fiction (Ishiguro) and a sample of academic prose (Morris), see *Sources*. They are attached in the Appendix.[1] The results of an analysis of the two texts are confronted with the description of noun phrase modification in different text sorts as presented in representative grammars, in pursuit of uncovering some less investigated, potentially novel, albeit minor points which might contribute to the overall description. Admittedly, the findings of the analysis are limited both by the number of the samples and the number of excerpts. Moreover, authors' styles vary, especially in fiction, and so does the style in academic prose, in particular between different fields of study. Nevertheless where the differences are consistent with the character of the respective text sort, they can be ascribed some stylistic relevance.

1. The overall material comprises 510 noun phrases almost equally drawn from running text of the fiction sample (256 instances) and running text of academic prose (254 instances). All noun phrases, i.e. both with and without modification, were counted except nouns in complex prepositions of the type preposition + noun + preposition (e.g. *on behalf of, for the sake of* etc.) and nouns in fixed phrases (like *of course, for example*, etc.). Since the point under study was the structure of the noun phrase, nouns in the possessive case are included among modifiers, although they mostly operate as

---

1   In the appended texts noun phrases containing one noun are denoted successively by Arabic numerals (1, 2, 3, ...); noun phrases functioning as components of modification structures are marked by Arabic numerals and letters (1b, 1c, ...). Clausal modifiers (non-finite and finite) are denoted by small Roman numerals (i, ii, iii, iv, ...), and lower dependency levels are indicated by Greek letters (α, β, ...). The marking is given in square brackets after each noun.

determiners (cf. Quirk et al. 1985: 326). Accordingly, the concept of determiner is here limited to the articles and the determinative function of pronouns and quantifiers.

The material includes some noun phrases with non-substantival heads, mostly indefinite pronouns, numerals and demonstrative pronouns functioning as substantival proforms. These instances, generally regarded as noun phrases[2], were registered where the head was modified and noted as NPs with non-substantival heads. As regards non-substantival NPs without modification, they lack either defining feature of the type of NP here studied. Containing neither a determiner, nor a noun in their structure, they were left out of account, i.e. they are not included in the group of non-modified NPs. Although this structure is of interest from the viewpoint of which non-substantival heads allow modification and what modification types, this aspect was not followed because in the examined samples the structure is marginal.[3] Noun phrases with non-substantival heads are illustrated in (1).

(1) a. nothing objectionable (Ishiguro 89)
　　 b. one of my pupils who first brought it to my attention (Ishiguro 47)
　　 c. those who had not wished the house to pass out of the family (Ishiguro 115ib)

In the analysis a problem sometimes arose as to how to class a prepositional phrase following an object, or the subject in the existential construction. Some prepositional phrases in this position presented neither a clear-cut instance of postmodification, nor of an adverbial. In these cases the adopted solution is only one of the ways of dealing with the problem and other solutions may be preferred. Conveniently for the quantitative data, these instances are again statistically insignificant. Compare (2):

(2) There is a label [1] on a cage [2] at a certain zoo [2b] (Morris)

Is the prepositional phrase [2] to be regarded as a modifier of *a label* (There is a label located on a cage ...) or as an adverbial of place (on a cage there is a label ...); and similarly does *at a certain zoo* modify *the cage* (a cage which is at a zoo...) or are both prepositional phrases separate locative adverbials (At a zoo, on a cage, there is a label ...)? Or finally do they both successively postmodify the head noun (a label stuck on a cage located at a zoo)? As shown by the marking in square brackets, the solution adopted here is classing the two prepositional phrases as one locative adverbial in which the second specifies the first. The tests applied here were alternative word order *On a cage at a certain zoo there is label* and the question test (*where is there a label?*). As pointed out above and shown by the other alternative forms, instances of this kind are mostly indeterminate and may be treated differently.

2　According to Huddleston and Pullum (2002: 326ff), pronouns are a subcategory of nouns.
3　For example, there were no instances of adjectival heads, such as *the poor, the city poor*.

2. Noun phrases in the two samples under study were first grouped according to whether or not the head noun was modified. The respective figures are given in Tables 1 and 2.

Table 1: Realization forms of noun phrases: Ishiguro

Noun modification		
Nouns without modifiers	**91** (100%)	35.5%
Common nouns	81 (89%)	
Proper names	10 (11%)	
Nouns with modifiers	**165**	**64.5%**
Total	**256**	**100.0%**

Table 2: Realization forms of noun phrases: Morris

Noun modification		
Nouns without modifiers	**78** (100%)	30.7%
Common nouns	77	
Proper names	1	
Nouns with modifiers	**176**	**69.3%**
Total	**254**	**100.0%**

The figures in Tables 1 and 2 show more or less expectable results, viz. that the noun phrase in academic prose is more complex than that in fiction: in the former, noun phrases without modification are by 5% more frequent. However, when we take into account the proportion of the two groups of nouns subsumed under non-modified nouns, this distinction appears in a different light. While non-modified noun phrases in academic prose are almost exclusively accounted for by NPs with determiners, there being only one proper noun (a geographical name, for that matter, cf. *Africa*, Morris [8]), in fiction the proportion of proper names is much higher (10 instances, 11%). Evidently, this reflects the nature of fiction: all proper nouns are here personal names referring to the characters of the story being told. If proper nouns are subtracted, the representation of non-modified NPs in the two samples differs only by 1% (77 instances out of 254 [30.3%] in academic prose, and 81 out of 256 [31.6%] in fiction). The relatively high representation of proper names in fiction may play a role in the relatively lower representation of modified NPs in this sample insofar as modification of proper names is in general greatly restricted, and hence rare (the examined sample contains no instance of a modified proper name). Thus the only distinction between the two texts sorts emerging from the group of non-modified NPs is the relatively high representation of proper names as a feature of fiction. This is doubtless one of fiction's general features, more or less independent of the style of the author and the role of the narrator.

3. The second point of potential relevance for the present discussion concerns the realization forms of the modifiers. The forms found in the two samples are presented in Tables 3 and 4.

Table 3: Realization forms of modifiers: Ishiguro

Types of modification	Abs.	%
Adjective	71	36.4
Prepositional phrase	61	31.3
Relative clause	18	9.2
Converted noun	12	6.2
Possessive case	9	4.6
ed-participle	9	4.6
Gerund	5	2.6
ing-participle	4	2.1
Infinitive	2	1.0
Apposition	3	1.5
Adverb	1	0.5
Total	195	100.0

The differences in the totals between Tables 1 and 2 on the one hand, and Tables 3 and 4 on the other, are due to instances of multiple modification, i.e. noun phrases with one head noun modified by more than one modifier none of which contains an NP in its structure, cf. the examples listed under (3):

(3) a. the fine cedar gateway (Ishiguro 21) (adjective + converted noun)
   b. the special food of the district (Morris 43, 43b)
      (adjective + prepositional phrase)
   c. The great advantage we have when studying ... (Morris 64)
      (adjective + relative clause)

Table 4: Realization forms of modifiers: Morris

Types of modification	Abs.	%
Adjective	92	45.3
Prepositional phrase	55	27.1
ing-participle	12	5.9
Relative clause	12	5.9
Converted noun	9	4.4
Apposition	9	4.4
Gerund	6	2.9
Possessive case	3	1.6
ed-participle	2	1.0
Adverb	2	1.0
Infinitive	1	0.5
Total	203	100.0

3.1 The two realization forms ranking highest in both samples are the adjective and the prepositional phrase, 36.4% and 31.3% in Ishiguro, and 45.3% and 27.1 in Morris, respectively. These results are in agreement with the data in Biber et al.: "Common adjectives (i.e. non-participial adjectives) are the most common category of premodifiers in all registers" (1999: 589). "Prepositional phrases are by far the most common type of postmodification in all registers" (1999: 606). In the examined texts prepositional phrases were more frequently registered in fiction than in academic prose. Here Biber et al. do not offer comparable data, relative frequencies of occurrence being presented only for the different forms of pre- and postmodifiers separately. Similarly, the considerable difference between the representation of adjectives and prepositional phrases in fiction and academic prose (5% and 18%, respectively) cannot be related to comparable data in Biber et al. As regards the noticeably higher representation of adjectives in academic prose than in fiction, partly comparable data can be found in Figure 8.7 (Biber et al. 1999: 589), but the difference between the two registers in this respect does not appear to be so prominent.

3.1.1 In the academic sample, the higher representation of adjectival premodification may be partly accounted for by the recurrence of collocates of the descriptive adjective *new* +*form* (3 instances), *species* (3 instances), *squirrel(s)* (2 instances), *type* (one instance) in reference to the hypertheme of the passage. The adjective *new* has altogether 11 occurrences in the text, its use with other head nouns being also connected with the novelty feature of the hypertheme, cf. (4) a. and b.

(4) a. new form (Morris 22, 28, 51), new species (46, 55, 102), new squirrel(s) (35, 73), new type (45b)
b. new trend (23), new medium (138)

Another factor contributing to adjectival modification in the academic sample is the realization form of some zoological terms, which includes, in addition to the head noun, a classificatory adjective denoting a subclass of the species designated by the head noun. The adjective performs this function alone or in conjunction with other premodifiers, cf. the examples listed under (5):

(5) a. black-footed squirrel (Morris 9, 65), the African black-footed squirrel (60)
b. aquatic animals (146), human animal (67), human being (71), tailless great apes (83b), reptilian ancestors (119), the naked mole rat (144b)

While the recurrence of the adjective *new* is connected with the treatment of a new hypertheme and is derivable from the text build-up, the two-word structure of zoological terms is a noticeable terminological feature in general and may be ascribed stylistic relevance.

3.1.2 The relatively higher representation of adjectives in academic prose than in fiction is also apparent in instances of multiple premodification, the prevalence of this type in the former being commensurate with the overall predominance of adjectival premodification in this sample (15 vs. 10 instances). In the examined samples, apart from coordinated adjectives multiple premodification includes converted nouns, participles and the possessive case, cf. (6) a. and b.

(6) a. this old and hidebound family (Ishiguro 91), certain interesting rumours (Ishiguro 107); various other anatomical features (Morris 75d), their protective furry covering (Morris 117)
b. the city's most respected and influential men [Ishiguro 19]; a constant high body temperature (Morris 121b), a thick hairy, insulating coat (Morris 127b).

The fiction sample contained two instances of a coordination type characteristic of informal speech, viz. modification with *or so* to express approximation (cf. Quirk et al. 1985: 981). Compare (7).

(7) for a year or so (Ishiguro 44)

Two instances of multiple modification by adjectives deserve to be mentioned for displaying special features. Fiction provides an example of discontinuous adjectival premodification due to the insertion of a comment clause in the function of parenthetical disjunct (cf. Quirk et al. 1985: 1112–117), a configuration indicative of the style of fiction.

(8) a most curious—some may say—foolish procedure (Ishiguro 28)

The other instance of discontinuous modification, found in the academic sample, represents a case of a complex modification structure constituted by multiple adjectival coordination and multiple apposition. The discontinuity involves two of three coordinated adjectives, and the entire multiple apposition, cf. (9).

(9) a new species (Morris 46) would have evolved, separate and discrete, a unique form (46b) of life (46ba), a three hundred and sixty-seventh kind (46c) of squirrel (46ca)

As regards other instances of postposed adjectives, apart from obligatory postposition in the case of indefinite pronoun heads (cf. (1) a., altogether three instances) and two occurrences of the adjective *worth* (cf. (20) a.), the texts under study did not provide any examples.

3.1.3 Potential stylistic relevance was further sought in the semantics of the modifying adjectives. Following the semantic classification in Biber et al. (1999: 508–515), the adjectives were first classed as descriptors or classifiers, the distinction between the two groups consisting in the delimiting or restricting function with respect to a noun's referent in the case of classifiers, while descriptors prototypically denote such features as colour, size, weight, age, etc. Needless to say, semantic classification, whatever model may be used, is hardly ever univocal. Hence the quantitative data are of the more-or-less kind rather than representing exact figures. In consequence of the overall larger number of adjectival modifiers in the academic sample, all semantic groups number more examples in this text, the only measure of comparison thus being the relative representation of the different semantic groups within each sample.

According to the corpus findings in Biber et al. (1999: 510–511) evaluative descriptors are equally represented in both fiction and academic prose, whereas the greatest difference is found in the case of relational classifiers, where the ratio of their representation in fiction and academic prose is 2:18 (cf. Table 7.2, p. 511). In the texts under study nearly a half of the adjectives found in fiction are evaluative, about 30% descriptive and 20% classificatory. In academic prose this scale is reversed: about 47% are classifiers, 35% descriptors and 18% evaluators. The semantic characteristics of adjectival modification in the two samples thus appear to consist in the prevalence of evaluators in fiction in contrast to the predominance of classifiers in academic prose. This has already been suggested by the adduced examples of adjectival modification. A qualitative distinction moreover emerges when the evaluators in the two text samples are compared. While fiction displays emotive or attitudinal evaluation, the evaluators in the academic sample are intellectual. Compare examples (3) a., (6), (8) and (10) a. with (3) c. and (10) b.

(10) a. the roof with its elegant tiles (Ishiguro 21ca), two haughty, grey-haired ladies (54c), an eccentric procedure (88), some bitter arguments (110)
  b. a primate of a very odd kind (Morris 76c), of vital importance (126), simple observation (104ib), a slight advantage (29)

Notably, the evaluator *simple* occurs three times (Morris 104, 59). Evaluating adjectives comparable with those found in the fiction sample are few: in addition to *odd in* (10) b., a clear example is *drastic* (this drastic step [136]).

3.2 Other realization forms of premodifiers found in the texts under study comprised converted nouns and the possessive case (see Tables 3 and 4). The representation of these forms in the two samples (converted noun and possessive case in Ishiguro 12 and 9 instances, respectively; in Morris 9 and 3 instances, respectively) suggests that only the possessive case may have some stylistic relevance.

3.2.1 According to Biber et al. (1999: 589) converted nouns account for c. 30% of all premodifiers in academic prose and judging from figure 8.7 (*ibid.*), they are approximately twice as common in this text sort as in fiction. Neither of these corpus findings corresponds with the data given in Tables 3 and 4. In the total of all premodifiers converted nouns account for some 8% in academic prose and for over 12% in fiction. As in several previous points, the fiction sample here appears to be rather atypical. Of the many semantic relations obtaining in the noun + noun sequences (cf. Biber et al. 1999: 590–591), most premodifying nouns in the academic sample express the genitive relation (*of*-relation), cf. (11) a. Other relations are illustrated in (11) b.

(11) a. squirrel family (Morris 16ba), primate species (93), skin surface (92), body temperature (121 ib), body processes (122b)
　　　b. heat loss (object relationship [129]), hair covering (source/composition [145])

The semantic relations expressed by noun modifiers in fiction are more varied, some of them fitting in none of the types listed in Biber et al.

(12) garden wall (location [21ba]), marriage negotiation (content [90]), gingko trees (kind [4b]), cedar gateway (material [21]), family members (partitive [150]), ink brush (purpose [75id]), art enthusiast (object [106b])

Whether variety of semantic relations in this form of premodification has stylistic relevance remains to be ascertained on the basis of larger and more varied text samples.

3.2.2 The possessive case appears to be more suggestive in this respect. Although the absolute figures do not exceed ten, there is a marked difference in the representation of this form in favour of fiction: nine vs. three occurrences (see Tables 3 and 4). This is expectedly connected with the nature of the head nouns in the two examined text sorts. Over a half of the instances drawn from fiction refer to the characters of the story, the remaining forms being comparable both in number and semantic type with the head nouns of the genitives found in academic prose, cf. (13) a. b. and c.

(13) a. our children's marriage prospects (Ishiguro 39b), Akira Sugimura's house (48b), their late father's house (60ca), the younger sister's words (104ba), the Sugimuras' high-handedness (148b)

    b. his patient's disease (Morris 54ba), one's moral conduct (Ishiguro 137iba), one's
       purse (Ishiguro 137ifa) (generic personal head)
    c. the animal's history (Morris 58b), the sun's rays (Morris 132ba), the city's most
       respected and influential men (Ishiguro 19b), half the property's true value
       (Ishiguro 26ba/a) (genitive of non-personal nouns)

As can be seen, the adduced instances of possessive genitive largely reflect the relatively high representation of proper names in fiction, noted in 1 as its special feature, thus contributing to this feature's stylistic relevance.

3.3 Of the realization forms that occur both as pre- and postmodifiers the texts under study contain *ing*- and *ed*-participles and the gerund. Biber et al. (1999) offer relative frequencies of occurrence only for each of these forms with respect to the other pre- and postmodifiers, but not for each form in regard to its occurrence in pre- and postmodification. While postmodifying past participles are described as more common in academic prose than in any other register (Biber et al. 1999: 606), occurrence in premodification is noted "as somewhat more common in academic prose than in the other registers" (Biber 1999: 589). Within fiction, the representation of *ing*- and *ed*-participle appears to be approximately equal, whereas in academic prose *ed*-participles predominate (cf. Biber et al 1999: 606, Fig. 8.13). The figures for the premodifying *ing*-participle presumably also include the gerund, since this category is not recognized. The occurrence of postmodifying gerunds can be only guessed at from the data for *of* + *ing* in comparison to *to*-infinitive, content *that*- and interrogative *wh*-clauses (*ibid*. 647, Fig 8.23), where *of* + *ing* is shown to be three-to-four times more frequent in academic prose than in fiction.

3.3.1 In the texts under study the *ing*-participle has 12 occurrences in academic prose and 4 in fiction. In the former it ranks third on the frequency scale, following the two most frequent modifers, whereas in fiction with four occurrences it falls in the group of the four least frequent forms. Out of the 12 *ing*-participles in Morris, seven occur in premodification and all operate here as classifiers, cf. (14):

(14) living species (Morris 15), independent breeding population (19), starting point
    (57), living mammals (116ba), flying mammals (139), burrowing mammals (143)

The fiction samples displays two *ing*-participles in premodification, both of which convey evaluative, qualifying meaning, cf. (15):

(15) a commanding position on the hill (Ishiguro 5, 5b), the imposing air of the house
    (10, 10b)

The semantic distinction appears to be connected only with the premodifying function of the *ing*-participle. In postmodification no similar distinction has been noted, cf. (16) a. and b.:

(16) a. special modifications, making interbreeding with other kinds … unlikely (Morris 41ib); a starting point, telling us … (57i)

    b. the steep path leading (2i) up from the little wooden bridge (Ishiguro 2i); its stylishly carved ridgepole (21cβ) pointing (ii) out over the view

As shown in (14), most premodifying *ing*-participles constitute components of zoological terms, thus performing the same function as many classifying adjectives (see 3.1) and may be regarded as style markers.

3.3.2 Noun modification by the *ed*-participle in the two texts presents a reversed picture, at least with respect to the relative frequency of occurrence: there is considerable prevalence of *ed*-participles in fiction, viz. nine occurrences against two in academic prose. This result is presumably due to the limited length of the samples, or else the relatively high representation of the *ed*-participle may be a specific feature of the style of the novel's author. Most *ed*-participles here occur in postmodification, again without evaluative colouring of meaning, cf. (17) a. and b.

(17) a. a simple descriptive name based (Morris 104i) on a simple observation

    b. the little wooden bridge still referred to (Ishiguro 2ibii) around here as the Bridge of Hesitation

The fiction sample contains three premodifying *ed*-participles, one of which conveys evaluative meaning by itself, and another is evaluatively modified, cf. (18):

(18) a. the exaggerated (Ishiguro 51i) respect my pupils always had for me

    b. its stylishly carved (Ishiguro 21cβ) ridgepole

3.3.3 The gerund is represented about equally, having five occurrences in fiction and six in academic prose (see Tables 3 and 4). While all instances in fiction illustrate the postmodifying function, the academic sample contains three premodifying gerunds (in one case gerunds in coordination) which, in connection with what has been observed about a notable number of premodifying adjectives and *ing*-participles in this sample, appears to be of stylistic relevance, cf. (19):

(19) their mating calls and displays (Morris 44ia, ib), heating and cooling problems [Morris 153id], on the dissecting table (Morris 72bαi)

These gerunds fall in the semantic class of classifiers, the instances themselves being well on the way to becoming terms.

Gerunds in the postmodifying function were found after several prepositions, of which only *of* had more than one occurrence (three instances), and two gerunds occurred as complements of *worth*, cf. (20) a. b. c.

(20) a. the importance of our having a house (Ishiguro 37i), the great physiological advantage of being able (Morris 121i) to maintain a constant, high body temperature

b. my surprise at receiving (Ishiguro 55i) such personal attention, a very powerful reason for abolishing it (Morris 134i)

c. one worth having suffered (Ishiguro 143i) a few inconveniences for, something worth pursuing (Morris 57non-sb head iii)

As noted in the case of adjectives and *ing*-participles, also here it is the premodifying use that appears to play a role as a marker of stylistic distinction.

3.4 The remaining noun modifiers occurred only in postmodification. Two of these, apposition and relative clauses, are represented by a number of examples that allows drawing some conclusions.

3.4.1 As regards apposition, in Biber et al. (1999: 639) it is described as a maximally abbreviated form of postmodification characteristic of registers with the highest informational density, viz. news and academic prose, where it accounts for about 15% of all postmodifiers. This is in agreement with the findings of the present study, apposition being represented by 9 examples in academic prose as against three in fiction (cf. Tables 3 and 4). In the total of all postmodifiers, in the academic text under study apposition accounts for 10%, which is less than the figure adduced in Biber et al., but still more than three times higher than the representation of apposition among the postmodifiers in fiction, viz. 3%.

However, as noted in several cases before, more illustrative than the quantitative findings are the qualitative differences in the types of apposition found in the two texts. Of the three instances of apposition drawn from fiction, two are of the kind most frequently displayed by this text sort, viz. equivalence involving appellation (Quirk et al. 1985: 1309), cf. (21) a.; a title in pre-position (*ibid.* 1319), cf. (21) b.; the third example expresses equivalence of the identification kind (*ibid.* 1309), cf. (21) c.

(21) a. Setsuko, our eldest (Ishiguro 41b)

b. Mr. Ono (in direct speech as a form of address [Ishiguro 99])

c. a nominal sum—a figure (Ishiguro 26b) probably not even half the property's true value

The examples found in the academic text express identification that further specifies the first appositive, cf. (22) a., exemplification or enumeration (22) b., and a consequence of the content of the first appositive, which is a finite clause (22) c.

(22) a. the symptoms, the rash (Morris 52b) that gives a doctor a clue; the markings of its fur—its black feet (Morris 50c); another species, a strange form (Morris 72b) of life; the flying mammals, the bats (Morris 139b)

b. the tailless great apes such as the chimpanzee and the gorilla (Morris 83c, d); the burrowing mammals—the naked mole rat, the aardvark and the armadillo

(Morris 144b, c, d); the aquatic animals such as the whales, dolphins, porpoises, dugongs, manatees, and hippopotamuses (Morris 146b, c, d, e, f, g); those abnormally heave giants, the rhinos and the elephants (Morris 153b, c)

c. we ourselves are not black-footed squirrels—a fact (Morris 65b) which forces us into an attitude of humility

Equivalence through identification that further specifies the concept denoted by the first appositive is found in both texts, but appears to be more frequent in academic prose. An obvious factor that plays a role here is the inherent need of academic texts to express meaning with maximal exactness. The other two types appear to be specific to the respective text sort, especially title in pre-position to fiction, cf. (21) b., and enumeration/exemplification in academic prose, as in (22) b.

3.4.2 Relative clauses are more numerous in the fiction sample than in academic prose in the texts under study, viz. 18 vs. 12 instances. This is in agreement with the data in Biber et al. (1999: 606, Fig. 8.13) which show relative clauses to be most frequent in news and least frequent in conversation, with fiction and academic prose ranking in between, the former taking the place next to news. Even the distribution of the relativizers and the registered types of relative clauses correspond with the description therein (*ibid.* 607–611). In the fiction sample a half of the relative clauses (9, i.e. 50.0%) identify or characterize personal antecedents. In all but one of these clauses the relative pronoun is *who* in the subject function. The only other relativizer with a personal antecedent is zero in the object function, cf. (23) a. and b.

(23) a. two haughty grey-haired ladies who turned out to be the daughters of Akira Sugimura (Ishiguro 54bi); the younger sister, who had barely spoken (Ishiguro 73i)

b. the house ... should pass to one our father would have approved of (Ishiguro 68ibi)

Inanimate entities were antecedents of relative clauses mostly where the relativizer performed the object function, viz. six instances, all displaying zero, cf. (24) a. As antecedents of subject relativizers inanimate entities occurred twice, cf. (24) b. In one clause the relativizer performed adverbial function, cf. (24) c.

(24) a. the exaggerated respect my pupils always had for me (Ishiguro 51i); the house our father built (Ishiguro 68i)

b. In the days which followed (Ishiguro 102i); things that will be to our advantage (Ishiguro 128i)

c. such a contest, in which one's moral conduct and achievement are brought as witnesses (Ishiguro 137i)

In the sample of academic prose the difference in the syntactic function of the relativizers is more prominent, cf. 9 subjects / 2 objects (within the total of 12 relative clauses) vs. 10 subjects / 7 objects in fiction (within the total of 18 relative clauses). As in the fiction sample, one relative clause contains an adverbial relativizer, *when*. Compare (25) a., b. and c.

(25) a. i.   Even for the zoologist, who is used to calling an animal an animal (Morris 68i)
      ii. a special kind of locomotion which has modified its basic form (Morris 88i); an attitude of humility that is becoming to proper scientific investigation (Morris 65icii)
      iii. abnormally heavy giants which have heating and cooling problems (Morris 153i); other species that appear to be closely related (Morris 74i)
    b. all we can be certain about (Morris 49i); The great advantage we have when studying such animals (Morris 64i)
    c. the moment would eventually arrive when it would be advantageous for them to become isolated (Morris 37i)

As regards the realization form of the relativizer, the two samples are basically comparable. In both the object relativizer is invariably zero (cf. (24) a. and (25) b.), while the subject function is implemented by *who* (referring to a personal antecedent, cf. (23) a. and (25) a. i.), and *which* and *that* (in reference to non-personal inanimate and animate antecedents, cf. (24) b. and (25) a. ii and a. iii). Whether *that* or *which* is favoured in the fiction sample cannot be judged since each occurred only once, there being two examples in all. In the academic sample *that* was found to be more common (five vs. three instances of *which*). This differs from the data in Biber et al. (1999: 611), where *which* is characterized as the most frequent relativizer in all registers of academic prose. Looking for potential factors motivating the choice between the two relativizers in the academic sample, a point that presents itself is the nature of non-personal antecedents, viz. animate vs. inanimate. However, the registered examples fail to suggest any tendency in this respect insofar as both *that* and *which* are used to refer to either antecedent type.

As suggested by the representation of the subject relativizers, the greatest difference between the two samples, apart from the prominent prevalence of the subject function over the object function in academic prose, appears to involve the antecedents of the subject relativizers. Whereas in fiction the antecedents are mostly personal, viz. the individual characters of the story, in academic prose there is only one instance of this kind, illustrated in (25) a. i. Notably, even in this instance the antecedent differs in having general reference. In the academic sample a large majority of the antecedents of subject relativizers were inanimate (6 instances), as in (25) a. ii., and non-personal animate (2 instances, cf. (25) a. iii).

Another point characteristic of formal writing is found in the modification structure of the noun phrase in (25) c. in that the postmodifying relative *when*-clause is discontinuous, the intervening element being the verb. Discontinuous postmodification as a feature of formal writing has also been noted in the case of apposition, cf. (9).

3.4.3 The two remaining realization forms of postmodification, the infinitive and the adverb, each represented by three examples, are mentioned for the sake of completeness.

(26) a. it is not a property to be endangered or discarded lightly (Morris 124i); nothing further to do with them (Ishiguro 121i); no attempts to hide (Ishiguro 151i) their hostility

b. the particular conditions there (Morris 25icα); their relatives nearby (Morris 27i); all others nearby (Ishiguro 6b)

Here a comment can be made on the passive form of the infinitive in academic prose, which is suggestive of formal text sorts, and on the phraseological nature of the infinitive *to do* postmodifying an indefinite pronoun in fiction.

3.5 The last point to be mentioned is the complexity of the modification structure by which is meant expansion through coordination and subordination. Both have been partly treated before, viz. coordination in the case of premodification (cf. 3.1.2) and enumerative apposition (cf. (22) b.), and subordination in the case of all modifiers on the first level of dependence. What remains to be discussed concerns coordination in the noun phrase structure occurring in the head noun and/or in postmodification, and subordination on lower dependence levels than the first.

Coordination appears to be more common in the academic sample than in fiction, cf. coordination in the head noun in (27) a. and in different kinds of postmodification in (27) b. Coordination in fiction is illustrated in (28).

(27) a. their mating calls and displays (Morris 44a, b); overheating and damage (Morris 131, 131b) to the skin;

b. other living species already known and described (Morris 15i); every aspect of its behaviour and structure (Morris 61b, c); species of monkeys and apes (Morris 78bα, β); conspicuous tufts of hair on the head, in the armpits and around the genitals (Morris 91bα, β, γ); small naked patches of skin on their rumps, their faces, or their chests (Morris 97bα, β, γ)

(28) a. one's moral conduct and achievement (Ishiguro 137ib, ic); the state of the house and alterations (Ishiguro 159b, c)

b. on grounds purely of good character and achievement (Ishiguro 66, 66b); a closer investigation of my background and character (Ishiguro 86b, c)

As regards instances of modification with more than one level of subordination, most examples in both texts display two subordination levels in different combinations. A frequent configuration comprises two prepositional phrases in successive dependence, cf. (29).

(29) at some point in the evolution of the squirrel family (Morris 16, 16b, 16bα), a rapid survey of the whole range of the living mammals (Morris 116, 116b, 116bα), at

one end of the row of the skins (Morris 82, 82b, 82bα); the idea of an 'auction of prestige' (Ishiguro 133, 133b, 133bα), the sentiments of a family with such a distinguished history (Ishiguro 118, 118b, 118bα)

Other configurations, illustrated in (30), are rarer, e.g.

(30) a. the symptoms, the rash that gives a doctor a clue (apposition + relative clause) (Morris 52bi)
b. the steep path leading up from the little wooden bridge still referred to around here as 'the Bridge of Hesitation' (Ishiguro 2, 2i, 2ii) (*ing*- and *ed*-participle)
c. a visit (Ishiguro 54) one afternoon (54b) from two haughty, grey-haired ladies (54c) who (54ci) turned out to be the daughters (prepositional phrase + relative clause)

Postmodification in noun phrases as constituents of non-finite clauses involves an additional dependency level, cf. (31).

(31) no attempts (Ishiguro 151) to hide (151i) their hostility (151ib) towards us (151ibα)

Still more complex instances of postmodification are illustrated in (32).

(32) a. a fact which (Morris 65bi) forces us into an attitude (65ic) of humility (65icα) that (65icii) is becoming to proper scientific investigation (two relative clauses in successive dependence, combined with postmodification by a prepositional phrase);
b. another species (Morris 72), a strange form (72b) of life (72bα) on the dissecting table (72bαi), awaiting (72ibi) analysis (two prepositional phrases in successive dependence, followed by a postmodifying *ing*-participle, the whole structure occurring in apposition);
c. the fine cedar gateway (Ishiguro 21), the large area (/Co-Ord/ 21b) bound (/-ed/ i) by the garden wall (21biα), the roof (/Co-Ord/ 21c) with its elegant tiles (21cα) and its stylishly carved (/-ed/ i) ridgepole (/Co-Ord/ 21cβ) pointing out (/-ing/ ii) over the view (21iiβd) (coordination of head nouns combined with postmodification by non-finite clauses and prepositional phrases)

According to Biber et al. (1999: 578–579), the complexity of noun phrases increases across registers with conversation at one extreme and academic prose at the other. Of the other registers the one closest to academic prose is news. The results obtained on the basis of the examined material diverge in that the modification structure of the two samples does not essentially differ but rather shows a fairly comparable degree of complexity. The differences that have been found consist in a greater representation of modified noun phrases in the academic sample, which provides ground for a higher representation of NPs with complex modification structure. As regards the complex modification structure itself, the most noticeable difference is the combination of multiple coordination and subordination in the academic sample, especially in the case of apposition. The similarity between the two text sorts in this respect is to be ascribed to the rather formal tenor of the fiction sample, shown in addition to the adduced features, even by one instance of discontinuous structure (cf. (30) c.)

4. The conclusions to be drawn from the foregoing discussion concern both non-modified and modified noun phrases. The higher representation of the former in fiction appears to be at least partly due to a relatively high frequency of occurrence of proper names, whose modification is greatly restricted in general. In the academic sample this category is marginal. On the other hand the higher representation of modified noun phrases in the latter sample appears to be at least partly connected with the structure of technical terms, which are frequently two-word formations, with the modifier specifying the meaning of the head noun or designating a subcategory of the concept denoted by the head noun.

Another feature of stylistic relevance was noted in the semantics of the pre-modifiers. While in the academic sample these modifiers, including not only adjectives, but also premodifying participles and gerunds, express classificatory meaning and often function as components of technical terms, in fiction they convey descriptive or evaluative meaning, and non-finite forms are rarer in this function.

Both quantitative and qualitative differences reflecting the subject matter of the texts were further noted in the case of the possessive case and apposition. While the possessive case, in connection with the relatively frequent occurrence of proper names, appears to characterize fiction, apposition, especially of the enumerative/exemplificatory type, reflects the expository nature of the examined academic text.

Minor differences connected with the subject matter were also found in the case of relative clauses. The syntactic functions of the relativizers differed in a marked prevalence of the subject function in the academic sample, whereas the fiction sample displayed great predominance of personal antecedents of the subject relativizers. In academic prose there was only one instance of this kind, a large majority of the antecedents of subject relativizers being inanimate.

As regards the degree of complexity in the modification structure, no major differences, either quantitative or qualitative, were noted in the two texts. This is ascribable to the formal, rather than informal tenor of the narrative, and may be classed as a feature of the author's style. Similarly, the high representation of apposition and the particular types in the academic sample may be due to the particular field of study from which the text is drawn. Nevertheless, some of the points that have been made, notably the role of proper names, the distribution and semantics of premodifiers, and possibly some others, may be afforded more general stylistic relevance.

APPENDIX

TEXT ISHIGURO

If on **a sunny day** [1] you climb **the steep path** [2] **leading up** [/-ing/ i] **from the little wooden bridge** [2ib] **still referred to** [/-ed/ ii] around here **as 'the Bridge** [2iic] **of Hesitation'** [2iicα], you will not have to walk far before **the roof** [3] **of my house** [3b] becomes visible between **the tops** [4] of **two gingko trees** [4b]. Even if it did not occupy **such a commanding** [/i/-ing] **position** [5] **on the hill** [5b], **the house** [6] would still stand out from all others [non-sb head] nearby [6b], so that as you come up **the path** [7], you may find yourself wondering **what sort** [8] **of wealthy man** [8b] owns it. But then I am not, nor have I ever been, **a wealthy man** [9]. **The imposing** [-ing/ i] **air** [10] **of the house** [10b] will be accounted for, perhaps, if I inform you that it was built **by my predecessor** [11], and that he was none other than **Akira Sugimura** [12]. Of course, you may be new **to this city** [13], **in which case** [14] **the name** [15] **of Akira Sugimura** [15b] may not be familiar to you. But mention it to anyone [non-sb head] who [/R clause/ i] lived here before **the war** [16i] and you will learn that for **thirty years or so** [17], **Sugimura** [18] was unquestionably amongst **the city's** [19b] **most respected and influential men** [19]. If I tell you this, and when arriving **at the top** [20] **of the hill** [20b] you stand and look at **the fine cedar gateway** [21], **the large area** [/Co-Ord/ 21b] **bound** [/-ed/ i] **by the garden wall** [21 biα], **the roof** [/Co-Ord/ 21c] **with its elegant tiles** [2lcα] **and its stylishly carved** [/-ed/ i] **ridgepole** [/Co-Ord/ 21cβ] **pointing out** [/-ing/ ii] **over the view** [21iiβd], you may well wonder how I came to acquire **such a property** [22], being as I claim **a man** [23] **of only moderate means** [23b]. **The truth** [24] is, I bought **the house** [25] **for a nominal sum** [26]—**a figure** [26b] **probably not even half the property's** [26bα/α] **true value** [26bα] **at that time** [27]. This was made possible **owing to a most curious**—some may say foolish—**procedure** [28] **instigated** [/i/ -ed] **by the Sugimura family** [28ib] **during the sale** [29]. It is now already **a thing** [30] **of some fifteen years** [30b] **ago. In those days** [31], when **my circumstances** [32] seemed to improve **with each month** [33], **my wife** [34] had begun to press me to find **a new house** [35]. **With her usual foresight** [36], she had argued **the importance** [37] **of our having** [/gerund/ i] **a house** [37ib] **in keeping** [/gerund/ ii] **with our status** [37iic]—**not out of vanity** [38], but for the sake of **our children's** [39b] **marriage prospects** [39]. I saw **the sense** [40] in this, but since **Setsuko** [41], **our eldest** [41b], was still only fourteen or fifteen, I did not go about **the matter** [42] **with any urgency** [43]. Nevertheless, **for a year or so** [44], whenever I heard **of a suitable house** [45] **for sale** [45b], I would remember to make **enquiries** [46]. It was **one** [non-sb head] **of my pupils** [47b] **who** [/R clause/ i] first brought it **to my attention** [47ic] that **Akira Sugimura's** [48b] **house** [48], **a year** [48c] **after his death** [48cα], was to be sold off. That I should buy **such a house** [49] seemed absurd, and I put **the suggestion** [50] down **to the exaggerated respect** [51] [/R clause/ i] **my pupils** [5 1ib] always had for me. But I made **enquiries** [52] all the same, and gained **an unexpected response**

[53]. I received **a visit** [54] one afternoon [54b] **from two haughty, grey-haired ladies** [54c] **who** [/R clause/ i] turned out to be the **daughters** [54id] of Akira Sugimura [54idα]. When I expressed my **surprise** [55] **at receiving** [/ gerund/ i] **such personal attention** [55ib] from **a family** [56] **of such distinction** [56b], **the elder** [57] **of the sisters** [57b] told me coldly that they had not come simply **out of courtesy** [58]. **Over the previous months** [59], **a fair number** [60] **of enquiries** [60b] had been received **for their late father's** [60cα] **house** [60c], but **the family** [61] had **in the end** [62] decided to refuse all but **four** [non-sb head] **of the applications** [63b]. **These four applicants** [64] had been selected carefully **by family members** [65] on grounds purely of **good character** [66] **and achievement** [Co-Ord 66b]. 'It is **of the first importance** [67] to us', she went on, 'that **the house** [68] [/R clause/ i] **our father** [68ib] **built** should pass to one [non-sb head] [/R clause/ 68ibi] he would have approved of and deemed worthy of it. Of course, **circumstances** [69] oblige us to consider **the financial aspect** [70], but this is strictly secondary. We have therefore set **a price** [71].' **At this point** [72], **the younger sister** [73], **who** [/R clause/ i] had barely spoken, presented me with **an envelope** [74], and they watched me sternly as I opened it. Inside was **a single sheet** [75] **of paper** [75b], **blank but for a figure** [75c] **written** [/-ed/ i] elegantly **with an ink brush** [75id]. I was about to express **my astonishment** [76] **at the low price** [76b], but then saw **from the faces** [77] **before me** [77b] that **further discussion** [78] **of finances** [78b] would be considered distasteful. **The elder sister** [79] said simply: 'It will not be **in the interests** [80] **of any** [non-sb head] **of you** [80b] to try to outbid one another. We are not interested in receiving anything [non-sb head] **beyond the quoted** [/ed/ i] **price** [81b]. What we mean to do from here on is to conduct **an auction** [82] **of prestige** [82b].' They had come **in person** [83], she explained, to ask formally on behalf of **the Sugimura family** [84] that I submit myself—along, of course, with **the other three applicants** [85]—**to a closer investigation** [86] **of my background** [86b] **and credentials** [/Co-Ord/ 86c]. **A suitable buyer** [87] could thus be chosen. It was **an eccentric procedure** [88], but I saw **nothing** [non-sb head] **objectionable** about it [89b]; it was, after all, much the same as being involved **in a marriage negotiation** [90]. Indeed, I felt somewhat flattered to be considered **by this old and hidebound family** [91] as **a worthy candidate** [92]. When I gave my consent [93] **to the investigation** [93b], and expressed **my gratitude** [94] to them, **the younger sister** [95] addressed me **for the first time** [96], saying: '**Our father** [97] was **a cultured man** [98], **Mr Ono** [99]. He had **much respect** [100] **for artists** [100b]. Indeed, he knew of **your work** [101].' **In the days** [102] **which** [/R clause/ i] followed, I made **enquiries** [103] **of my own** [103b], and discovered **the truth** [104] **of the younger sister's** [104ba] **words** [104b]; **Akira Sugimura** [105] had indeed been **something** [non-sb head] **of an art enthusiast** [106b] **who** [/R clause/ i] **on numerous occasions** [106ic] had supported **exhibitions** [106id] **with his money** [106ie]. I also came across **certain interesting rumours** [107]: **a significant section** [108] **of the Sugimura family** [108b], it seemed, had been against selling **the house** [109] at all, and there had been **some bitter arguments** [110]. **In the end** [111], **financial pressures** [112]

meant **a sale** [113] was inevitable, and **the odd procedures** [114] **around the transaction** [114b] represented **the compromise** [115] **reached** [/-ed/ i] with **those** [115ib non-sb head] **who** [/R clause/ii] had not wished **the house** [115iic] to pass **out of the family** [115iid]. That there was something [non-sb head] high-handed **about these arrangements** [116b] there was no denying; but **for my part** [117], I was prepared to sympathize **with the sentiments** [118] **of a family** [118b] **with such a distinguished history** [118ba]. **My wife** [119], however, did not take kindly to **the idea** [120] **of an investigation** [120b]. 'Who do they think they are?' she protested. 'We should tell them we want nothing [non-sb head] further to do [/inf/ 121i] with them.' 'But where's **the harm** [122]?' I pointed out. 'We have nothing [non-sb head] [/R clause/ i 123] **we wouldn't want them to discover**. True, I don't have **a wealthy background** [124], but **no doubt** [125] **the Sugimuras** [126] know that already, and they still think us **worthy candidates** [127]. Let them investigate, they can only find **things** [128] **that** [/R clause/ i] **will be to our advantage** [128ib].' And I made **a point** [129] **of adding** [/gerund/ i]: '**In any case** [130], they're doing no more than they would if we were negotiating a marriage [131] with them. We 'll have to get used **to this sort** [132] **of thing** [132b]. Besides, there was surely much to admire **in the idea** [133] **of an auction** [133b] **of prestige** [133ba], as **the elder daughter** [134] called it. One wonders why **things** [135] are not settled more often **by such means** [136]. How so much more honourable is **such a contest** [137], **in which** [/R clause/ i] **one's** [137iba] **moral conduct** [137ib] **and achievement** [Co-Ord 137ic] **are brought** as **witnesses** [137id] rather than **the size** [137ie] **of one's** [137ifa] **purse** [137if]. I can still recall **the deep satisfaction** [138] [/R clause/ i] **I felt** when I learnt **the Sugimuras** [139]—**after the most thorough investigation** [140]—had deemed me the most worthy **of the house** [141] [/R clause/ i] **they so prized**. And certainly, **the house** [142] is one [non-sb head] worth having suffered [/gerund/ 143i] **a few inconveniences** [143ib] for; **despite its impressive and imposing [/-ing/ i] exterior** [144], it is inside **a place** [145] of soft, natural woods [145b] selected [/-ed/ i] **for the beauty** [145ib] **of their grains** [145iba], and all [non-sb head] of us [146b] who lived in it [/R clause/ i] came to find it most conducive to relaxation [147] and **calm** [Co-Ord 147b]. For all that, **the Sugimuras'** [148b] **high-handedness** [148] was apparent everywhere **during the transactions** [149], **some family members** [150] making **no attempts** [151] **to hide** [/inf/ i] **their hostility** [151ib] **towards us** [151iba], and **a less understanding buyer** [152] might well have **taken offence** [153] and abandoned **the whole matter** [154]. Even **in later years** [155] I would sometimes encounter **by chance** [156] **some member** [157] **of the family** [157b] **who** [/R clause/ i], instead of exchanging **the usual kind** [157b] **of polite talk** [157bia], would stand there **in the street** [158] interrogating me as **to the state** [159] **of the house** [159b] **and any alterations** [Co-Ord 159c] I had made [/R clause/ i]. **These days** [160], I hardly ever hear of the **Sugimuras** [161]. I did, though, receive **a visit** [162] shortly **after the surrender** [163] from the younger [non-sb head b] **of the two sisters** 162ba] **who** [/R clause/ i] had approached me **at the time** [162baic] **of the sale** [162baica]. **The war years** [164] had turned her **into a thin, ailing old woman** [165].

TEXT MORRIS

THERE is **a label** [1] **on a cage** [2] **at a certain zoo** [2b] [/R clause/ i] that states simply,
'This **animal** [3] is new **to science**' [4]. **Inside the cage** [5] there sits **a small squirrel**
[6]. It has **black feet** [7] and it comes **from Africa** [8]. **No black-footed squirrel** [9]
has ever been found **in that continent** [10] before. Nothing is known about it. It has
no name [11].

For the zoologist [12] it presents **an immediate challenge** [13]. What is it
about **its way** [14] **of life** [14b] that has made it unique? How does it differ from
the three hundred and sixty-six other **living** [/*ing*-participle/ i] **species** [15] **of
squirrels** [15b] already known and described [Co-Ord /*ed*-participle/ i]? Somehow,
at some point [16] **in the evolution** [16b] **of the squirrel family** [16ba], **the ancestors** [17] **of this animal** [17b] must have split off **from the rest** [18] and established
themselves **as an independent breeding** [/*ing*-participle/ i] **population** [19]. What
was it in **the environment** [20] that made possible **their isolation** [21] as **a new
form** [22] **of life** [22b]? **The new trend** [23] must have started out **in a small way**
[24], **with a group** [25] **of squirrels** [25b] in **one area** [25bα] becoming [/*ing*-par-
ticiple/ i] slightly changed and better adapted **to the particular conditions** [25ic]
there [/adverb/ α]. But **at this stage** [26] they would still be able to interbreed
with their relatives [27] nearby [/adverb/ i]. **The new form** [28] would be **at a
slight advantage** [29] **in its special region** [30], but it would be no more than **a
race** [31] of **the basic species** [31b] and could be swamped out, reabsorbed **into
the mainstream** [32] **at any point** [33]. If, as **time** [34] passed, **the new squirrels** [35] became more and more perfectly tuned-in **to their particular environment** [36], **the moment** [37] would eventually arrive when [/R clause/ i] it would
be advantageous for them to become isolated from possible **contamination** [38]
by their neighbours [38b]. **At this stage** [39] **their social and sexual behaviour**
[40] would undergo **special modifications** [41], making [/*ing*-participle/ i] inter-
breeding [41ib] with other kinds [41ic] of squirrels [41icα] unlikely and eventually
impossible. At first, **their anatomy** [42] may have changed and become better at
coping with **the special food** [43] **of the district** [43b], but later their mating [/
gerund/ i] **calls** [44a] and **displays** [Co-Ord 44b] would also differ, ensuring that
they attract only **mates** [45] **of the new type** [45b]. At last, **a new species** [46]
would have evolved, **separate and discrete, a unique form** [46b] **of life** [46bα], **a
three hundred and sixty-seventh kind** [46c] of **squirrel** [46cα].

When we look **at our unidentified squirrel** [47] **in its zoo cage** [47b], we can
only guess **about these things** [48]. All [non-sb head] [/R clause/ 49i] we can be
certain about is that **the markings** [50] **of its fur** [50b]—**its black feet** [50c]—indicate that it is **a new form** [51]. But these are only the **symptoms** [52], **the rash**
[52b] that [/R clause/ i] gives **a doctor** [53] **a clue** [54] about **his patient's** [54bα]
disease [54b]. To really understand **this new species** [55], we must use **these clues**
[56] only as a starting [/-*ing* participle/ i] **point** [57], telling [/-*ing* participle/ ii]
us there is something worth pursuing [non-sb head] [/gerund/ iii]. We might try

to guess at **the animal's** [58b] **history** [58], but that would be presumptuous and dangerous. Instead we will start humbly by giving it **a simple and obvious label** [59]: we will call it **the African black-footed squirrel** [60]. Now we must observe and record **every aspect** [61] **of its behaviour** [61b] **and structure** [Co-Ord 61c] and see how it differs from, or is similar to, **other squirrels** [62]. Then, little by little, we can piece together **its story** [63].

    The great advantage [64] we [/R clause i] have when studying such animals [64ib] is that we ourselves are not **black-footed squirrels** [65]—**a fact** [65b] which [/R clause i] forces us into an **attitude** [65ic] **of humility** [65icα] that [/R clause/ ii] is becoming **to proper scientific investigation** [65iid]. How different **things** [66] are, how depressingly different, when we attempt to study **the human animal** [67]. Even **for the zoologist** [68], who [/R clause/ i] is used to calling **an animal** [68ib] **an animal** [68ic], it is difficult to avoid **the arrogance** [69] **of subjective involvement** [69b]. We can try to overcome this **to some extent** [70] by deliberately and rather coyly approaching [/ gerund/ i] **the human being** [71i] as if he were **another species** [72], **a strange form** [72b] **of life** [72bα] **on the dissecting** [/gerund/ i] **table** [72bαi], awaiting [/-ing participle/ i] **analysis** [72ibi]. How can we begin?

    As with the new squirrel [73], we can start by comparing him **with other species** [74] that [/R clause/ i] appear to be most closely related. From **his teeth** [75], **his hands** [Co-Ord 75b], **his eyes** [Co-Ord 75c] and **various other anatomical features** [Co-Ord 75d], he is obviously **a primate** [76] **of some sort** [76b], but of a very odd kind [76c]. Just how odd becomes clear when we lay out in **a long row** [77] **the skins** [78] of the **one hundred and ninety-two living** [/-ing participle/ i] **species** [78b] **of monkeys** [78bα] and **apes** [Co-Ord 78bα], and then try to insert **a human pelt** [79] at **a suitable point** [80] somewhere in **this long series** [81]. Wherever we put it, it looks out of place. Eventually we are driven to position it right **at one end** [82] **of the row** [82b] **of skins** [82bα], next to **the hides** [83] **of the tailless great apes** [83b] **such as the chimpanzee** [83c] and the **gorilla** [Co-Ord 83d]. Even here it is obtrusively different. **The legs** [84] are too long, **the arms** [85] are too short and **the feet** [86] are rather strange. Clearly **this species** [87] **of primate** [87b] has developed **a special kind** [88] **of locomotion** [88b] which [/R clause/ i] has modified its **basic form** [88bic]. But there is **another characteristic** [89] that [/R clause/ i] cries out for **attention** [89ib]: **the skin** [90] is virtually naked. Except **for conspicuous tufts** [91] **of hair** [91b] on the head [91bα], **in the armpits** [Co-Ord 91bβ] and **around the genitals** [Co-Ord 91bγ], **the skin surface** [92] is completely exposed. When compared **with the other primate species** [93], **the contrast** [94] is dramatic. True, **some species** [95] **of monkeys** [95b] **and apes** [Co-Ord 95c] have **small naked patches** [96] **of skin** [96b] **on their rumps** [97bα], **their faces** [Co-Ord 97bβ], or their chests [Co-Ord 97bγ], but nowhere **amongst the other one hundred and ninety-two species** [98] is there anything [non-sb head] even approaching [/-ing participle, i] **the human condition** [99i]. **At this point** [100] and **without further investigation** [101], it is justifiable to name **this new species** [102] the 'naked ape' [103]. It is a **simple, descriptive name** [104] based [/-ed participle/ i] **on a simple observation** [104ib], and it makes no **special assumptions** [105]. Perhaps it will help us to keep **a sense** [106] **of proportion** [106b] and maintain **our objectivity** [107].

Staring **at this strange specimen** [108] and puzzling over **the significance** [109] **of its unique features** [109b], **the zoologist** [110] now has to start making **comparisons** [111]. Where else is **nudity** [112] **at a premium** [113]? **The other primates** [114] are **no help** [115], so it means looking farther afield. **A rapid survey** [116] **of the whole range** [116b] **of the living** [/-*ing* participle/ i] **mammals** [116bα] soon proves that they are remarkably attached **to their protective, furry covering** [117], and that **very few** [non-sb head] **of the 4,237 species** [118b] **in existence** [118bα] have seen fit to abandon it. Unlike **their reptilian ancestors** [119], **mammals** [120] have acquired **the great physiological advantage** [121] of being [/gerund/ i] able to maintain **a constant, high body temperature** [121ib]. **This keeps the delicate machinery** [122] **of the body processes** [122b] tuned in **for top performance** [123]. It is not **a property** [124] to be [/ infinitive/ i] endangered or discarded lightly. **The temperature-controlling devices** [125] are **of vital importance** [126] and **the possession** [127] **of a thick, hairy, insulating** [/-*ing* participle/ i] **coat** [127b] obviously plays **a major role** [128] in preventing [/gerund i] **heat loss** [129]. **In intense sunlight** [130] it will also prevent **over-heating** [131] and **damage** [Co-Ord 131b] **to the skin** [131bα] **from direct exposure** [132] **to the sun's** [132bα] **rays** [132b]. **If the hair** [133] has to go, then clearly there must be **a very powerful reason** [134] for abolishing [/gerund/ i] it. **With few exceptions** [135] **this drastic step** [136] has been taken only when **mammals** [137] have launched themselves **into an entirely new medium** [138]. **The flying** [/-*ing* participle/ i] **mammals** [139], **the bats** [139b], have been forced to denude **their wings** [140], but they have retained **their furriness** [141] elsewhere and can hardly be counted **as naked species** [142]. **The burrowing** [/ -*ing* participle/ i] **mammals** [143] have **in a few cases** [144]— **the naked mole rat** [144b], **the aardvark** [Co-Ord 144c] and **the armadillo** [Co-Ord 144d], for example—reduced **their hair covering** [145]. **The aquatic animals** [146] such as **the whales** [Co-Ord 146b], **dolphins** [Co-Ord 146c], **porpoises** [Co-Ord 146d], **dugongs** [Co-Ord 146e], **manatees** [Co-Ord 146f] and **hippopotamuses** [Co-Ord 146g] have also gone naked as **part** [147] **of a general streamlining** [147b]. But **for all the more typical surface-dwelling mammals** [148], whether scampering **about on the ground** [149] or clambering around **in the vegetation** [150], **a dense hairy hide** [151] is **the basic rule** [152]. Apart from those abnormally heavy **giants** [153], **the rhinos** [153b] and **the elephants** [Co-Ord 153c] (which [/R clause/i] have heating and cooling [/gerund/ ii] **problems** [153id] of their own [153ida], **the naked ape** [154] stands alone, [marked off by his nudity from all the thousands of hairy, shaggy or furry land-dwelling mammalian species.]

SOURCES

Morris, D. *The Naked Ape*. London: Triad Grafton Books, 1977, 13–16.
Ishiguro, K. *An Artist of the Floating World*. London: Faber and Faber, 1990, 7–11.

REFERENCES

Adam, M. (2003), "Religious text: the thematic and rhematic layers within a distributional macrofield." Unpublished doctoral dissertation. Brno: Masaryk University.

Adam, M. (2013), *Presentation Sentences (Syntax, Semantics and FSP)*. Brno: Masaryk University.

Biber, D. et al. (1999), *Longman Grammar of Spoken and Written English*. London: Longman.

Bolinger, D. (1977), *Meaning and Form*. London: Longman.

Breivik, L. E. (1983), *Existential THERE*. Bergen: University of Bergen.

Brown, G. and G.Yule (1987), *Discourse Analysis*. Cambridge: Cambridge University Press.

Brůhová, G. (2015), "Passivization of ditransitive verbs from the FSP point of view." *Linguistica Pragensia* 25/1, 27–36.

Carlson, L. (1983), *Dialogue Games. An Approach to Discourse Analysis*. Dordrecht: D. Reidel.

Čermák, J. et al. (eds) (2005), *Patterns*. Prague: Ústav anglistiky a amerikanistiky FFUK / Kruh moderních filologů.

Čermáková, M. (1999), "Větněčlenské korespondence podmětu mezi angličtinou a češtinou" [Syntactic counterparts of the subject between English and Czech]. Unpublished diploma dissertation. Prague: Charles University / Faculty of Arts.

Chamonikolasová, J. and M. Adam (2005), "The presentation scale in the theory of functional sentence perspective." In: J. Čermák et al. (eds), 2005, 59–69.

Chesterman, A. (1991), *On Definiteness. A Study with Special Reference to English and Finnish*. Cambridge: Cambridge University Press.

Christophersen, P. (1939), *The Articles: A Study of their Theory and Use in English*. Copenhagen: Munksgaard.

Daneš, F. (1964), "A three-level approach to syntax." *Travaux linguistiques de Prague* 1, 225–240.

Daneš, F. (1966), "The relation of centre and periphery as a language universal." *Travaux linguistiques de Prague* 2, 9–21.

Daneš, F. (1974), "Functional sentence perspective and the organization of the text." In: F. Daneš (ed.), *Papers on Functional Sentence Perspective*. Prague: Academia, 106–128.

Daneš, F. (1979), "O identifikaci známé (kontextově zapojené) informace v textu" [On identification of given (context-dependent) information in text]. *Slovo a slovesnost* 40, 257–270.

Daneš, F. (1986), *Věta a text* [Sentence and text]. Prague: Academia.

Daneš, F. et al. (eds) (1987), *Mluvnice češtiny 3: Skladba* [A Grammar of Czech 3, Syntax]. Prague: Academia.

Dušková, L. (1971), "On some functional and stylistic aspects of the passive in present-day English." *Philologica Pragensia* 14, 117–143. Reprinted in Dušková 1999, Part 1, Chapter 6.

Dušková, L. (1973), "*Man*-Sätze in Czech and in English." *Philologica Pragensia* 16, 5–37. Reprinted in Dušková 1999, Part 2, Chapter 17.

Dušková, L. (1975), "On some semantic and FSP aspects of the subject in Czech and in English." *Philologica Pragensia* 18, 199–221. Reprinted in Dušková 1999, Part 2, Chapter 32.

Dušková, L. (1977), "A note on *there is* in Present-day English." *Philologica Pragensia* 20, 97–105. Reprinted in Dušková 1999, Part 2, Chapter 18.

Dušková, L. (1984), "A contrastive view of grammatical means of textual cohesion." In: J. Kořenský and J. Hoffmanová (eds), *Text and the Pragmatic Aspects of Language*, Prague: Ústav pro jazyk český, 141–162.

Dušková, L. (1985), "The role of definiteness in functional sentence perspective." In: Z. Hlavsa and D. Viehweger (eds), *Aspects of Text Organization*, Prague: Ústav pro jazyk český, 57–74. Reprinted in Dušková 1999, Part 2, Chapter 35.

Dušková, L. (1986a), "A note on the thematic character of the subject in English in comparison with Czech." *Prague Studies in Mathematical Linguistics* 9, 95–102. Reprinted in Dušková 1999, Part 2, Chapter 33.

Dušková, L. (1986b), "On the type of definiteness expressed by the English possessives." *Philologica Pragensia* 29, 197–207. Reprinted in Dušková 1999, Part 1, Chapter 12.

Dušková, L. et al. (1988), *Mluvnice současné angličtiny na pozadí češtiny* [A Grammar of Contemporary English against the Background of Czech]. Prague: Academia.

Dušková, L. (1991), "An attempt at a classification of irregular sentences and nonsentences." *Prague Studies in English* 19, *Acta Universitatis Carolinae, Philologica* 1, 1990, 71–81. Charles University in Prague / Karolinum Press. Reprinted in Dušková 1999, Part 2, Chapter 25.

Dušková, L. (1993), "On some syntactic and FSP aspects of the cleft construction in English." *Prague Studies in English* 20, *Acta Universitatis Carolinae, Philologica* 1, 1993, 71–87. Reprinted in Dušková 1999, Part 2, Chapter 37.

Dušková, L. (1995), "On the language specific vs. general nature of syntactic discontinuities." In: B. Palek (ed.), *Proceedings of LP'94*, Prague: Charles University Press, 302–318. Reprinted in Dušková 1999, Part 2, Chapter 20.

Dušková, L. (1999), *Studies in the English Language*, Parts 1 and 2. Prague: Karolinum Press.

Dušková, L. (2012), "Vilém Mathesius and contrastive studies, and beyond." In: M. Malá and P. Šaldová (eds), *A Centenary of English Studies at Charles University: from Mathesius to Present-day Linguistics*. Prague: Charles University, Faculty of Arts, 21–48.

Dušková, L. (2015), "Textual roles of two forms of rhematic subjects: initial rhematic subjects vs. subjects rhematized by *it*-clefts." *Linguistica Pragensia* 25/1, 49–66.

Dvořáková, B. (1988), "České protějšky anglické vytýkací konstrukce" [Czech counterparts of the English cleft sentence]. Unpublished diploma dissertation, Prague: Charles University / Faculty of Arts.

Enkvist, N. E. (1964), "On defining style." In: J. Spencer (ed.), *Linguistics and Style*, Oxford: Oxford University Press, 1–56.

Enkvist, N. E. (1973), *Linguistic Stylistics*. The Hague: Walter De Gruyter.

Firbas, J. (1961), "On the communicative value of the Modern English finite verb." *Brno Studies in English* 3, 79–104.

Firbas, J. (1966), "Non-thematic subjects in contemporary English." *Travaux linguistiques de Prague* 2, 239–256.

Firbas, J. (1967), "It was yesterday that … " *Sborník prací filosofické fakulty brněnské university* 16, 141–146.

Firbas, J. (1980), "Post-intonation-centre prosodic shade in the modern English clause." In: S. Greenbaum, G. Leech, and J. Svartvik (eds), *Studies in English Linguistics for Randolph Quirk*, London: Longman, 125–133.

Firbas, J. (1991), "On some basic issues of the theory of functional sentence perspective III." *Brno Studies in English* 19, 77–92.

Firbas, J. (1992), *Functional Sentence Perspective in Written and Spoken Communication*. Cambridge: Cambridge University Press.

Firbas, J. (1994), "Substantiating Daneš's view of givenness as a graded phenomenon." In: S. Čmejrková and F. Štícha (eds), *The Syntax of Sentence and Text*. Amsterdam: John Benjamins, 119–129.

Firbas, J. (1995), Retrievability span in functional sentence perspective. *Brno Studies in English* 21, 17–45.

Grzegorek, M. (1984), *Thematization in English and Polish*. Poznan: Uniwersytet im. Adama Mickiewicza.

Hajičová, E. (1993), *Issues of Sentence Structure and Discourse Patterns*. Prague: Charles University.

Hajičová, E. (1994), "Topic/Focus and related research." In: P. A. Luelsdorff (ed.), *The Prague School of Structural and Functional Linguistics*. Amsterdam: John Benjamins, 245-275.

Hajičová, E., B. H. Partee, and P. Sgall (1998), *Topic-focus Articulation, Tripartite Structures, and Semantic Content*. Dordrecht: Kluwer Academic Publishers.

Halliday, M. A. K. and R. Hasan (1976), *Cohesion in English*. London: Longman.

Hasselgård, H. (2004), "Adverbials in *it*-cleft constructions." *Language and Computers* 49, 195-211.

Hawkins, J. (1978), *Definiteness and Indefiniteness*. London: Croom Helm.

Hedviková, O. (1996), "Developmental tendencies in the passive use: comparing the present state of the passive with the situation at the beginning of this century." Unpublished diploma dissertation. Prague: Charles University / Faculty of Arts.

Hewson, J. (1972), *Article and Noun in English*. The Hague: Mouton.

Hladký, J. (1961), "Remarks on complex condensation phenomena in some English and Czech contexts." *Brno Studies in English* 1, 105-118.

Huddleston, R. and G. K. Pullum (2002), *The Cambridge Grammar of the English Language*. Cambridge: Cambridge University Press.

Jakobson, R. (1936), Beitrag zur allgemeinen Kasuslehre. *Travaux du Circle linguistique de Prague* 6, 240-288.

Jespersen, O. (1940), *A Modern English Grammar on Historical Principles*, Part V. *Syntax*. Fourth Volume. Copenhagen: Ejnar Munksgaard.

Johansson, S. and S. Oksefjell (eds) (1998), *Corpora and Cross-Linguistic Research*. Amsterdam: Rodopi.

Klégr, A. (1996), *The Noun in Translation*. Prague: Karolinum Press.

Komárkova, J. (2000), "Constancy of syntactic function." Unpublished seminar paper. Prague: Charles University / Faculty of Arts.

Koubová, V. (2002), "Větněčlenská konstantnost příslovečného určení mezi češtinou a angličtinou" [Syntactic constancy of adverbials between English and Czech]. Unpublished seminar paper. Prague: Charles University / Faculty of Arts.

Kuno, S. (1978), "Generative discourse analysis in America." In: W. U. Dressier (ed.), *Current Trends in Textlinguistics*, Berlin: de Gruyter, 275-294.

Leech, G. and Lu Li (1995), "Indeterminacy between noun phrases and adjective phrases as complements of the English verb." In: B. Aarts and C. F. Meyer (eds), *The Verb in Contemporary English*, Cambridge: Cambridge University Press, 183-202.

Lyons, J. (1971), *Introduction to Theoretical Linguistics*. Cambridge: Cambridge University Press.

Mathesius, V. (1911), "O potenciálnosti jevů jazykových." In: J. Vachek (ed.), *U základů pražské jazykovědné školy, Prameny české a slovenské lingvistiky* 1, Prague: Academia, 1970, 5-34. English translation On the potentiality of the phenomena of language. In: J. Vachek (ed.), *A Prague School Reader in Linguistics*, Bloomington: Indiana University Press, 1964, 1-32.

Mathesius, V. (1915), "O passivu v moderní angličtině" [On the passive in Modern English]. *Sborník filologický* 5, 198-220.

Mathesius, V. (1929), "Zur Satzperspektive im modernen Englisch." *Archiv fur das Studium der neueren Sprachen und Literaturen* 155, 202-210.

Mathesius, V. (1937), "Double negation and grammatical concord." In: *Mélanges de linguistique et philologie offerts à Jacques van Ginneken*, Paris: Klincksieck, 79-83.

Mathesius, V. (1947a), "O funkci podmětu" [On the function of the subject]. In: *Čeština a obecný jazykozpyt*, Prague: Melantrich, 277-285.

Mathesius, V. (1947b), "O tak zvaném aktuálním členění větném" [On the so-called functional sentence perspective]. In: *Čeština a obecný jazykozpyt*, Prague: Melantrich, 234-242.

Mathesius, V. (1961), *Obsahový rozbor současné angličtiny na základě obecně lingvistickém*, Prague: Nakladatelství Československé akademie věd.

Mathesius, V. (1975), *A Functional Analysis of Present Day English on a General Linguistic Basis*. Prague: Academia.

Mráz, M. (1998), "Užití some s počitatelnými substantivy v singuláru" [The use of *some* with countable singulars]. Unpublished diploma dissertation. Prague: Charles University / Faculty of Arts.

Nehls, D. (1986), *Semantik und Syntax des englischen Verbs, Teil II, Die Modalverben*. Heidelberg: Julius Groos.

Nekvapilová, S. (1998), "Větněčlenské korespondence podmětu mezi angličtinou a němčinou" [Syntactic counterparts of the subject between English and German]. Unpublished diploma dissertation. Prague: Charles University / Faculty of Arts.

Neústupný, J. V. (1966), "On the analysis of linguistic vagueness." *Travaux linguistiques de Prague* 2, 39–51.

Nosek, J. (1989), "Jazyková typologie a kategorie určenosti" [Linguistic typology and the category of determination]. In: *Abstracts of the Brno Conference of English Studies* 31, Brno: Masaryk University.

Nosek, J. (1990), "The category of determination and auxiliary words in language." *Philologica Pragensia* 33, 177–189.

Nosek, J. (1991), "Nejnovější bádání o kategorii určenosti (členu) v jazyce" [The latest research into the category of determination (article) in language]. *Časopis pro moderní filologii* 73, 38–43.

Panevová, J. (1981), "K otázkám homonymie a neutralizace ve stavbě věty" [On questions of homonymy and neutralization in sentence structure]. *Jazykovedné studie* 16, 85–89.

Prince, E. F. (1978), "A comparison of wh-clefts and it-clefts in discourse." *Language* 54, 883–906.

Pyles T. and J. Algeo (1993), *The Origins and Development of the English Language*. New York: Harcourt Brace Jovanovich College Publishers.

Quirk R. et al. (1972), *A Grammar of Contemporary English*. London: Longman.

Quirk, R. et al. (1985), *A Comprehensive Grammar of the English Language*. London: Longman.

Rieser, H. (1978), "On the development of text grammar." In: W. U. Dressier (ed.), *Current Trends in Textlinguistics*, Berlin: de Gruyter, 6–20.

Sahlin, E. (1979), *Some and Any in Spoken and Written English*. Uppsala: Uppsala University.

Sgall, P. (2002), "Moravská a pražská (malostranská) koncepce aktuálního členění" [The Moravian and the Prague (Lesser Town) conception of functional sentence perspective]. In: Z. Hladká and P. Karlík (eds), *Čeština—univerzália a specifika* 4, Brno: Masaryk University, 51–58.

Sgall, P., E. Hajičová, and E. Buráňová (1980), *Aktuální členění v češtině* [Functional sentence perspective in Czech]. Prague: Academia.

Sgall, P., E. Hajičová, and J. Panevová (1986), *The Meaning of the Sentence in Its Semantic and Pragmatic Aspects*. Dordrecht: Reidel.

Slunečková, L. (2005), "Syntactic constancy of the object between Czech and English in fiction and technical writing." Preliminary notes. In: J. Čermák et al. (eds), 2005, 197–207.

Smolka, V. (2007), "The Position of Finite and Nonfinite Subject Clauses." Unpublished doctoral dissertation. Prague: Charles University / Faculty of Arts.

Strnadová, J. (1998), "Anglické překladové ekvivalenty českého určitého slovesa" [English translation equivalents of Czech finite verbs]. Unpublished diploma dissertation. Prague: Charles University / Faculty of Arts.

Svartvik, J. (1966), *On Voice in the English Verb*. The Hague: Mouton.

Svoboda, A. (1968), "The hierarchy of communicative units and fields as illustrated by English attributive constructions." *Brno Studies in English* 7, 49–101.

Svoboda, A. (1981), *Diatheme*. Brno: Masaryk University.

Svoboda, A. (1983), "Thematic elements." *Brno Studies in English* 15, 49–85.

Svoboda, A. (1987), "Functional perspective of the noun phrase." *Brno Studies in English* 17, 61–86.

Svoboda, A. (1989), *Kapitoly z funkční syntaxe* [Chapters from functional syntax]. Prague: Státní pedagogické nakladatelství.

Svoboda, A. (2005), "Firbasian semantic scales and comparative studies." In: J. Čermák et al. (eds), 2005, 217–229.

Travaux linguistiques de Prague 2 (1966), "Les problèmes du centre et de la périphérie du système de la langue," Prague: Academia.

Trnka, B. (1954), *Rozbor nynější spisovné angličtiny II. Morfologie slovních druhů (částí řeči) a tvoření slov.* [An analysis of present-day Standard English II. Morphology of the word classes (parts of speech) and word formation]. Prague: Státní pedagogické nakladatelství.

Trnka B. (1956), *Rozbor nynější spisovné angličtiny III. Syntaxe jména a jmenných tvarů slovesných* [Syntax of the noun and non-finite verb forms]. Prague: Státní pedagogické nakladatelství.

Trnka, B. (1967), *Rozbor nynější spisovné angličtiny* I. *Rozbor fonologický* [Phonological analysis]. Prague: Státní pedagogické nakladatelství.

Trnka, B. (1982), *Selected Papers in Structural Linguistics: Contributions to English and General Linguistics written in the years 1928–1978*. Ed. V. Fried, Berlin: Mouton.

Trnka, B. (1982a), "On the combinatory variants and neutralization of phonemes." In: B. Trnka 1982, 119–124.

Trnka, B. (1982b), "On some problems of neutralization." In: B. Trnka 1982, 149–159.

Trnka, B. (1982c), "A few remarks on homonymy and neutralization." In: B. Trnka 1982, 356–360.

Trnka, B. (1982d), "Morphological oppositions." In: B. Trnka, 1982, 303–316.

Trnka, B. (1982e), "The change of Middle English -erC into -arC in Early New English." In: B. Trnka 1982, 276–280.

Trnka, B. (1982f), "On morphemic homonymy." In: B. Trnka 1982, 336–339.

Trnka, B. (1982g), "On the basic categories of syntagmatic morphology." In: B. Trnka 1982, 340–349.

Trnka, B. (1982h), "Principles of morphological analysis." In: B. Trnka 1982, 320–332.

Trnka, B. (1982i), "The phonemic development of spirants in English." In: B. Trnka 1982, 224–231.

Trnka, B. (1990), *Kapitoly z funkční jazykovědy* [Studies in functional linguistics]. Ed. J. Nosek, Prague: Charles University.

Trnka, B. (2014), *Rozbor nynější spisovné angličtiny. Díl I, II, III* [An analysis of present-day standard English. Parts I, II, III]. Prague: Karolinum.

Uhlířová, L. (1974), "On the role of statistics in the investigation of FSP." In: F. Daneš (ed.), *Papers on Functional Sentence Perspective*, Prague: Academia, 208–216.

Vachek, J. (1955), "Notes on the English 'possessive case.'" *Časopis pro moderní filologii* 37, 11–15.

Vachek, J. (1961), "Some less familiar aspects of the analytical trend of English." *Brno Studies in English* 1, 9–78.

Vachek, J. (1964), "On peripheral phonemes of modern English." *Brno Studies in English* 4, 7–109.

Vachek, J. (1966), "On the integration of the peripheral elements into the system of language." *Travaux linguistiques de Prague* 2, 23–37.

Valehrachová, L. (2002), "Větněčlenská konstantnost předmětu mezi angličtinou a češtinou" [Syntactic constancy of the object between English and Czech]. Unpublished diploma dissertation. Prague: Charles University / Faculty of Arts.

Valehrachová, L. (2003), "Syntactic constancy of the object between English and Czech." *Linguistica Pragensia* 13, 5–15.

Vaňková, L. (2014), "Expressing indefiniteness in English with reference to body parts." *Prague Studies in English* 26, *Acta Universitatis Carolinae, Philologica* 3/2013, 159–180.

Yotsukura, S. (1970), *The Articles in English: A Structural Analysis of Usage*. The Hague: Mouton.